Women's Voices
in Experiential Education

Karen Warren

Association for Experiential Education
2305 Canyon Blvd. Suite 100
Boulder, Colorado 80302-5651

KENDALL/HUNT PUBLISHING COMPANY
4050 Westmark Drive   Dubuque, Iowa 52004

Cover design concept by Maryanne Pratt

Special thanks to everyone who contributed photos for the cover:
       Woodswomen
       Shawn Malarcher and Joseph Pfeifer, Kiwanis Camp
       Haley Pepper
       Mary McClintock
       Priscilla McKenney, Lois Lane Expeditions

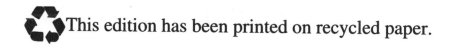This edition has been printed on recycled paper.

Copyright © 1996 by Association for Experiential Education

Library of Congress Catalog Card Number: 96-76627

ISBN 0-7872-2059-0

Printed in the United States of America
10   9   8   7   6   5   4   3   2   1

Dedication

This book is dedicated:

To my partner Sue Tippett and my daughter Amelia Hua Ye Tarren, whose love and encouragement have both supported my professional work and kept it in perspective.

To the memory of two wise women, May Sarton and Helen Nearing, who left us this year. Their voices taught me about learning, the natural world, simplicity, and solitude.

To women and girls everywhere who strive to have their voices heard.

Table of Contents

Section I: Questioning Voices   7

Section II: Professional Voices   61

Section III: Leading Voices   105

About the Association for Experiential Education

The Association for Experiential Education (AEE) is a not-for-profit, international, professional organization with roots in adventure education, committed to the development, practice, and evaluation of experiential learning in all settings.

AEE sponsors local, regional, and international conferences, and publishes the *Journal of Experiential Education*, the *Jobs Clearinghouse*, directories of programs and services, and a wide variety of books and periodicals to support educators, trainers, practitioners, students, and advocates.

AEE's diverse membership consists of individuals and organizations with affiliations in education, recreation, outdoor adventure programming, mental health, youth service, physical education, management development training, corrections, programming for people with disabilities, and environmental education.

To receive additional information about the Association for Experiential Education, call or write: **AEE, 2305 Canyon Blvd., Suite 100, Boulder, CO USA 80302, phone (303) 440-8844, FAX (303) 440-9581, e-mail aeemikal@nile.com**

About the Women in Experiential Education Professional Group

The Women in Experiential Education Professional Group of AEE has its roots in educational programming and research for women and girls. The group consists of members who share a commonality of concerns as women engaged in all areas of the experiential education field. The Women in EE PG serves a dual function. First, it provides a structure to voice the interests, needs, and concerns of women within AEE and in the larger professional community. Second, it serves as a safe place/space to connect around the joys, pains, and problems we meet as women within our work settings.

Foreword

Rita Yerkes

As an adventurous young child, I loved the thrill of challenge experiences and learning by doing. I did not understand or accept the message that those were only for my many brothers to do. You see, I was only a child filled with the joy to be all that I could be.

It was only later, in my adolescent years, that voices told me to take my proper woman's role in society and leave the challenges to others. It left me confused because I knew that society's role perception for women was not a comfortable fit for me. It was a lonely time. I was unaware of the many women's lives and voices from the past that could have spoken to me of their uniqueness. Even much later, as a graduate student and young experiential education professor, I had little access to their journeys and commitments to experiential education.

In this book, Karen Warren and her authors capture the personal, instructional, and scholarly contributions of women. The readings of her stories, philosophy, feminist pedagogy, and women's experiential programming will elevate the reader's awareness and understanding of perspectives held by girls and women. It is a timely addition to the fields of experiential education and women's studies and for those professionals and organizations committed to inclusion.

Why feature women's voices in experiential education? Why, when we have moved toward inclusiveness in the workplace and in our communities? Haven't we done enough? There are two important responses to this question. First, history teaches us that women's achievements, and even more importantly, their central concerns and values, are easily forgotten or submerged. Voices can be stilled through sheer amnesia. The fact is that the presence of women's activities and contributions still remain under-represented in experiential education literature. Second, as will be seen in this volume, women's voices are varied. Women's experiences are mediated by class, race, ideological, and lifestyle differences. We must continue to provide opportunities for women to make representations to one another of their struggles, dreams, and discoveries.

Women's Voices in Experiential Education, therefore, is first written by and for women—students, participants, teachers, adventurers, thinkers, and leaders. It does justice to the diversity and ingenuity that women bring to the field. But it will enable all women and men alike to enlarge their understanding of the wide range of roles in women's experiences. No previous work has pulled together the major publications of women in the field in one volume. To make note of this fact is another way of saying that this book offers a fuller understanding of experiential education itself, including its history, problems, and potential for advancement. If it succeeds on this score, we may advance enough so that in the future, instead of asking why such knowledge is needed, the real question will be, "Have we recorded *all* of the voices of those who have committed their lives and work to the advancement of experiential education?"

Rita Yerkes, Ed.D.
Dean, George Williams College
School of Physical Education & Recreation Administration
Aurora University
Aurora, IL 60506

Acknowledgments

This book is the result of the collective energy of many women who nurtured the idea to light as it languished on my desk as my "guilt file," waiting for me to believe it was possible. Martha Bell and Marg Cosgriff, two friends and colleagues in New Zealand, offered encouragement in the earliest stages. During our writing group sessions, Angel Russek convinced me the book could fit into my life. Denise Mitten, Rita Yerkes, Wilma Miranda, Mary McClintock, and Ellen Winiarczyk offered support at critical junctures.

I am indebted to Pia Renton, AEE Publications Manager, who skillfully guided me through this publishing venture. Her professionalism and ability to quickly and cheerfully find an answer to my many questions was a tremendous help.

I received considerable support from my colleagues and students at Hampshire College. I am thankful for Hampshire's unique system of learning and teaching that has contributed to my work in experiential education and feminist outdoor leadership.

The AEE Review Group of Marty O'Keefe, Nina Roberts, and Pam McPhee provided valuable insight, encouragement, and attention to the true spirit of collaboration in the review process.

Many women served as manuscript reviewers, offering indispensable feedback and suggestions to authors. I am grateful to Karla Henderson, Wilma Miranda, Nina Roberts, Rita Yerkes, Denise Mitten, Heidi Mack, E. J. George, Mary McClintock, Marianne Scippa, Marty O'Keefe, Connie Russell, Deb Jordan, Angel Russek, Mary Hulbert, Robyn DuBoff, Ruth Rohde, Gayle Stoner, Anji Estrellas, and T.A. Loeffler for their insightful reviews.

Two women stand out for their constant encouragement throughout the entire project and are undoubtedly a key reason this text exists. Marty O'Keefe would call regularly to check in on the book. We shared not only the process of bringing the book to life but also strategized about the challenges we both faced in blending parenting with our professional lives. Nina Roberts, with her incredible energy and dedication, was always ready to tackle the next job necessary to make this book a reality. Both Marty and Nina are inspirational women, trusted friends, and valuable colleagues.

Finally, my special thanks goes to my partner, Sue Tippett, for encouraging my dream of having women's voices in the experiential education field recognized and celebrated. Her input at various stages and steadfast support in helping me carve out time to work on this project made it possible.

The Quilt of Women's Voices

We all should know that diversity makes for a rich tapestry,
and we must understand that all the threads of the tapestry
are equal in value no matter their color;
equal in importance no matter their texture.

Maya Angelou

When I became a mother several years ago, students and co-workers at Hampshire College made a patchwork quilt for my family. That cherished quilt became a guiding vision for this book. I took each carefully stitched quilt square of this book, each a special representation of a single woman's voice, and joined it with other panels that had been entrusted to me to make a whole. Together they create a work of beauty, a stunning compilation of diverse experiences and voices. While each square is a story by itself, the pattern of repeating squares holds together a unity of ideas that are important to women and girls in experiential education.

Yet as resplendent as a quilt may be, often its real distinction is in the unseen process of its fabrication: women working together in community for a common end. This concept of quilting has defined the creation of this book. As a shared vision of women hungering for the representation of their lives within the present literature of experiential education, this work was an astonishing volunteer effort. I was deluged with support and encouragement from women who shared the dream. Many women accepted responsibility for a piece of the hard work necessary to bring this volume to life. My role as editor was more as a conduit of the immense energy that accompanied the ideas in these chapters. Clearly resonant was the heartfelt assertion by women and male allies that it's about time to hear what is important to women in experiential education.

In keeping with the spirit of volunteer service, all profits from the sale of this book will be donated to the Association for Experiential Education, with half of the money directed to the Women's Professional Group for scholarships and awards to enhance women's research, writing, and participation in experiential education.

Finally, in piecing together this quilt of women's voices, I was reminded of how much quilts are a chronicle of a way of life that can be passed on to the next generation. Women rarely quilt solely for themselves; the quilt regularly serves as an endowment expressing love and care. I sense that the women who worked tirelessly on this book see it as an endowment of care and commitment to be handed down to the next generation of women and girls in experiential education.

The ability to speak from one's own experience is the best remedy to powerlessness. Yet the access to an audience through the wide dissemination of the written word has frequently been closed off to women. Women face a multitude of constraints in their attempt to gain a voice in the field of experiential education. My own process with this book is illustrative.

The seeds of this book germinated from my own work as a woman in a male-dominated field. As I became more involved in the Association for Experiential Education (AEE), I wondered where the women authors were and why very few women's voices existed in the literature of experiential education. I personally knew countless women who were doing amazing things in experiential education programming but I didn't see this reflected in the writings about the field.

Then I read a letter in the *Journal of Experiential Education* (*JEE*) from Peggy Walker Stevens addressed to the women members of the association. (Peggy mentions that letter in her story in the last chapter of this book.) Her letter infuriated me. In it, Peggy pointed out that the number of women on the AEE Board was decreasing, that women were absent in the major volunteer roles within AEE, and that women authors in the *Journal* were virtually nonexistent. She implored women to stop complaining about AEE being a male-dominated organization and get involved. The letter made me angry because I didn't feel Peggy had considered the constraints to involvement that kept women on the outside of the power center of the association. I knew from experience that women are wonderful writers, tireless volunteers, valuable proponents of experiential education. So what impeded their involvement in the literature and leadership of experiential education? As it certainly wasn't because women did not wish to be involved, the answer must lie elsewhere.

In thinking about constraints for women, I am reminded of Marilyn Frye's (1983) essay about oppression. She uses the analogy of a bird cage to show the barriers that exist for oppressed people. If you look at the wires of a bird cage microscopically, one wire at a time, it seems inconceivable that any one wire could prove an obstacle to the bird's escape to freedom. Yet if you step back and view all the wires together, macroscopically, then it is apparent that the wires are an impediment to the bird's freedom. As Frye (1983) points out:

> It is perfectly *obvious* that the bird is surrounded by a network of systematically related barriers, no one of which would be the least hindrance to its flight, but which, by their relations to each other, are as confining as the solid wall of a dungeon. (p. 5)

Similarly, barriers to women's involvement and ability to have a voice in the field of experiential education have often been complex, difficult to articulate, and cumulative.

I will use my journey in conceptualizing and completing this book as an example of the obstacles women encounter. My story certainly does not reflect the experiences of all women in the field because we have all come up against different barriers and found different solutions; however, I share my process to give a face to the complicated challenge of claiming a voice.

Doubt played a part in this book's evolution. It took me a long time to believe in the possibility of this book. On these pages are the words I wanted to see 20 years ago as an entry-level, outdoor experiential educator. If not for wonderful mentors and carefully developed support networks in the field, this book would still be on my wish list.

As a first-generation college graduate in a working-class family, I struggled against the feeling that I was an impostor in the academic community. How could my working-class language put me in association with polished scholars? Upon viewing the draft manuscript, my dad asked me very sincerely, "What makes you an editor?" I stumbled on the answer, "I just decided I am."

There are other hurdles that many women must surmount in order to gain a voice in this field. I knew financial resources and families had a bearing, but didn't realize how much until my own experience with being a mother while employed in the outdoor experiential education field. Right in the middle of this book project, my partner and I got the call saying our daughter was waiting for us in China. I returned from a nine-day canoe trip in Georgia and left for China two days later. The book went in the piles on my desk left in my office darkened by maternity leave. When I finally got my wits together enough to pick up the book project again, it was often amid baby bottles and rattles, between diaper changes. I got so I could quickly look at a manuscript and determine how many of my daughter's naps it would take to edit it.

The time spent in the field was also a constraint as well as an inspiration. Many times chapters were tucked in a dry bag or backpack to be read later in my tent by flashlight. I edited and wrote at the solo basecamp, during school visitations, on rest stops and rain delays. I composed ideas during my morning run. The all-consuming nature of working as an outdoor experiential educator often limits those immersed in the field from putting the innovative ideas of their practice into writing. Yet those voices are essential if we are to resist the inclination to be experience rich and theory poor.

Even the actual putting together of the book reflected the challenge of claiming a voice. There is a way of editing other women's voices that I am just beginning to tentatively understand. I struggled with how to nurture contributors' voices, how to encourage them to be stronger and more accessible to their vast and varied audience yet still maintain the integrity of their uniqueness. In working with the chapter authors, I reminded myself that I must resist writing my own article with their pen. The editor's job is as mentor, guide, supporter, and reframer but not as rewriter; I left it up to the authors to be true to their own voices as women. I did not attempt to standardize spelling, instead preserved the British English used here by Canadian and New Zealand authors.

I find it noteworthy that no authors in this volume use quantitative justification as a basis for their essays. Similar to the work of Carol Gilligan and other noted feminist researchers, the experiences and voices of women are the foundation for hypothesis and analysis for contributors to this text. The common threads in this collection involve questions about how experiential education fits women's ways of learning, being, and experiencing in the world.

This book is intended for all practitioners and programmers of experiential education, both women and men. As the ideas contained here have influenced and will continue to reshape the thinking in the entire field of experiential education, those practitioners desiring to stay abreast with a changing field will pay heed to the contents of these chapters. Like the utilitarian nature of a quilt, the thoughts contained in this book are meant to be used. Those working in the field will find insights they can directly apply to their teaching and leading. Theorists will find novel variations on contemporary experiential education thought. Program administrators will find blueprints to make their program design and management more receptive to the needs of their female staff and students.

I guarantee that some of the ideas advanced here will be at times inspiring, and at times disconcerting. As you read this book, I ask you to remember that when moved out of our comfort zone, we sometimes tend to invalidate the challenging idea. I encourage you to neither discard nor take the ideas here as the absolute truth. I urge you to sit with these ideas, to act on them, to discuss them, to disagree not in isolation but by entering into dialogue. In a book about voices, dialogue is an essential goal.

There are panels of the quilt that are still empty; missing are the voices of women in mainstream education and in the corporate training world. The voices of women with disabilities, older women, and women in experiential education outside the adventure realm are also absent. Additionally, the voices that are here can in no way represent the final word on women's issues in the field. There is much quilting yet to be done; the empty squares are beautiful, open pieces of fabric awaiting a new voice of women in experiential education. I hope we have the courage, the persistence, and the care to bring those panels to life.

Many people have told me that they have waited a long time for the arrival of this quilt of women's voices. I am happy that they will now be able to wrap themselves in it.

Karen Warren
January, 1996

References

Angelou, M. (1993). *Wouldn't take nothing for my journey now.* New York: Random House.

Frye, M. (1983). *The politics of reality: Essays in feminist theory.* Trumansburg, NY: The Crossing Press.

Questioning Voices

*Wholeness may have something to do
with speaking in one's own words.*

May Sarton

Not too long ago I stood with a group of women in front of the Spider's Web.[1] It was early in a class I was teaching on women and girls in the outdoors where we were doing group initiatives both to build our group and to examine issues important to us as women in outdoor adventure. Before we attempted to pass group members through the openings in the web, I stressed physical and emotional safety. I had used the Spider's Web initiative with groups countless times previously to foster trust, problem-solving skills, and cooperation, and expected similar results this time. I anticipated that this tried-and-true activity would further help us to bond and feel safe with each other.

As we stood before the various size openings of the web, the women began to speak. I listened empathetically as one by one, the women started to tell their stories of how body image had been such a difficult issue for them throughout their lives. As the women in my class assessed the challenge before them, they did not see potentials for cooperation or community building, but instead self-doubt and questioning about their bodies. Even after they decided to try it, their conflicting feelings of body image loomed larger than feelings of accomplishment at completing the initiative. I was poignantly reminded on that day that the popular techniques of experiential education must be constantly subjected to critical examination. I witnessed once more how women's experience in the outdoors does not necessarily fit neatly into the recipes for success common to the field of experiential education.

So, too, the chapters in this section question and critique some of the commonly accepted ideas and practices in experiential education. The section begins with a piece I wrote which theorizes about women's experience in outdoor adventure programming by examining five prevalent myths which may serve as stoppers for women who seek meaningful outdoor challenges. Next, Mary McClintock addresses the often-asked question, "Why have all-women's outdoor trips?" by recording the rich variety of women's answers. McClintock supports the rationale for all women's programming through this collection of diverse voices of women explaining why

7

adventuring with other women is imperative to them. Heidi Mack looks at the use of metaphor practiced widely in the field, particularly by therapeutic adventure practitioners. She draws on her work with women with eating disorders to question the applicability of imposed metaphors for women, suggesting instead that women be encouraged to derive their own distinct metaphoric meaning from each experience. Anjanette Estrellas's chapter suggests that the research on stress and eustress has been misinterpreted and that creating stressful situations for participants in the outdoors could be suspect. Estrellas proposes a feminist model for decreasing stress in wilderness adventure programming. Finally, Ruth Rohde offers an analysis and critique of program models used to work with survivors of incest. She disputes the use of a stress model by therapeutic wilderness programs and makes key recommendations for leaders and program designers working with groups of adult women incest survivors.

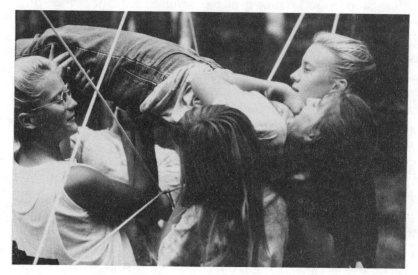

Photo courtesy of Kendall Kalkstein

The questions raised by authors in this section can encourage experiential educators to scrutinize some of the practices that have been taken for granted in the past. This new look promises to contribute to new theories and practices, particularly ones that support the experience of women and girls, in the field of outdoor experiential education.

Endnote

[1] The Spider's Web is a group problem-solving initiative where members of the group are passed through openings in nylon strands roughly configured in the shape of a spider's web. See K. Rohnke, (1984), *Silver Bullets*, Hamilton, MA: Project Adventure, Inc., for a description, and M. Gass, (1995), *Book of Metaphors*, Dubuque, IA: Kendall/Hunt, for possible applications.

Reference

Sarton, M. (1973). *Journal of a solitude.* New York: W.W. Norton.

1

Women's Outdoor Adventures: Myth and Reality

Karen Warren

Two decades ago, Outward Bound opened its doors to women, initiating a trend in providing women access to institutionalized outdoor adventure. By creating courses for women, adventure organizations took great preliminary strides in validating women's outdoor experiences. It is now time to move on. Adventure leaders must recognize that a woman's experience in the wilderness is unique and that programming should correspond to this different perspective. To simply sign up a group of women for a standardized course and enlist the services of available women instructors ignores the specific needs of this special population.

In looking at adventure programming from a feminist perspective, we need to ask questions and ultimately redefine our assumptions. Is outdoor experiential education an effective methodology for women's growth? How can existing wilderness models be adapted to respond to women's needs? How is the outdoor experience of this clientele unique and what implications does that have for programming? To answer these questions, it is useful to explore several myths which underlie our conceptions of women's adventure experiences. These myths, which cause adventure programs to be unresponsive to women through ignorance rather than intention, also serve as stoppers for women at various stages in their pursuit of meaningful outdoor challenges. After defusing the myths by recognizing their existence and reconciling their impact, adventure programs can respond to the special needs of women in the wilderness.

The Myth of Accessibility

The myth of accessibility is based on the misconception that outdoor experiences are widely available to women. As more women participate through organized coed programs as well as through emerging women's tripping businesses, the appearance of equal access is fostered. However, women's reality doesn't support this notion.

Social and economic factors limit women's participation; a new vision which postulates alternative avenues to include women in outdoor activities is in order.

Women's economic inequity, well documented in their statistically lower earning power, is the first deterrent to involvement in adventure programs. A woman struggling with the grocery bills may not be able to consider a backpacking trip. Furthermore, while a man has a sense of the value of adventure experiences based on previous exposures, a woman with no prior experience may not be willing to assume the financial risk for an unknown commodity. She is unsure if adventure-based education makes economic sense.

Adventure programs intent on increasing access need to pay more attention to providing scholarships, instituting sliding-scale fee structures, and offering course price discounts. The Hurricane Island Outward Bound School's policy of offering reduced course fees to Women Outdoors, Inc., members is a positive step in this direction. For other programs to follow suit would signify a commitment to equitable accessibility.

Photo courtesy of Moon Joyce

The primary factor that advances the myth of accessibility is a woman's social conditioning. When deciding between the needs of her loved ones and her own desire for adventure, an outdoor trip seems frivolous and trivial compared to a child who might need her. Making the choice to take for herself when she is trained to always give to others creates an internal conflict. Guilt at pursuing her own needs is a powerful deterrent from seeking adventure experiences.

Besides, social conditioning inundates a woman with the insistent message that the woods is no place for her. Not only must she then reconcile her own doubts on a personal level (i.e., guilt at leaving the family alone, economic stress, etc.), a woman faces substantial societal risks in pursuing adventure experiences. Historically a masculine domain, the wilderness trip is painted by the message bearers of the media and tradition as a scary, uncomfortable, and intimidating event. The moment she steps into the woods, her femininity is in question. Faced with these odds, it is a great social risk for women to be involved in outdoor programs. By not being a part of the male network that validates outdoor challenges, a woman misses the external prompting and support to seek the offerings of adventure programs.

Outdoor programs with a mandate for equal access will work along avenues women trust to minimize factors that prevent women's full participation in wilderness activities. Forming networks of women who have found value in the outdoors, promoting adventure options through women's educational and social organizations, and offering short courses which allow women to sample the wilderness without making a huge time or financial commitment are all possibilities for adventure institutions to pursue to avert inaccessibility.

The Myth of Egalitarianism

This myth is predicated on the notion that the wilderness is an ideal place to revise prevailing social conditioning. As outdoor experiential educators, we are imbued with the power of the mountains to enact changes in people's lives. We therefore believe that a viable corollary to the wilderness-as-social-healer axiom is that the outdoors is the perfect place to eradicate any inequalities based on gender. We can encourage women to light stoves while the men do the cooking and in the process redefine acquired sex roles. The fallacy of this aspiration lies in the fact that the wilderness is not a natural place to break stereotypes. When it's pouring rain, the group has been hiking all day, and it's growing dark, the most expedient way to set up camp is for people to do tasks that are comfortable and familiar to them. In spite of our noble intentions of egalitarianism, when efficiency is important in a trying situation women often do end up cooking.

The coed wilderness trip also serves as a constant, insidious reminder to women that their intrinsic worth on the course is in doubt. Weight distribution on a backpacking course illustrates this point. Since women have lower weight-carrying capabilities than men, when it comes time to divide up group gear and food, women should realistically carry less of the load. Yet in a group situation where participants ideally have an equal commitment to group responsibilities, the message that subtly prevails is that the woman is not carrying her weight. Someone else is doing it for her. What the woman makes up for in load transporting by her nurturing, endurance, and facilitation is often not given comparable acclaim because her contribution to the trip is more intangible.

It is important for adventure course leaders to understand how wilderness experiences that subtly emphasize physical prowess perpetuate the myth of egalitarianism and undermine a woman's experience outdoors. Since research has demonstrated that women have proportionately less absolute strength than men, wilderness course components that favor strength discriminate against women. Yet this discrimination is rarely blatant; therein lies its tyranny. My favorite example to show this elusive dynamic is about learning to single-carry a canoe while I was portaging in the Boundary Waters of northern Minnesota. As I repeatedly struggled unsuccessfully to raise a 77-pound Grumman to my shoulders, my male counterparts who also had not yet mastered the technique could still succeed by muscling the canoe. My friends constantly reminded me that upper-body strength was unimportant if I had perfect technique. These encouraging exhortations made it no less obvious that I was a failure because my technique was unrefined while my equally inexperienced male friends were shuffling down the portage trail with the canoe on their backs. This example shows that while both male and female participants may be similarly skilled in a particular course component, if the task is better suited to the male body type, the woman faces initial failure and feelings of inadequacy. Instead of changing the emphasis of the task, women are expected to be perfect and, therefore, may be discouraged from seeking additional adventure situations.

Adventure programs sensitive to the myth of egalitarianism will alter course components that unconsciously discriminate against women. Obviously I am not suggesting that adventure programs make courses easier for women; that idea has been justly put to rest by those who realize that simply advocating an easier version of a standard course is condescending to women and not a useful methodology for their growth through adventure experiences. I do, however, envision a different experience for women outdoors. For example, egalitarianism at the climb site means concentrating on climbs that emphasize less upper-body strength and more grace. It means selecting ropes course events that will offer realistic challenges based on women's skills and abilities in endurance, flexibility, and balance, and avert the predetermined failure intrinsic to elements which invalidate women's strengths. It also means elevating perceived risk while de-emphasizing intensive physical strength in challenging situations. By extending the feminist philosophy of comparable worth to the outdoor adventure field, the myth of egalitarianism could be unequivocally denied.

The Myth of Square One

The myth of square one is apparent at the start of most beginning-level wilderness education courses. Outdoor instructors often assume that beginners arrive with the same lack of skills and similar disadvantages—in other words, all participants start at square one. This unfortunate assumption can be detrimental to women, especially as it affects the type of instruction they receive because of it. Lacking the same precursory experiences which men have acquired through their conditioning, women embark upon a wilderness adventure at a disadvantage. I have identified three major precursory experiences which directly influence the quality of women's outdoor undertakings. Because women lack technical conditioning, role models, and an internalized assumption of success, they are thwarted in maximizing wilderness learning situations.

The first precursory experience denied women, technical conditioning, affects a woman's aptitude to easily and enjoyably learn wilderness skills. Mechanical unfamiliarity may hinder her ability to grasp stove use and repair, while math anxiety prevents her from learning map-and-compass skills as quickly as her male counterparts. Rock climbing, an activity which usually creates some anxiety in participants regardless of gender, becomes more problematic for a woman because she has not had the same opportunity to handle ropes and tie knots as her Boy Scout-trained cohorts. Therefore, it is paramount that enlightened adventure programs take women's shortage of technical training into account when planning instruction. When instructors do not recognize that they must first peel back the layers of technical apprehensiveness that trouble most women, they promulgate the myth of square one.

The invisibility of acceptable role models also prevents women outdoors from starting at square one. I remember very distinctly my first day instructing at the Outward Bound School in Minnesota when I found out that the student patrol groups were named MacKenzie, Pond, Radisson, and Hennepin after the explorers and traders of the northwoods. Where were the women? It's not that no role models exist; women have been active in the outdoors throughout history, yet their story is hidden or unspoken. It's time to reclaim the Isabella Birds, the Fanny Workmans, and the Mina Hubbards from their historical burial grounds and restore them as role models to young and old adventurous women.

The final precursor deficient in a woman's outdoor experience is an internalized assumption of success. A woman who constantly encounters surprise that "she got as far as she did in the wilderness" will soon internalize the message that she is expected to fail. So not only is the woman's presence in the wilderness questioned, her ability to cope once there has been traditionally discredited. Realizing this social prejudice, it is understandable that when a woman is faced with a challenging situation in the outdoors, the little voice of anticipated failure comes back to color her response. She is no longer simply figuring out how to fix a broken tent pole or taking a compass bearing; the woman is first forced to wrestle with her fear of defeat, her fear frequently becoming a self-fulfilling prophecy.

The uniqueness of how women learn intervenes as well. While men have been urged to learn experientially, women are often left to learn by observation. Wilderness skills, which are usually task oriented, allow a man to step forward buoyed up the supposition that he will succeed. So inspired, he masters the task. On the other hand, the woman who watches the demonstration of an outdoor skill has the weight of a double doubt bearing down on her. Her confidence is undermined both by the absence of an internalized expectation of accomplishment and by her inexperience in learning by doing. Seeking alternative creative ways of teaching is the answer adventure programs must embrace to confront this paradox. Adventure educators must be prepared to advocate for different styles of learning and to critically examine how their own attitudes may unconsciously contribute to women's inner predictions of failure.

The Myth of the Superwoman

While the effects of this myth eventually filter down to all outdoorswomen, the myth of the superwoman most acutely maligns women outdoor leaders. In order to achieve an advanced rank in the outdoor field, women leaders acquire exemplary competence in all outdoor skills. In this common scenario, she can carry the heaviest pack with a smile on her face. She demonstrates complete command of her campstove, compass, and canoe. She is comfortable in the mountains and woods, confident in her unequaled proficiency. Yet the Catch 22 is exactly that competence which women leaders have worked years to gain and refine. For with superior abilities, she becomes the superwoman, a woman unlike the rest of the population. Her students no longer have to view her competence for what it is—the ongoing struggle to gain parity in a male-dominated profession.

The effect of the superwoman on wilderness course participants is unintentionally detrimental. Participants, both men and women, struggle with the dissonance created by the conflict between their indoctrination that implies a woman doesn't belong in the wilderness and the reality of the woman outdoor leader guiding them. The existence of the superwoman gives them a way out of this nagging conflict. Due to her exemplary outdoor achievements, the superwoman is the exception to other women. She's extraordinary, unique, not normal. As an anomaly, the superwoman instructor can be cast aside and made invisible in the minds of the students. When she is perceived as being unrepresentative of ordinary women, participants are no longer forced to deal with their sexist conditioning; they need not reappraise their world view of women. They merely write off this one superwoman as incongruous and leave the course with the same cultural baggage they had when they arrived.

The implications for women participants are notably profound. While the woman instructor might serve as a wonderful role model to other women, her superwoman status disallows this. Women, especially beginners in the outdoor field, may feel great admiration for the superwoman but are intimidated by this woman who, in addition to her superlative outdoor skills, may display no apparent fears. The "I can never be like her" statement that rings in the minds of her female students robs the competent outdoor leader of her opportunity to be a role model.

Adventure program leaders and administrators can counter the myth of the superwoman by being conscientious of the style of leadership they value. Sharing leadership by consensus decision making, demystifying competency, and revealing vulnerabilities may be one method of confronting the myth. With attention to the tenets of a feminist vision of outdoor leadership, the superwoman has no impetus to come into being.

The Myth of the Heroic Quest

The final myth to be explored centers on women's spiritual identity in a wilderness adventure situation. A metaphor employed by adventure programs is a model of the heroic quest prevalent in classical and contemporary literature. The participant undergoes a real-life experience in the wilderness that parallels the mythical quest of the hero. The student hears a call to adventure, leaves home, encounters dragons on the way and slays them, reflects on his conquest, and returns home as a hero with a clearer understanding of himself.

Upon closer examination, the heroic quest is a metaphor that has little meaning to women. Each stage of a woman's journey in the wilderness is a direct contradiction of the popular quest model. A woman rarely hears a call to adventure; in fact, she is more often dissuaded by the factors discussed in the myth of accessibility from leaving home to engage in adventurous pursuits. The dragons looming in a woman's path on a wilderness course are equally ambiguous. Are these metaphoric limitations a personal block or are they societally imposed? It's impossible for her to sort out. Which dragons should she slay? Needing a point of reference to discern the difference, a woman finds confusion at this stage of the model. Furthermore, a woman's experience often is not compatible with viewing challenges in the wilderness in a militaristic framework; she is more likely to ally with the metaphoric dragons than to conquer them. Returning home is also problematic for women if the myth of the heroic quest is given credence. While a man's mythical journey in the wilderness parallels his everyday situation, a woman's does not. Encouraged to be bold and aggressive in the woods, this style transfers readily for a man upon return. The woman who has learned to be strong, assertive, and independent on a wilderness course encounters intense cognitive dissonance back home because these traits are not presently valued for her in society. Transfer of her newly acquired understanding of her strengths to her real world life is jeopardized. Finally, as argued in the section on the superwoman, the generic model of heroism, because it necessitates the emergence of a hero or superperson, incites a tradition that is a disservice to women.

The answer, therefore, is not to engage women in the heroic quest cycle, but to inspire a new heroic for adventure programming. A heroic based on bonding with the natural world rather than conquering it may be the foundation of a new metaphor for outdoor adventure experiences for men and women alike. Adopting women's emphasis on merging with nature and the attention to spiritual complete-ness and process valued by many women outdoors, wilderness programs may increase the spiritual and, eventually, the social significance of their course offerings.

Conclusion

What emerges from this analysis of the myths prevalent in the adventure experi-ence of women is not only a cogent rationale for women's outdoor programs, but also a call for a feminist standard integral to all courses. Enlightened programs for women must strive to follow the tenets of John Dewey who cautioned against trans-ferring a body of knowledge from one generation to the next—especially if that body of knowledge is skewed and inappropriate to a woman's view. When Dewey urged educators to learn new role borders, to recodify ingrained habits, and to ques-tion old ideas, he was epitomizing a feminist approach to outdoor adventure.

The goal of this discussion has been to point out that women bring to adventure experiences not only distinct needs that programs must acknowledge but also a unique perspective that would be beneficial if incorporated in all facets of outdoor experiential education. By labeling myths that impede our realization of gender dif-ferences, we take the first step in ensuring that outdoor adventure will be a positive, holistic experience for women. The demise of the myths frees adventure leaders to conceive and restructure programs that will be on the cutting edge of growth for men and women alike.

Endnote

This chapter was originally published in the 1985 *Journal of Experiential Education, 8*(2), 10-14.

References

Andrews, R. (1984, May/June). No spare rib. *Mountain, 97,* 22-29.

Bacon, S. (1983). *The conscious use of metaphor in Outward Bound.* Denver, CO: Colorado Outward Bound School.

Christ, C. P. (1980). *Diving deep and surfacing.* Boston, MA: Beacon Press.

Del Rey, P. (1978, Spring). Apologetics and androgyny: The past and the future. *Frontiers, 3,* 8-10.

Dewey, J. (1938). *Experience and education.* New York: Collier.

Fielder, E. (1979, March, April, May). Women and leadership. *Women in the Wilderness Quarterly,* 4-15.

Galland, C. (1980). *Women in the wilderness.* New York: Harper & Row.

Hardin, J. A. (1979). *Outdoor/wilderness approaches to psychological education for women: A descriptive study.* Ed.D. dissertation, University of Massachusetts, Amherst.

Maughan, J. J. (1983). *The outdoor woman's guide to sports, fitness and nutrition.* Harrisburg, PA: Stackpole Books.

2

Why Women's Outdoor Trips?

Mary McClintock

I have lost track of the number of times I have been asked, "Why are you going on an all-women's trip?" Nor can I remember the wide variety of responses, ranging from flippant to serious, that I have given over the years. Sometimes, the question is asked with a genuine interest and support, but often the question is asked in a hostile, offensive manner. Other all-women's groups and organizations regularly face similar questions, especially if their activity or purpose challenges traditional gender roles. After twenty years of experience on all-women's outdoor trips, I thought that the question would not be asked anymore. But I continue to hear "Why?"

I didn't think much about the question until I participated in a course in the Hampshire College Outdoors Program entitled, "Mountains, Back Roads, Rivers and Women," taught by Joy Hardin in 1976. Prior to that course, my women's trip experience had been with the Outing Club from the women's college I attended. When out on the trail or the water, responding to questions about why there weren't any men with us was easy . . . we just said we were from a women's college.

But Joy's course made me finally stop and think: Why did I choose all-women's trips? I was stunned by what I heard the first day of the course when, after cross-country skiing all afternoon, we talked about our reasons for taking the course. I was excited at the chance to develop more outdoor skills and go on a number of trips. As we went around the circle, most of the women described reasons that focused on doing outdoor activities with other women. Their reasons fell into themes I've heard many times since then:

1. the emotional and physical safety of all women's trips;
2. the freedom to step out of gender role stereotypes;
3. the opportunity to develop close connections with other women;
4. and the comfortable environment for being a beginner and learning new skills and, alternatively, for being highly skilled.

18

At the time, I was amazed to hear such a range of reasons different from my own and the passion with which these women had sought out an opportunity to be with other women outdoors. I realized I needed to examine my own reasons, beyond outdoor skill development, for choosing a women's course. After all, if what I wanted was skill development, there were many coed programs available to me. I didn't really have words for it at the time, but somehow I knew that I could be comfortable and stretch and grow in a group of women.

That course was almost twenty years ago, and the question, "Why a women's trip?" is still asked today. Any woman who considers an all-women's trip has to first answer the question for herself. In answering to herself, a woman often has to overcome the social conditioning that has trained her not to choose to meet her own needs, but rather, to meet the needs of others. After answering the internal question, she then often has to answer to someone else—her spouse, boyfriend, parent, friends, co-workers, boss, or children. Even strangers we meet on the trail or on the water question why we choose women's trips, or as they often see it, why we exclude men.

Photo courtesy of Mary McClintock

There seem to be two questions: "Why are there women-only trips?" and "Why would a woman choose a women's trip?" Parallel questions don't seem to be asked of men. Are men who are going fishing with the guys asked, "Why a *men's* trip?" I had hoped the growing popularity of women's trips would point to the obvious answer to the question of why they exist: because women want to be in the outdoors with other women. Many outdoor-trip businesses run all-women's trips for the simple reason that they sell.

In planning this chapter, I had hoped to offer a definitive answer so I could keep copies in my pack to pass out to each person who asks. I have since realized that while many women have written in the experiential education and recreation literature about this topic, there is no one definitive answer. Every woman, at any given moment, has her own answer.

What I choose to do is record some of the answers women give to this question and to encourage women to continue to do women's outdoor trips for whatever reason. The following is a collection of answers drawn from many sources: from other women I asked specifically for this chapter, from myself, and from other women I've encountered outdoors over the last twenty years. I collected answers from friends while sea kayaking off the coast of Maine, from answers written on large sheets of newsprint I posted on the wall at the Northeast Women Outdoors Gathering, and from women I know who are leaders and participants in women's outdoor trips.

I invite you to sit back and imagine that you are sitting in a circle of women outdoors somewhere on a trip—next to a whitewater river, in the desert, on a mountainside, wherever women travel together. Imagine that one woman has just said, "I know my reason for choosing this women's trip, but I don't know everyone else's reason. I'm curious . . . WHY DID YOU CHOOSE A WOMEN'S OUTDOOR TRIP?"

AND THE WOMEN ANSWERED:

- Because I like spending time with other women outdoors.
- When I was growing up, my father and brother and uncle and boy cousins went on overnight, whitewater canoe trips, while my mother and sister and I stayed at the cabin. Now I want to learn how to do all the paddling and camping skills, but I feel like such a beginner, I thought I'd be more comfortable with other women who didn't get to learn this stuff when they were kids.
- My husband doesn't like going on extensive paddling trips, and I do. But I don't like going with coed groups where everyone is already coupled or there is an underlying assumption that those who aren't paired up are looking for a "trip fling."
- There is a special support and camaraderie that happens when a group of women spend time with each other outdoors. I really treasure the times I get to spend with women where our complete focus is on each other and the outdoors. It seems like we are all able to relax with each other and ourselves in a way that doesn't happen when we are in our regular city lives.
- For years, I went on coed trips where, as a highly skilled outdoorswoman, I found myself caught between connecting with the men around our shared competence and skills or with the women around our identity as women. On these trips, I often found the women became resentful of me or were

intimidated by my skill level. Now, I prefer to go on trips with women who share my skill level.

- I work year-round in an outdoor program for adolescent boys and need time to be with other women to be reminded that I am not the only woman in the world who likes the outdoors.

- Because I love women.

- In coed settings, I've been embarrassed to ask questions about things like how to tie a bowline, how to coil a rope, and other stuff that you're already supposed to know somehow. I'm afraid I'll get kidded for not knowing basic stuff. On women's trips, I can ask for guidance without being talked down to. I can compete at my own level and achieve what I can, encouraged by others while in the company of and inspired by strong role models.

- I'm trying to understand what it means to be a woman and not be defined by men. In mixed groups, I feel like I am either going along with the men's image of who I should be or rebelling against that image. With other women, I think I can sort out a definition of myself as a woman that comes from inside of me and other women.

- As a lesbian who works in a setting hostile to lesbians, trips with women are a chance for me to relax into all of who I am, rather than be compartmentalized like I have to be at work.

- I'm widowed and want to go hiking in another country, but don't feel comfortable traveling as a woman alone. When I used to do trips with my husband, I felt safe. I don't need a man to protect me. A group of women traveling together can take care of each other.

- With women, I can relax and not feel judged as to how I fit or don't fit the way women are "supposed to be."

- The outdoor activities—skiing, winter camping, biking, and canoeing—on the course sound like great fun and I qualify because it's a women's course and I'm a woman.

- I think women come into their own in women-only events. Men are empowered and privileged in our culture, and women are often intimidated and self-conscious when men are around. The power dynamics are unequal. Women tend to be more confident in women-only events.

- I don't have to watch (as much) where I pee. I can be more open about my body and not feel like the men are checking me out as a potential sexual partner.

- It's really not so much what anyone else does or doesn't do that impacts my experience, but more the degree to which I let my inhibitions go. The inhibitions that limit me are emotional, so the more interdependent the companions, the more I feel at ease. Life experience has given me many more self-regulating habits when men are involved. I can meet my goals successfully and with more satisfaction when I'm free of that baggage.

- Because I like women and can enjoy outdoor activities without all the male superiority bullshit our society throws at us.
- Because I feel less self-conscious and more self-confident in women-only groups. I feel proud to be a woman. I go home feeling renewed.
- There's a different competition level when men are involved. Being stronger, they will always throw farther, hit harder, run faster, spike the ball harder, etc. When involved with women, a woman who can run faster, hit harder, etc., is someone I can admire. She provides a model and a resource for information on how I can better myself.
- It's the women in my world who nurture me. Spending time together outdoors is a chance to be surrounded by that nurturance.
- I enjoy experiencing outdoor activities free from the male ego and men's tendency to make decisions/take charge and women's/our tendency to allow or even encourage men to do so. The adventure experience is much more equal with women-only groups.
- I used to just do outdoor trips with my boyfriend and other male/female couples. I realized after many canoe trips, that I didn't know how to paddle in the stern or how to clean the campstove, or how to set up the tent by myself. When I mentioned this to others in the group, they said it was easier for everyone to do what they know how to do best and that it takes too much time and effort for everyone to learn new things. Well, I want to learn new things. Maybe I'll like stern-paddling better.
- As a woman leader on coed trips, I've often been challenged by male participants who push me to prove my competence and ability to be a leader. Often this happens with men who are at a beginner skill level in an activity that I am at an expert skill level. It feels as if they challenge me because they can't believe a woman could really be an expert in an outdoor activity. I have never experienced this kind of "testing" on women's trips I've led.
- As a rape survivor, I don't feel emotionally and physically safe living so closely with men I don't know. I feel more comfortable and able to relax in my body with a group of women.
- When I was a kid, I used to resent being forced to do things in groups of girls. Boys and girls weren't allowed in the same groups and teams. I always thought that I was missing out on the adventures the boys were having. Now, I CHOOSE to be with groups of women because with women, I feel free to challenge the rules about how women are supposed to behave.
- The key thing is for women to be able to choose to be in coed or in women's groups. People keep telling me that we should all be together now, because segregation is bad and exclusive. But the world isn't equal yet. Discrimination and prejudice happen every day to me and other women. To have men, for whatever reason, even in the interest of equality, make the choice

for me about what kind of group I can be in or not, continues the power imbalance of the genders. I and other women need to have choices, to be able to choose a place to be all of who we are without being prejudged or discriminated against.

- Just because we're out in the woods doesn't mean we all left our socialization behind. Men's socialization to take control and my own socialization to be passive mean that on mixed-gender trips, I end up stepping back and deferring to the men on the trip. On women's trips, there is a chance to stretch past my socialization.

- Outdoor trips with women are a great way to meet other lesbians as friends, lovers, traveling companions.

- When I spend time with women in the outdoors, I feel a deep healing connection with the earth. I need that connection to help me through the times I am back living in the human-manufactured world.

- It is tremendously exciting and rewarding to lead a group of women who begin a trip with little confidence in their abilities and very few technical skills and to watch them gain skills and a sense that they are capable and competent. On trips like that, I feel like I have made a small step toward combating the disabling forces that work on women every day—the forces, internal and external, that say to a woman, "You're not as good as, not as capable as, not okay. . . ."

These are some of the many reasons that women choose to go on all-women's trips. Many of the reasons relate to women's desire to escape the bounds and limits that sexism and gender roles have placed on women. So, if sexism disappeared tomorrow, would women still want to do outdoor trips with other women? My answer is an absolute YES! I would still want to do trips with other women because I love being in the company of strong, competent, fun women outdoors. Would any other woman still want to go outdoors in the company of women? I don't know. You'll have to ask her!!

Acknowledgments

The inspiration for this chapter came from countless women over the last twenty years— women I've done trips with and women I've had long talks with about "why *women's* trips." I want to acknowledge all of those women as well as a few specific women: Anne Garretson, Franny Osman, and Sondra Spencer, and others for writing on the wall at the Gathering; Margaret Anderson, my co-worker, who offered great editorial advice and said, after reading the article, "Reading all these reasons makes me want to go on a women's trip!"; Karen Warren for taking the dream of this book and making it into a reality, and for encouraging me to write this chapter; and Anne Hazzard, my life partner and paddling companion, who helped edit this article and who has supported my need to go off on trips with other women.

3

Inside Work, Outdoors: Women, Metaphor, and Meaning

Heidi Mack

Outdoor and experiential educators and, more specifically, adventure therapists, recognise metaphor as an effective method for transferring participant learning into functional change in situations outside the experiential learning setting (Bacon, 1983; Gass, 1993). Metaphors, used in the field of adventure therapy and experiential education, are usually in the form of activities created to map directly onto the experience of the participants and make the therapeutic intent more memorable (Gerstein, 1993). Although metaphors have profound healing potential, there is a subtle and important difference in methods for implementing their use through outdoor activities—a difference that is particularly meaningful for women. Examining the difference between adventure metaphors that are created and directed *for* participants (imposed metaphors), and metaphors that are created and directed *from within* the experience of the participants (derived metaphors), will be the focus of this chapter.

The belief that metaphors are an effective way to bring about change in individuals does not necessarily mean that existing metaphoric constructs address the specific needs and voices of women, how we learn and how we experience. Carol Gilligan (1982) speaks of "theories in which men's experience stands for all of human experience—theories which eclipse the lives of women and shut out women's voices" (p. xiii). Further, Joyce (1988) writes that this difference may reflect how men and women create experience: "Men create through a mechanism or extension outside of their bodies and women create from within their bodies: external/internal, tangible/intangible" (p. 22). Therefore, outdoor instructors for women populations cannot assume that existing theories about metaphors consider women's experience and women's ways of learning. Existing strategies for the use of metaphors with women should be carefully evaluated and restructured and, at times, discarded altogether.

In my experience as an outdoor and experiential support-group facilitator for women recovering from the eating disorder *bulimia nervosa,* it has become apparent that women have an incredible capacity to internalize information about their situation but lack the tools to transfer that knowledge to their lives. Appropriately framed settings, where metaphors can be created by women, can assist in the transfer of knowledge and aid in healing and empowerment.

Through exploration of the differences between imposed metaphors and derived metaphors, it will be clear that metaphors assume meaning when women, given the opportunity to rely on their own expertise, create personal metaphors that characterize their present experience. Derived metaphoric activities enable women to explore and reorder issues in their lives and communicate the many levels of meaning of their experience.

Karen Warren (1985) suggests that it is critical for instructors to look carefully at assumptions about suitability of outdoor adventure activities for women. Among other things, Warren recommends that adventure leaders ask themselves how existing outdoor adventure course models can be adapted to respond to the specific needs of women. Making activities reflect the needs of women is crucial in creating effective outdoor programs.

In the process of adapting existing activities, there may be a desire to discard the imposed metaphor constructs altogether, including the instructions that accompany them. For example, many women are weary of the word "adventure," which conjures up heroic quests and intense physical endurance. However, women instructors and programmers of feminist adventure therapy can work *within* existing constructs to create a place for women to derive meaning.

Altering Existing Metaphoric Constructs

Many of the alterations/adaptations needed to improve existing metaphoric constructs come from a shift away from directed learning and toward giving women control of their learning, changing, and healing. A trip to a local rock face to climb with a women's group this year was testimony to the effectiveness of altering an oft-used therapeutic metaphor situation. Once safety rules were instilled, we proceeded to climb, without choosing perfectly worded instructions to initiate the metaphoric activity. The post-climbing debrief moved smoothly through technical discussion, feelings of support, and communication, but more importantly, several women found moments of truth and connection in some of the most obscure places. For one woman, the colour and texture of the rock three inches from her nose became a four-by-six-inch snapshot of the only options she felt were available to her. Information and direction from women on the ground represented her "real options"—for the climb and for her situation outside the group. She was grateful for this, realising that there was more to her experience with bulimia—truths that she was not able to see without help and support.

Facilitating Derived Metaphor

Inherent in the imposed metaphoric construct is the assumption that the adventure instructor is responsible for creating and directing metaphoric activities. The antithesis of this view is a metaphor created by and derived from the participant's experience. Nadler and Luckner (1992) recognize the need for metaphors derived from the individual rather than imposed by the instructor. They suggest that the responsibility of the instructor is to create themes or frames within which metaphors can be created by the learners. Feminist adventure therapists advocate for this view and carry it further by giving participants a choice in activities.

Let's examine a hike to a local bog. In an imposed-metaphor setting, the facilitator may expect the bog to represent the same thing for every woman, that is, a problem to overcome. Participants may be expected to "conquer" the bog in the hope that success in the physical world would transfer to parallel success in the quagmires of their world away from the woods. In the activity and metaphor, as designed by the instructor, the solution to the problem would be to "go through the bog" to find success. But what if going through the bog is a solution that has no meaning in a woman's experience? Possibly, "going through the bog" could mean failure if a participant was unable to complete the task.

Consider an alternate scenario for success. The instructor provides a framework for metaphor creation, a hike. The bog that is encountered on the hike is not suggested to represent anything. There is no expected outcome or "right" way to interpret it. Without the imposition of a particular metaphoric representation, the bog takes on a more significant meaning for women who are working from within their own experience; there can be more profound, individualized interpretations. One woman may choose to stay completely away from the bog and find something else that entices her; another may decide to join another woman in finding its bottom or touching it and smelling it; another still may quietly and carefully move around the exterior to examine it from the outside for a while, assessing its depth and length before she decides she will walk through it. All of these solutions/interpretations have significant meaning for individual women.

However, the information encountered in the literature on the use of metaphor in the outdoors is not this inclusive. Instead, directing women from the outside by imposing expected outcomes of what the bog should represent, delineating the main issues of women's problems and identifying critical areas of change *for* them (Gass, 1993), is an example of imposed metaphor development popular in outdoor experiential education today. This practice is further exemplified by Bacon's (1983) description of how to "dress a metaphor":

> Once assessment is completed, the instructor needs to introduce an appropriate metaphoric experience designed to remedy whatever deficits exist in the patrol ... an instructor must be able to vary the meaning of an

upcoming event so that any prescheduled activity can meet any particular patrol needs. (p. 23)

In this case, it is assumed that it is the instructor's responsibility for metaphor creation and direction. In Gass's (1993) description of the Trust Fall, an activity where a participant stands on a 4- to 5-foot object and falls backward into the arms of the group, directions are given to the group before the activity begins:

> Each of you will be getting up here and holding on to this tree before falling backwards. Before you fall, I'm going to ask you to close your eyes and imagine that the tree is part of your personality—that piece of you most responsible for your drinking and drugging. I don't want you to think of this as a tree anymore; I want you to think of it as the most powerful factor responsible for your using. And I want you to hug it like you love it—like it's all you've got. (p. 225)

While it may be argued that direction is necessary in specific populations of clients in adventure therapy, I believe this highly directed and imposed metaphor is inappropriate for women. Telling women exactly what each component of the activity metaphorically represents creates a learning space crowded with expectations of how this activity should be interpreted. For women living in a world of externally imposed expectations, this activity may be inappropriate, replicating expectations that exist in their experience in a patriarchal society.

When outdoor instructors direct and impose metaphors, rather than encourage women to try what is best for them, they further disenable women by modeling that "others know what is best." Meaningful metaphors begin with value placed on the expertise and capacity of women. The result is a chance that the experience will more effectively be "bridged with personal meaning for the individual . . . the experience as a metaphor can then stand for the learning and be used in an abundance of ways and situations" (Nadler & Luckner, 1993, p. 96).

The Trust Fall activity would be framed differently from a derived metaphor perspective; the activity would not have imposed counterparts of meaning. Women would choose to fall from a self-selected height and would then explore what this meant for them. Perhaps this would have less to do with letting go and more to do with an undisclosed part of a woman's experience. The debrief following this activity would be a time when women might make connections between the activity and their life outside the group. This reflection would not exclusively rely on verbal communication; instead, women would choose their most effective way of reflecting, be that using journals, drawing, silent reflection, or discussion.

Effective adventure therapists use derived metaphors to reflect and celebrate women's differences. In my experience working with women with bulimia, it has been crucial that I acknowledge each woman's individual experience with bulimia— each woman comes to the group setting with a different history and will find a unique path to wellness. It is a difficult task to create an effective activity that reflects the needs of an entire female population if the circumstances that have brought each woman to the adventure therapy setting are different. Women may gather together in a group because they share issues that cause them to use similar coping strategies, like compulsive eating. However, there is a wide spectrum of ways women arrived at this point in their lives, and how they will heal.

Facilitators must respect and validate the various, unpredictable components of women's experiences and take care not to homogenize these experiences with expected learning outcomes. The use of derived metaphors facilitates the necessary task of treating each woman's experience as unique.

The Role of the Facilitator

Gass (1993) asserts that one of the complexities of his metaphoric model is that instructors have a substantial amount of responsibility. In the imposed metaphor model, not only must the instructor assess the client's needs, provide a safe physical environment, and ensure transfer of the experience to real-life settings, but she/he "must also provide appropriate framing and structuring of the experience for the client" (p. 226). This means an application of what might be considered a heavy and paternalistic hand in creating and directing the metaphoric activity.

While Gass assumes that it is the responsibility of the instructor to create and direct metaphors, Nadler and Luckner (1992) have a more individualized approach for the use of metaphors. They believe that it is important to fit learners' stories into existing frames or themes. They draw from Milton Erickson whose explanation of a mountain climb demonstrates a derived-metaphor model and follows a feminist philosophy of adventure therapy:

> [Erickson] frequently told his patients to climb a nearby peak where they would learn something significant. Typically, they would come down with a profound experience, discovering why he sent them there. He used these experiences metaphorically, allowing his patients to come back with whatever learning they needed. (p. 95)

The Feminist Facilitator

The complexity of instructor responsibility is lessened in a derived metaphoric model (or what might be termed a feminist metaphoric model). The facilitator acts as a situational thermostat. She is interactive and egalitarian, guiding women in their creation of metaphors within a broader framework or theme. Adler (1993), a feminist social worker who uses metaphors for healing self-harm behaviours, sees the role of the facilitator as one who "plays a supportive role and sets the backdrop for the metaphors to unfold, facilitating insight as required" (p. 275).

Adler (1993) believes that there are many reasons why the use of metaphor can be a very powerful and effective tool for healing in feminist therapy. The use of derived metaphors can allow women to maintain the locus-of-control in the adventure therapy setting. Through the creation of metaphors within frameworks, like the bog on the hike, women can express their own reality in a non-threatening way with as little or as much detail as feels comfortable. In Ozick's (1986) words, "Metaphor uses what we already possess and reduces strangeness" (p. 67). Women work at a recovery speed that is comfortable for them and rely on their own intuition, stopping when their healing process becomes too painful or too threatening (Adler, 1993).

Metaphors may also help women achieve a balanced perspective on the many "voices" that are at play in their worlds. Cooper (1991) believes that:

> Through the use of metaphor, the student begins to integrate the voice of societal expectations with the voice from within. She is listening to her inner feelings even as she attends to her world, attempting to balance the voices she hears from each, in order to develop a central integrated voice. (p. 102)

These voices are often represented in a group setting. Metaphors in group work may also allow women to imagine the experience of other women. "In a group, women can often see, understand and accept in other women what they cannot see, understand or accept in themselves" (Malmo, 1991, p. 396).

The use of metaphor can account for the individual differences in women's past experience, present interpretations, and future expectations. If women create their own metaphors to match their experience, then they can return to those metaphors and "add or change the elements when new learning or changes take place" (Nadler & Luckner, 1992, p. 95). When women make connections between their experience and the metaphor they have created, they gain trust in their own expertise. This guidance from within and trust of self to know what is best is empowering. By deriving metaphors, women are able to take responsibility for the choices they have made and are less likely to feel unsuccessful as a result of working with expectations imposed on them by a facilitator predetermining their needs.

An Environment Conducive to Derived Metaphor Creation

The facilitator can create an environment where derived metaphors are possible by using the following guidelines.

In general:

1. Establish that there are no expected outcomes in activities.
2. Enable women to create their own programme goals.
3. Show interest in women's histories and goals.
4. Encourage women to look within themselves for answers and expertise.

5. Ask women to examine and document their unique ways of healing so that they may refer to these on an ongoing basis.
6. Promote the power of individuality; discourage comparison to others.
7. Discourage "paralleling experience," that is, one woman's story drowns in the memories it sparks in other women's minds.
8. Encourage discussion among participants about the variety of goals that exist in the group.

More specifically:

9. Model analogies. Speak early in your programme about your own experience through the use of metaphoric language.
10. Use stories to create metaphoric language and connections.
11. Use art to draw feelings.
12. Use quick metaphoric activities (e.g., if I were a building, I would be a _____) to seed abstract thinking.
13. If a woman speaks about her experience in terms of a metaphor, ask questions within the context of the metaphor she has created.

Limitations of Metaphors

If an outdoor instructor plans to implement derived metaphoric constructs, it must be acknowledged that the use of metaphors is not appropriate for everyone. Since metaphors require the use of language and not everyone feels comfortable expressing themselves through words and discussion, not all women will respond to the abstract form of metaphor creation. A very logical thinker may have difficulty expressing her experience in anything other than concrete terms. Other tools for expression and reflection such as movement, writing, or art should be introduced.

Women may possibly become too absorbed in finding connections between their metaphors and their life. The facilitator may need to guide and model metaphors and help a woman see that sometimes metaphors do not fully map onto her life and experience. Relaxation and spontaneity are often needed to begin to explore personal metaphors or to make connections between metaphoric activities and actual life settings. This relaxation may be difficult for women who are afraid of losing control (Adler, 1993). It may be more appropriate to begin by a process of metaphoric training (Nadler & Luckner, 1992) where a woman can work through short fill-in-the-blank similes. For example, I am like a ____ because ____. There may be situations where it would be more useful for a facilitator to suggest a metaphor for a woman who is having difficulty getting started. If this is the case, several metaphors might be offered from among which a woman could choose (Adler, 1993).

The use of metaphor in outdoor settings for women has great potential for healing. When women instructors and programmers do not assume that the existing imposed metaphoric constructs are appropriate for women, and when women are given the opportunity to interpret therapeutic activities and derive meaning according to their own situations and experiences, the metaphors will have greater symbolic meaning and will inherently transfer to real-life situations.

References

Adler, M. (1993). Metaphors for healing self-harm behaviours. In C. Brown and K. Jasper (Eds.), *Consuming passions* (pp. 274-287). Toronto: Second Story.

Bacon, S. (1983). *The conscious use of metaphor in Outward Bound.* Denver, CO: Colorado Outward Bound School.

Cooper, J. E. (1991). Telling our own stories: The reading and writing of journals or diaries. In C. Witherell and N. Noddings (Eds.), *Stories lives tell.* New York: Teachers College Press.

Gass, M. (1993). *Adventure therapy: Therapeutic applications of adventure programming.* Dubuque, IA: Kendall/Hunt.

Gerstein, J. S. (1993). *High power group facilitation: A training manual for adventure-based counsellors.* Jaclyn S. Gerstein home publishing.

Gilligan, C. (1982). *In a different voice.* Cambridge, MA: The Harvard University Press.

Joyce, M. (1988). Rocks, rivers, men & women: Learning from each other at Outward Bound. *The Journal of COBWS Education, 4*(1), 22-25.

Malmo, C. (1991). Feminist therapy. *Canadian Journal of Counselling, 25*(4), 392-406.

Nadler, R. S., & Luckner, J. L. (1992). *Processing the adventure experience.* Dubuque, IA: Kendall/Hunt.

Ozick, C. (1986, May). The moral necessity of metaphor. *Harper's Magazine,* pp. 62-68.

Warren, K. (1985). Women's outdoor adventures: Myth and reality. *Journal of Experiential Education, 8*(2), 10-14.

Witherell, C. (1991). The self in narrative: A journey into paradox. In C. Witherell and N. Noddings (Eds.), *Stories lives tell.* New York: Teachers College Press.

4

The Eustress Paradigm:
A Strategy for Decreasing Stress in
Wilderness Adventure Programming

Anjanette Estrellas

Introduction

Ethical questions abound in the discussions of the role of stress in adventure programming. If stress, "a condition which arouses anxiety or fear" (Ewert, 1989b, p. 70), is a consistent element of wilderness adventures, to what extent should it be further manipulated or lessened? If risk taking is urged upon a client from a position of stress, is there a tendency to jeopardize or enhance physical and emotional safety? I investigated these questions by analyzing both the traditional and feminist perspectives on adventure education. In light of my inquiry, I propose that the use of "stress" has been mishandled in traditional adventure education. Furthermore, I believe the concept of "eustress" is vaguely and incorrectly interpreted and applied in traditional adventure education. The original writings on eustress are more congruent with a feminist perspective. I present a new model for risk taking that is based on the literature on stress and feminist perspectives in adventure education. The Eustress Paradigm is a strategy for decreasing unnecessary stress and increasing psychological and physiological benefits which result from eustress. Because I first began to conceptualize this model when I was exploring key differences and similarities between traditional and feminist perspectives on wilderness adventure programming, the first section of this chapter will review both perspectives.

The Traditional Perspective

I define the traditional perspective of adventure education as the philosophical movement which arose from the Outward Bound model created by Kurt Hahn. Originally, Outward Bound was a survival school created to meet the needs of young British seamen (Miner, 1990). The traditional perspective has its roots in a model which was created in a different country for specific cultural and gender needs. Evidence of this historical influence is found in Miner's statement on applying Outward Bound in the United States:

> The first major break with our constituency precedent was the introduction and astonishing success of courses for young women, along with the equally "astonishing" discovery that girls could handle—at times even with a superior blitheness—the same courses of the same degree of difficulty, that had been designed for boys. (p. 63)

Clearly, there is sex discrimination in the history of Outward Bound. Fortunately, since the 1960s, the field of adventure experiential education has been evolving philosophically. One example is the recent trend toward considering issues of emotional safety as well as physical safety (Priest, 1991). However, it is important to acknowledge the feminist roots of this methodology to include emotional safety as a priority (Mitten, 1994; Warren & Rheingold, 1993). This example, which some may call appropriation, serves as an illustration that the traditional perspective needs to acknowledge its historical roots.

Traditional Perspective on Stress

Proponents of the traditional perspective state that "the intentional use of stress is central to the change process of wilderness therapy. Stress is often magnified by the students' tendencies to exaggerate the level of risk. . . . The resulting anxiety sets the stage for a potentially transformational experience" (Kimball & Bacon, 1993, p. 21). I propose that physical and emotional safety are jeopardized when transformation is dependent on a participant experiencing stress. However, the traditional perspective is contrary to this premise.

Traditional-perspective followers argue that most adventure programs set physical safety as a priority. Within these programs there is a significant gap between perceived risk and the actual risk of an activity (Kimball & Bacon, 1993; Nadler, 1993). Those working from this perspective advocate enhancing the perception of risk when appropriate. For example, Nadler (1993) suggests "increasing the constructive level of anxiety. . . increasing the sense of the unknown and unpredictable by doing what is unexpected . . . developing behavior contracts of emotional and behavioral risks . . . withholding or increasing the amount of information given about activities . . ." (p. 68). Justification for this approach is offered by Ewert (1989a) who proposes that "just enough" fear needs to be present in adventure activities. Evidently, this fear can be increased by manipulating information since it is the information which provides an individual with a sense of control. Ewert, therefore, concludes that the "greater the perceived risk in the situation, the greater the individual's felt need for information" (p. 21).

Priest and Baillie (1987) suggest increasing the perception of risk when working with timid or fearful clients:

> The role of the facilitators is to build confidence by increasing the perceived risk of an activity until these participants are expecting a condition of misadventure to ensue. Then, after successfully coaxing the participants through to a condition of adventure, the facilitators further aid them by reflecting back on the experience and drawing out the key points of learning. (p. 20)

They are suggesting that the actual risk of an activity be manipulated, known as "structuring for failure," in order to deflate the ego of a fearless or arrogant participant (Priest, 1993; Priest & Baillie, 1987). Clearly, advocates of the traditional adventure education perspective propose utilizing inherent stressors for the growth of the participant. This technique of manipulating stress and anxiety is a crucial point of difference between the traditional and feminist perspectives.

The Feminist Perspective

I believe the feminist perspective is found within the writings on adventure education which question the socio-political structure of the field of experiential education. For example, supporters of this perspective are willing to analyze current or past gender discrimination within the field. They critique the usefulness of experiential methods with populations which do not represent the mainstream dominant culture (e.g., women, girls, people of color, etc.). Finally, those with this perspective advocate for creating new paradigms and dialogue which address these discrepancies.

The Feminist Perspective on Stress

It is the feminist commitment to analysis that led to questioning the use of stress in the traditional perspective. Instead of condoning the manipulation of stress, those working from a feminist perspective attempt to lessen the experienced stress of participants. Woodswomen, a women's outdoor adventure company founded in 1977, can be used as an example. The instructors at Woodswomen do not purposefully create stressful situations. As Woodswomen director Denise Mitten (1985) points out, "The less stress the participants are feeling, the better able they are to cope with new activities, participate as a constructive group member and handle challenging physical situations" (p. 22). The guides do not "pull surprises, even in the name of building character or creating a learning situation" (p. 21). Encouraging risk taking and minimizing stress is encouraged at Woodswomen through "discussing the risk and working to remove the mystery about the activity or encounter. Discussing fears. Clarifying with participants why the risk may be worth it to them (or why it might not be). Helping participants set their own goals" (Mitten, 1986, p. 33). This emphasis on minimizing stress, creating dialogue about risk, and encouraging personal choice sets the stage for what I term "authentic risk taking."

The possibility for authentic risk taking is developed within an environment which encourages appropriate risk taking. Rachel Holzwarth (1994), the founder of Alaska Women in the Wilderness, believes in appropriate risk taking which de-emphasizes competition and encourages risk, not stress. Similar to Holzwarth's distinction between risk and stress is Mitten's (1986) belief that women learn from risk taking. This is supported by Parrino's (1979) parallel of risk taking to the principle of adaptive exposure. Parrino claims risk taking is habit changing and anxiety reducing.

In order for risk taking to be effective, Mitten (personal communication, April 5, 1994) underscores the necessity of "making sure a person is getting a choice" in all activities. According to Mitten, a person's internalized esteem is what allows them to own their risk taking and their challenges. In other words, a person already brings esteem to an activity and what they need is affirmation. This outlook differs from the traditional perspective which claims that risk, challenge, and success build esteem.

These sentiments are echoed in Tippett's (1993) distinction between stress and challenge. Tippett draws from the work of Lazarus and Launier (1978) and contends that stress is similar to a sense of jeopardy. Thus, stress decreases self-esteem, whereas challenges increase self-esteem. Despite a perceived risk with challenges, the individual or group expects success. Tippett elaborates by stating:

> The subjective experience of an activity determines whether it is defined as a stress or challenge. Almost any activity will be experienced as a stress if it is imposed on participants. Yet the same activity can improve self-esteem if participants choose it themselves. For example, being forced to continue on a difficult rock climb is likely to undermine self-esteem even if the climb is completed. However, if participants know they can choose which climb to attempt and can come off a climb if necessary without loss of face, they will experience climbing as a challenge. Self-esteem will increase and the holding environment will be supported. (1993, pp. 91-92)

This comparative analysis reveals key differences in how stress and subsequent risk is viewed in both perspectives. In the traditional model, stress is viewed not only as central and desirable, but there is approval for manipulating stress levels and/or intentionally creating stress as a companion to risk taking. In the feminist perspective, there is no advocacy for intentionally manipulating stress levels, nor is stress viewed as central to a client having a transformative experience. Rather, the feminist perspective relies on the subjective experience of a client and the importance of personal choice as preparation for risk-taking behavior. Risk taking is supported through acknowledgment of a person's esteem, strengths, personal awareness, and power of choice. I believe that this approach to risk taking contains sound judgment and is supported by the research on stress and eustress.

Stress Research

Originally, Dr. Hans Selye (1974) borrowed the word "stress" from physics to describe the body's response to environmental and emotional stressors. A stressor may be pleasant or unpleasant (Selye, 1974). The degree of intensity and duration of a stressor will vary. Stressors affect the entire human system: our thoughts, our physiology, and our behaviors all work together to produce an effective response strategy (Parrino, 1979). It is important to note that the definition of stress has evolved to include both the stressor and the body's stress response. Commonly, the interpretation of the word stress is negative and defined as synonymous to distress (Davies, 1980).

Stress causes our bodies to experience a "flight or fight" response to a threat. Conditions which produce the "greatest perceived threat in a given situation are the following: lack of predictability, lack of control, lack of outlets for frustration. When these elements are present, innocuous situations can turn stressful, sometimes far out of proportion to their actual stimulus" (Chopra, 1993, p. 156). Our bodies undergo physiological changes in order to gather enough energy to respond to the threat. In order to cope, our bodies switch from normal anabolic metabolism, which builds tissues, to catabolic metabolism, which breaks down tissues (Chopra, 1993). If we experience catabolic metabolism for prolonged periods, it is harmful to our bodies and may lead to disease and/or death (Chopra, 1993; Davis, Eshelman, & McKay, 1982).

Clearly, the physiological effects of stress are harmful, yet life presents us with stressful events on a daily basis. The phases of our response to these stressors are: "1) the stressful event; 2) your inner appraisal of it; 3) your body's reaction" (Chopra, 1993, p. 154). One point of agreement in the writings on stress is the importance of an individual's perceptions and interpretation of a stressor (Cherry, 1978; Chopra, 1993; Davis, Eshelman, & McKay, 1982; Edwards & Cooper, 1988; Parrino, 1979; Selye, 1974, 1983). Why is a person's subjective experience so critical in regard to stress? The point of interpretation is where an individual has the potential to control or transform their body's stress response (Chopra, 1993). It is this juncture of interpretation that allows an individual to experience eustress rather than stress.

Eustress: Good Stress

Eustress, named by Selye (Cherry, 1978) for the Greek prefix *eus* meaning good, is a term that appears in experiential education literature as an important dynamic of risk taking (Mason, 1987; Priest, 1993; Schoel, Prouty, & Radcliffe, 1988). This is exemplified in Priest's (1993) theoretical model of competence for human risk-taking behavior. Priest's model juxtaposes distress and eustress as the two possibilities a person experiences as they test perceived self-efficacy against actual competence. In this model, a person's entry into eustress is based on successful task accomplishment, while the entry into distress is based on task failure. I contend this is a misinterpretation of the concept of eustress. A review of literature on stress research reveals that certain internal conditions must be present in order for eustress to occur. In fact, there is no dependence on task completion. Rather, the focus is on process and how one perceives and internalizes situations. In my opinion, based on various readings, the following nine conditions are necessary for eustress to occur:

1. Self-awareness of perceptions, feelings, attitudes, and behaviors (Cherry, 1978; Parrino, 1979).
2. Valuing the subjective experience of the individual. A person's attitude defines experience as pleasant or unpleasant. Therefore, a person has the power to convert distress into eustress (Cherry, 1978).
3. Self-determination in setting attainable goals (Cherry, 1978).
4. Self-awareness of one's optimal personal stress level (Cherry, 1978).
5. An ability to meet the demands placed on an individual (Edwards & Cooper, 1988).
6. The person must desire and consider it important to meet the demand placed upon them (Edwards & Cooper, 1988).
7. The individual must appraise the current situation as meeting or exceeding their desired state (Edwards & Cooper, 1988).
8. The individual views the coping activities as enjoyable, regardless of the impact on stress (Edwards & Cooper, 1988).
9. The individual derives pleasure from the success of the coping activities (Edwards & Cooper, 1988).

These nine conditions will be further interpreted with a narrative example in the Eustress Paradigm section.

Eustress is a powerful way to experience life. Evidently, eustress puts far less demand on the body than other types of stress (Cherry, 1978). Edwards and Cooper (1988) speculate that "eustress may directly influence health, and perhaps improve it by stimulating the production of anabolic hormones, HDL cholesterol, and other health-enhancing biochemical substances" (p. 1448). Clearly, eustress has the inherent potential to directly and positively benefit physical health.

Positive benefits exist indirectly for psychological health as well. Edwards and Cooper (1988) suggest that eustress helps to facilitate coping abilities and efforts. In fact, eustress may ease social interaction, thereby increasing social support and enhancing a person's coping abilities. Another way that eustress enhances coping abilities is by facilitating feelings of mastery and control. Eustress may promote a sense of "self-efficacy and optimism, particularly when the source of eustress is relevant to the coping task at hand" (p. 1449). In other words, a new rock climber who has experienced eustress in other climbing situations may transfer feelings of self-efficacy and optimism to a current situation on the rocks.

In summary, eustress is not dependent on task completion. Rather, eustress is manifested through an individual's subjective experience. Eustress is not a factor which can be manipulated by a course instructor. If a participant experiences eustress, the potential exists to positively affect self-efficacy and competency, as well as transfer to other situations where coping is necessary.

Stress and Eustress in Wilderness Adventures

What is the relationship of stress, which is omnipresent in everyday life, to wilderness adventures? First, it is logical to conclude that adventure programs contain inherent stressors, just as everyday life has stressors. Therefore, every participant will experience these stressors. A study by Dickinson (1992) found that the "levels of anxiety (stress) and arousal during adventure activities are constantly changing as different situations arise" (p. 36). The literature also shows there can be too much stress in adventure programs (Ewert, 1989a; Hendee & Brown, 1987). This leads us to the pivotal question, asked by Ewert (1989a, p. 19): "Can instructors be sure, however, that the level of stress and anxiety that their students experience is both appropriate and beneficial?" I believe that the negative outcomes of stress far outweigh any possibility of benefit.

What are the potential negative implications of stress in a wilderness program? First, it is questionable whether true community forms under crisis conditions. Mitten (1986) states:

> If people bond under stress it is often bonding together against something or someone. This can lead to scapegoating or groups fractioning. For some people bonding under stress can feel familiar and even comfortable. This is especially true for people from families where bonding often took place during or after conflict. These people may leave a course believing that they have made a meaningful, honest connection with another person(s). However, this bonding does not lead to community building nor does it in the long run increase self-esteem. (p. 32)

Scott Peck (1987), the author of *A Different Drum*, a book on community and peace making, concurs with Mitten: "Once the crisis is over, so—virtually always—is the community. The collective spirit goes out of the people as they return to their ordinary lives, and community is lost" (p. 77).

Beyond the loss of authentic community is the possibility of psychological harm and/or emotional distress being experienced by individuals. Mitten (1986), asked workshop participants to describe what situations are stressful:

> Too much to do and not enough time, lack of sleep, too heavy loads, physical illness or injury, external standards to meet, getting up early, lack of food, being wet and cold . . . someone not being honest, nonchoiceful risky situations, clashes of ideas and value systems, miscommunication, pressure from a boss, and when someone puts pressure on you to make a decision. (p. 30)

Mitten also asked the workshop participants how they feel in stressful situations:

> Alone, tense, like a child, irritable, defensive, frustrated, depressed, hyper, immobilized, like they want to cry, scream, and that they often want others to feel bad too. Women also notice changes in their behavior. Some may get more aggressive, or others more quiet or passive. Some women withdraw, or feel numb physically and emotionally. Others get hostile, blame and are impatient with the group. Some neglect personal care, sleep a lot or feel tired all the time, are apologetic, or abuse substances. Some women become accident prone, walk into things, and can't focus. (p. 30)

While this poll of participants was specific to women, it offers indications that stressful experiences do not facilitate learning. More research needs to be done on how stress is experienced by a wide variety of populations on adventure outings.

Another downfall of experiencing stress is the lack of long-term benefit. Tippett (1993) states:

> While stress may be helpful for learning to push past self-imposed limits, it is counter-indicated for in-depth reparative work. Psychic growth requires a holding environment where anxiety is reduced. Since anxiety has been responsible for solidifying maladaptive behaviors, increasing it will only interfere in the process of true change. (p. 92)

While Tippett's observations pertain to a group of borderline adolescents, the main point is salient for other clientele—short-term gain is an illusion. The literature clearly shows that long-term benefits are the outcome of experiencing eustress.

In summary, it is clear that stress is not a desirable state in life or in adventure situations. Stress causes long-term negative outcomes, both physiologically and psychologically. How should this information affect a wilderness program? I believe it furthers the case for a eustressful model, one which does not create unnecessary stress for participants. I advocate a model where the inherent stress and risks in adventure activities are acknowledged, and eustress rather than stress occurs.

The Eustress Paradigm: A Strategy for Decreasing Stress in Wilderness Adventure Programming

The Eustress Paradigm is my method for addressing a basic need of human beings to decrease stress in their lives and invite in health, balance, and well-being. The primary goal is to support clients in engaging in adventures and authentic risk taking which facilitates the experience of eustress. This paradigm is based on feminist adventure education literature (Holzwarth, 1994; Mitten, 1985, 1986, 1992, 1994; Warren, 1985, 1993; Warren & Rheingold, 1993) and on the nine conditions of eustress which were previously outlined. The seven components of this paradigm will be presented in a narrative example as we follow "Maria" as she travels on a three-day women's canoe outing.

1. The Individual as the Beginning Point

Two instructors, Shari and Marissa, offer a women's canoe outing. Both instructors believe in and model these principles:

- A person is complete in and of themselves.
- A person's inner strengths and knowledge are viewed as a resource.
- A person's internal esteem is to be acknowledged and validated.

Shari and Marissa encourage the participants to practice being aware of perceptions, feelings, attitudes, and behaviors by having participants self-assess their optimal personal stress levels. Within this framework, the importance of subjective experience is acknowledged. It is an individual's perception which defines experience as pleasant or unpleasant. Therefore, a person does have the ability to convert stress into eustress.

2. Preparation for Risk Taking

Before the trip, group members meet and begin the natural process of building community. Shari and Marissa share trip information and logistics with participants. While both instructors are skilled outdoor educators, the "expert instructor" status is discouraged. All participants offer rich experiences and their own expertise. Acknowledging this helps to maintain equitable relationships between participants and instructors.

The instructors model and facilitate the establishment of group norms of emotional and physical safety. Part of this process is to collaboratively discuss and decide upon program goals and objectives. Another important aspect of establishing safety is to share and validate feelings. Specifically, fears are named and discussed. Maria shares that she has a fear of water and hopes to overcome it on the canoe outing. All participants are asked for their interpretations of the words stress, eustress, and risk. Educational information on stress and eustress is shared with participants. This is followed by brainstorming different stress-management techniques individuals can use while on the outing.

3. Entrance into a Novel Setting

As the participants enter the novel setting, physical and emotional safety remain a priority. Therefore, no information is withheld from participants. Marissa and Shari do not manipulate perceived risk or actual risk. Major decisions are made through consensus with all voices heard. Participants are encouraged to monitor their stress levels. Maria is discovering that near the water, her stress level is high, yet she is able to function and concentrate on learning paddling skills. She is practicing her stress-management techniques of conscious breathing, focusing her attention on the beauty of the natural surroundings, and doing a safety check on her life vest.

4. Choice

Even though the objectives of the canoe trip are to learn specific canoeing skills and complete a particular route, flexibility of schedule is maintained by offering choices within the structure of a day. Options to all activities are made available unless an issue of safety arises. The instructors do not impose goals upon individuals. Rather, participants self-determine attainable personal goals. Maria's goals are to learn basic paddle strokes, practice her stress-management techniques, spend time on the water in the hope of overcoming her fear, enjoy her surroundings, and make new friends.

5. Authentic Risk Taking

In order to support an environment of authentic risk taking, both instructors believe in and model these principles:

- Task completion and noncompletion are not dichotomized as task success and task failure. It is important to remember that both eustress and stress can be felt with either of these outcomes. Therefore, external environmental outcomes are not helpful. Rather, attention must be paid to the internal process of the individual and her subjective interpretation of events.
- Process is valued over task outcome.
- Personal choice and control is maintained, acknowledged, and validated. Interventions without participant approval are reserved for cases of immediate physical danger or intense emotional distress.

Eustress promotes authentic risk taking. For example, Maria is given safety information and skill instruction. She is progressing with her goals and has the ability (physical and emotional skills) to meet the demands placed upon her in this environment. Maria desires and considers it important to meet these demands placed upon her. Both of these conditions help to create an experience of eustress.

Another aspect of eustress is that Maria appraises her current situation as meeting or exceeding her desired state. Initially, Maria felt less safe in the bow of the canoe. She decided that her goal would be to spend one hour a day in the bow as a way to work on this fear. By the third day, she found her comfort level increasing and spent three hours in the bow, even though her feeling of fear was slightly present. Maria perceives this specific risk-taking incident as eustressful because her situation exceeds the original goal of one hour in the bow.

6. Appraisal of Experience

The group schedules time for individual and group reflection. An environment of emotional safety is maintained as participants discuss perceptions of events, feelings, stress, and methods used for coping.

7. The Individual as the Ending Point

One of the two final conditions of eustress to be addressed is that the individual views the coping activities as enjoyable, regardless of the impact on known stressors. Additionally, the individual derives pleasure from the success of the coping activities. In other words, Maria chose to participate in a supervised canoe outing as a way to cope with the stress of fearing water. She finds the outing very enjoyable, regardless of how it impacts her fear of water. Even though Maria experiences stress while canoeing, she also feels a sense of accomplishment, success, and eustress when the outing is finished. Therefore, this experience for Maria offers both physiological and emotional benefits.

Conclusion

Stress is a consistent element of wilderness adventures, just as it is a consistent part of life. However, stress should not be manipulated further in the guise of facilitating transformative experiences. Stress is known to cause physiological and psychological damage. To purposefully create stressful situations as a companion to risk taking blatantly fosters an environment of negative outcomes. In addition, this approach also denies the participant personal choice. Since the necessary conditions which facilitate eustress call for self-determination, if a person is denied personal power, the possibility of experiencing eustress is forsaken. To forsake eustress is to invite stress. Risk taking from a position of stress has greater potential for jeopardizing physical and emotional safety. I believe the role of a wilderness instructor is to support authentic risk taking through honoring process, self-determination, and subjective experience. Authentic risk taking is based on a position of power and choice and this has greater potential to lead to eustress.

As eustress is proven to elicit physiological and psychological benefits, I have offered the Eustress Paradigm as a method for increasing eustress in adventure programming. I believe this paradigm is applicable to diverse populations, since a commonality among human beings is the benefit of eustress and the harm of stress. Wilderness instructors and participants in adventure programs have the potential to cultivate eustress to reap profound benefits.

Acknowledgments

I would like to thank the following people for their support, encouragement, and editorial comments: Karen Warren, two anonymous reviewers, Denise Mitten, Rachel Holzwarth, Ellen Cole, Joan Clingan, Lyn Holiday, Elizabeth Peeler, Sara Chase, and Shari Weinstein.

References

Bertolmi, C. (1981). *Effects of a wilderness program on self-esteem and locus of control orientations of young adults.* (Report No. RC 015 711). Paper presented at the Annual Canadian Conference on the Application of Curriculum Research, 6th Annual, Winnipeg, Manitoba, Canada, November 26-27, 1981. (ERIC Document Reproduction Service No. ED 266 928)

Cherry, L. (1978, March). On the real benefits of eustress. *Psychology Today*, pp. 60-70.

Chopra, D. (1993). *Ageless body, timeless mind.* New York: Harmony Books.

Davies, P. (Ed.). (1980). *American heritage dictionary of the English language.* New York: Dell.

Davis, M., Eshelman, E. R., & McKay, M. (1982). *The relaxation and stress reduction workbook* (2nd ed.). Oakland, CA: New Harbinger.

Dickinson, S. (1992). Measurement of anxiety and arousal in outdoor adventure activities. *Journal of Adventure Education and Outdoor Leadership, 9*(1), 35-36.

Edwards, J. R., & Cooper, C. L. (1988). The impacts of positive psychological states on physical health: A review and theoretical framework. *Social Science Medicine, 27*, 1447-1459.

Ewert, A. (1989a). *Outdoor adventure pursuits: Foundations, models, and theories.* Columbus, OH: Publishing Horizons.

Ewert, A. (1989b). Managing fear in the outdoor experiential education setting. *Journal of Experiential Education, 12*(1), 19-25.

Hendee, J. C., & Brown, M. H. (1987). *How wilderness experience programs facilitate personal growth: The Hendee/Brown model.* (Report No. SE 050 098). Paper presented at the Annual Meeting of the World Wilderness Congress, 4th Annual, Estes Park, Colorado, September 16, 1987. (ERIC Document Reproduction Service No. ED 300 255)

Holzwarth, R. (1994, April). Alaska Women in the Wilderness. In Psychology of Women course at Prescott, Arizona.

Kimball, R. O., & Bacon, S. B. (1993). The wilderness challenge model. In M. A. Gass (Ed.), *Adventure therapy: Therapeutic applications of adventure programming* (pp. 11-41). Dubuque, IA: Kendall/Hunt.

Lazarus, R., & Launier, R. (1978). Stress-related transactions between person and environment. In L. Pervin and M. Lewis (Eds.), *Perspectives in interactional psychology.* New York: Plenum.

Mason, M. J. (1987). Wilderness family therapy: Experiential dimensions. *Contemporary Family Therapy, 9*(1-2), 90-105.

Miner, J. L. (1990). The creation of Outward Bound. In J. C. Miles and S. Priest (Eds.), *Adventure education* (pp. 55-66). State College, PA: Venture Publishing.

Mitten, D. (1985). A philosophical basis for a women's outdoor adventure program. *Journal of Experiential Education, 8*(2), 20-24.

Mitten, D. (1986). Stress management and wilderness activities: Women's experiential education. In L. Buell & M. Gass (Eds.), *Association for Experiential Education 1986 Conference Proceedings,* (pp. 29-33). Boulder, CO: Association for Experiential Education.

Mitten, D. (1992). Empowering girls and women in the outdoors. *Journal of Physical Education, Recreation and Dance, 63*(2), 56-60.

Mitten, D. (1994). Personal communication on April 5, 1994.

Mitten, D., & Dutton, R. (1993). Outdoor leadership considerations with women survivors of sexual abuse. *Journal of Experiential Education, 16*(1), 7-13.

Nadler, R. S. (1993). Therapeutic process of change. In M. A. Gass (Ed.), *Adventure therapy: Therapeutic applications of adventure programming*, (pp. 57-69). Dubuque, IA: Kendall/Hunt.

Nadler, R. S., & Luckner, J. L. (1992). *Processing the adventure experience: Theory and practice.* Dubuque, IA: Kendall/Hunt.

Parrino, J. J. (1979). *From panic to power: The positive use of stress.* New York: John Wiley.

Peck, S. (1987). *The different drum.* New York: Simon & Schuster.

Priest, S. (1991). The ten commandments of adventure education. *Journal of Adventure Education and Outdoor Leadership, 8*(3), 8-10.

Priest, S. (1993). A new model for risk taking. *Journal of Experiential Education, 16*(1), 50-53.

Priest, S., & Baillie, R. (1987). Justifying the risk to others: The real razor's edge. *Journal of Experiential Education, 10*(1), 16-22.

Schoel, J., Prouty, D., & Radcliffe, P. (1988). *Islands of healing: A guide to adventure based counseling.* Hamilton, MA: Project Adventure.

Selye, H. (1974). *Stress without distress.* New York: J. B. Lippencott.

Selye, H. (1983). The stress concept: Past, present, and future. In C. L. Cooper (Ed.), *Stress research* (pp. 1-20). New York: John Wiley.

Tippett, S. (1993). Therapeutic wilderness programming for borderline adolescents. In M. A. Gass (Ed.), *Adventure therapy: Therapeutic applications of adventure programming* (pp. 83-94). Dubuque, IA: Kendall/Hunt.

Warren, K. (1993). The midwife teacher: Engaging students in the experiential education process. *Journal of Experiential Education, 16*(1), 33-38.

Warren, K., & Rheingold, A. (1993). Feminist pedagogy and experiential education: A critical look. *Journal of Experiential Education, 16*(3), 25-31.

5

The Value of Therapeutic Wilderness Programs for Incest Survivors: A Look at Two Dominant Program Models

Ruth Rohde

This chapter explores the question of whether wilderness trips have therapeutic value for women incest survivors, and if so, which model of trip is best suited to this population. Although a limited body of empirical research has developed on the question of whether wilderness trips benefit women victims of violence generally—a term which includes women who have been victims of battering, rape, or incest (Israel, 1989; Oliver, 1988; Phirman, 1987)—to date, no studies[1] have examined specifically the value of therapeutic wilderness programs for women survivors of incest. Based on the studies on women victims of violence, in which positive changes in behavior were noted, one might presume that wilderness programs offer the same therapeutic benefits for women survivors of incest. This, however, may not be true, since women survivors of incest may have adverse reactions to being in the wilderness and to being in a group with other incest survivors—reactions that may be different from those of the more general group of women victims of violence. Because of this, it cannot be assumed that a wilderness treatment model used with women who have been victims of violence generally is appropriate for use in working with incest survivors whose trauma profile may be distinctly different. These differences are critical to consider when designing a trip for this particular population. Furthermore, as one very important article, entitled "Outdoor Leadership Considerations with Women Survivors of Sexual Abuse" (Mitten & Dutton, 1993), points out, wilderness experiences can be countertherapeutic for some incest survivors, but may, if well planned for a particular group, offer therapeutic benefits.

The second question raised in this chapter is, if, in fact, wilderness trips have therapeutic value for incest survivors, which model of outdoor trip is best suited to working with this population? In the research I conducted, two dominant models of outdoor programs emerged. The first, commonly referred to as a "stress" model, has been utilized by many outdoor programs throughout the country. This model uses increasingly difficult experiential activities to induce stress and, thereby, motivate the participant. Under these pressured circumstances, individuals are forced to "try out" behaviors and rely on the group for help and support (Israel, 1989; Oliver, 1988; Phirman, 1987; Webb, 1993). The second dominant model, while sharing similar goals, utilizes a different approach. This second model—a "challenge" approach— minimizes the deliberate or contrived use of stress to bring about change and uses instead challenges that are more graduated or ones which naturally evolve on a trip, to maximize group and individual learning.

Many variations of both of these models exist in outdoor programs throughout the country. Also, each model has been adapted in a variety of ways to fit the particular needs of the population for which it is being used. For the purposes of this chapter, I will look at some of the basic features of each of these models as they relate to incest survivors.

In the process of conducting research for this chapter, a number of other questions arose, such as: At what stage of recovery are women incest survivors best suited for this type of experience? What types of personal and interpersonal problems might emerge on a trip for incest survivors? What length trip is best suited for working with this population? And lastly, what staff training should be required?

To support my exploration of the questions I have posed, I will begin by reviewing some of the current theoretical writings and research on the impact of incest on females and the symptomatology that commonly develops. This will be followed by a discussion about the recovery process using a model from Judith Herman's recent book, *Trauma and Recovery* (1992).

The Impact of Incest

Theoretical and clinical writings and research on incest and its impact are a relatively recent phenomenon. Important contributions to this field, in the last ten to fifteen years, have been made by such researchers as Gelinas (1983), Finkelhor and Browne (1985), and Herman (1992). Herman's latest book, *Trauma and Recovery* (1992), has been an important addition to the field, and one which has firmly established incest as a traumatic event. This event can lead to a post-traumatic stress disorder exhibiting the same symptomatology as other categories of trauma victims, including combat veterans, survivors of concentration camps, rape victims, and battered women. As Herman (1992) points out, the history of incest is one which entails a tradition of "episodic amnesia" (p. 7). Just as the individual is prone to repress the atrocious events of the past, so, too, is society. This is evidenced in the appearance and subsequent disappearance of clinical attention to, and integration of, this phenomenon into the mental health community.

The effect of incest on the individual depends upon a number of factors, including: age at which incest began; duration of the incest; relationship between perpetrator and victim; temperament of the incest victim; and quality of the incest victim's attachments, insight, strengths, and sensitivities. Other compensatory factors may include support and resources available to the victim at the time of the abuse and the reactions of people close to the individual if the incest is disclosed (Finkelhor & Browne, 1985; James, 1989).

Although a host of factors, in combination with one another, can serve to either exacerbate or alleviate the negative consequences that result from incest, a child's fundamental need for safety, trust, connection, and empowerment are inevitably compromised by the trauma of incest and by the social and familial dynamics which collude to create an environment ripe for abuse. While incest is a form of trauma that can result in either short- or long-term effects, it is an experience that is recognized as having impact on all levels of an individual's development and growth, including cognitive, physical, emotional, and spiritual realms. Herman (1992) writes:

> Traumatic events call into question basic human relationships. They breach the attachments of family, friendship, love and community. They shatter the construction of the self that is formed and sustained in relation to others. They undermine the belief systems that give meaning to human experience. They violate the victim's faith in a natural divine order and cast the victim into a state of existential crisis. (p. 51)

In order to accommodate and assimilate the traumatic experiences of incest which impinge upon a child's fundamental needs and primary relationships, the child must make adaptations that will become forever inscribed in the signature of his or her personality (Herman, 1992, p. 62). While some of these adaptations may serve the person well in certain areas of life, others may become problematic as the incest survivor advances through various life stages and events.

Finkelhor and Browne concluded in their seminal research on *The Traumatic Impact of Child Sexual Abuse* (1985) that there are four traumagenic dynamics that are at the core of the psychological injury to the child who is sexually abused (p. 106). These are identified as: "traumatic sexualization, betrayal, stigmatization, and powerlessness" (p. 106). These four areas are seen by the authors as the "links between the experience of sexual abuse and the sequelae that have been widely noted" (p. 110). These sequelae include the following: feelings of helplessness, powerlessness, hopelessness, terror, loss of control, isolation, loss of trust and connection, loss of spirituality, shame, guilt, loss of a sense of self-worth, loss of a sense of meaning and purpose (Chu, 1988; Finkelhor & Browne, 1985; Gelinas, 1983; Goodwin & Talwar, 1989; Herman, 1992; Janoff-Bulman, 1985; Miller, 1990; and Webb, 1993).

Many incest survivors, because of the existence of these sequelae and a natural tendency to reenact past events, may become predisposed to revictimization through rape, battering, neglect, and abuse of all kinds. Other more specific problems that may develop include somatic complaints, pervasive anxiety, relational problems, dissociative episodes, panic and eating disorders, self-mutilation, substance and alcohol abuse, suicidality, depression, flashbacks, nightmares, and psychotic episodes (Courtois, 1988, p. 90).

Today, incest is recognized as a form of trauma which can produce "profound and lasting changes in physiological arousal, emotion, cognition, and memory" (Herman, 1992, p. 34). There are three main categories used to describe the symptomatology of post-traumatic stress disorder which can develop as a consequence of trauma. These are: hyperarousal, intrusion, and constriction (Herman, 1992; van der Kolk, 1987). Hyperarousal depicts the state of constant alert and danger that frequently plagues victims of trauma. Intrusion reflects the "indelible imprint of the traumatic event" (Herman, 1992, p. 35) that can intrude on the individual's consciousness at any moment. Lastly, constriction is the term used to describe the process of contraction, withdrawal, and surrender which naturally evolves as a by-product of trauma (Herman, 1992; van der Kolk, 1987). These are the features of post-traumatic stress that, coupled with the problems listed above, can wreak havoc in an individual's life.

Characteristics of Families in Which Incest Occurs

Incest is not confined to any one segment of society. It is a problem that pervades every class, race, and ethnic group in America. Each of these factors—a person's race, a person's class, a person's ethnic heritage—will have an impact on how the experience of incest affects the individual.

When we look at families in which incest occurs, some general characteristics emerge. Incestuous families are often isolated, chaotic, and lacking in structure and cohesion (Alexander, Neimeyer, & Follette, 1991). An imbalance in power relations between men and women and the patriarchal assumption that women and children should be available for the sexual pleasure of men (and in a few cases, adult women) play a primary role in creating a climate in which incest can occur (Bograd, 1986; de Young, 1985; Herman, 1992). Alcoholism and/or substance abuse are also often present in incestuous families (Harney, 1992).

Typically, incestuous families display rigid external boundaries and fluid internal boundaries between family members (Courtois, 1988). Enmeshed relationships among family members is not uncommon. Parents in incestuous families, because of their own developmental deficits, are often unable to self-nurture, nurture each other, or nurture their children (Courtois, 1988; Harney, 1992). Accordingly, one or both of the parents may turn to their children, rather than each other, to get their needs met, both emotionally and sexually (Harney, 1992; Courtois, 1988).

Courtois (1988) points out that in spite of the factor of enmeshment in incestuous families, there is often very little physical or emotional nurturing present. Instead, affection is expressed sexually and often in secrecy. Families with incest often have well-developed systems of denial in which all family members participate (p. 46). The silence and secrecy which this promotes transmits a powerful message to the victim that his or her reality, however painful, must not be disclosed. This is compounded by other factors, such as the use of bribery or coercion, the threat or use of violence, and the imbalance of power and authority between perpetrator and victim. This dynamic creates a "double-bind" for the victim who is caught between the real and false realities created within the family. Courtois writes, "In order to contend with the paradox inherent in the bind, they transform their reality and ultimately themselves to suit the family rules and injunctions" (p. 46). This transformation of self, to accommodate the reality of the incestuous family, has many far-reaching implications for the development and growth of the incest victim.

Due to the overwhelming nature of the experience of incest, some victims may lose all or partial memory of the actual events. It is not uncommon, therefore, for incest survivors to seek therapy, not because of any knowledge or interest in their incest histories, but because of various secondary elaborations or symptoms, such as chronic depression, nightmares, depersonalization, dissociative disorders, panic attacks, and self-destructive behaviors which are causing stress in their lives (Gelinas, 1983). Over time, incest memories may emerge but often are not included in the initial presentation or reason for entering therapy.

While much of the literature examines the negative impact of incest on the individual, it should be pointed out that many incest survivors develop extraordinary strengths and abilities, in large part due to the compensatory behaviors they have been forced to develop over the years. Linda Sanford (1990), who takes a nonpathologizing view when discussing the impact of trauma on individuals, writes, "All human beings, traumatized as children or not, are 'checkerboards of strengths and weaknesses.' Perhaps with trauma the strengths are a little stronger and the weaknesses a little weaker" (p. 16). However, while the extraordinary capacities of incest survivors may result in successful careers and ostensibly successful lives, the negative effects of incest may continue to persist in, and impair, even the most seemingly resilient individuals.

The Recovery Process

Herman (1992) describes the core experiences of psychological trauma as "disempowerment and disconnection from others" (p. 133). Other terms that are more commonly used in the literature to describe these same experiences, and which Herman also uses synonymously, are "helplessness and isolation" (p. 197). Recovery, according to Herman and many of her compatriots in the field, involves two primary objectives. These are "empowerment and reconnection" (p. 197).

As Herman (1992) has noted, recovery occurs in three stages. In the first stage, the central task is to establish "safety" and "trust"; in the second stage, the central task is "remembrance and mourning"; and in the third stage, the central task is "reconnection with ordinary life" (p. 155). Each of these stages builds on the one that came before it. For instance, recalling the sexual abuse and disclosing the details—an essential task of healing—can only take place after safety and trust have been firmly established (Gelinas, 1983; Herman, 1992; and Miller, 1990). If safety and trust are not established and the memories are revealed too soon, the individual may become retraumatized, flee from the overwhelming and intolerable pain of remembering, and revert to unsafe coping behaviors (Chu, 1988; Gelinas, 1983).

According to Herman (1992) and van der Kolk (1987), both group and individual treatment are important to the recovery process. While individual treatment "allows for a detailed examination of a patient's mental processes and memories that cannot be replicated in a group therapy setting" (van der Kolk, p. 163), groups provide the "social relational dimension" (Herman, p. 232). It is during the final stage of recovery, termed by Herman as the "reconnection" stage, that group therapy that involves relational and dynamic work is clearly indicated. This stage focuses on "reintegrating the survivor into [a] community" of interpersonal relationships (Herman, p. 217). At this stage, "recovery can only take place within the context of relationships; it cannot occur in isolation" (Herman, p. 133).

The value of group experience at the third stage of recovery—the "reconnection" stage—is that it allows for reconnection within a context of mutually enhancing, mutually rewarding relationships (Herman, 1992, p. 216). Mirroring and normalization are important aspects of recovery at this stage, which only a group can offer (Goodwin & Talwar, 1989; Herman, 1992). Similarly, learning about the "commonality" of incest survivor's experiences can lead to greater self-acceptance, empowerment, and a reduction in feelings of stigmatization and shame (Goodwin & Talwar, 1989; Herman, 1992; van der Kolk, 1987). "Discussing the abuse in a group challenges the continued power of vows of secrecy even more profoundly than does one-to-one disclosure" (Goodwin & Talwar, 1989, p. 285).

This final stage of recovery is the stage at which survivors might best benefit from a therapeutic wilderness experience. In fact, Herman (1992) makes reference to wilderness experiences as an optional form of therapeutic treatment at this stage (p. 198). The experiences that she highlights as important on a wilderness trip are the "opportunity to restructure the survivor's maladaptive social responses as well as her physiological and psychological responses to fear" (p. 199).

Positive Benefits of Therapeutic Wilderness Programs

Therapeutic wilderness experiences differ from more traditional forms of therapy in several respects and, therefore, may offer unique benefits not found in more traditional forms of therapy. Some therapists believe that one such benefit is that wilderness therapy, when used as an adjunct to other therapy, can result in more time-efficient and effective treatment (Abarbanel, 1988; DePaul, 1988; and Wartik, 1986). In several research studies of outdoor programs working with a variety of clientele, many of the same positive results attributed to traditional forms of therapy were duplicated in a briefer experiential model. These included the following:

increased feelings of self-esteem, empowerment, control, competence, and trust; the development of healthier coping skills, including learning new ways to cope with fear; and a decrease in feelings of powerlessness, hopelessness, and disconnection (Bacon & Kimball, 1993; Gass, 1993; Goodwin & Talwar, 1989; Israel, 1989; Mitten, 1990; Oliver, 1988; Pfirman, 1987; Tippett, 1993; and Webb, 1993).

Helping individuals reestablish a spiritual connection or framework from which to draw strength and sustenance is an aspect of recovery from incest that is under-emphasized in many treatment modalities. As van der Kolk (1987) points out, "The essence of psychological trauma is the loss of faith that there is order and continuity in life. Trauma occurs when one loses the sense of having a safe place to retreat within or outside of oneself to deal with frightening emotions or experiences" (p. 31).

On wilderness trips, the experience of being in a natural setting can ignite a sense of spiritual connection, order, and continuity that can help restore an individual's faith in the existence of a larger order. Many individuals who attend wilderness programs report feeling more grounded, empowered, and spiritually connected to themselves, humanity, and to nature (Miles, 1993; Mitten, 1990; Stringer & McAlvoy, 1992; and Webb, 1993). The fact that many contend that being in the wilderness can be powerfully transformative and healing on a physical, mental, and spiritual plane (Miles, 1993; Mitten, 1990; Stringer & McAlvoy, 1992; and Webb, 1993) is something which sets wilderness experiences as a therapeutic modality apart from many traditional forms of therapy (Bacon & Kimball, 1993; Canda, 1988; Goodwin & Talwar, 1989; Miles, 1993; Mitten, 1990; Stringer & McAlvoy, 1992). This can be of particular value to incest survivors for whom relationships to self and others, including nature, have been significantly impaired and for whom the existence of some kind of faith has often been severely damaged (DePaul, 1986; Israel, 1989; Mitten & Dutton, 1993; van der Kolk, 1987; Webb, 1993).

Because wilderness experiences combine activities which employ the use of different faculties and involve individuals in both verbal and nonverbal experiences, as well as in group and individual activities, they offer a unique multidimensional therapeutic experience. Israel (1989), in her dissertation on the effect of a wilderness program in the treatment of battered women, cites the work of Gilligan, who noted that because "the experience of being sexually or physically abused is a non-verbal experience . . . non-verbal experience might more powerfully address underlying processes" (Israel, 1989, p. 110).

The physical activity required on a wilderness program can be of particular value to incest survivors, many of whom have distorted, dissociated relationships with their bodies, the place where they were abused. As a woman learns to use her physical self in new ways and to feel more comfortable in her body, her perception of herself and her body may change and she may begin to feel a greater sense of groundedness, integration, control, competence, and power. As Mitten and Dutton point out, "Working in harmony with nature and seeing others do so as well can help a survivor gain positive memories through her body which was often experienced as a place of pain because of the abuse and to recover a feeling of power and pride in herself and in her body" (Mitten & Dutton, 1993, p. 12).

From my own experiences leading women's trips, including trips for women who are incest survivors, I have found that women's wilderness programs offer experiences which can provide both "empowerment" and "reconnection." The day-to-day challenges that arise offer each individual opportunities to try out new skills, develop new strengths, and learn about resources they may not previously have been aware of in themselves. On an all-women's wilderness trip, participants also have an opportunity to share vulnerabilities and strengths in a context that neither dilutes nor diminishes them. Experiencing the energy and support that women in community offer one another can be healing and can provide a new sense of belonging to those who have led lives of isolation and, in some cases, of quiet desperation.

Countertherapeutic Situations in Therapeutic Wilderness Programs

While outdoor experiences offer some distinct therapeutic opportunities and benefits, a number of adverse situations can arise which can become countertherapeutic for some people. For instance, although being in the wilderness can offer a restorative, healing experience, this same experience can become retraumatizing for individuals who may have been abused in an outdoor setting and for whom the outdoors represents a dangerous, threatening place. Furthermore, a number of activities commonly used in outdoor programs, such as guided imagery, Trust Walks using blindfolds, or various kinds of rituals can trigger memories of similar experiences that took place during the course of abuse. These sorts of activities also exhort the incest survivor to relinquish control and place their trust in the hands of another person who may be a complete stranger. This dynamic hearkens back to the loss of power and control experienced during abuse and may be retraumatizing and disempowering. For this reason, these types of activities are often inappropriate to use when working with this population.

Another problem that can evolve in groups of incest survivors is retraumatization when incest stories and memories are shared. Even when individuals have done considerable work on themselves, and safety and trust have been established in a group, hearing another's story may trigger other participants' memories. In some instances as well, hearing a story which contains horrific details can cause vicarious traumatization to one or several members of a group (McCann & Pearlman, 1990).

On the other hand, it is in group settings that individuals who are incest survivors may regain their connection to humanity. And, it is through the process of sharing their stories and being heard—sometimes for the first time—that incest survivors have an opportunity to receive the validation and support they have long deserved. In a discussion of the importance of disclosure in groups, Sanford (1990) quotes Thoreau who said, "It takes two to tell the truth. One to say it, the other to hear it" (pp. 23-24).

Similarly, in groups of incest survivors, individuals may encounter situations which reenact the same dynamics they experienced in their families of origin (Herman, 1992; Mitten & Dutton, 1993). For instance, other group members may inadvertently take on a familial role, such as perpetrator, accomplice, bystander, victim, or rescuer (Herman, 1992, p. 217). While this might provide an opportunity to work through old relational patterns, if not facilitated properly, these types of group dynamics can turn into reenactments that may be harmful to individuals and lead to the demise of the group. Because of this, Herman writes, "A group must have a clear and focused understanding of its therapeutic task and a structure that protects all participants adequately against the dangers of traumatic reenactment" (p. 217).

Other potential problems can arise when working with incest survivors in an outdoor setting. For instance, encounters with insects, adverse weather, sleeping in a tent with another person, or being touched by another person can feel intrusive and threatening (Mitten & Dutton, 1993). These experiences can trigger memories of other more traumatic intrusions which may cause the individual to feel in physical and psychological jeopardy. In a wilderness setting that is unfamiliar and less physically bounded, helping group members contain the anxiety and distress that may arise can be challenging at best. This, in turn, can lead to one or several people experiencing dissociative episodes, flashbacks, nightmares, suicidal ideation, or sleeping disorders, all of which can cause significant risk to the individual and to the group if not properly managed.

All of these are difficult issues and dynamics to control and manage, given the nature of wilderness travel. This emphasizes the importance of having a well-thought-out program that is designed specifically for incest survivors, as well as having sufficient numbers of staff who are well trained in working with incest survivors, and a screening process designed to help determine whether these types of wilderness experiences are suitable for each and every participant. Because of the myriad problems that can develop, many outdoor programs are used adjunctively with more traditional treatment programs. In these situations, staff from both organizations can be utilized, providing additional support and continuity for participants.

Positive and Negative Aspects of
Two Wilderness Program Models

Problematic Issues Related to Achieving the Goal of "Reconnection"

For many women survivors of incest, learning to trust can be exceedingly difficult and painstaking and may take months, even years, to accomplish. This is why it is commonly acknowledged that individuals who have been the victims of trauma and show persistent signs of post-traumatic stress, will require long-term treatment. A brief treatment model, therefore, may be counterindicated and may result in a frustrating experience for both the clinician and the client.

In "Ten Traps for Therapists in the Treatment of Trauma Survivors," Chu (1988) writes:

> The most common trap for therapists, particularly those unfamiliar with the treatment of trauma survivors, is the assumption of the presence of trust. It is crucial to recognize that patients who have backgrounds of abuse, neglect, and abandonment, often at the hands of their caretakers, do not know the meaning of trusting human relationships. . . . A reasonable level of trust often takes months or years to develop, and a normal level of trust usually exists only when the treatment nears its end. (p. 25)

The difficulty incest survivors have establishing trust and connecting in a healthy manner with others, raises a number of questions about whether wilderness programs, particularly those of short duration, have therapeutic value. This leads to the second question of which elements should be included or excluded in an outdoor program to maximize therapeutic benefit. Based on my experiences leading outdoor trips with incest survivors and with women in general, it seems that a longer, rather than a briefer, trip format is more conducive to allowing a foundation of trust to be established. However, on a longer trip, there is more opportunity for difficult situations to arise. Working in conjunction with an already existing group for incest survivors and their staff offers an optimal therapeutic situation, particularly when compared with trips which consist of individuals who are strangers to one another and to the staff, and, therefore, have no shared experiences and history.

While there are many programs that utilize an adjunctive approach, a number of these also use a brief program format, which has both advantages and disadvantages. The advantages of a brief program format are that it keeps costs down and requires less of a time commitment. These factors enable more women to participate (Webb, 1993). Because of their brevity, however, these types of programs often utilize contrived "stress"-inducing experiences to effect change which can be problematic for incest survivors. For instance, in many such programs, a combination of activities may be used to intensify the experience and accelerate the group bonding process. The intensity and stress created by these activities often replicates the intensity and stress experienced by incest survivors in their families of origin. Under duress, individuals naturally engage in a kind of superficial bonding that is familiar and comforting, but does not necessarily provide the basis for healthy intimacy, which needs to be developed slowly and deliberately over time. Mitten (1990) writes:

> When two or more women share a crisis before they establish friendship, even though they are bound in an intense and intimate relationship

involving immediate emotional release, these relationships flourish if they
can look at themselves as more than fellow survivors. It is important therefore, to allow the time and space during an outdoor experience for relationships to develop. (p. 15)

According to Mitten, it is through the process of sharing and disclosing things to one
another over time that women establish closeness and intimacy. The opposite is true,
however, for many men for whom intimacy and closeness may be more easily
established through sharing in an activity (p. 16). For this reason, initiative games and
trust activities, often used in conjunction with a "stress" model, may work well for
men, but run counter to the natural bonding process of women (Mitten, 1990).

Another problem with a "stress" model is that it encourages women who are
incest survivors to revert to instinctive behaviors in order to negotiate the stressful
experiences they encounter. For instance, many incest survivors have learned how to
endure stressful experiences by dissociating—a defense that may serve an individual well in certain circumstances, but may be a reflexive behavior that is counterproductive, even dangerous, in other situations. Using "stress"—the original stimulus
that produced the behavior—as a catalyst for change, runs the risk of invoking and
reinforcing instinctive survival behaviors. This approach, therefore, can be counterproductive to the therapeutic goals of recovery. As Tippett (1993) points out:

> While stress may be helpful for learning to push past self-imposed limits, it
> is counter-indicated for in-depth reparative work. Psychic growth requires a
> holding environment where anxiety is reduced. Since anxiety has been
> responsible for solidifying maladaptive behavior, increasing it will only
> interfere in the process of true change. (p. 92)

A "challenge" model that offers individuals the chance to challenge themselves at a
pace that is comfortable for them, rather than at a predetermined, stressful pace,
therefore, offers an environment that is more conducive to trying out new behaviors
rather than reacting with old, ingrained ones.

Problematic Issues Related to Achieving the Goal of "Empowerment"

One of the primary goals of the recovery process is to help incest survivors
become more empowered. One of the ways to help women achieve this on wilderness trips is to give them opportunities to be involved at appropriate points in the
planning, decision making, and leadership of a course. How a program is structured
overall can have a major impact on the experiences of participants. Trips that are rigidly structured and inflexible do very little to empower individuals and may
encourage incest survivors to transform themselves to fit the "family rules and
injunctions" (Courtois, 1988, p. 46). At the other end of the spectrum, trips that are
too loosely structured run the risk of not providing enough support. While it is critically important to provide a balance of structure in an outdoor program for incest

survivors, it can also be important to allow for unstructured time and leisure. For many women whose lives have been filled with the demands of others, having free time can be a rare gift. Therefore, allowing time on a trip for participants to commune with nature and with fellow participants, and enjoy the more common aspects of day-to-day travel can be an invaluable, restorative experience (Mitten, 1990; Tippett, 1993). For those for whom more structure is needed, providing alternative activities can offer a good balance. On brief trips, allowing time for these types of interludes is often impossible and on trips that are *too* activity oriented, such experiences may be undervalued (Mitten, 1990; Tippett, 1993).

Helping women who have been the victims of incest gain a sense of control over their lives is key to measuring the success of any program. One of the ways this can be enhanced on an outdoor trip is to support an incest survivor's choice to discontinue or not engage in an activity. For a woman to successfully say "No" is an empowering experience. For many incest survivors, however, saying "No" takes both courage and practice. The more opportunities women are given to say "No" and to observe others daring to say "No," the more empowered a woman can become. Castor-Lewis (1988) writes:

> Replete in the survivor's history are instances in which she was not only *not* encouraged to say "no" in order to protect herself from something uncomfortable, but was also *not* listened to when she *did* say "no." The ability to protect oneself, to set limits, to say "no" and to expect to have it respected are often central conflicts for the survivor. (p. 76)

Providing opportunities for women to say "No" and assert themselves on a trip is another feature that can become compromised due to the pressures created by time and program design. Also, many programs fundamentally believe that urging participants to push through their "self-imposed" limits will deliver positive benefits, a stance that can be counterproductive when working with incest survivors. Mitten and Dutton (1993) write:

> It is not useful to foster an attitude of "pushing through" one's feelings to get to a "better" place. The meaning of being sexually abused is to be pushed physically and emotionally, against one's will, beyond what a person can manage. This approach is dangerous for a survivor and can cause unnecessary stress for other members as well. In fact, encouraging women to push-on either emotionally or physically can reinforce women not listening to their bodies and minds. (p. 11)

Mitten and Dutton (1993) promote the idea of a graduated approach to working with groups of women who are incest survivors. In their experience, offering a series of trips that present graduated challenges over time, rather than a single trip packed into a weekend or a week, offers women more opportunities to gradually build their skills and confidence so that they can take on more responsibility and leadership and feel more comfortable in what for many of them may be a foreign environment. In general, it seems that programs that offer a series of experiences that build participants' skills, demystify outdoor experiences, and help participants learn how to gain access to and pursue outdoor activities on their own, can be particularly empowering and therapeutic. Activities such as backpacking, hiking, and canoeing, which require the least amount of equipment and tend to be more accessible to most people, are activities that are perhaps more ideally suited to promoting continued use of the new skills and strengths cultivated. Programs that utilize more technical equipment and activities such as ropes courses and rock climbing, may, on the other hand, be more intimidating and difficult for women to pursue on their own, and, therefore, do little to enhance a woman's chances of utilizing this new experience in the future.

Conclusion

The issues that I have discussed in this chapter are ones that I have been made aware of through my experiences leading outdoor trips for incest survivors and for women in general. While it is not my intention to give an exhaustive review of every issue that may arise, I want to encourage anyone who works with incest survivors to think critically about the question of whether wilderness experiences have therapeutic value for incest survivors. If wilderness programs do have therapeutic value, then which model or which elements from the different models can be combined to create a situation that will help achieve rather than undermine the therapeutic goals of recovery, of which "empowerment and reconnection" (Herman, 1992) are of foremost importance?

In summary, today, while insurance companies are demanding ever briefer forms of treatment, wilderness programs which offer brief treatment models have a distinct opportunity to fill a need in the market. As I have attempted to show, however, brief models which often necessarily utilize a "stress" approach may offer positive therapeutic opportunities and benefits working with certain populations, but may be countertherapeutic working with incest survivors. Also, given the complexities of the recovery process, while wilderness programs may create momentary breakthroughs and insights into old behavior, the building of new skills and experience requires slow deliberate work over time. This must be made explicit to participants for whom change is often greatly desired, but hard won, and for whom false hope can be devastating.

Recovery from incest is a lifelong process in which "new conflicts and challenges at each new stage of the life cycle will inevitably reawaken the trauma and bring new aspects of the experience to light" (Herman, 1992, p. 195). Given this fact, while wilderness programs offer unique experiential opportunities that can aid individuals in their healing process, in part by providing new challenges, due to the unpredictability of wilderness travel and the insidious nature of post-traumatic stress, no matter how carefully planned, any wilderness program can become countertherapeutic and dangerous at a moment's notice.

Due to the unique needs and experience of most incest survivors, longer programs, and in particular, graduated programs, that work in conjunction with an ongoing therapy group, seem to offer optimal therapeutic conditions for working with incest survivors in the wilderness. Many factors need to be considered, however, when planning a therapeutic wilderness program for this population. These range from careful selection and screening of participants, to training of staff in the latest theory on incest and post-traumatic stress disorder, to correct ratios of staff to participants and the utilization of experiences that will offer challenges that enhance growth rather than challenges that trigger instinctive survival behaviors.

Endnote

[1] Since this chapter was written, an important addition to the literature on wilderness therapy has been published: Cole, E., Erdman, E., & Rothblum, E. D. (Eds.). (1994). *Wilderness therapy for women.* Binghamton, NY: The Haworth Press.

References

Alexander, P. C., Neimeyer, R. A., & Follette, V. M. (1991, June). Group therapy for women sexually abused as children. *Journal of Interpersonal Violence, 6*(2), 218-231.

Arbarbanel, S. (1988, April 17). Conquering the mountain: How victims of sexual abuse regain their self-respect. *Family Circle,* 66-68.

Bacon, S. B., & Kimball, R. O. (1993). The wilderness challenge model. In M. A. Gass (Ed.), *Adventure therapy: Therapeutic applications of adventure programming* (pp. 11-41). Dubuque, IA: Kendall/Hunt.

Bograd, M. (1986). A feminist examination of family systems models of violence against women in the family. In M. A. Riche (Ed.), *Women and therapy* (pp. 34-51). Rockville, MD: Aspen Publications.

Canda, E. (1988). Spirituality, religious diversity, and social work practice. *Social Casework, 69*(4), 238-247.

Castor-Lewis, C. (1988). On doing research with adult incest survivors: Some initial thoughts and considerations. *Women & Therapy, 7*(1), 73-80.

Chu, J. A. (1988). Ten traps for therapists in the treatment of trauma survivors. *Dissociation, 11*(4), 24-31.

Courtois, C. A. (1988). *Healing the incest wound.* New York: W. W. Norton.

DePaul, A. (1986, April 18). From victim. . . . to victor. *The Washington Post,* Section D, p. 5.

DeYoung, M. (1985). *Incest: An annotated bibliography.* Jefferson, NC: McFarland.

Finkelhor, D., & Browne, A. (1985). The traumatic impact of child sexual abuse: A conceptualization. *American Journal of Orthopsychiatry, 55*(4), 530-541.

Flannery, R. B. (1987). From victim to survivor: A stress management approach in the treatment of learned helplessness. In B. A. van der Kolk (Ed.), *Psychological trauma.* Washington, DC: American Psychiatric Press.

Gass, M. A. (1993). Foundations of adventure therapy. In M. A. Gass (Ed.), *Adventure therapy: Therapeutic applications of adventure programming*, (pp. 3-10). Dubuque, IA: Kendall/ Hunt.

Gelinas, D. J. (1983). The persisting negative effects of incest. *Psychiatry, 46*, 312-332.

Gillis, H. L. (1993). Annotated bibliography for the therapeutic uses of adventure-challenge-outdoor wilderness: Theory and research. In M. A. Gass (Ed.), *Adventure therapy: Therapeutic applications of adventure programming*, (pp. 371-407). Dubuque, IA: Kendall/ Hunt.

Goodwin, J. M., and Talwar, N. (1989). Group psychotherapy for victims of incest. *Psychiatric Clinics of North America, 12*(2), 279-293.

Harney, P. A. (1992). The role of incest in developmental theory and treatment of women diagnosed with borderline personality disorder. *Women & Therapy, 12*(1/2), 39-57.

Herman, J. L. (1992). *Trauma and recovery.* New York: Basic Books.

Israel, E. (1989). *Treatment intervention with battered women.* Unpublished manuscript, University of Northern Colorado, Greeley, Colorado.

James, B. (1989). *Treating traumatized children: New insights and interventions.* New York: Lexington Books.

Janoff-Bulman, R. (1985). The aftermath of victimization: Rebuilding shattered assumptions. In C. R. Figley (Ed.), *Trauma and its wake* (pp. 15-35). New York: Brunner/Mazel.

McCann, L., & Pearlman, L. A. (1990). Vicarious traumatization: A framework for understanding the psychological effects of working with victims. *Journal of Traumatic Stress, 3*(1), 131-149.

Miles, J. (1993). Wilderness as healing place. In M. A. Gass (Ed.), *Adventure therapy: Therapeutic applications of adventure programming*, (pp. 43-55). Dubuque, IA: Kendall/Hunt.

Miller, D. (1990). The trauma of interpersonal violence. *Smith College School of Social Work Journal*, (Fall/Winter), 313-318.

Mitten, D. (1990). *Meeting the unknown: Group dynamics in the wilderness.* Minneapolis, MN: Woodswomen.

Mitten, D., & Dutton, R. (1993). Outdoor leadership considerations with women survivors of sexual abuse. *Journal of Experiential Education, 16*(1), 7-13.

Oliver, J. (1988). *An evaluation of the Outward Bound School's Victim of Violence Recovery Program.* Unpublished manuscript, Colorado Outward Bound School, Colorado.

Pfirman, E. S. (1987). *The effects of a wilderness challenge course on victims of rape in locus of control, self-concept, and fear.* Unpublished manuscript, University of Northern Colorado, Greeley, Colorado.

Sanford, L. T. (1990). *Strong at the broken places.* New York: Avon.

Stringer, A. L., and McAvoy, L. H. (1992). The need for something different: Spirituality and wilderness adventure. *Journal of Experiential Education, 15*(1), 13-20.

Tippett, S. (1993). Therapeutic wilderness programming for borderline adolescents. In M. A. Gass (Ed.), *Adventure therapy: Therapeutic applications of adventure programming*, (pp. 83-94). Dubuque, IA: Kendall/Hunt.

van der Kolk, B. A. (1987). The role of the group in the origin and resolution of the trauma response. In B. A. van der Kolk (Ed.), *Psychological trauma.* Washington, DC: American Psychiatric Press.

Wartik, N. (1986, April). Learning to dare again. *Ms. Magazine, 14*(1), 20.

Webb, B. (1993). The use of a three-day therapeutic wilderness adjunct by the Colorado Outward Bound School with survivors of violence. In M. A. Gass (Ed.), *Adventure therapy: Therapeutic applications of adventure programming*, (pp. 95-102). Dubuque, IA: Kendall/ Hunt.

Professional Voices

I look to life as a day in school;
an opportunity to learn, to develop skills,
to contribute to the general welfare,
and to see all as part of the great whole.
Experiential education ought to be the core of everyone's life.

Helen Nearing

Current dialogue within the Association for Experiential Education revolves around the role of professional groups within the association. There is persistent sentiment that the Women's and NAALA[1] groups are identity groups rather than a professional affiliation and therefore should be accorded a different and essentially less important status than such groups as Therapeutic Adventures or Experience-Based Training and Development. As experiential educators struggle with questions of professionalism, this is an important debate.

While identity-based support and politics are foundational to the Women's Professional Group (PG), professionalism remains a vital part of its mission. Ewert (1989) proposes six criteria used to define a profession. A profession must satisfy an indispensable social need, provide a guarantee of competence, possess a body of specialized knowledge and skills, have a body of literature, demonstrate professional goals and responsibilities, and develop a set of ethical standards and practices. Further, Michalec (1995) suggests that "professions are collections of practice-oriented individuals who are guided in their actions by theory and professional standards of conduct" (p. 34). Throughout its history, the Women's Professional Group has remained faithful to these conditions of professionalism.

The Women's PG has consistently sought ways to include new members and mentor them in the professional milieu of the group. Many in academia have carved out a niche researching and writing about the complex facets of gender issues in experiential education. The application of the new scholarship on women and girls to adventure programming, using that groundbreaking research as the basis of program design rather than solely as subsequent justification, has strengthened the professional standards of the entire profession. Further, single-gender programs have served as a microscope to look at the experience of women and girls in the outdoors in order to gain specialized skills and knowledge about how to create female-friendly experiential education programs. Finally, feminist ethics have been examined in AEE workshops and in the formation of the Women's PG mission statement.

Women authors in this volume add their voices to the dialogue about professionalism. Wilma Miranda and Rita Yerkes uncover the history of women in the American camping movement to remind us of the importance of women in the professionalization of experiential education. They write women back into the picture of the outdoor professions that have often ignored, hidden, or trivialized their contributions. Denise Mitten sums up principles of leadership and program design that are particularly important to a women's outdoor adventure program. She stresses that these principles come from the women who participate, rather than from an abstract outside source, thereby further validating all-women's programs as the laboratory where women's experience can be studied. Related to this section theme, Mitten provides one set of professional standards useful for women's outdoor programs. In Nina Roberts and Ellen Drogin's examination of the participation of African American women in outdoor recreation, the authors point out how women of color have been extremely underrepresented in leisure research. They assert that this research must be undertaken to identify and overcome the constraints to participation faced by many African American women. In a profession where research must inform practice, the inclusion of women of all races in experiential education demands the solid research base suggested by Roberts and Drogin. To end the section, T.A. Loeffler details strategies for experiential education programs to use to support female staff and enhance women's career development. Condensed from her timely study of women outdoor leaders, Loeffler outlines some of the limitations to advancement for women in the profession and offers informative suggestions to break the glass ceiling. These chapters contribute significantly to a continuing reach for more professionalism in experiential education.

Endnote

[1] NAALA is the acronym of the Natives, Africans, Asians, Latinos(as), and Allies Professional Group of the Association for Experiential Education.

References

Ewert, A. (1989). *Outdoor adventure pursuits: Foundations, models, and theories.* Columbus, OH: Publishing Horizons.

Michalec, P. (1995). The future of experiential education as a profession. In R. Kraft & J. Kielsmeier (Eds.), *Experiential learning in schools and higher education* (pp. 32-39). Dubuque, IA: Kendall/Hunt.

Nearing, H. (February 20, 1986). Personal correspondence to editor.

6

The History of Camping Women in the Professionalization of Experiential Education

Wilma Miranda and Rita Yerkes

Origins in Organized Camping

In the late 1970s, experiential educators were taken by surprise by a groundswell of interest in women-only outdoor pursuits programs. This demand has swelled unabated throughout the 1980s to the present (Yerkes & Miranda, 1982; Mitten, 1992).

The program responses to women's interests have generated an accompanying expansion of feminist-based theory in experiential education. With the growth of a broad range of programs to choose from, women from diverse backgrounds have built female community across cultural and racial differences. Leadership philosophy itself is grounded in women's experience, skills, and needs (Warren, 1985; Mitten, 1986; Pfirman, 1988; Roberts, 1993).

Not since the rise of the girls' camping movement at the beginning of this century has an autonomous women's movement so directly impacted outdoor programs and professional discourse. Indeed, we should understand the present wave not as something new, but rather, as a resurgence of neglected feminist traditions in experiential education. When a new breed of women leaders began in the 1980s to rethink their profession along feminist lines, their claims exceeded the usual demands for employment equity and participant access. What made them appear transgressive to some was their willingness to reconstruct definitions of outdoor pursuits leadership in light of the principles of feminist pedagogy (Mitten, 1985; Henderson & Bialeschki, 1987). They used the normative concepts in experiential education to interrogate assumptions in the field. Whose experience was really addressed? Whose left out? Critiques showed how gender blindness in service to a universalist notion of experience unwittingly masked the tailoring of "experience" to fit men's experience (Bialeschki, 1992).

Fifty years and historical amnesia separate us from the earliest campaign in the 1920s to achieve professional autonomy by and for women. Female leaders in organized camping, the only form of outdoor experiential education then available, shaped the very meaning of professionalism and for over seven years, held organizational structures and policies in their control. We take their achievement to be paradigmatic of women's professional struggles in the outdoor pursuits professions in this century.

This case study shows how camping women acted to define the first institutional expression of what we term experiential education today. The originality of their achievement lay in uniting educational theory with a conception of associational democracy that assured them parity with men. Gender equality was to be virtually definitive of the field. The lessons they offer are still relevant to all experiential educators, women in particular, since the barriers they faced have yet to be overcome, and perennial dilemmas in professional self-definition remain urgent. To recover the story of their attainments and limitations, therefore, serves to clarify our own.

We shall show how first in the National Association of Directors of Girls Camps, and later in the Camp Directors Association, women came to view their work through two contradictory interpretive screens. First, they borrowed the gender-based logic of their male prep-school colleagues to craft a heroic reading of "the director"; and second, as association founders and members, they deployed this romantic image of the woman leader in service of their status in *professional* organization. Their professional self-definition was rooted in both a communitarian feminist pedagogy and a vision of rigorous professional standards (Brown, 1913).

Reconstructing the Education of Girls

It all started with only eight women who, in the fall of 1916, met to plan what would soon be known as The National Association of Directors of Girls Camps (NADGC) (Eells, 1986, p. 163). The meeting included such luminaries as Mrs. Luther Gulick, co-founder with her husband of The Campfire Girls, and her sister, Mrs. Charles Farnsworth, headmistress of the Horace Mann School for Girls at Teachers College, Columbia University, whose husband was also on the faculty there. Mary Schenck Woolman, founder of the Manhattan Training School for Girls and once professor of Household Arts at Columbia, and Florence Marshall, director and head of the Manhattan Trade School for Girls, were pioneers in the development of home economics education. Though Dr. Susan Kingsbury, director of the Women's Educational and Industrial Union of Boston could not attend, it was she who had issued the invitations.

These women represented an elite coalition of academic and philanthropic interests in women's progressive education. The overriding belief they held in common was that a new American golden age depended on the liberation of girls. In other words, it depended on them. The problem was not what to do, but where to do it!

The impressive popularity of the organized camping movement seemed to offer a way. Camp sessions could be short and flexible, the required investment was modest, and the outdoors was an idyllic setting to counter traditional homes and schools.

One of the attendees, Laura Mattoon, had earned her fame as owner/director of Kehonka, a showpiece girls' camp in New Hampshire. Porter Sargent, a key promoter of private school camping, had identified Mattoon as among the "pioneers in everything pertaining to the progress of the summer camp" (Sargent, 1924, p. 263). Yet, at the age of 43, neither she nor any of the other 200 women then directing camps were eligible to join the Camp Directors Association of America, founded in 1910 (Eells, 1986). The story of women's power in the NADGC and later in the merged Camp Directors Association, was also Mattoon's story. Long before 1916, she had become an honored pioneer, but she was not yet deemed a colleague.

The men who began camping for boys in the 1890s had been seeking not progress, but restoration. Deploring the "effeminizing" drift of modern life (Miranda, 1985), they blamed the decadent city and hothouse "indoors" prep schools. To counter these threats to American virility, they launched a movement toward rugged outdoor education (Hamilton, 1930, p. 69). With Thoreauvian defiance, they constructed communal Walden Ponds to serve as masculine incubators against the twin evils of temptation and coddling. Never much interested in professionalizing this new work, they crafted a romantic image of the director as mentor—an educational adventurer capable of inspiring a community of "real" men and boys (Hamilton, 1930, p. 4). The "chief" was cast as an outdoorsman of breeding, character, and style. By definition, this was a male role (Balch, 1893, p. 251). There is irony in the fact that it would be for this vision of educational community, this lost cause of 20th-century American education, that Mattoon and her feminist allies would work so fervently for over twenty years.

The public infatuation with camps had turned them into the first stable leadership training bases for girls. Freed from the domesticating influences of home, camps became centers for envisioning new lives. Yet camping education itself needed reform, if the work was to advance. Women directors modeled shared leadership in contrast to "control from the top," a feature in boys' camping they deplored. Girls would learn "cooperative government in which campers have a very real part. . . . We are teaching attitudes of mind more than anything else" (Mattoon, 1923, p. 21). Women directors were to be the charismatic models of the *new* woman.

Their first target was outdated attitudes toward physical activity. As a close colleague of Mattoon put it: "The camps reveal . . . a deplorable lack in the present system of education for women. It is the failure to put the proper emphasis on physical development" (Coale, 1919, p. 16).

Though these new educational executives (as they called themselves) modeled feminine independence which tested class and gender-appropriate mores of the times, they stopped short of open repudiation (Miranda, 1987). However, they directly challenged the intrusions of industrialism on what today we call womanspace: "Just as in industry women have been working under conditions designed for men, so it would seem, in the school and college, a man's program is being imposed upon the girl student" (Coale, 1919, p. 263).

Directors of girls' camps, therefore, needed a strong professional association which could serve as a counterweight against such imposition. By 1920, a coalition of girls' camp directors had established to their own satisfaction a fact largely doubted by their contemporaries. "The girls' camp has proved that there can be just as great esprit de corps among girls as among boys" (Coale, 1919, p. 263). Only a strong professional association would provide the needed leverage to support these embryonic communities.

The National Association of Directors of Girls Camps

By 1910, camps were at the heart of the incipient recreation professions, as potential employers of newly trained camp personnel. The men in organized camping were aware that this expansion of camping would bring problems of control. Alarmingly, some parents even pressed for co-educational scouting (Buckler, 1961, p. 29). The "ladies," of course, were very welcome to start their own girls' camps along with an organization of camp directresses. The men understood, of course, that these camps would be less rigorous imitations of the real thing, and that their activities, while educationally virtuous, had no bearing on the business of the Camp Directors Association of America (CDAA).

Since the stakes over the control of camping were rising, male leaders eagerly counterproposed a separate girls' organization, agreeing that girls had special needs and should be preparing for different adult roles (Gulick, 1912). After 1910, leading men took keen interest in the formation of carefully defined "opportunities" for girls. Luther Gulick himself led the way. But other prominent men, such as Daniel West, head of the Boy Scouts, also insisted on separate arrangements—both for girls' camping *and* for a separate organization of girls' camp directors (Gulick, 1912). The purpose of Camp Fire Girls, as outlined by Gulick, was to glamorize female domestic duties. Women would be trained to find adventure at home in service to the industrial age built by men. Not the wildfire but the hearthfire was to be the symbolic source of outdoor romance for girls (Gulick, 1912, p. 325).

Few women were independent owners of boys' camps, while men often owned girls' camps directed by their spouses. A separate organization admitting both men and women would assure that the CDAA could avoid female membership and, through the men who joined both associations, retain influence in the direction of the largely women's association. They hadn't reckoned on the influence of those at the 1916 planning session, who were not so compliant with this agenda as were their own spouses. Laura Mattoon, Florence Marshall, and Susan Kingsbury resisted not only the simplistically domestic agenda of Camp Fire programming, but the idea of a subordinate professional association as well. Marshall was soon to resign from her role in the Camp Fire Association after charges were brought against Gulick for fiscal malfeasance (*New York Times*, 13 March, 1915, p. 9). Kingsbury, an economy professor at Vassar, had established her camp explicitly as an experiment in socialist principles (McMullen to Eells, 8/31/76).

The National Association of Directors of Girls Camps was by definition an association of directors of both genders. For the first time, married women, along with singles, would hold independent association membership in their own right in an association that included both genders. Though the old guard in the CDAA no doubt expected men to shape the fledgling association, younger males really functioned as conduits, carrying the NADGC agenda back into the deliberations of the CDAA. L. B. Sharp, Director of Life Camps, and William Gould Vinal, President of the CDAA at the time of the merger in 1924, pushed for the progressivism that literally defined the NADGC. Its priorities, in fact, were identical with the goals of educational progressivism—program certification, safety standards, program development, training, and the expansion of camping opportunities for middle- and lower-class youngsters (Lehman, 1925).

Enter the Kingmaker

As the NADGC's first secretary, Laura Mattoon played the pivotal role in protecting the interests of the large cadre of women directors. Her wealth helped. By subsidizing its activities, she was able to chart the direction of the new association. Born in 1873 in Springfield, Massachusetts, to a socialite opera singer and a financier, Mattoon used her inherited wealth and her connections to establish an associational structure that would ensure a voice for women. She had graduated from Wellesley College in 1894 with a degree in the natural sciences. There she had been inspired by the lingering spell of Alice Freeman Palmer, the young and brilliant former president of Wellesley. Palmer's educational vision for women would inspire Mattoon's own throughout her long and amazing career. Of Palmer, she later wrote in a book of camp devotions, "We love the mind courageous which no dread of failure ever daunted, whose control of gentleness all opposition stole" (Mattoon & Bragdon, 1947, p. 133). For almost fifteen years, Mattoon was to ply this art of gentleness with consummate skill before its severe political shortcomings were to be revealed. Yet Palmer showed Mattoon's generation of young educated women how to be daring and also perfectly ladylike. "O Leader of Leaders," Mattoon wrote, "Thy life was set, to counsel—to be a friend" (Mattoon & Bragdon, p. 133). This was the stirring image of moral leadership she took to the forums of the NADGC, exhorting others to follow the old Wellesley dictum—"Not to be ministered unto, but to minister."

Mattoon was out to educate the new woman in new ways. Her intentions at Kehonka were always explicit:

> Among the many things we are trying to do in camps is to develop a keen
> and solid sense of responsibility toward the new voting citizenship that now

has become a part of a woman's life. Energy, time, and thought have been put into the long fight for the right to vote. Much has been won for America's girls. (Mattoon, 1925, p. 11)

Though friendly to the Camp Fire leaders and sympathetic toward programs in the household arts, her main goal was to challenge old boundaries set for girls. For reasons different from the men, she lay great stress upon the rigors of the "primitive camp." While men were trying to recapture the ideals of the past for boys, Mattoon aimed to overcome them for girls (McMullen to Eells, 1976).

The basic pedagogical responsibility for the education of girls opposed the one set out by Gulick (Brown, 1913, p. 30). Mattoon and others expected their campers to sleep in tents, take backcountry hikes, and learn the skills detailed in campcraft as developed by Ernest Thompson Seton and the Woodcraft League (Coale, 1918, p. 263). In an era, particularly after World War I, when most progressives were arguing for coeducation, these progressive educators remained staunchly committed to a separate female education. Even more important than "roughing it" were the aesthetic and spiritual links between a robust girlhood and nature. A distinctly female aesthetic along the Palmer model was promoted: "Artistic expression comes naturally and spontaneously in the solitude and beauty of the woods. . . . A leader has only to foster and nourish it" (Eells, 1978).

A professional association of such leaders, however essential, would not be sufficient. A democratic organization congruent with their feminist commitments would be required. Eleanor Eells comments (interview, 1978) that "the women stuck it out. In amazing fashion [they] made it a full-time profession . . . very much in response to social issues." Dr. Anna Brown, head of the Young Women's Christian Association, held that ". . . the duty of democratizing intercourse lies chiefly at the door of women in our country." For her, outdoor play was "the most democratizing single influence we can exert upon the artificial social standards of our time" (1913, p. 30).

Given the domination of men in numbers, prestige, and wealth, it would be difficult at best to establish equal participation in professional association with them. Yet, in spite of their commitment to a separate female education, this is precisely what the women set out to accomplish. A women-only association would only replicate the gender relations they hoped to reverse. Only in a professional association where they wielded equal power with men, could they provide themselves the base to influence norms beyond the association itself.

Pedagogy and professional association democracy, therefore, were of one piece. The constitution of the National Association of Directors of Girls Camps reflected the values of the well-run camp community. It became a professional model for gender inclusivity. Under Mattoon's leadership, the NADGC comprised a remarkable group of men and women directors who briefly achieved congruence between their educational ideology and their organizational structure. Within a few years of its official beginning in 1916, the young association would attract some of educational progressivism's biggest stars. Like the older, exclusively male CDAA, it remained in the hands of private camp directors, but in this case, those hands were female.

Secretary Mattoon nurtured an effective alliance against a perceived common enemy—"quickbuck operators," busily degrading the professional standards of true camping:

> The secretary notes that among the newer camps there is a growing tendency toward modern commercial procedure in publicity... the ethics and dignity of our educational profession are ignored. . . . Even I who have been conducting a camp for twenty-six seasons, have been included in these purchased lists as a desirable "miss" of camping age. (Mattoon, 1928, p. 18)

Mattoon's influence owed much to her great skill in balancing interests. Prominent men did not dominate the association, but she could ill-afford to alienate them or their spouses. Never seeking the limelight for herself, she saw to it that the ambition of others was served. She was never president. It was her unchallenged incumbency in the secretary's position that assured her a continuous seat on the executive committee whose meetings she held at her own camp. She maintained a surprisingly resilient coalition of interests between progressive school camp directors, independent camp women, large agency directors and administrators, and a growing number of teacher education faculty. More than money and personal finesse were at work here. Mattoon knew how to deploy constitutional and parliamentary regulations against any challenges to her own agendas (Gibson, 1936, p. 23). Since the constitution stipulated that the presidency and vice-presidency must be alternated annually between a man and a woman, and since she herself was returned annually as executive secretary, at least *two* women would always be on the executive committee (Lehman, 1925, p. 133). Usually, there were more.

From this position, Mattoon worked unremittingly on behalf of her primary long-term goal—amalgamation with the CDAA. Merger negotiations were kept entirely covert for two years to prevent conflicts from breaking into an open hostility that would dash her hopes (Eells, 1986). Why amalgamation? Because only in a unified association could camp directors compete as equals with other educational leaders. Further, if women were to retain the same power after merger that they had already achieved in the NADGC, their advance would range far beyond the camping movement itself.

Only the Name is the Same

"As Eve was created from one of Adam's ribs, so, in this case, the girl's camp organization is but a highly developed rib from the masculine parent" (Eells, 1986, p. 42). So intoned William Gould Vinal at the great March 1924 Meeting of the National Association of Directors of Girls Camps and the Camp Directors Association of America. This perhaps intentionally patronizing remark may have been said to soothe the pride of the men of the CDAA, honoring male chivalry in allowing "the ladies" to join them. The truth, as Vinal well knew, was directly to the contrary. The terms of the merger were a NADGC diplomatic triumph, imposing gender equality and progressive policies on the field as a whole. It had proudly stood for "all that was best" in scientific education, standardization of health and safety practices, and expanded curricula (Gibson, 1936, p. 25). "It was at this historic meeting that 'A Statement of Basic Standards for Organized Summer Camps as prepared by the New England Section of the NADGC,' was presented by Mrs. Dwight Rogers, and adopted" (Gibson, 1936, p. 23). The NADGC had redefined camping education:

> The word "camp" shall be construed to mean an educational and recreational organization occupying ample grounds in the country, in which systematic instruction is given primarily in the branches of outdoor activities, nature lore, and handicraft, by trained counselors to an organized group of young people, for a period of not less than seven weeks. (Lehman, 1925, p. 133)

As the men of the old CDAA knew, the NADGC had not been the child of the wilderness but of the city, born in New York where not only Teachers College but also the burgeoning private agencies in camping had their headquarters—the Girl Scouts, the YWCA, the settlement houses. By the twenties, Teachers College had become the center of post-World War I educational progressivism. It provided graduate degrees for personnel not only in education, but in new social service and recreational fields. Young people attended in huge numbers, seeking legitimation for new professions, including organized camping, the playground movement, and YMCA programs. To the horror of some New England directors, camping had been recaptured by the city, bringing standardization, hierarchy, and conformity in the name of progress (Wack, 1923, p. 42).

The NADGC had owed its rapid rise to this concentration of new education and recreation interests. As Teachers College drew increasing numbers of graduate students seeking advanced degrees, the NADGC drew prestigious faculty support, including John Dewey's disciple, William Heard Kilpatrick. He claimed the camp to be the quintessential form of progressive and experiential education:

> I want the camp to set an example to the school that brings education in, instead of setting it up so that it is hard to get an education at all . . . so that when people watch the camp they would come back to the school teachers and say "Now look here, we have had enough of your kind of education." (Kilpatrick, 1933, p. 20)

Young protégés of Kilpatrick, among them E. K. Fretwell and L. B. Sharp, who were soon to become important leaders in camping and, later, in what came to be known as outdoor education, derived much of their own influence in the NADGC from their faculty positions at Teachers College-Columbia. Though supported by

Mattoon, the coalition came at a price for the women. Feminist progressives retained their alliance with conservative, private-camp men against a headlong rush to management expertise. They held out for the autonomous model of charismatic leader so indispensable to their own professional identities (Mattoon, 1925, p. 11). Interestingly, feminist directors and the conservative chiefs of private boys' camps found themselves allied and on the defensive against urban voices calling for managerial reform.

The consolidation in 1924 masked these tensions under the rhetoric that the interests of all camp directors were the same. To many curmudgeons of New England, however, the amalgamation was a bad show led by owners of the "Vest-Chesty Biltmore Hotels in the woods" (Wack, 1923, p. 42). This corruption they blamed on Teachers College and the hordes of women, their own colleagues at last, who had grown strong in the NADGC. They knew a merger would promote the influence of the agencies at the expense of the individual private camp. Yet by 1924, most outdoor educators, like all educators, were loathe to be thought *un*progressive. In an era when universities, recreational agencies, and private camps all were competing to shape the definitions and norms of the "progressive" outdoor professions, camping was key; it would not do to retreat from the fray.

Mattoon's balancing act became unsustainable in spite of her continued support from both independent and agency camp constituencies. She exhorted camps to "guard like a jewel" their own individuality since the independent camp must remain the cornerstone of the profession (Mattoon, 1925, p. 13). Social service and teacher education interests should nonetheless be welcomed, she warned the old guard, since they were powerful promoters of the true camping idea. As her position was equivocal, so, too, were her marching orders to the new organization:

> They included a housecleaning among our present members to bring us up
> to the same standards we demand of our new camps; [and] . . . the need of a
> centrally located headquarters with a permanent full time executive secre-
> tary. (Gibson, 1936, p. 23)

Temporarily, at least, she was in control. As executive secretary *and* treasurer, she presided over annual business meetings while continuing the monthly executive committee meetings at her own camp—just as she had for the NADGC. She would continue to underwrite the costs of association initiatives. From 1924 until her resignation in 1931, she stayed in office as others rotated on and off the executive committee. Though she had a firm hand on the tiller, trouble churned below.

Reversal

Evidence of tension and her response appear early—in her 1925 convention report, where the laconic statement appears that, "The plan which existed in the

NADGC of having its members grouped in different sections has been continued in the new organization" (Mattoon, 1925, p. 11).

This was a key issue. The association was a federation of sections where each section was equally represented on the executive committee, irrespective of their membership numbers. Since an individual's primary membership was in the section rather than in the national association, this assured a large measure of sectional influence. The arrangement particularly suited the interests of the New England section which, with its small membership compared to that of New York, had a voice at the national level disproportionate to its actual size. It also assured the general pre-eminence of private camps and, therefore, the relative power of the independent camp women.

With Mattoon subtly guiding most association matters, and the protections provided by a sectional confederation, neither agency progressives nor conservative interests could marginalize the independent camp women. A centralized hierarchical organization, however, with primary membership in the national association, would wipe out this sectional advantage.

A second bone of contention was the criteria for membership. On this question turned the whole definition of the profession. From the private camp perspective, the Camp Directors Association ought clearly to be an association of camp directors:

> Active membership shall be open to any man or woman who shall have directed an organized and approved camp for boys or girls or for both boys and girls, during a period of at least two consecutive seasons, and who shall be conducting such a camp at the time of election. (Lehman, 1925, p. 133)

Feminist independents held out against their powerful progressive allies, by holding tenaciously to both the federation concept and restrictive membership criteria. Between 1924 and 1930, Mattoon, "The Godmother of Organized Camping," warded off a barrage of constitutional challenges, playing off interests so as to put a brake on moves either to dominate or to secede. As the only assured member of the executive committee for over six years, she learned how to ride out the storms. Her gender, reputation, and class status ensured deference from members of her own class and even from the ambitious young New York members seeking to define the profession in less elitist terms. Women directors supported her not only because she was an admired director herself, but also because she held the line against encroachments on their position. In a typical tribute, her supporters expressed the "love and appreciation of the directors":

> Miss Mattoon has served the association since its organization and much of the success of the CDA is due to her unselfish and sacrificial devotion to the organization. (Atlantic City Annual Meeting, 1929)

She had become their Alice Freeman Palmer. Yet the balance struck between the ambitious partisans of New York agencies and their New England resisters could not last. The fulcrum coalition of feminist women began to disintegrate. Girls' camp leaders who were positioned between conservatives and progressives became themselves fragmented after 1929 as the Depression hit new independent camps especially hard. As many dropped out of the association, independent camp leaders became more defensive in organizational skirmishes.

By 1930, the executive secretary's legendary patience was wearing thin. Her annual reports became sermonettes on the proper conduct of camping education and the association's business. "The secretary notes . . ." was the typical introduction to a literate scolding. Her frustration mounted. The old tactics were failing. No longer could she play off relatively equal forces in the organization. The New York section chafed under the indignity of having full membership denied to some of its most influential members. Prestigious faculty might write the books on professional standards, but if they didn't run a camp, they were barred from full voting membership. This situation could not last.

Mattoon's influence after 1929 eroded so rapidly that critics openly sniped at her retreat into a "cabal," a secret controlling group (Hamilton, 1931, p. 11). In spite of hard times, the association had outgrown its dependence on her financial support. Universities and philanthropic agencies became increasingly important sources of funding. From Mattoon's perspective, more substantive setbacks had taken their toll. The educational rhetoric upon which organized camping had grounded its professional claims failed to convince most of its own members. Behind Mattoon's merger agenda had been the hope to create an association of directors whose voice would count in larger educational forums. She complained that the Camp Directors Association was "missing" from the Child Study Association, the Progressive Education Association, and the National Educational Association. "We should seek direct understandings and contacts with educational organizations" (Mattoon, 1929, p. 12). On this, the conservatives prevailed. For them, the whole point of camp had been to escape the school, not to become one. For their part, teacher education experts had little specific interest in the private-school-based independent camp of either the old CDAA men or the progressive feminists. They would maintain their ties with agencies, public schools, and teacher education. In 1929, Mattoon gave it one more try:

> We begin to wonder whether we have given enough thought about the idea of each section having an office that would meet the requirements of local conditions. There is lacking a definite and comprehensive, and progressive plan. . . .
>
> Why not, then, before we leave this convention consider the appointment of a commission "truly" representative of the association and camping movement? Each section might be permitted to appoint representatives . . . in proportion with section membership. (Mattoon, 1929, p. 12)

This is vintage Mattoon. She hoped this plan to funnel resources to the local sections would forestall constitutional attacks. Unfortunately, the call for true representation begged the question of the criteria for membership. As things stood, New England members, mostly heads of private camps, as well as the independent camp directors in New York, favored the status quo. Certainly, the private girls' camps directors would benefit by retaining the federation concept and the criteria for membership. Agency staff women, however, decreasingly looked to the independents to speak for their interests. Coeducational, municipal, or state park personnel had no roots in girls' camping and few now defined themselves as educators. Their professional identity owed little to the older tradition of the camp director. Less restrictive membership criteria and changes in organizational structure met their concrete needs (Lehman, 1930, p. 23). For a new generation of women, neither gender, nor feminist pedagogy, nor sectional autonomy was a compelling issue. The coalition had finally broken down.

When in 1931, Mattoon finally retired from her role, it marked the end of a struggle toward one form of associational democracy. A constitution assuring collegial relationships among equal proprietors holding membership in a confederation of independent sections was rejected by former progressive allies. Teacher education professionals, social service personnel, support personnel in camps, and those in outdoor recreation agencies clamored for "an association of all camps and camp groups recognizing each other as members of the same function" (Final Report of the Committee of Seven, 1932).

In 1932, a commission along lines suggested by Mattoon presented its blunt report. Active voting membership would henceforth be open to all persons interested in educational/recreational camping. A strong national organization was *the* priority. Sections should be fostered but never at the expense of the national (Final Report of the Committee of Seven, 1932). This became the organizational model for an again-renamed American Camping Association, established in 1932, and remains so to the present.

Conclusion

By the late twenties, the romantic conception of the camp director lost ground to the expert manager:

> The genial delusion that a camp is good for a child in proportion to the moral or ethical characteristics of the director still persists. As well persuade a municipality to hire an engineer to build a bridge because he is a pillar of the church and pays his graces. Camping becomes more highly technical every year. (Solomon, 1931, p. 3)

New bureaucratic professionals, many of them women, understandably pressed for an end to membership restrictions. Yet there is irony here. University programs in management, safety standards, or tests and measurement were now the centers of legitimation for otherwise diffusing fields in outdoor recreation/education. Women flocked to classes preparing them for new job opportunities, but as students, employees, and professional association members, their activities were subsumed under hierarchical organizations. Though their numbers grew exponentially, they found themselves again at the margins of power.

Women directors had implemented a model of outdoor experience designed to nurture female independence in community. The necessary associational form to support their aspirations amounted to a structured gender parallelism, one that provided a bulwark against masculine privilege. Theirs was not an errand in futility. Female leadership in the NADGC made possible a form of association democracy through which women's aims helped to establish norms constitutive of outdoor professionalism.

In 1926, Laura Mattoon delivered a paper to the Camp Directors Association, entitled, "The Need of Professional Leadership in Camps." In it, she successfully urged those assembled to pass a motion agreeing to begin an assessment of camp programs in cooperation with representatives of the Child Study Association. Nothing concrete would come of this. But its aim was clear—professionalism was to be developed from the ground up, its standards upheld by those closest to the work, and regulated within professional associations. Not external experts, but directors as educators in community were to legitimate the profession.

The rise of feminist-based women's adventure programs in the 1980s represents a new attempt to link feminist educational thought to activist social ends. This time, the programs were addressed to adult women rather than to younger girls. Non-hierarchical networks were formed between voluntary associations, university faculty, and independent private businesses. Understandably, this ferment originated, though it did not remain, outside the professional associations. By 1986, strong women's professional subgroups were established within recreation and outdoor experiential education organizations. The relative importance of sectional membership was again debated. In the Association for Experiential Education, for example, this took place in a political context friendlier to confederation principles—moving centers of control from centralized organizations to more powerful independent sections. Women outdoor pursuits leaders from disparate professional constituencies, including outdoor educators, wilderness trippers, social workers, scouting leaders, and professors, came together to redefine the work they held in common across diffuse professional boundaries. Once again, the substantive and strategic issues inherent in establishing professional visibility are being faced.

The 1990s are witness to the breakdown of bureaucratic systems. To guide the future, it will be important to grasp that more than one version of professionalism and professional association was for a time viable and successful. A deeper reading of the conditions and constraints under which women in the experiential professions strove to define themselves and their work provides a historical basis for understanding the challenges and dilemmas today. Many detailed studies are required before a full and undistorted history of women in the varieties of experiential education can be written. Included must be analyses of women's roles in physical education, the national recreation association movement, and Outward Bound. Until detailed stories like this one are added to the professional literature base, all experiential education professionals will lack a sure grasp of their own diverse and fruitful foundations.

References

Atlantic City Annual Meeting of the Camp Directors Association. (1929). *Camping, 4*(1).

Balch, A. (1893). A boy's republic. *McClure's Magazine, 1,* 242-254.

Bialeschki, M. D. (1992). We said, "Why not?"—A historical perspective on women's outdoor pursuits. *Journal of Physical Education, Recreation, and Dance, 63*(2), 52-55.

Brown, A. (1913). The training of recreation secretaries. *The Playground, 7,* 28-32.

Buckler, H. (1961). *Wo he lo: The story of the Camp Fire Girls: 1919-1960.* New York: Holt, Rinehart, & Winston.

Coale, A. W. (1918). Joys of a hike in a girl's camp. *St. Nicholas, 45,* 724-729.

Coale, A. W. (1919). The college and the camp. *Outlook, 122,* 263.

Coale, A. W. (1919). *Summer in the girl's camp.* New York: The Century Co.

Constitution of the Camp Directors Association, *Camps and camping,* New York: Spauldings Athletic Library, American Sports Publishing Company, *no. 105X,* 133-135.

Eells, E. (1978). Oral History, Lake Geneva Campus of the George Williams College, Sept. 2, 1978, Eleanor Eells Collection, Department of Recreation Administration, Aurora University, Aurora, Illinois.

Eells, E. (1986). *History of organized camping: The first hundred years.* Martinsville, IN: The American Camping Association.

Gibson, H. (1936). *History of organized camping.* Reprinted with the permission of The American Camping Association. Oregon, IL: Lorado Taft Field Campus of Northern Illinois University.

Gulick, L. (1912). The Campfire Girls and the new relation of women to the world. *Proceedings of the National Education Association,* 322-327.

Hamilton, A. E. (1930). *Boyways.* New York: John Day.

Hamilton, A. E. (1931). Muckraking—or constructive criticism. *Camp Life, 3*(6), 11-17.

Henderson, K., & Bialeschki, M. D. (1984). Viva la differencia! *Camping Magazine, 59*(4), 20-22.

Kilpatrick, W. (1933). True and false education: The camp vs. the school. *Camping Magazine, 5*(6), 2-4, 20.

Lehman, E. (1930). What's ahead in the camping movement? In E. Lehman (Ed.), *Camps and Camping,* (pp.18-26). New York: Spauldings Athletic Library, American Sports Publishing Company.

Luther Gulick Obituary. (1918, August 14). *New York Times,* p. 9.

Mattoon, L. (1923). Secretary—treasurer's report. *Proceedings of the National Association of Directors of Girls Camps,* November 1922. In E. Lehman (Ed.), *Camps and Camping,* (p. 21). New York: Spauldings Athletic Library, American Sports Publishing Company.

Mattoon, L. (1925). Secretary's report and resume of the work of the association. *Camps and Camping*, New York: Spauldings Athletic Library, American Sports Publishing Company, 11-13.

Mattoon, L. (1926). The need of professional leadership in camps. Camp Directors Association of America Convention, New York.

Mattoon, L. (1929). Secretary's report. Proceedings of the Camp Directors Association. In E. Lehman (Ed.), *Camps and Camping.* New York: Spauldings Athletic Library, American Sports Publishing Company.

Mattoon, L., & Bragdon, H. (1947). *Services for the open.* New York: Association Press.

McMullen, J. to Eleanor Eells, 8/31/76. Eleanor Eells Collection, Department of Recreation Administration, Aurora University, Aurora, Illinois.

Miranda, W. (1985). Heading for the hills and the search for gender solidarity. *Journal of Experiential Education, 8*(2), 6-9.

Miranda, W. (1987). The genteel radicals. *Camping Magazine, 59*(4), 12-16.

Mitten, D. (1985). A philosophical basis for a women's outdoor adventure program. *Journal of Experiential Education, 8*(2), 20-24.

Mitten, D. (1986). Women's outdoor programs need a different philosophy. *The Bulletin of the Association of College Unions—International, 54*, 5.

Mitten, D. (1992). Empowering girls and women in the outdoors. *Journal of Physical Education, Recreation and Dance, 63*(2), 56-60.

Pfirman, E. (1988). The effects of a wilderness challenge course on victims of rape in locus-of-control, self-concept, and fear (Doctoral dissertation, University of Northern Colorado). *Dissertation Abstracts International, 49-07B* (University Microfilms No. AAC8818574).

Report of the Committee of Seven to the National Executive Committee, Camp Directors Association, 3 May, 1932, Eleanor Eells Collection, Department of Recreation Administration, Aurora University, Aurora, Illinois.

Roberts, N., & Drogin, E. B. (1993). The outdoor recreation experience: Factors affecting participation of African-American women. *Journal of Experiential Education, 16*(1), 14-18.

Sargent, P. (1924). *A guide to summer camps.* Boston: Wright and Potter Printing Company.

Solomon, B. (1931). Negative issues. *Camp Life, 3*(6), 3.

Wack, W. (1923). *Summer camps for boys and girls.* New York: The Redbook Magazine.

Warren, K. (1985). Women's outdoor adventures: Myth and reality. *Journal of Experiential Education, 8*(2), 10-14.

Yerkes, R., & Miranda, W. (1982). The need for research in outdoor programs for women. *Journal of Physical Education, Recreation and Dance, 53*(4), 82-85.

7

A Philosophical Basis for a Women's Outdoor Adventure Program

Denise Mitten

Many women prefer to adventure with other women, and the trip styles that emerge are different from those of mixed groups and from all-men's groups.

Women come to outdoor programs with a different acculturation than men. Margaret Mead (1976) and Nancy Chodorow (1974) relate this to a difference in gender role identification from early socialization. Women and men grow up learning different ways of being and coping in our society. An important factor contributing to this difference in socialization is that women have been almost exclusively responsible for early child care. Young girls relate to their mothers and even if they never choose to have children, they still tend to define themselves in connection to others. Women learn and accept from an early age that others often have different needs and different timing, even for such routine activities as eating, sleeping, and playing.

Another cultural difference is women's tendency to put persons higher than principles on a scale of values. This sense of responsibility for the well-being of others is evident in women's belief that you can solve conflicts so that no one is hurt and "everyone comes out better off" (Gilligan, 1982). Women often choose to sacrifice their self-interest so that others may survive or prosper. Gilligan contrasts this to a masculine system which is more inclined to sacrifice people to "truth" if necessary, like "Abraham who prepared to sacrifice the life of his son in order to demonstrate the integrity and supremacy of his faith." In contrast, the woman (nameless) who came before Solomon "verifies her motherhood by relinquishing truth in order to save the life of her child" (Gilligan, 1982).

One setting where women can experience this feminine reality is in an all-women's group. We know from our experience at Woodswomen, and other research supports this, that women react differently and have significantly different experiences when in an all-women's group, outside traditional male society.

Woodswomen, Incorporated, is an adventure program for women of all ages that for the past nine years has been offering women's wilderness trips. Our philosophy developed from our personal beliefs and our knowledge of social dynamics, and from observing what consistently happened in individual and group behavior on trips. Woodswomen's philosophy encourages women to interact in ways that they feel comfortable doing. Another way to say it is that we merely reinforce commitments and beliefs that women already hold but which they do not always express in society. On these trips, women feel freer to interact using these explicitly "feminine" behaviors. What we have done is to observe and document how women help one another, and we have made a conscious choice to use these discoveries to develop principles of leadership and program design. The ultimate source for these principles is the women who participate.

Principles Used on Woodswomen Trips

The following ten principles of leadership and program design are derived from the Woodswomen, Inc., philosophy:

- The guides' primary responsibility is to set the stage so that women feel and are safe, **emotionally** and physically.
- The trip environment is supportive of differences in client needs.
- We travel the wilderness for its own sake, not using it as a means to an end, not to create situations to take risk, or prove competency.
- We are flexible about goals and contend that there are many workable ways to learn skills and be outdoors.
- We encourage women to accomplish their own goals, not pre-set program goals.
- We believe individual needs are varied, valid, and possible to meet. Individual accomplishments are different and special to each woman.
- We strive for collectivity as much as possible, by sharing decision making and using matrix leadership.
- We see leadership as a role, not a personality type, and believe that constructive, safe leadership can take many forms.
- Women do not need to be changed to fit into adventure programs or "taught" in order to be good enough.
- Women's strengths are an asset to programs.

A Feeling of Safety or Security

It is important to start a trip with the participants feeling as secure as possible given all of the inevitable fears people have about joining a group and about the other unavoidable trip unknowns. If they feel safe, women will often respond by:

- Reaching out to others.
- Taking initiative to try new activities and skills.
- Cooperating as individuals to accomplish group tasks/goals.
- Allowing themselves to recognize and fulfill individual needs and wants.
- Feeling good and having fun.

Exactly what the instructor/guide does to encourage this will depend on her particular personality and that of each of the participants. However, one of the most important traits for a guide to project is a genuine feeling of comfort and ease in the outdoors and especially in the area chosen for the trip.

Participants need to know that they can depend on the guide in case of an emergency and for reliable information about safety and risk. If women know that they can "check in" with the guide, they often enter into the decision-making process early in the trip. This feeling of security actually makes it easier for women to learn new skills and enables them to handle routine activities comfortably and safely. Women also need to know that the guide is available for emotional support, though more than likely much of this support will come from other participants.

Photo courtesy of Karen Warren

Guides should encourage a participant to feel included in the group, which is very different from "belonging to a group." If an individual feels like she belongs to a group, she will be less likely to recognize or attend to her own needs. She may feel pressure to comply with pervasive group norms, which can result in her feeling inhibited and not included at all. Feeling included, of course, is simply feeling that she has a right to be there, and is welcomed and accepted just as she is today.

This also means that the guide cannot pull surprises, even in the name of building character or creating a learning situation. Participants should have a good idea of the course content before arriving, including information about the route, packing suggestions, and what to expect in physical exertion, bugs, and weather. Answers to the myriad questions from group members at the beginning of a trip need to be given in a direct, patient, and positive way.

At the beginning of a trip, the guide should explain safety considerations, stating whether a suggestion she makes is for safety (in which case **do** it) or if it is simply a suggested alternative way to accomplish a task. The guide can encourage women to say if they feel unsafe and to acknowledge and affirm when a woman makes a choice for her feeling of safety. A woman might say, "I don't think I want to run those rapids this afternoon—I just don't feel up to it." Leaders should acknowledge that her decision is **not** irrational and may well avert a potential disaster. Another gesture that builds individual security is giving each participant her own amount of high-energy snack food. Although it may seem like a small gesture, to some individuals it helps to provide a feeling of confidence that they will be able to meet trip challenges. These efforts to create a comfortable atmosphere and encourage women to take care of their own needs decrease the stress that participants feel. Our experiences at Woodswomen confirm the observations of various stress management courses, that the less stress the participants are feeling, the better able they are to cope with new activities, participate as a constructive group member, and handle challenging physical situations.

Fostering Constructive Attitudes

An attitude or social structure that needs to be avoided is "One-Up-One-Down" relationships. Anne Wilson Schaef gives a good explanation of the effects of these relationships in her book, *Women's Reality* (1981). If relationships are defined in terms of one person being superior and the other inferior, then cooperation is sabotaged from the beginning. This attitude can be in all relationships: among participants, between the group and the guide, between an individual and the guide, or between the environment and the group. Again, the guide sets and reinforces the appropriate tone of the experience.

Delighting in group diversity is important. Recognize differences. The melting pot theory that you learned in the fourth grade really isn't true. It assumes that everyone turns out white, middle class, heterosexual, and male. We look for cues from the participants, and when they are extended, we accept them. On one trip, an extremely novice participant decided that the guide might benefit from learning Yiddish. This made her feel more equal by being able to offer a skill and contribute to the group. Meanwhile, the guide had great fun practicing and using Yiddish. Reinforce that a "sunset watcher" can be as important as a "fire builder." Equal is not that we each carry 55 pounds, but rather that we all contribute appropriately. One woman may carry a limited amount due to a weak back, but she may cook a little more often, or sing wonderful songs as the group portages. Often, given the space and support, participants will equal out the tasks. In fact, with women, being sure everyone "does her part" is usually no problem. It is more common to have to suggest to someone to slow down, relax, or give someone else a chance to cook.

Vocabulary choice is important on trips. We are careful to avoid "survival mode" conversation, which can imply a win/lose or conflict situation, as well as words that connote domination, such as "attack the trail," "conquer the summit," "assault the mountain," or "hit the water." Instead, we use adapting or coping language.

Individual Choice to Participate in Activities

In order for a person to internalize an experience as her own, she has to choose it and acknowledge that she chose it. It is not necessarily a choice to say, "I'll go on the program" and then be up for all activities, carte blanche. Some people feel that they chose the program and want it all—the more, the better. Others choose a program and need to choose each step thereafter, from eating granola to whether they will climb that day, or ever.

Guides have a lot of power in defining choice. It is not a real choice to say, "This is what we are doing today and you can either do it or not." Or, "Today we are climbing, tomorrow taking a day hike, the next day learning knots, and you can do it or not." Choosing not to do something is not really choosing. And a person who says, "No," can too easily feel "one-down" or a failure or left out.

The choices need to be informed choices, not "I'll do it because you say we should." There are times when guides do have better judgment, because of experience, than the participant. A participant might say, "I want to do this but I'm not sure I have the skill." Guides can certainly give an opinion, but then they should let the participant think over the options and make her own choice.

One way to offer genuine choice in a program is to have a flexible schedule. For example, on a three-week canoe trip, we may have four portages a day, need to build fires or use stoves, and paddle varied distances. It may be on Day 12 that a woman decides to portage her first canoe, or Day 1 when she jumps in to help with cooking, or Day 6 when she is really tired and decides to sleep through breakfast. The guide is working hard through all of this, encouraging participants and being active herself. She is inviting women to go fishing with her. Perhaps in private, she asks Joan or Sally if she would like to carry a canoe or if one of them would like to paddle with her to learn stern. There isn't one day to carry or not, to learn knots or not. If there was only one day when we'd be able to climb because of location, we would certainly say that, but still have other activities available on that day. The guide must make this explicit to the group and be accepting of participant decisions and choices.

We use a co-guiding system, which gives us the option of subdividing groups. This encourages individual choices and immediately gives the group more flexibility. Part of the group can start moving early to catch the sunrise. Or one group may want to take the high road and the other the low road.

How does this relate to encouragement or support from the guide? There is a thin line between pushing and encouraging. A participant needs to feel that the guide and the group are plugging for her. The go-for-it attitude is compatible with women having a choice. So is the attitude, "I came on this course to learn a few skills, relax, and get away from the hustle of my city life."

Avoiding a Success/Failure Approach to Challenges

It is important not to pre-set program goals or agendas for participants' growth. If participants spend energy meeting course standards or see everyday activities in terms of succeeding or failing, or of being watched or tested, they respond by giving up too much power to the instructor. This can inhibit or limit their growth and enjoyment and can lead to unsafe situations. Participants in outdoor programs can more fully internalize their accomplishments if they do not feel analyzed, graded, or critiqued. Unfortunately, people will come to programs conditioned to think in terms of success/failure. We take care not to have covert or subtle agendas that may imply that there was a way "it should be done" or "it should have been done."

We try to use language that gets out of a right/wrong way of describing actions. Words like "useful," "workable," "not useful in this situation," and "efficient" can help describe what's going on without being critical or judging. These words convey a different feeling than "that's right," or "no, that's not the way to do it," or even, "you did it perfectly," which implies you **could** do it wrong. If you can do it right, then you can do it wrong. If you can succeed, you can fail.

Many women seek fun and adventure in outdoor experiential education. Women specifically enroll in women's programs because they feel they will have a better chance to learn and practice skills and share common interests. Yerkes and Miranda report that 90% of the women that they surveyed denied that all-women groups were "easier" (1982). In our program, we cope with hardships or difficult situations that arise, from the weather, trail conditions, choices that participants make, and other predicaments that occur in the wilderness. However, we do not purposefully create stressful situations.

Groups and individuals often choose hard climbing routes, long portages (sometimes lined with plump blueberries), paddling days that last long into the evening, and even playful canoe races across the lake. Individuals and groups set goals, work toward goals, and achieve them without being obsessed with the end results.

Conclusion

Because women grow up with different acculturation than men, women often bring different strengths and have different expectations for outdoor programs. It is important for experiential educators to examine their program's agenda carefully, as well as their own personal agendas that they may communicate to participants. As much as possible, allow and encourage participants to set their own goals and agendas. Adding women to men's programs does not automatically mean that the strength of women will be felt. Mixed programs can be men's programs with women allowed to participate. We have found that through the implementation of the Woodswomen philosophy and program design, an experiential learning environment can be created which is supportive of the strengths and attitudes that women bring to a group. This kind of environment enables women to grow and change in ways they have not yet experienced.

Endnote

This chapter was originally published in the 1985 *Journal of Experiential Education, 8*(2), 20-24.

References

Chodorow, N. (1974). Family structure and feminine personality. In M. Z. Rosalda & L. Lamphere (Eds.), *Woman, culture and society* (pp. 43-66). Stanford, CA: Stanford University Press.

Gilligan, C. (1982). *In a different voice.* Cambridge, MA: Harvard University Press.

Mead, M. (1976). Presentation at Yale University, New Haven, Connecticut.

Schaef, A. W. (1981). *Women's reality.* Minneapolis, MN: Winston Press.

Yerkes, R., & Miranda, W. (1982). Outdoor adventure courses for women: Implications for new programming. *Journal of Health, Physical Education, Recreation and Dance* (April).

8

The Outdoor Recreation Experience: Factors Affecting Participation of African American Women

Nina S. Roberts and Ellen B. Drogin

All individuals inherently search for ways in which to improve the quality of their lives. Recreational activities, specifically those in the outdoors (e.g., biking, hiking, fishing, camping, skiing, canoeing, wildlife viewing, and the like), are an important means by which individuals attain satisfaction, thereby improving the quality of life. Although an increasing number of women are enjoying the outdoors and participating in outdoor activities, the representation of black women among them is relatively low. What are the factors contributing to the nonparticipation of African American women in outdoor recreation activities?

In order to address this question, relevant research was synthesized and interviews were conducted with African American women in the Washington, DC, area regarding their thoughts, feelings, and insights on the subject of outdoor recreation participation and nonparticipation. Acknowledgment of cultural diversity among women mandates that women of color be looked at as a group that may indeed pursue different goals, and subsequently, engage in different activities toward meeting these goals.

The voices of those interviewed are limited. However, if experiential education is to address the growing and altering needs of all individuals, the comments of those interviewed should be taken as illustrative of the imperative to investigate reasons for nonparticipation by individuals of varied ethnic backgrounds. The nonparticipation of African American women in outdoor recreation can be viewed in the contexts of: historical oppression and racism; stereotyping by race and gender; lack of role models; insufficient exposure to activity options; limited accessibility to outdoor recreation areas; and oppressive economic conditions.

Historical Perspective

The uniqueness of outdoor adventure experiences for women, in general, has been explored and well documented (LaBastille, 1980; Miranda & Yerkes, 1982; Warren, 1985; Bialeschki, 1992). These historical perspectives indicate that women have traveled adventurously for years, yet social barriers and gender roles have limited many women from attaining a quality experience in outdoor adventure activities. Understanding what the nature of black women's experience has been with respect to outdoor adventure is a difficult task.

There has historically been an emphasis on representation of blackness that supports and maintains a sense of oppression, exploitation, and overall domination of black people (hooks, 1992). For instance, oppression is driven by the belief that because skin color is different or individuals simply "look" different, then that, in itself, makes their lives different. If life for women of color is different, then their experiences (including outdoor pursuits) are going to be different. Just how different are the needs of women of color? Even today, more than twenty years after the onset of the Civil Rights movement, "which served to enlighten the dominant culture" (Boyd, 1990), many black women (in particular) continue to suffer from a negative self-image:

> The woman of color's self-image, her confidence (or lack of it), as well as her perceptions of the world around her have evolved out of her personal experience. Many of these experiences are rooted in myths and stereotypes surrounding her ethnic and cultural heritage and gender. (p. 151)

Perceptions of Race and Gender

Are there any ingredients manifest in diverse cultural backgrounds which have an effect on or alter the outdoor experience? Chavez (as reported in Henderson & Bedini, 1992) explored diversity among various ethnic groups. In her studies, she found that outdoor activities and those factors which affect the quality of the experience do not vary significantly by group; activities are enjoyed and appreciated equally. The most significant difference reported between ethnic groups was perceived exposure to discriminatory acts. Individuals with a minority background were more likely to believe that they may be further imperiled by these acts. Recommendations were directed to resource managers and incorporated suggestions for interaction and communication with the visitors.

Zelda Lockhart, a graduate student of English literature, poet, and former president of the Board of Directors of the Women's Wilderness Network, says, "I do not think that black women are not aware of outdoor activities; it's just that black women may think it's a white thing. They seem to be socialized to believe that participating in outdoor adventure is a white person's thing to do; it's not a white thing, it's a life thing."

In order to survive, women of color have become masters in the art of being bicultural. Smith (1983), in her article "Some Thoughts on Racism," writes, "There is a lot of propaganda in this culture for the normality of the rightness of whiteness" (p. 27). According to Smith, generations of exposure to the socially accepted norms of "whiteness" have made it virtually impossible for women of color not to adopt specific behaviors (i.e., standards of beauty, language, and mannerisms associated with white culture that would allow them to survive). It is still apparent that what is known about women pursuing outdoor adventures comes primarily from studies of white women; the interests and experiences of women of color need further exploration (Freysinger, 1990; Roberts, 1992).

Women of color are learning that a valuable benefit of outdoor experiences is the opportunity for spiritual enrichment and growth. A connection can be made with their own lives because, for many women of color, establishing a sense of identity through rituals and traditional customs is important in developing a "stronger sense of self individually and collectively" (Boyd, 1990).

The leisure service professionals and outdoor educators of tomorrow will have to effectively translate culture into leisure and perform the role of facilitator in order to truly meet the needs of diverse cultures. In order to have dignity in difference, professionals must have an understanding of and established place within the community, before reaching out to community members (Colston, 1991). Leaders must convey that outdoor recreation experiences may occur in a variety of outdoor settings, from city parks to pristine wilderness. The opportunity for spiritual experiences, particularly in terms of solitude, as a part of outdoor activities may largely depend on the natural attributes of these environments. The quality and naturalness of the environment, including physical attributes, may have an influence on the type and intensity of the emotional and psychological experience of each woman.

Lack of Role Models

Professionals need to bridge the gap between the ideal of wilderness activities available for all and the reality of stereotypes that convey the outdoors as a white privilege. The discrepancy can be a problem if not handled properly:

> If groups and individuals are more sensitive to cultural differences, then women of color will be attracted to the outdoors on a more positive level. Other stereotypes such as perceptions of racial tension, although very real, are exaggerated. If black women really want to try these activities they will. (Kathy Billingslea)

The cultural aspect plays a role, but for the most part, black women must deal with stereotypes actively or place them internally:

> I don't pay any attention to color differences. It's being with women and enjoying the experience that matters. If the need were real and actual then the need would be met, but if the need were to provide for a stigma or cultural stereotype, the need would not be met. It bothers me to hear other black women saying "they" aren't providing for us. Who is "they"? White women or wilderness/outdoor organizations? (Zelda Lockhart)

Other black individuals often pave the way for black women who need to have someone else "do it first." Similarly, Diane, a 33-year-old administrative associate employed with a DC-based marketing firm, believes that most black women do not look to or search for adventure in their lives:

> There is a need for encouragement from other women of color who have done such activities (i.e., adventure-based) to aggressively encourage these women to try certain outdoor pursuits, possibly sparking their interest. African American women need to feel that they are not the only black person participating. On the other hand, they must have a more positive attitude of self; outdoor activities are very individual. (Diane)

Diane tells about her recent purchase of a new bike. "I know I must do for myself. Although most of my friends don't have bikes I learned that it's o.k. to be an individual, and biking is something I really enjoy." Although she's never participated in more "risk-taking" activities, she wants to try rock climbing and whitewater rafting someday. Diane continues: "There is a stereotype of wanting to be with other people of color; not being around others of similar cultures is an uncomfortable feeling for some people."

Boyd (1990) recognizes that although there are women of color who may not look to their ethnic traditions for subsistence, it is very likely on some level many women of color will seek a source of comfort and/or nurturing that only her family or community can provide (p. 159).

"Adventure activities make you brave no matter what your level. Outdoor successes make you feel strong and courageous. They make you reach out of your everyday life, and expand your day to day routine" (Zelda Lockhart). Zelda asserts that having black women as leaders would be a recognizable means of connecting other black women with the experiences and opportunities of outdoor activities. Denise Mitten, executive director of Woodswomen (Minneapolis), affirms this:

> As part of our guide network, our recruiting aspect will work to include women of color in the Leadership Training. This in turn will increase the role models for ethnically diverse women who participate, and conceivably increase involvement of women of color as a whole.

Lesley, a computer analyst, states, in terms of increasing involvement of black women in general, "attracting more women of color on a social basis may be a factor." Similarly, Diane suggests that "advertising and marketing do not use black women in photographs or commercials, and this hurts the promotion of outdoor activities." The publication of outdoor-related magazines and brochures is often very discriminatory (textually and graphically). A change is necessary to fairly represent that the outdoors is a place for all people.

Lack of Exposure

"Black women don't get any push or motivational force in this direction," says Pam Rigby, 33, a research assistant. "It's not so much that black women have a lack of interest, but since we don't get exposure to these activities growing up, we are not as aware of the opportunities. Black women use different methods to release stress and enjoy themselves. They need exposure to the outdoors to see it as an alternative." Pam enjoys hiking, traveling, and photography. Although she doesn't participate that often in outdoor activities, Pam would love to try whitewater rafting where everyone paddles. "I like the idea of excitement and challenge in a more controlled activity; in addition, I like having a guide in the raft because if I lose control someone is there to take over!"

Through outdoor experiences, women of color can enhance their pride in themselves as individuals and as women. For African American women, in particular, society has indicated that lighter skin makes one more worthy and valuable in the eyes of others (hooks, 1992). Despite efforts to educate African Americans in an affirming black context, they may internalize white "aesthetic" values, "a way of looking and seeing the world" that negates their value as black individuals (p. 3). Increased exposure to outdoor recreation/adventure activities can enhance self-confidence. Self-confidence is an admired trait. Life goes on outside the neighborhood and beyond the family; self-confidence is one springboard to personal richness.

Kathy Billingslea grew up in West Point, Georgia. She feels, as does Pam, that many black women are unaware of outdoor and adventure activities. When asked about some of the ways in which black women might become involved, their responses were similar. "Because of the continued perception of racial stereotypes, women of color will be more likely to participate through sponsorship of a minority group or social club or other support system" (Kathy Billingslea). Similarly, Pam believes that one method of reaching out would be to introduce the outdoors to an organized group and begin with low-key activities (e.g., easy hiking vs. backpacking, lake canoeing vs. whitewater rafting).

> Make all possible options and opportunities available—don't push, but encourage gently. Black women need to know outdoor activities are not threatening and can be facilitated to enhance positive experience. It would do more damage than good to have a bad experience.

Kathy was a Physical Education major in college when she lived in the South, and as an avid outdoor enthusiast, she says it was easier to participate in adventure activities because she knew people with the same interests.

> I find that as I've traveled (and now live) further north on the east coast, people don't know how to relax. Being in the outdoors is often real time for me. It helps me realize whether I am able to spend time with myself. I can determine whether I am at peace with myself, where I am in life. People grow accustomed to a city lifestyle and just don't enjoy the benefits of a secluded natural environment.

Accessing Wilderness from Urban Areas

The opportunities to participate in leisure activities or experiential programs were once limited (and for many still are) to the geographic boundaries of the urban environment. Once women of color experience an activity in the outdoors, the desire and subsequent opportunity for increased participation may be enhanced. We cannot expect women from inner cities who have had only minimal exposure to outdoor areas through the media, to feel good about adventuring beyond their personal/familiar environment unless there is sufficient time to interact with other areas, develop an enjoyable relationship with the outdoors, and want to explore.

> If black women are not in a double income family, participation in outdoor programs becomes even more difficult. Moreover, for those black women living in the inner city without personal means of transportation, their "activity world" is often restricted or bounded by public transportation routes. If these women are aware of activities happening in the suburbs or the wilderness, many must rely on friends for transportation and may not ask. (Kathy Billingslea)

Economic Conditions

Economic conditions affect everyone; however, the degree of effect varies significantly. Economics is frequently noted as a barrier or constraint to outdoor recreation participation. Research shows that women of color bear more economic burdens than any other group in this country: maintaining single-parent households (44% of black women, 23% of Hispanic women, 23% of Native American women, 13% of white women); heading households living in poverty (52% of black households, 53% of Hispanic households, and 27% of white households); and, supporting large families of four or more (40% of black women, 60% of Hispanic women, 20% of white women) (Hurtado, 1989). In addition, teenage mothers are more likely to be black (58% black, 13% white). "White women also suffer economically, but their economic situation is not as dire as that of women of color" (p. 837).

Of course, there is a population of black women who live within solid financial means and can well afford participation in a variety of recreational activities. Over the past twenty years, new class divisions within the black community have emerged. Most women (including African American women) assume that all black women share the same material and social interests; this must be re-examined (Albrecht & Brewer, 1990). Many middle-class black women are no longer rooted within the culture of a black working-class community. How exactly does class structure fit into participation in the outdoors? Are black women who are more self-sufficient more likely to participate in a canoe expedition or hiking adventure, for instance, than those having less income? A lack of economic means, however, does not completely explain the disproportionately small number of black women choosing involvement in adventure activities. For the woman engaged in outdoor adventure pursuits, there is an opportunity to gain a more intimate view of one's strengths, weaknesses, and character. The outdoors provides an experience that no amount of money could ever buy.

Denise Mitten states that during the first year of their Women and Kids program (canoeing, camping, and rock climbing), about 85% of their participants were comprised of African Americans, Hispanics, or Native Americans. "A large factor in the success of this program is the effective and valuable outreach to families who are socially and economically disadvantaged," affirms Mitten. "Unfortunately, during our second year, this diverse participation decreased to about 50% as our budget did not allow for the same pace and level of outreach as we would have liked" (personal communication, October 1991).

Conclusion

Ethnic and cultural differences cannot be ignored. In general, women of color have been largely underrepresented in leisure research in the wilderness, in part because of their predominantly urban residence and the failure to account for these individuals in national or state surveys and in interviews in sufficient numbers for detailed statistical and behavioral analysis (Hutchison, 1988). Primarily, the criticisms for lack of emphasis are because of methodological concerns. Hutchison explains that more important, and more damaging, is the fact that contemporary leisure research has bypassed blacks and other minority populations in the United States because of the lack of specificity given to definitions of "race" and "ethnicity"; the lack of published research in race and ethnic relations; and the lack of attention given to the activities of other ethnic groups (p. 16).

Understanding participation levels and leisure patterns of black women in the outdoors is difficult. Planning initiatives to reduce barriers for women of color on the part of outdoor recreation and experiential education professionals must be undertaken to comprehend and overcome, if appropriate, unique constraints to participation faced by black women. The outdoors has become a vital force in the lives of millions of people and increasing opportunities for people of color will call for cooperation and communication between individuals, community groups, and public and private agencies.

Black women have expressed intrinsic satisfaction and quality experiences from outdoor participation. There is a sense of personal freedom that can be acquired from the out-of-doors which all women regardless of ethnicity can experience and share. There are a great many outdoor adventures which can be undertaken at very little cost. Economically, options for participation exist. Diverse role models must be identified to encourage and educate those willing, yet hesitant to participate. These models should serve to facilitate and strengthen the unique differences among women of color. Women of color look for a source of comfort and/or nurturing that only their community can offer. The community can then be strengthened and enriched by these participants gaining and, in turn, passing on the benefits of outdoor pursuits. The outdoors provides a rich assortment of possibilities that may not be discovered without some degree of knowledge and risk.

It is only with the passage of time coupled with a gradual acceptance and understanding by society that women have more fully experienced the opportunities and benefits of outdoor pursuits (Bialeschski, 1992). For African American women, the issue is to live beyond the societal and self-imposed boundaries and constraints to participation in the outdoors. From what experiential perspective do black women dream, look, create, and take action? For those who dare to escape the conventional "black urban environments," the issue becomes more than simply moving beyond social barriers, just criticizing the status quo. It is about transforming the image of the outdoors to be a place for all people; transforming the scope and opportunities available within the outdoors beyond the boundaries of the city limits.

Endnote

This chapter was originally published in the 1993 *Journal of Experiential Education, 16*(1), 14-18.

References

Albrecht, L., & Brewer, R. (1990). *Bridges of power: Women's multicultural alliances.* Philadelphia, PA: New Society Publishers.

Bialeschski, M. D. (1992). We said, "Why not?"—A historical perspective on women's outdoor pursuits. *Journal of Physical Education, Recreation and Dance, 63*(2), 52-55.

Boyd, J. A. (1990). Ethnic and cultural diversity: Keys to power. *Women and Therapy, 9*(1/2), 151-167.

Colston, L. (April, 1991). *Dignity in difference: Leisure programming for a multi-cultural society.* Paper presented at the Maryland Recreation and Park Association State Conference, Ocean City, Maryland.

Freysinger, V. J. (1990). A lifespan perspective on women and physical recreation. *Journal of Physical Education, Recreation and Dance, 1,* 48-51.

Henderson, K. A., & Bedini, L. A. (1992). NRPA Leisure Research Symposium Showcases Current Park & Recreation Research. *Parks & Recreation, 1,* 16-25, 90.

hooks, b. (1992). *Race and representation.* Boston: South End Press.

Hurtado, A. (1989). Relating to privilege: Seduction and rejection in the subordination of white women and women of color. *Journal of Women in Culture and Society, 14*(4), 833-855.

Hutchison, R. (1988). A critique of race, ethnicity, and social class in recent leisure-recreation research. *Journal of Leisure Research, 20*(1), 10-30.

LaBastille, A. (1980). *Women and wilderness.* San Francisco, CA: The Sierra Club.

Miranda, W., & Yerkes, R. (1982). The need for research in outdoor education programs for women. *Journal of Physical Education, Recreation and Dance, 4,* 82-85.

Roberts, N. S. (1992). *The portrayal of women climbers in Climbing magazine 1970-1990: A content analysis.* Unpublished master's thesis, University of Maryland, College Park, MD.

Smith, B. (1983). Some thoughts on racism. *Aegis, 27,* 34-36.

Warren, K. (1985). Women's outdoor adventures: Myth and reality. *Journal of Experiential Education, 8*(2), 10-14.

9

Leading the Way: Strategies That Enhance Women's Involvement in Experiential Education Careers

T.A. Loeffler

Introduction

I probably should have been a career counselor. Ever since grade school, I can remember helping classmates sort out the answer to the question, "What do you want to be when you grow up?" It seems natural that when I finally chose a dissertation topic it focused on career development (Loeffler, 1995). I was fortunate to combine my love of career counseling with that of my other love, outdoor leadership. Reflecting on my own career in outdoor leadership, I realized that I had several questions and sought to find answers to them by doing extensive research. I learned a great deal about women's career development in the past year. I had the privilege of interviewing 25 women about their careers in outdoor leadership. I heard many voices telling rich stories of challenge, success, struggle, and growth. I shared much laughter and some tears with the women as they spoke. Five of the women in the study were field instructors, five were program administrators, five were college instructors, five were executive directors, and five women had left the field of outdoor leadership. The women ranged in age from 22 to 44, and they ranged in years of experience from one to 25.

As part of the research process, I asked each woman to suggest strategies for outdoor organizations, strategies that outdoor and experiential education organizations could implement to support women in becoming even more successful in their careers and to increase the number of women employed in the field of experiential education. This chapter highlights and illustrates the women's answers to that particular question. Table 1 contains a summary of the strategies. It is my hope that these women's voices will be heard and that these strategies will be put into action at outdoor organizations around the world.

Table 1
Potential Strategies for Supporting Women's Career Development

Hire and promote more women into administrative and executive positions. Develop a management training program for women. Develop formal and informal mentoring programs for women at all levels within outdoor organizations.

Offer advanced skills training in single-gender environments. Single-gender training allows women to learn in a safe and nurturing environment where they feel more comfortable taking risks. Provide a wide variety of professional development opportunities.

Commit to equal opportunity, affirmative action, and other non-discriminatory hiring policies. Value people skills as highly as technical skills when hiring. Adopt a sexual harassment policy and strongly enforce it. Provide training in sexual harassment prevention. Pay men and women equally for equal work. Provide a livable salary.

Actively recruit and encourage women to apply for outdoor leadership positions. Set up recruiting networks between organizations. Provide scholarships for women to attend instructor training programs.

Educate staff and participants about gender issues. Provide training in gender-issue resolution for staff. Provide assertiveness training for female staff. Support increased diversity awareness and sensitivity in all program areas.

Increase the number of female participants by offering single-gender programs for women and girls and by using new marketing approaches. Outdoor programs for girls will provide opportunities for interest, skill, and self-esteem building. Gender-sensitive marketing will attract more women and girls to attend outdoor programs.

Create an organizational climate that is appealing to women. Reduce bravado and macho-ness in programs. Focus on curriculum and work environment which provides support, is free of harassment, and dispels stereotypical roles of women and men.

Assist in the creation of networking and support systems for female outdoor leaders, both within and between organizations. Encourage the formation of a national women's outdoor organization. Give women the opportunity to work with other women.

Recognize women's achievements in and contributions to the field of outdoor leadership. Publish books and articles by women authors and about women's accomplishments in the outdoors. Assist women in becoming recognized and visible in national organizations.

Assist women in balancing work with family and relationship commitments. Provide daycare, staff housing that works for families, parental leave, courses where children can go along with parents, and flexible scheduling options to support parents. Allow partners to work courses together or have field times that coincide.

Hire and Promote More Women into Administrative and Executive Positions

This strategy was mentioned by the vast majority of the women in the study. These women believed that having more women in administrative and executive positions would effect change in at least three ways. Firstly, according to one of the women, "If more women get into more leadership roles, then you don't have as much of the old boys network." Additionally, a second woman thought that "hiring a greater number of administrators who are female will draw and keep more women." Another woman suggested that outdoor organizations develop management training programs where women could be taught the necessary skills to be successful at the administrative level.

Secondly, an increase in the number of women at administrative and executive levels would increase the number of available female role models and mentors. Ninety-four percent of the women said that it is extremely important for women to have strong, female role models and mentors. "Mentoring was really crucial for me, having someone to say 'you'd be good at that so why don't you work toward it' made all the difference in my career success," is how one woman described the role that mentoring had on her career. Another woman outlined her ideas about mentoring in outdoor leadership:

> Women need to take on being role models and mentors. This is one of the jobs we have as women. Not only do I train outdoor leaders but I must be a role model for women so they know it is possible. I think it is the responsibility of any woman who has made it in the field to act as a role model and mentor for up and coming women.

Thirdly, three of the interviewees thought that an increase in the number of women in positions of power would cause a "paradigm shift," whereby organizational structures would become less hierarchical, more accessible, more humanistic, and more nurturing. They believed that this paradigm shift would enable outdoor organizations to hire and retain more women.

Offer Advanced Skills Training in Single-Gender Environments

Many of the women in the study suggested that single-gender training opportunities allow women to learn new skills in a safe and nurturing environment. When women feel more comfortable, they are often more willing to take risks of either a physical or emotional nature. Since many outdoor leadership skills require women to act outside traditional gender roles, a single-gender group can provide support and opportunity to push beyond previously held limits.

"There has to be advocating for women-only space, a place where women learn from women," one woman summarized. A long-time field instructor noticed that when female instructor candidates were allowed to learn rock climbing in a single-gender environment, "they finally learned they were already competent and as a result, they were more willing to jump out during their instructor's course at the same level as their male counterparts—they no longer held themselves back fearing they weren't good enough." One of the administrators interviewed believed that "women need the leg up to develop technical skills and access to skill acquisition without always having to fight the same old battles of sexism. There is a dire need to embrace all-women trainings." Another woman noticed that the women she worked with liked learning new outdoor skills in a formalized setting rather than "just going out and doing it on their own." She advocated that outdoor organizations provide lots of professional development opportunities, both mixed-gender and single-gender, to assist women in furthering both their skill base and overall career development.

Commit to Equal Opportunity, Affirmative Action, and Other Nondiscriminatory Hiring Policies

Women in the study noticed that the application process in outdoor organizations tends to emphasize technical skill competence at the expense of human interaction skills. Several people believed that outdoor organizations need to value and balance these two competency areas when hiring, both to increase staff competence and to increase the number of women they employ. One interviewee described how her organization had implemented this strategy:

> Because we value lots of different kinds of experience, we've broken the application process down into parts so it doesn't look so foreboding. This makes it possible for more women to apply. Also, we've coupled intense internships and trainings with the first year of someone's employment.

Some women tended to stress hiring policies such as equal opportunity and affirmative action as strategies for helping women be more successful in their outdoor leadership careers; whereas other women stressed correcting pay inequities, increasing salaries, and providing quality benefits as strategies to help women to be more successful.

Actively Recruit and Encourage Women to Apply for Outdoor Leadership Positions

Several of the women mentioned the value of being recruited and/or encouraged by an outdoor organization. "I would never have thought about applying to the instructor's course until they sent me the application. I didn't think I was qualified enough," is how one woman described how a recruitment program got her career started. Another woman values her organization's commitment to recruiting women staff members:

> My organization is doing a great job of encouraging women right now. We track talented female students from our courses and encourage them to apply for staff positions. We provide all-women training seminars and then provide mentoring over the length of their careers with us.

In addition, several women mentioned how scholarships had helped them acquire outdoor leadership skills. These women thought scholarships and other forms of financial assistance would aid women in becoming more successful in their careers by giving them greater access to training in outdoor leadership skills.

Educate Staff and Participants about Gender Issues

"I've found that in-house trainings which bring up gender issues in a nonconfrontational way are hugely beneficial," is how one woman described this strategy. Another suggested that "gender-related issues and needs must be an important part of an organization's agenda and mission rather than waiting to see if something comes up." Assertiveness training for female staff was recommended by two program administrators because they felt that such training assists women in dealing with "macho" co-workers. Finally, several program administrators advocated for awareness and education for all diversity issues facing outdoor organizations.

Increase the Number of Female Participants by Offering Single-Gender Programs for Women and Girls

Many of the women interviewed suggested that it is valuable for girls and women to have both mixed-gender and single-gender outdoor experiences. Since the majority of organized outdoor experiences for adults are currently mixed-gender, they advocated for increasing the number of single-gender options available. As previously mentioned, single-gender outdoor courses may provide greater learning opportunities for women. In such environments, women may be able to gain a more accurate sense of their interests and abilities. These women believe that as the number of female outdoor participants increases, there will be a parallel gain in the number of female outdoor leaders.

Another group of women advocated for increasing the number of outdoor program options available for girls. One woman, a founder of a single-gender outdoor program for girls said the following:

> Self-confidence building is a thing that needs to start at an early age for girls. We need to increase the number of organized outdoor programs available

for girls so their self-esteem can be salvaged before and as it gets thrashed by adolescence.

"As more girls participate in outdoor programs, more will become aware of outdoor leadership as a career option. We need to let girls and young women know this is a work option that they can choose," declared one long-time field instructor.

Increase the Number of Female Participants by Using New Marketing Approaches

Many interviewees mentioned redesigning marketing and promotion materials as a strategy for assisting women's career development in outdoor leadership. They thought the number of female participants could be increased through marketing that was designed to appeal to women and that made outdoor activities seem accessible to women. One program administrator mentioned that "marketing is huge." Her organization is very conscious about good gender representation in all of its brochures and photos. She believes it is very important for women to see images of women doing outdoor activities. She concluded by saying, "Only when an individual woman can see herself in the [brochure] picture, can she imagine signing up for a course." Another woman said that organizations need to examine the language in their marketing materials to see if it portrays their programs in a way that appeals to women. Finally, it is important for outdoor programs to advertise their courses in a broad spectrum of media that women read and see in order to expand their current reach beyond outdoor magazines.

Create an Organizational Climate that is Appealing to Women

According to many of the women, outdoor organizations can create a climate that is appealing to women. One female program administrator expressed her opinion: "Outdoor organizations need to ask women what they need and then try their hardest to provide it." She went on to say, that for her, she was looking for an organizational climate that was supportive, free from harassment and oppressive "machoness," and allowed people to step outside traditional roles and stereotypes.

During their interviews, several women mentioned that the "macho" elements or values present in outdoor leadership "turn them off." They wished the "conquering spirit" and other war-like metaphors could be removed from their programs' ambiance. One woman described how her organization made such a shift:

> I think [organization name] is farthest along in putting a value on the process, the context, the relationship rather than having something to prove or conquer. We've been working with our physical aspects of our program to

set a norm that is healthy and accessible for everyone such as using two-person portage lifts for canoes and single pack carries across portages.

Another woman described how instructors in her program now teach rock climbing: "We've shifted the emphasis when we teach rock climbing. We try to find initial climbs that favor balance and grace rather than upper body strength because such climbs encourage women's success."

Assist in the Creation of Networking and Support Systems for Female Outdoor Leaders, Both Within and Between Organizations

Many of the interviewees spoke of the value of professional and support networks they had set up for themselves. They also shared the difficulties of maintaining these networks during transitory times. Many of the women used their professional networks for information about career options and movement, political and organizational reform ideas, and overall professional development. "We need networks so we have someone to bounce ideas off of and someone to turn to when the times get rough," said one woman.

Some of the women interviewed wanted a new, national women's outdoor organization to be formed. Others believed that every female outdoor leader should be a member of one of the mixed-gender professional organizations that already exist. It was suggested that outdoor organizations pay the membership costs for any staff member who wished to belong to a professional organization. Two women proposed that a national women outdoor leaders conference be held every two years so women can come together to learn from and support each other. Finally, many women suggested that women instructors be allowed to work together frequently, even if it means that some other courses only have male instructors, as a way of building support networks and confidence in their professional abilities.

The value of support networks was also mentioned by many of the interviewees. They used support groups or close friends within an organization to lend assistance during harder times that were either professional or personal. Since it can be difficult to maintain support networks while leading a field-based existence, several women suggested that outdoor organizations help set up formal or semi-formal support systems for their staff.

Recognize Women's Achievements in and Contributions to the Field of Outdoor Leadership

Several interviewees had very strong feelings about this particular strategy. They called for women's achievements and contributions to the field of outdoor leadership to be recognized. One woman said that it was time for female outdoor leaders to reclaim their history:

> We need to acknowledge and recognize the contributions that women have already made to the field of outdoor leadership. Women's contributions have been co-opted. And I don't mean co-opted in a vicious and stealing way, but in a subtly sexist way. A lot of the contributions that originally came from women's programs have become part of the field and no one knows or acknowledges where they came from. Women have had a strong influence on how the whole field has become more open to diversity, more cooperative, less competitive, more gentle, and more process-oriented. This movement has come from women's voices in the field and is not recognized. We need to rewrite that history.

It was also suggested that outdoor organizations assist their female staff in becoming visible and recognized in national organizations. "I think we need to get more women into positions where they can influence the outdoor leadership field as a whole," declared one of the interviewees.

Another strategy that was mentioned for women to become both influential and visible is through writing and publication. Several women suggested that outdoor organizations make a concerted effort to highlight female staff within organizational publications and to publish the writing of female authors more frequently. Another woman hoped several more anthologies of women's outdoor experiences[1] would be published in the near future. She thought these anthologies were valuable tools for women's career development because they give women a powerful voice in the outdoor literature and provide quality images of women outdoors that may inspire other women to adventure and lead.

Assist Women in Balancing Work with Family and Relationship Commitments

According to most of the interviewees, there is a real need for recognition on the part of outdoor organizations that outdoor leadership is a long-term career choice for many staff. Outdoor organizations need to grapple with the same family issues as the rest of the corporate world: child care, parental leave, and quality-of-life issues. One interviewee suggested that outdoor organizations "make field positions saner so that people can have their lives, outside the field, work. This will improve the environment for everyone and will make it more inviting to women." A frequent question that arose during the interviews was: "Why can't outdoor organizations restructure how they hire staff so there are more full-time positions where staff can make a living wage and raise a family at a normal age?" Another woman offered her opinion:

> Unless outdoor organizations change their staffing philosophies, this field is never going to be that attractive to people that have debt, families, or children. It is really hard to deal with these things which means the field has a lot of single people. The more that organizations encourage relationships and families and help people make a living, the more women are going to stay. Organizations need to pay more attention to people in partnerships being on the same courses together, or starting and ending together. This will assist women in staying in outdoor careers longer.

Several women advocated for job sharing and other flexible scheduling arrangements to assist women in balancing work and family commitments.

One woman believed that outdoor programs needed to rethink how they structure courses because the current structure does not support staff with families or primary relationships. She related her experience of working at an outdoor program in Britain:

> At the program, 90% of the staff were married and most have kids at the normal times, and we still ran 21 day courses out there. The courses were more base site oriented than U.S. courses are, but I don't think it was any less of an outdoor experience. The base camp situation made it so that when you were in camp, people were able to go home at night because there would be mass first aid sessions and two instructors would be responsible for 125 students. It was do-able. The rest of the people got to go home to their spouses and they had decent family housing. It worked.

Another woman mentioned that she was drawn to outdoor organizations that have a strong sense of community. She thought this sense of community was improved by the organization providing quality housing for the entire season, not just transitional housing. She described the housing situation provided by her current employer:

> At [organization name], you have housing for the entire season, a space that is yours and your stuff is there. No one else is sleeping there. You share it, but it feels like home and it really helps over the long-haul.

It was mentioned by several women that "the world" doesn't understand their careers. One woman thought outdoor organizations needed to educate the general public about the value of the outdoor leadership profession and the reality of the work load. She explained that most of her friends think she has "the most wonderful job in the world and it must be great to get paid to play." She finds it hard to explain to them the enormous responsibility and work load she carries and she wishes her organization would assist people in understanding the demanding nature of the profession. Finally, a program administrator suggested that outdoor organizations examine "what they are accepting as givens," because she believed a few changes could make outdoor careers easier to manage for everyone.

Conclusion

This chapter highlighted many potential strategies for outdoor leadership organizations to adopt to assist women in being more successful in their careers. As experiential education enters the next millennium, it is imperative that experiential education organizations address the career and life development needs of women in order to ensure the viable continuation of this valuable education process.

This is only an initial list of strategies. I encourage every outdoor organization to ask their female staff members to generate their own list of strategies. Asking this and other questions gives women an opportunity to speak and have their voices be heard, and it begins the process of change. This process will also result in a list of strategies that will be specific to a particular organization. It is my belief and hope that with these and other strategies in place, women's career development in outdoor and experiential education can and will soar to new heights.

Endnote

[1] See the following references for more information: da Silva (1992); Galland (1980); La Bastille (1980); Lewis (1992).

References

da Silva, R. (1992). *Leading out: Women climbers reaching for the top.* Seattle, WA: Seal Press.

Galland, C. (1980). *Women in the wilderness.* New York: Harper & Row.

LaBastille, A. (1980). *Women and wilderness.* San Francisco, CA: Sierra Club.

Lewis, L. (1992). *Water's edge: Women who push the limits in rowing, kayaking, and canoeing.* Seattle, WA: Seal Press.

Loeffler, T.A. (1995). *Factors that influence women's career development in outdoor leadership.* Unpublished doctoral dissertation, University of Minnesota, Minneapolis, MN.

Leading Voices

*Women need a reorganization of knowledge,
of perspectives, and analytical tools that can help us know our
foremothers, evaluate our present historical, political,
and personal situations, and take ourselves seriously as agents
in the creation of a more balanced culture.*

Adrienne Rich

I haven't always been a feminist outdoor leader. When I started leading trips over twenty years ago, an outdoor leadership career was an anomaly for women. Early in my outdoor career, I was molded and mentored primarily by male supervisors, peers, and co-workers who were trained in the hierarchical, technical-skill-valuing paradigm of outdoor leadership popular during that time. Spurred on by the women's movement, the emergence of my feminist consciousness in the late '70s and '80s helped me begin to question the traditional training I had received.

Now, many years later, I'm fairly direct with the students of my outdoor leadership class. I tell them they will be exposed to many models of leadership over the course of the semester, but they should know that my particular leading and teaching style is feminist based. Invariably they are quite curious about what a feminist leadership model entails, as most of the leadership models they know are based on the premise that there is a universal approach to leadership.

So what, then, is feminist outdoor leadership? Some assume feminist leadership is what you use when you work with women's groups. However, I know from years of experience the value it has for coed groups as well. I believe it is evolving, fluid, and subjective, so while there is not one definition of feminist outdoor leadership, there are some qualities I would identify as being part of a feminist outdoor leadership style.

Feminist leaders give attention to relationship, often believing that accomplishment of task hinges on the initial and continued establishment of connection between all involved in the experience. Issues of power relations are often examined in feminist leadership models, with authority redefined to encompass more egalitarian principles. Decision making might be more consensual, problem-solving skills

105

more collective than the traditional "the buck stops here" leader utilizes. The validation of personal experience, especially of those who are not privileged in the dominant social structure, might also be part of a feminist outdoor leader's style. Success/failure and right/wrong dichotomies are eschewed. Risk management, based on the belief that the participants are the ultimate authority on what is risky to them, is shared by all who are involved. A feminist outdoor leader might consider that each group member brings unique contributions to the outdoor experience, both process skills and technical skills. It is the leader's job to facilitate the emergence of these contributions while honoring the choices each participant makes.

Readers of this section will find a variety of ideas about how feminism has influenced outdoor leading and teaching. Karla Henderson shows how feminist perspectives might be applied to outdoor leadership. She presents a feminist critique of outdoor experiences and examines the pros and cons of several approaches currently used to correct the biases that exist. Henderson proposes a transformational feminist model which has potential to further change some of the traditional perspectives on outdoor leadership. Alison Rheingold and I undertake a critical feminist analysis of the pedagogy of experiential education. We point out intersections between feminist pedagogy and experiential education and give suggestions to experiential educators who wish to embrace a more feminist way of learning and teaching. Denise Mitten and Rosalind Dutton offer advice to outdoor leaders who work with general populations of women as well as to those who work with programs for survivors of sexual abuse. Given that one in three women and one in seven men have experienced some sort of sexual violence, this is important information for all outdoor leaders. Finally, Martha Bell questions some of the assumptions outdoor experiential educators have about outdoor leadership, particularly the prevalent belief that there is a generic leadership model with objective and abstract norms. She brings in the voices of women outdoor leaders to examine how feminism can inform their practice as outdoor teachers and facilitators. Each of these chapters builds on an evolving and growing body of knowledge and experience about feminist outdoor leadership.

Reference

Rich, A. (1979). *On lies, secrets, and silence.* New York: W.W. Norton.

10

Feminist Perspectives on Outdoor Leadership

Karla Henderson

Several years ago I was teaching a class on "camping skills for women" through the university continuing education program. I spent several classes talking about and demonstrating camping skills. The practical experience was a weekend, flatwater-canoe camping trip. All of the participants said that they had canoed before, but a refresher course on canoe safety was conducted before the weekend. After a brief introduction on land, I asked the women to go to the bow or the stern of the canoe where they planned to paddle. Every woman went to the bow of the canoe. None had ever been in the stern or "steering" position. When I commented about the situation, the women indicated that fathers, husbands, boyfriends, or significant others had generally taken that position. This predicament led me to ask questions about women's involvement in the outdoors and how feminist perspectives might enhance outdoor experiences for females, as well as males.

The purpose of this chapter is to show how feminist perspectives might be applied to outdoor leadership. This purpose will be accomplished by using the categories of critique, correction, and transformation to describe outdoor involvement from feminist perspectives (Eichler, 1980). Although many questions remain unanswered concerning how the traditional male model of leadership dominates expectations of outdoor leadership, this analysis will challenge the assumptions of traditional leadership models and make applications to outdoor involvement.

A Grounding in Feminism

Feminist perspectives provide a basis for examining the nature of participation, the goals of leadership, and the meanings associated with the outdoors. Feminism is concerned with the correction of both the invisibility and distortion of female experience in ways relevant to social change and the removal of all forms of inequality and oppression in society (Henderson, Bialeschki, Shaw, & Freysinger, 1989). These perspectives are useful for understanding outdoor leadership experiences. For example, liberal feminists would suggest that women ought to have equal rights in outdoor participation and that their leadership opportunities ought to be similar to those of men. Cultural feminist philosophy focuses on seeing and celebrating the uniqueness of women's outdoor experiences and leadership styles; radical feminists provide a basis for how women ought to choose their own models of outdoor leadership that may not resemble male models at all. No one view of feminism, however, provides all the perspectives necessary. Together, the philosophies of feminism can give a broader understanding of outdoor experiences.

One important aspect of the outdoors is the recognition of the diversity among women that exists. In this discussion, space and time require talking about women in general. Leaders, however, must keep in mind the potential differences in experiences of girls and women related to culture, race, age, class, physical and mental ability, motherhood, sexual orientation, ethnicity, or other social constructions. In the following sections, perspectives on feminism and the diversity of women's experiences will serve as a critique of existing practice, a means for correcting biases that exist, and a groundwork for the transformation (Eichler, 1980) of outdoor participation and leadership.

A Feminist Critique of Outdoor Experiences

Any feminist analysis begins with a critique of the existing structures. This critique allows issues and challenges to be uncovered. In addition, the body of knowledge about women and their interests and abilities in the outdoors is also increasing due to various critiques of literature and practice. According to Henderson (1994), Tetreault's (1985) feminist phase theory provides a useful perspective on the critique and evolution of research on women's recreation/leisure and outdoor experiences. Five conceptual phases were identified that will be applied to a discussion of women's outdoor leadership: womanless, add women and stir, dichotomous differences, women-centered, and gender/gender relations.

The womanless phase of research and practice has hidden women's outdoor involvement. As outdoor historians have begun to discover, women have always been leaders, albeit often silent, in the outdoors. For example, in the early 1900s, some women found the value of activities such as mountaineering, canoeing, and exploring to symbolically represent freedom from traditional Victorian roles and a move toward independence and equality (Bialeschki, 1990). Women commonly participated in outdoor activities, but were often obscured in the literature by the exploits of male colleagues, by their relegation to a helpmate role, or by their achievements being questioned or trivialized (LaBastille, 1980; Lynch, 1987). Many women know little about the active involvement of women in the outdoors in the last 100 years. A 1905 ascent of Mt. Rainier, for example, had 112 ascent members— 46 of whom were women (Kaufmann, 1986). Historically, women have been invisible in outdoor pursuits and have been inaccurately depicted because of the incompatibility between traditional perceptions of women's roles and their participation in outdoor activities. As women's roles in society change, the opportunities they have for visible leadership are also changing.

More women than ever before are participating in outdoor activities. Today the number of women involved in physical activities often equals or outnumbers men (*Statistical abstract*, 1991). For example, in 1989 almost 26 million women in the United States went backpacking and camping, 29 million rode bicycles, 16 million went fishing, and 7 million went skiing. In the 1990s, in all aspects of outdoor recreation, the participation of women will be increasing faster than that of men (Kelly, 1987). Thus, the outdoors is not "womanless" and a need exists for women in outdoor leadership positions.

Related to the invisible aspects is the "add women and stir" phase of research and practice where people are conscious that women might be missing from the outdoors and that some examples or exceptions to the universal male experience might be important to note. Underlying the idea of "adding women" is a notion that women ought to be acknowledged, but such acknowledgment generally means that women are judged in terms of their contributions based on typical male standards. Although examples of prominent women such as Annie Oakley and Mary Shaeffer (the first explorer of the Jasper area of Canada) have been inspirational, they have not provided role models for how many of us experience the outdoors on a day-to-day or vacation-to-vacation basis.

The realization that women participate in the outdoors and that they might be "different" than men resulted in many discussions, particularly in the 1970s and 1980s, that focused on dichotomous sex differences as a third phase applied to the critique of feminist outdoor leadership. Leadership has been an especially important topic for examining male and female differences. Although the study of differences can be helpful in understanding behavior, studying differences can also be problematic (Henderson, 1990). Some say that identifying differences affirms women's value and special nature; others say it reinforces the status quo. Differences can seem to imply hierarchy; in other words, one group is seen to be superior or better than the other group. Another risk is that such research can oversimplify and overclaim, and it may also reinforce inequalities through the often-unstated implication that if differences occur, they must be inevitable or "natural."

A critique of what is known about women as outdoor leaders arises to some extent from the roots of leadership research and particularly, research about leadership differences (Henderson & Bialeschki, 1991). The historic identification of stereotypical masculine personality traits has been an artifact of the overwhelmingly large number of men in leadership positions (Friesen, 1983). In the past, males were typically in leadership positions, including outdoor leadership, at the time when leadership was first studied. Thus, a number of models that were developed were based on typical male virtues and values such as the desire for practicality and the utility of things and ideas; a search for rational truth, power, and influence; objective power and reasoning; and gaining the influence and admiration of others (Loden, 1985). Female values, not traditionally linked with leadership, were associated with a priority on form and harmony; concern for people, unity, and spirituality; a desire to help and care for others; and a concern for beauty and creative expression. These differences in male and female values produced differences in perceptions, attitudes, and behaviors in many areas of life, including perceptions of outdoor leadership. For example, in leadership situations, researchers have identified that females are more concerned with the decision-making process while males tend to be more concerned with the outcomes of the decision (Henderson & Bialeschki, 1991).

The impact of socialization on the differences in leadership roles of women and men is an area that requires acknowledgment when discussing differences in outdoor leadership between women and men. Adkinson (1981) suggested a number of reasons for why women have not been visible in leadership positions in organizations. In some cases, girls and women have not been socialized toward positions of power. Further, women may have low aspirations for leadership positions because they have been socialized to see their role as the bearer of emotion, not power. In addition, some women may have negative attitudes about what leadership means that are inconsistent with how they define themselves (Weller, 1988). For example, leadership sometimes connotes authoritarianism which may not be the style that fits many women.

Examining outdoor leadership from a feminist perspective suggests that researchers and practitioners are only beginning to understand why women have been ignored, acknowledged primarily when they conformed to male standards, or compared to men in outdoor leadership style. Questions need to be addressed concerning whether gender differences exist at all in outdoor leadership and what bearing gender differences may have on the outcomes of outdoor experiences. A critique of outdoor leadership, however, provides a starting point for examining the meaning of leadership for women and has resulted in possible corrective approaches that can be taken.

Corrective Approaches Related to Outdoor Leadership

Tetreault's (1985) feminist phase theory has also addressed two corrective phases that have particular salience for understanding outdoor leadership for women: women-centered and gender analyses. As a result of collecting additional information about outdoor experiences, more empowering models may be offered to enhance the experiences of women in the outdoors.

Cultural feminists believe that it is women's qualities and experiences, not men's, that should be the measure of significance in society. The women-centered phase examines the experiences of women in an attempt to understand the importance and meaning of women's lives, not as a comparison to men. In this women-centered perspective, what was formerly devalued (e.g., everyone feeling like they have a say in group decision-making) in the context of women's participation and involvement assumes new value. Women-centered notions have also challenged some of the traditional androcentric ideas about the outdoors. Cultural feminism has helped to generate new ideas, patterns, and ways of examining outdoor experiences. For example, the language used in the outdoors such as "assaulting mountains" has been questioned by feminists who find different meanings in these words. Thus, the focus on women has made the outdoors visible for women and has also opened the door for reinterpreting previous ideas about outdoor behavior for both women and men.

Gender analyses about the outdoors offer the most recent attempt to correct our understanding of women's experiences. Gender or gender relations refers to cultural connections and relationships associated with one's biological sex. Thus, when biological sex is determined at birth as female or male, a huge number of cultural expectations are immediately associated with the child. Gender, then, refers to how women and men contribute to and are influenced by society (Henderson, 1994). One's biological sex leads to a lifetime of relationships and expectations based on gender that have implications for outdoor participation and leadership. The meaning of gender is constructed by society and each of us is socialized into that construction.

The analysis of gender and gender relations appears to offer the most potential in the 1990s for understanding outdoor leadership for both females and males. Gender scholarship addresses the complexity of expectations, roles, and behavior associated with being male, as well as being female. Overgeneralizations about feminine and masculine behavior result in stereotypes which limit people's options (e.g., assuming that females will become too emotional in a dangerous situation or that males cannot be sensitive to a participant's personal problems). Individuals may be deprived of originality and initiative if they are limited to only certain gender-appropriate behaviors.

Thus, as the experiences of women as well as the analysis of gender relations have been factored into research and practice, the need for understanding both the process and product variables of outdoor leadership has become more apparent (Loden, 1985). Most of the literature of the last fifteen years that has examined gender roles and leadership suggest that gender per se is not necessarily significant, but that sex-role stereotypes and power differences are reflected in the leadership styles of men and women (Adkinson, 1981; Kanter, 1977).

Leadership, as generally defined today, is a function of two types of behaviors (Jordan, 1989). The first is categorized as instrumental or initiation behaviors. This category is concerned with orientation toward task, production, outcomes, or initiating structure. These behaviors are traditionally equated with the masculine stereotype. The second category is labeled as consideration or expressive behaviors. Orientation toward the affective, socio-emotional support relationships and people is the primary component of this category. Consideration and expressive behaviors have traditionally been identified with the feminine stereotype. The expressive category originally was not considered as valuable or necessary to good leadership as was the instrumental category (Friesen, 1983; Jordan, 1989; Naisbitt & Aburdene, 1990). The importance of a variety of leadership patterns and the expressive dimensions that women often bring to leadership situations is becoming evident (Denmark, 1977; Naisbitt & Aburdene, 1990), but much more research is necessary to demonstrate how leadership styles and performance effectiveness are related in an area such as the outdoors.

Two contrasting approaches (Fasting, 1987) provide an initial framework for how feminism can provide a corrective mechanism for providing women with opportunities for outdoor leadership. These corrective approaches include the possibilities of: a) women becoming more like men in their leadership, and b) women participants and leaders preserving and developing what has been defined as typically female. Neither of these approaches is agreed upon by feminists as THE perspective to follow, but they offer examples for examining how feminism might correct some of the ways we have previously viewed outdoor leadership.

Women becoming like men is an outgrowth of liberal feminism and the equal rights struggle (Henderson & Bialeschki, 1991). It implies that women should be given the same opportunities in outdoor involvement and leadership as men. This perspective means equality on men's terms with women striving to get more of what men have always had. The approach is based on the attempt to remove or compensate for the social impediments that have prevented women from competing on equal terms with men, without challenging traditional hierarchical structures (Hargreaves, 1990). Examples of the success of this pragmatic approach are seen when *more* outdoor opportunities are *more* accessible to *more* women. It assumes no biological explanations for women's subordination and assumed participation rates; thus, an assumption of culture, not biology, acts as the barrier to women in outdoor leadership, a barrier that can be removed through rational intervention.

Major problems exist with the approach of women becoming more like men. The underlying assumption that women just need to "catch up" with the men would appear to be more concerned with quantitative rather than qualitative changes. This vision of women's involvement in the outdoors is idealized with no real question as to where the values about participation and leadership originate or whose interest they serve. Questions about equality for which particular women, for what purpose, and according to what criteria are ignored (Hargreaves, 1990). Another problem is that achievement of this approach would lead one to view women as a homogeneous group where increased participation in leadership roles is an improvement for women in general. Women from different backgrounds, however, may not experience the outdoors in the same way and often have different expectations and opportunities. In reality, this approach may actually benefit only a small minority of women. Lastly, this approach assumes that women want to be leaders in the same way in which men are; rather than challenge the masculine concept of leadership, liberalism endorses it (Fastings, 1987; Hargreaves, 1990). As a consequence, the values that dominate male outdoor culture and male leadership will be internalized by females who wish to be leaders. Nevertheless, the liberal feminist approach to leadership through equal opportunity seems to be a popular approach and is accepted by many people interested in getting women more involved in outdoor experiences.

A second feminist approach to outdoor involvement proposes that women should preserve and develop what has been defined as typically female. This approach has evolved from cultural and radical feminism as a result of women's feelings of powerlessness, frustration, and anger resulting from discrimination and male chauvinism in the outdoors. Proponents of this view suggest that the very definition and conduct of leadership must be changed to allow a woman's voice to emerge in outdoor activities and leadership interactions. The meanings women attribute to their involvement in the outdoors become the focus in preserving and developing typical female styles.

This corrective approach proposes that the characteristics associated with male participation and leadership are sometimes undesirable and that women should build alternative models of leadership that are intrinsically more liberating, rather than emulate the traditional, masculine-based models (Henderson & Bialeschki, 1991). Thus, the characteristics normally ascribed to men in the outdoors, such as competitiveness, aggression, and authoritarianism, are rejected and replaced with characteristics popularly defined as female, such as cooperation, nurturance, and consensus. This approach addresses a "pro-woman" stance that asserts women's difference from men and strives to create an environment where women feel free from discrimination and sexism, and where a greater sense of control and autonomy is felt.

Two major problems appear when examining this approach of preserving and developing what has been defined as typically feminine. First, focusing on femaleness supports the idea that there are distinctive biological natures of males and females which are treated as if they are culturally and historically universal; the idea of "feminine-appropriate" and "masculine-appropriate" participation or leadership locks people into a fixed concept of the "natural," which is blind to history and ignores changing feminine and masculine identities and different gender relations (Hargreaves, 1990). The second problem is that the women-centered approach can create social divisions not only specifically between women and men, but also even between different groups of women and different groups of men. The experience of males in the outdoors has been a dominant paradigm, but not necessarily universal for all males. In relation to the diversity of our society, a female perspective may not represent all female perspectives any more than all males have been represented by the traditional male approach.

A Time for Transformation

I would like to propose a third perspective that offers potential for using feminism as a way to transform women's (and men's) leadership in the outdoors. This transformational feminist perspective is based on the notion that leadership is not necessarily defined by gender or gender-related traits (Cimperman, 1986), but that females have contributions in the outdoors. This transformational feminist perspective is both radical and commonsensical. Many people agree that gender-biased leadership styles must change in ways that will empower all participants.

Karsten (1994) has offered some specific aspects of organizational structure change that may provide a foundation for feminist transformative models regarding outdoor involvement. If we are to avoid situations where women are channeled into traditional roles, such as in the case of the canoe story told at the beginning of this chapter, and if we are to enable women and men to provide outdoor experiences that empower participants, new models are appropriate. The dimensions of the models are not unlike many of the characteristics of organic, as opposed to mechanistic, organizations. Organic organizations allow for changes and enable each individual to see how she/he fits within a particular experience.

In one example of a transformative feminist model, outdoor leadership tasks would not be highly specialized. All individuals would have an opportunity to learn a variety of skills with the focus on the process and not necessarily the product. The leadership power from a feminist perspective would be based on expertise, not necessarily position. Along with this notion of power would be the desire to allow all participants to develop expertise so they can assume leadership positions. A feminist transformative perspective would suggest that conflict resolution would be addressed by interaction among those in conflict. In addition, communication would be upward, downward, and lateral. The content of that communication would be oriented toward advice, counsel, and collective decision making. Certain rules or guidelines for safety and for effective group interaction would be necessary, but they would be understood and enforced by all participants, not just the designated leader. Thus, control would be the internal responsibility of each individual. Loyalty to the group would also be the focus of this type of interaction in the outdoors.

This evolving feminist organizational model has been successfully used by some outdoor groups. The staff at Woodswomen, Inc., for example, consciously apply a transformational feminist approach to all their groups with the mission of empowering girls and women through the outdoors. Mitten (1992) has identified three goals that guide their programs:

1.   A program philosophy that respects women and adds to self-esteem building;
2.   Leaders who are skilled in implementing the program philosophy; and
3.   Participants who have choices about and within the experience. (p. 56)

These goals are then translated and transformed into action in the way that participants and leaders work together toward providing empowering outdoor experiences. Specifically, the ways that feminist transformational leadership is applied at Woodswomen, Inc., can be seen in these principles and objectives:

- To create an atmosphere that is safe and encourages women to feel emotionally, spiritually, and physically safe
- To travel in the wilderness for its own sake, not using it as a means to an end, not creating situations to take risks or prove competency. Respect and care for the environment during trips is important.
- To be aware that having fun is essential to many people's growth and learning process and that it helps in developing self-esteem
- To create a trip environment supportive of differences in participants' needs and to support the belief that individual needs vary, are valid, and are possible to meet
- To be flexible about goals and understand that there are many workable ways to learn skills and be outdoors
- To recognize that individual accomplishments are different and special to each woman and to encourage women to have their own standards
- To recognize that women do not need to be changed to fit into adventure programs or taught in order to be good enough to participate on outdoor trips
- To emphasize that women's strengths are an asset to outdoor groups
- To understand that leadership is a relationship, not a personality type, and to believe that constructive safe leadership can take many forms
- To avoid a success/failure approach to challenges

(Mitten, 1992, p. 58)

This application of feminist outdoor leadership is not the domain of women only. A number of scholars are discussing the notion of transformational leadership which involves distributing the power for accomplishing tasks to group members (Jordan, 1992). The approach to participation and leadership, however, does have a feminist orientation that has only become evident in the leadership literature since the reemergence of the contemporary feminist movement thirty years ago. The major problem with a feminist transformative approach to outdoor leadership is similar to the problem discussed in the women-like-men equity view—the difficulty in changing traditional perceptions of female and male gender roles when applied to leadership. These changes will not be the result of legislative actions, but rather of a culture that allows women and men both instrumental and expressive characteristics, and does not value males more than females, or products more than processes. The traditional attitudes toward leadership and organizational structures, however, will not be given up easily since they are the underpinnings of political and economic hegemony and power.

Moving Onward

The variety of feminist perspectives presented in this chapter provides a starting point for further examining leadership by women in the outdoors. These analyses help to deconstruct the social structures surrounding traditional involvement in ways that encourage women and men to exhibit outdoor leadership that empowers themselves as well as others. Old authoritarian behaviors are being transformed toward a new mode of leadership designed to coach, inspire, and gain people's commitment (Naisbitt & Aburdene, 1990). Much is yet to be learned about how feminist perspectives can affect outdoor experiences; evolving models will likely emerge in the coming years.

Feminism offers one means for transforming views about outdoor leadership. Feminist perspectives critique and challenge traditional concepts and practices. These perspectives make us ask questions about why women are "supposed" to paddle in the bow of the canoe. Through feminist analyses, the notion of power as domination can also be transformed to focus on empowerment so that all individuals feel comfortable paddling anywhere in a canoe. The concept of empowerment through feminist transformational leadership—where power is shared, differences in leadership styles are valued, and individuals have a high level of control over their environment—is needed by women as well as men to challenge the traditional androcentric views of outdoor participation and provide the highest quality of outdoor leadership for the future.

References

Adkinson, J. A. (1981). Women in school administration: A review of the literature. *Review of Educational Research, 51*(3), 311-343.

Bialeschki, M. D. (1990). The feminist movement and women's participation in physical recreation. *Journal of Physical Education, Recreation and Dance, 61*(1), 44-47.

Cimperman, R. M. (1986, April). *Women in leadership roles: A field study of women administrators' perception of self.* Paper presented at the annual meeting of the Central States Speech Association, Cincinnati, OH.

Denmark, F. (1977). Styles of leadership. *Psychology of Women Quarterly, 2,* 99-112.

Eichler, M. (1980*). The double standard: A feminist critique of feminist social science.* New York: St. Martin's.

Fastings, K. (1987). Sports and women's culture. *Women's Studies International Forum, 10*(4), 361-368.

Friesen, L. (1983). Women and leadership: Focus on research. *Contemporary Education, 54*(3), 223-230.

Hargreaves, J. (1990). Gender on the sports agenda. *International Review for the Sociology of Sport, 25*(4), 287-305.

Henderson, K. A. (1990). Anatomy is not destiny: A feminist analysis of the scholarship on women's leisure. *Leisure Sciences, 12,* 229-239.

Henderson, K. A. (1994). Perspectives on analyzing gender, women, and leisure. *Journal of Leisure Research, 26*(2), 119-137.

Henderson, K. A., & Bialeschki, M. D. (1991). Feminist perspectives on women in recreation leadership. *Journal of Applied Recreation Research, 16*(4), 281-296.

Henderson, K. A., Bialeschki, M. D., Shaw, S. M., & Freysinger, V. J. (1989). *A leisure of one's own.* State College, PA: Venture Publishing.

Jordan, D. J. (1989). A new vision for outdoor leadership theory. *Leisure Sciences, 9,* 35-47.

Jordan, D. J. (1992). Effective leadership for girls and women in outdoor recreation. *Journal of Physical Education, Recreation and Dance, 63*(2), 61-64.

Kanter, R. M. (1977). *Men and women of the corporation.* New York: Basic Books.

Karsten, M. F. (1994) *Management and gender.* Westport, CT: Praeger.

Kaufmann, P. W. (1986). Early women claim parklands for adventure and aspiration. *Courier, 31*(10), 16-18.

Kelly, J. (1987). *Recreation trends: Toward the year 2000.* Champaign, IL: Management Learning Laboratories.

LaBastille, A. (1980). *Women and wilderness.* San Francisco, CA: Sierra Club.

Loden, M. (1985). *Feminine leadership, or how to succeed in business without being one of the boys.* New York: Times Books.

Lynch, P. (1987). Scaling the heights: They called it 'an easy day for a lady.' *New Zealand Women's Studies Journal, 3*(1), 59-73.

Mitten, D. (1992). Empowering girls and women in the outdoors. *Journal of Physical Education, Recreation and Dance, 63*(2), 56-60.

Naisbitt, J. & Aburdene, P. (1990). *Megatrends 2000.* New York: William Morrow.

Smith, H. W. (1982). *Gender and leadership in organizations: Critical review.* Unpublished doctoral dissertation, Texas Tech University, Lubbock, Texas.

Statistical abstract of the United States: 1991. (1991). Washington, DC: U.S. Government Printing Office.

Tetreault, M. K. (1985). Feminist phase theory: An experience-driven evaluation model. *Journal of Higher Education, 56*(4), 364-384.

Weller, J. (1988). *Women in educational leadership.* Center for Sex Equity, Monograph 3(4). Ohio State University, Columbus, Ohio. (ED 304 742).

11

Feminist Pedagogy and Experiential Education: A Critical Look

Karen Warren and Alison Rheingold

It is becoming increasingly difficult
to keep feminism out of education.

Dale Spender

We have been intrigued for quite some time about how feminist pedagogy and experiential education compare. This interest culminated in our co-teaching an experiential education course at Hampshire College with considered attention to feminist pedagogy. For one class, we used creative dramatics to act out a dialogue between John Dewey (complete with mustache, bifocals, and gravelly voice) and a feminist scholar (with requisite radical armband). Besides serving as a captivating method to comprehend Dewey and feminist theory, we left the session further convinced of the connections between the two methodologies that our characters represented.

In this chapter, we look at existing intersections between the two theories, particularly as they are applied in the current field of experiential education (see Table 1). We offer ideas about the ways in which feminist pedagogy can inform and strengthen the practice of experiential education. We also include a feminist critique of experiential education in an effort to encourage critical thinking about how experiential-education practice benefits or inhibits the direct experience of women and girls. We have narrowed our examples to adventure education even though applications to all facets of experiential education are possible.

Feminist Pedagogy

Feminist pedagogy is the educational manifestation of feminist theory, translating feminist thought into practice in a classroom setting. Although all feminist theorists do not subscribe to the same thinking, feminism is based on the premise that we live in a male-dominated society that unequally distributes power according to gender. Power is defined by economics, politics, social standing, and personal worth.

Feminist educators strive to equalize power imbalances by investigating the power and privilege individuals (both teachers and students) hold within the classroom. In an attempt to address different oppressions without a hierarchical approach, many feminist pedagogists look at how issues of gender, race, class, sexual orientation, and ability are linked and how these connections are played out in learning situations. It is through this critical analysis that feminist pedagogists hope to create egalitarian learning environments.

While feminist pedagogy has links to other educational movements, particularly the liberatory or critical pedagogy advanced by Paulo Freire, it can be distinguished by its acknowledged attention to women in the consideration of oppression (Maher, 1985). Furthermore, while the stratification within oppressed groups (i.e., a white woman has privilege not accorded a woman of color) is identified by feminist pedagogy, it is not emphasized by Freire (Weller, 1991). Ellsworth (1989) concurs:

> As long as the literature on critical pedagogy fails to come to grips with issues of trust, risk, and the operations of fear and desire around such issues of identity and politics in the classroom, their rationalistic tools will continue to fail to loosen deep-seated, self-interested investments in unjust relations of, for example, gender, ethnicity, and sexual orientation. (pp. 313 314)

Feminist Pedagogy and Experiential Education

There are three areas to be examined in applying feminist pedagogy to experiential education. The first area makes explicit an analysis of power in the teacher/learner relationship and how power differentials might be acknowledged and mitigated. The conscious use of personal experience as a valid and vital teaching tool is the second area of interest. Finally, the social justice work that has been fundamental to women's studies curriculums is considered as an excellent addition to a curriculum utilizing experiential education.

The fact that some readers may see familiar practices in this chapter may demonstrate that experiential education practitioners have already integrated, or some would say co-opted without clear attribution, portions of feminist pedagogy into experiential programs. For example, the idea behind the now popular "challenge by choice" practice used in experiential education programs (Schoel, Prouty, & Radcliffe, 1988) was originally a hallmark of early women's adventure programs operating under feminist theory (Hardin, 1979; Mitten, 1985).

Table 1
Shared Methods, Goals, and Objectives

(Although all terms listed can apply to both feminist pedagogy and experiential education, they may have a stronger connection to one or the other.)

Experience = Knowledge	Communication
Valuing Experience	Cooperation
Multi/Interdisciplinary	Conflict Resolution
Rejection of Either/Or Thinking	Non-Competitive
Discovery Learning	Power Sharing
Liberatory	Gender Justice
Participatory	Anti-oppression
Active and Engaging	Overcoming Hatred
Empowering	Acknowledging and Validating Difference
Synthesis of Mind, Body, Spirit	Student Centered
Attention to Process	Learner Responsibility
Class as Community	Internal Motivation
Risk Taking	Student-based Evaluation
Commitment to Growth	Teacher as Facilitator and Guide
Articulation of Needs	Still Evolving as a Methodology

Marginalized or Fringe to Mainstream Education

The Use of Power

A critical look at power in educational relationships is central to any discussion of using feminist theory to inform experiential learning. Feminist scholars have struggled with the power dynamics which exist in the teacher/learner relationship and how to transform traditionally vested power into situations of mutually held power. An analysis of gender, race, and class is often at the root of feminist educators' critique of power.

One way to equalize power is to divest experiential education practitioners of the "expert" label. For the teacher to maintain a cloak of expertise denies students both connection to the teacher as a fallible human being and witness to the teacher's ability to work through difficult situations (Belenky, Clinchy, Goldberger, & Tarule, 1986; MacDermid, Jurich, Myers-Walls, & Pelo, 1992). For example, the preface one of us uses when teaching map-and-compass skills is that it has always been a diffi-cult topic for her because of math anxiety, requiring more preparation to teach it than would other subjects.

Yet, there is irony to a woman teacher striving to disperse power in educational situations where people are conditioned to give less authority to women than men (Friedman, 1985; Weiler, 1991). One author had a professional experience on an out-door trip as a co-leader with two first-time student leaders, a female and a male. Throughout the trip, the three leaders noticed that when the male leader addressed the group, there was silent listening from the participants. When either of the female leaders spoke, however, the trip participants tended to keep talking, have side con-versations, or ask for things to be repeated.

Evaluation is a primary source of power often unilaterally maintained by the teacher. An unspoken but omnipotent power relationship makes most systems of evaluation punitive instead of a welcome opportunity for students' growth and self-reflection. An evaluation system popular in feminist classrooms is to remove the teacher from direct evaluation in favor of a partnership model between students (Bright, 1987; Beckman, 1991). In the partnership model, a student team works together to create evaluation criteria that fit the needs of each individual as well as satisfy the institutional requirements. The students then work together throughout the course to monitor their progress continually and reflect on and refine its direc-tion. We have used this system of evaluation buddies in several experiential educa-tion programs with success, finding that students are energized by the idea of evaluation as helpful feedback.

Belief in the learner as primary teacher (Spender, 1981) can be extrapolated beyond evaluation to learner-created syllabi and experiences. Many feminist educa-tors establish only guidelines for the curriculum, encouraging students to work cooperatively to create their own syllabus (Bright, 1987; Warren, 1988). By allowing students to control what they learn, feminist teachers foster responsibility in learners and use their granted power of position constructively.

Another form power sharing has taken in feminist education is in de-emphasiz-ing competition in educational settings. Sapon-Shevin and Schniedewind (1991) document the critical link between competition and oppression by suggesting that competition is the inevitable result of the struggle for scarce resources, a scarcity often contrived by the teacher. Since the resultant division into haves and have-nots only benefits those with privilege, the charge of the feminist educator who wants to foster student empowerment is to eliminate competition where there is a clear loser. Applied to experiential education, this might mean using win-win games in our team-building exercises, enhancing chances for collaboration, and eliminating suc-cess/failure dichotomies (such as implying that to run a rapid or to reach a summit is the ultimate goal).

Casting a critical eye on co-teacher relationships in outdoor education is also important. Institutionally supported hierarchical leadership in adventure programs (i.e., head instructors, primary leaders) detracts from creating collaborative teaching relationships that model for students a situation in which power is shared rather than wielded. In co-teaching outdoors, there are power differentials between teachers that need to be worked with rather than ignored or institutionalized by designating one teacher more senior. In any educational situation where modeling a shared leadership style is revered, these power differentials must be named, acknowledged, and actively addressed. Our own experience of teaching is illustrative. By naming the power based on age and experience one of us had in our teaching relationship, we worked together to create situations that valued the contributions the less-experienced leader brought to the class. Her ability to establish rapport with participants, her novelty in approaching routine situations, and her understanding of the beginner's mind were a few of the contributions we emphasized. Creating power balances is often time consuming and challenging, but the example of egalitarian cooperation it models for students is important in feminist pedagogy.

Feminists have shown that language is a profound purveyor of power, an institution that defines the norm (Spender, 1985; Giroux, 1989). Besides the language already mentioned that subordinates one leader in a co-teaching relationship, teachers are prone to use terms that subtly deride students. Therefore, for teachers to use language such as "my students" instead of "the students I work (or learn) with" or to refer to adult college students as "kids" can perpetuate the firm grasp the teacher has on power. In adventure programming, use of discriminating language such as "two-man ten" and referring to a coed group in the masculine can often lead to a silencing of women's and girls' experiences.

The new scholarship on women provides the groundwork for a critique of stress challenge and questions it as a methodology useful for women. Stress-challenge, experiential-education models with their adversarial relationship to the environment may be wrong for women who favor a more connected way of approaching the outdoors. In stress-challenge programs, participants encounter a novel situation, experience doubt about whether they can successfully confront the challenge, and, with the teacher's skilled facilitation, are encouraged to resolve the challenge in a manner that facilitates personal reflection. However, research by Belenky et al. (1986) found that the adversarial doubting model of education does not resonate with the ways women construct knowledge:

> We do not deny that cognitive conflict can act as an impetus to growth; all of us can attest to such experiences in our own lives. But in our interviews only a handful of women described a powerful and positive learning experience in which a teacher aggressively challenged their notions. (p. 227)

They propose, instead, a midwifery model of education (see Chapter 16 for Warren's midwifery model of experiential education) in which the focus of power is on the student's rather than the instructor's knowledge.

The Value of Personal Experience

Although both experiential and feminist teachers believe experience is an essential part of learning, there are distinct differences between the approaches. Many feminist educators encourage students to examine their life experiences and to treat these experience as valid forms of knowledge (Lewis & Simon, 1986; Schniedewind, 1987; Giroux, 1989; Ryan, 1989; Dewar, 1991; Brown, 1992). By using students' personal experiences as learning tools, feminist teachers illuminate the political realities of society in which various forms of oppression affect different people. As Romney, Tatum, and Jones (1992) point out:

> Honoring life experiences in a cooperative environment is fundamental because those experiences serve as a springboard for examining and understanding the dynamics of oppression. This emphasis is based on feminist ideas of connection, context, and partnership, which expand our vision of human capacity. (p. 96)

The value of experience is located differently within experiential theory. While feminist teachers value students' articulation of past and present life experiences, experiential educators actually *create* experiences for students as the center of learning. Created experiences are based on the common assumption that knowledge must be "out there," rather than on a belief that what knowledge the student already has is valid and should be used for further learning. Feminist scholar Dale Spender (1981) calls the use of personal experience "knowledge 'made' rather than 'received' by all who participated" (p. 167). Therefore, using only created experiences—which are frequently based on task or activity rather than on personal experiences—not only may deny women and girls a place in experiential learning, but also may limit the methodology useful for all.

A feminist use of experience is an opportunity for experiential educators to expand their notion of experience. While McClintock (1992) points out that using student life experience is a valid tool in teaching about social justice issues, we argue for a general inclusion of this feminist principle in all topics taught experientially. Another foundation feminist educators add to their concept of experience concerns the place of social change in education (the personal is political). Whereas experiential educators promote the transformation of self through learning, feminists seek the transformation of society (Gordon, 1982; Shrewsbury, 1987; Lewis, 1990). Feminist teachers create societal change by working toward a goal of social justice. For example, the life experience of urban kids in dealing with conflict in their lives is worthy as knowledge and is as poignant as a facilitated adventure experience in conflict resolution.

The Goal of Social Justice

The trend in the current experiential education movement has been toward creating an ethical base for experiential education (Hunt, 1990; Gass, 1993) with little focused attention on a sustained and realized social justice agenda. Experiential education more often concentrates on effectiveness than on equity. This is an area where experiential practitioners can be mentored by feminist educators to create true liberatory practice.

One objective of feminist educators is to teach students the tools for overcoming the oppression of targeted social groups. They attempt to create classroom communities which are supportive and promote growth and risk. In her feminist classroom, Shrewsbury (1987) encouraged students to be "engaged with others in a struggle to get beyond . . . sexism, racism, classism, homophobia and other destructive hatreds and to work together to enhance . . . knowledge" (p. 6). Methods feminist teachers employ include conflict resolution, communication skills, attention to group process, and the use of personal experience.

Although experiential educators often use similar methods, many do not include the encompassing goal of working for social justice. Experiential education teachers who fail to address issues of diversity risk creating a climate where oppression will exist if it is not repudiated.

For experiential educators to address these issues, anti-oppression theory has to be an integral part of every experience that is created: it must be a part of the developmental process of curriculum planning and carried out in practice. Therefore, adding a few multicultural activities to an experiential curriculum that lacks an integrated social change agenda and associated pedagogy will *not* make a difference. Lasting results require risk taking, developmental planning, and training for teachers to understand their conditioned bias.

We often encounter educators who have absorbed the "treat everyone as individuals" myth of addressing oppression. We have found some glaring incongruencies with what Schaef (1981) calls the humanistic leveler position with its attendant line of "let's not look at the ways in which we're different; let's focus on the ways in which we're alike." As the world is weighted to favor privileged social categories (white, male, heterosexual, Christian, able-bodied, etc.) over targeted categories, giving equal power to both only maintains the power imbalance, providing little reparative work to bring the experience of the targeted group on the level of the dominant group. As Lewis (1990) asserts, "A pedagogical approach that fails to acknowledge how such inequality silences serves to reinforce the powerlessness of the powerless" (p. 478).

We have often seen, particularly with homogeneous groups of the dominant culture, that there is an assumed normative of the Euro-American culture in which marginalized groups remain invisible. Yet, because of the pervasive structures of oppression, there is no such thing as passive anti-bias work. If the educator does not raise social justice issues, especially in apparently homogeneous groups, they risk perpetuating the invisibility of oppressed groups.

One place to start would be to question our profession's interpretation of the history of experiential education and seek the obliterated voices that have been silenced by bias. This means that experiential education didn't start with John Dewey, Kurt Hahn, and William James as we are led to believe. Experiential education existed for the working-class tradespeople who passed their craft along experientially; for the indigenous people throughout the world who take lessons from experience in nature, for women who taught life's lessons to their children long before university-educated white men started to write about it.

Toward a Feminist Experiential Education

If the challenge for the teacher in experiential education programs is to embrace a more feminist way of learning/teaching, then we offer the following suggestions.

1. Work to minimize power differentials

Experiential teachers using a feminist approach will need to recognize their power as teachers and seek methods to redistribute power between themselves and students and co-leaders. A personal assessment of one's privilege and assumptions based on gender, race, age, class, religion, sexual orientation, and ability is the first step in creating power balances.

2. Value students' personal experiences

Experiential educators can integrate the value of personal experience by making a conscious effort to foster learning experiences which promote an analysis of students' backgrounds. This helps students feel more comfortable about who they are, and their reflection on life experiences can aid in the processing of created experience. The result is students who are critical thinkers, able not only to critique what they are taught but also to look insightfully at how they are taught.

3. Create a vision of social change

Currently, the field of experiential education addresses change on an individual level (i.e., self-esteem building, knowledge acquisition) and a group level (i.e., team building). Feminist education goes one step further to include institutional change, helping students translate abstract ideas into concrete realities (Thompson & Disch, 1992). Certainly experiential education has promise as an excellent methodology to use for social justice work and this may be the richest potential for growth that exists in the field today.

4. Advocate for female learners

Given that women and girls have a distinctly different educational experience than men and boys (Gilligan, 1991; Belenky et al., 1986; MacDermid et al., 1992), and unique needs in outdoor adventure programs (Warren, 1990), support for female learners in experiential education programs is necessary to counteract inequality. This might take the form of not just tolerating, but advocating for women-only space on coed trips; supporting women and girls in undertaking untraditional tasks; incorporation of ritual, ceremony, imagery, and women's life stories in addition to the content and task orientation of the experience; being aware of the "air time" men and women/boys and girls have available in discussion; and eliminating elements that subtly discriminate (ropes course events that require upper-body strength are prime examples).

Kurt Hahn's ethic of service fits well with women's needs if it truly involves both an ethic of caring and a focus on women's experience. Yet, regretfully, it is the service component that has faded from many experiential education programs. Furthermore, experiential educators must include not only soup kitchens and trail maintenance projects in service learning programs, but also experiences in battered women's shelters, AIDS crisis hotlines, and women's centers. To validate the experience of women and girls, it is crucial to include the real issues of their lives.

5. Use teaching methods which support the learning experiences of women

These might include: consensus decision making, student responsibility for evaluation, cooperative learning, constructive feedback, collective problem solving, conflict resolution, and peer mentoring.

For example, outdoor professionals might consider that given women's and girls' attention to relationship over achievement (Gilligan, 1982), it may be equally if not more valuable for women/girls to participate in a Trust Fall initiative exercise than in the highest element on the ropes course.

6. Make gender issues an integral part of the curriculum

Waiting for gender issues to create controversy before addressing them is similar to ignoring risk management strategies in adventure education and waiting to use First Aid and emergency procedure protocol after the accident has happened. Proactive treatments of gender create opportunities for students to examine their roles in society critically. An exercise one of us uses is to have students switch typical sex roles while loading and unloading a 400-pound North Canoe on the van and paddling to a local island. In the role play, only the women (who are playing masculine roles) are allowed to handle the canoe, tie it on top of the van, and paddle out to the island. The men's role (playing the feminine role) is to be supportive and encouraging. While this gender-bending exercise usually creates some extremely stereotypic actions by the students, when we process the experience while on the island, students are usually astounded by their reactions and the issues raised. Their understanding of gender dynamics in outdoor experiential education, which was piqued by previously assigned readings, is furthered by personal experience and reflection.

7. Create structures that prevent the marginalization of women

Experiential education programs need to establish policies for parity between women and men. Pay equity, clear paths of advancement, skill development, and equal voices in decision making for women are a start. Policies for dealing with sexual harassment, for teacher/student relationships, and for preventing discrimination are also important.

8. Bring a critical consciousness to experiential education

Anti-oppression work as a foundation of *all* experiential education programming is imperative in a system that has such strong roots in the white male system. Issues of oppression must be scrutinized in programs promoting experiential learning. To do so, we must be able to look critically at what we do. Ask ourselves questions. Is using expensive high-tech equipment in adventure programs insensitive to class issues? Do we schedule course events with no awareness of Jewish holidays? Why are our programs unappealing or impractical for certain ethnic minorities (Ashley, 1990)? Do students have equal access to role models who are women, people of color, or gay, lesbian, or bisexual? Are our service projects one-shot, quick-fix forays into disadvantaged communities?

Conclusion

Feminist education practice infused in experiential education has the potential to create a just society. Experiential education, when done without a critical look at issues raised by feminists, replicates nonliberatory practices and reinforces a status quo of oppression. Throughout our research, we have been continually excited that feminist pedagogy and experiential education dovetail. To infuse experiential education with feminist pedagogy is difficult because we believe the pedagogy to be evolving and not an established technique; yet, having used feminist pedagogy in countless experiential education programs, we are convinced of its value for both women and men. Therefore, we invite experiential educators to attempt to integrate feminist pedagogy into their own theory and practice.

Acknowledgments

The authors would like to thank Sue Tippett, Angel Russek, and an anonymous reviewer for their helpful comments on this chapter.

Endnote

This chapter was originally published in the 1993 *Journal of Experiential Education, 16*(3), 25-31.

References

Ashley, F. B. (1990). Ethnic minorities' involvement with outdoor experiential education. In J. C. Miles & S. Priest (Eds.), *Adventure education* (pp. 369-373). State College, PA: Venture.

Beckman, M. (1991). Feminist teaching methods and the team-based workplace: Do results match intentions? *Women's Studies Quarterly, 19*(1 & 2), 165-178.

Belenky, M. F., Clinchy, B. M., Goldberger, N. R., & Tarule, J. M. (1986). *Women's ways of knowing.* New York: Basic Books.

Bright, C. (1987). Teaching feminist pedagogy: An undergraduate course. *Women's Studies Quarterly, XV*(3 & 4), 97-100.

Brown, J. (1992). Theory or practice—what exactly is feminist pedagogy. *Journal of General Education, 41,* 51-63.

Dewar, A. (1991). Feminist pedagogy in physical education: Promises, possibilities, and pitfalls. *Journal of Physical Education, Recreation and Dance, 62*(6), 68-77.

Ellsworth, E. (1989). Why doesn't this feel empowering? Working through the repressive myths of critical pedagogy. *Harvard Educational Review, 59*(3), 297-323.

Friedman, S. S. (1985). Authority in the feminist classroom: A contradiction in terms? In M. Culley & C. Portuges (Eds.), *Gendered subjects: The dynamics of feminist teaching* (pp. 203-208). Boston, MA: Routledge.

Gass, M. A. (1993). Ethical principles for the therapeutic adventure professional group. In M. A. Gass (Ed.), *Adventure therapy: Therapeutic applications of adventure programming* (pp. 451-461). Dubuque, IA: Kendall/Hunt.

Gilligan, C. (1982). *In a different voice.* Cambridge, MA: Harvard University Press.

Gilligan, C. (1991). Teaching Shakespeare's sister: Notes from the underground of female adolescence. *Women's Studies Quarterly, 19*(1 & 2), 31-51.

Giroux, J. B. (1989). Feminist theory as pedagogical practice. *Contemporary Education, 61*(1), 6-10.

Gordon, S. A. (1982). *Experiential education, women's studies, and feminist pedagogy: A comparison.* Unpublished master's thesis, Mankato State University, Mankato, MN.

Hardin, J. (1979). Outdoor/wilderness approaches to psychological education for women: A descriptive study. (Doctoral dissertation, University of Massachusetts). *Dissertation Abstracts International, 40*(8), 4466-A.

Hunt, J. (1990). *Ethical issues in experiential education.* Dubuque, IA: Kendall/Hunt.

Lewis, M. (1990). Interrupting patriarchy: Politics, resistance, and transformation in the feminist classroom. *Harvard Educational Review, 60*(4), 467-488.

Lewis, M., & Simon, R. I. (1986). A discourse not intended for her: Learning and teaching within patriarchy. *Harvard Educational Review, 56*(4), 457-472.

MacDermid, S. M., Jurich, J. A., Myers-Walls, J. A., & Pelo, A. (1992). Feminist teaching: Effective education. *Family Relations, 41,* 31-38.

Mayer, F. (1985). Classroom pedagogy and the new scholarship on women. In M. Culley & C. Portuges (Eds.), *Gendered subjects: The dynamics of feminist teaching* (pp. 29-48). Boston, MA: Routledge.

McClintock, M. (1992). Sharing lesbian, gay and bisexual life experiences face to face. *Journal of Experiential Education, 15*(3), 51-55.

Mitten, D. (1985). A philosophical basis for a women's outdoor adventure program. *Journal of Experiential Education, 8*(2), 20-24.

Romney, P., Tatum, B., & Jones, J. (1992). Feminist strategies for teaching about oppression: The importance of process. *Women's Studies Quarterly, 29*(1 & 2), 95-110.

Ryan, M. (1989). Classrooms and contexts: The challenge of feminist pedagogy. *The Feminist Teacher, 4*(2/3), 39-42.

Sapon-Shevin, M., & Schniedewind, N. (1992). Cooperative learning as empowering pedagogy. In C. E. Sleeter (Ed.), *Empowerment through multicultural education* (pp. 159-178). Albany, NY: SUNY.

Schaef, A. W. (1981). *Women's reality.* Minneapolis, MN: Winston Press.

Schniedewind, N. (1987). Teaching feminist process. *Women's Studies Quarterly, 15*(3 & 4), 15-31.

Schoel, J., Prouty, D., & Radcliffe, P. (1988). *Islands of healing: A guide to adventure based counseling.* Hamilton, MA: Project Adventure.

Shrewsbury, C. (1987). What is feminist pedagogy? *Women's Studies Quarterly, XV*(3 & 4), 6-14.

Spender, D. (1981). Education: The patriarchal paradigm and the response to feminism. In D. Spender (Ed.), *Men's studies modified* (pp. 155-173). Oxford, England: Pergamon Press.

Spender, D. (1985). *Man made language.* London, England: Routledge & Kegan Paul.

Thompson, B., & Disch, E. (1992). Feminist, anti-racist, anti-oppression teaching: Two white women's perspectives. *Radical Teacher, 41,* 4-10.

Warren, K. (1988). The student directed classroom. A model for teaching experiential education theory. *Journal of Experiential Education, 11*(1), 4-9.

Warren, K. (1990). Women's outdoor adventures. In J. C. Miles & S. Priest (Eds.), *Adventure education* (pp. 411-417). State College, PA: Venture.

Warren, K. (1993). The midwife teacher: Engaging students in the experiential education process. *Journal of Experiential Education, 16*(1), 33-38.

Weiler, K. (1991). Freire and a feminist pedagogy of difference. *Harvard Educational Review, 61*(4), 449-474.

12

Outdoor Leadership Considerations with Women Survivors of Sexual Abuse

Denise Mitten and Rosalind Dutton

To many outdoor leaders and educators, the wilderness represents home. Many leaders feel comfortable there, connected to the earth, themselves, and others. Many people choose this profession in order to share these feelings with participants. Outdoor leaders want to help others receive the gifts of the wilderness and experience the joys of "coming home." In contrast, for a person who has been sexually abused, an outdoor or wilderness situation can make them feel "out of their element" and trigger feelings of fear, being out of control, or invaded. With a thorough understanding of how outdoor settings can affect survivors of sexual abuse, outdoor leaders can help women and men experience the healing and comforting qualities of nature and regain a sense of power over their lives.

Through a positive outdoor experience, a survivor can learn to manage her/himself in an environment that can feel out of control. A survivor can find ways to feel safe, set clear limits and boundaries, and still experience a oneness with nature. Most concretely, a survivor can experience her/his traumatized body as powerful, supportive, and full of vital information. Sensitive, aware, and respectful leaders are key elements in the quality of the outdoor experience (Mitten, 1986a).

An outdoor leader's understanding of possible reactions that a survivor of sexual abuse (hereafter referred to as "survivor") may have to a wilderness experience and to group interactions can greatly influence the success of the trip for survivors and the safety of the trip for all. Practitioners who work in outdoor programs especially designed for survivors have had specific training to work with this population therapeutically, and are aware of special needs and certain reactions to the wilderness that these women and men may have. However, because of the high incidence of sexual abuse in the United States and the fact that many survivors do not remember the abuse that happened to them, there is a high probability that survivors will be part of outdoor groups that are not designed specifically for them.

This chapter is intended to be used by outdoor leaders who work with groups that include a general population of women, as well as by outdoor leaders who work with programs whose clients are survivors. The purpose is to create an awareness of the discomfort and feelings that may surface for survivors during an outdoor experience. Outdoor leaders should be able to recognize behavioral indicators of sexual abuse and use that information to increase their sensitivity to the participant's experience. In order to assist outdoor leaders, issues of self-perception that survivors have, how these issues affect their outdoor experience, and the impact of natural elements on survivors will be discussed. The names we use are fictitious. The information in this chapter is based on observations by both authors as well as on supporting literature.

There are numerous definitions of sexual abuse. For this chapter, we consider that childhood sexual abuse is a social issue. It is an abuse of power expressed through sexual behavior. It is the imposition of one's will through sexual acts, or acts with sexual overtones, upon children to meet the distorted sexual/emotional needs of their caretakers. The natural imbalance of power between caretakers and their charges creates an environment in which unhealthy adults can act abusively (Blume, 1990).

Studies show that in the United States at least 38% of girls and 24% of boys are sexually abused before the age of 18 by someone designated as a caretaker (Giarretto, 1982; Russell, 1986). This means that for individuals signing up for any outdoor program, more than one out of three women and more than one in seven men may be survivors. In fact, some survivors who do not remember being sexually abused join outdoor trips and remember their experience during the course of the trips. Other individuals who know they are survivors have no idea that being in an outdoor environment may trigger certain feelings of discomfort. It may be an overestimation to say that 38% of women and 14% of men on all outdoor trips will be survivors because some will anticipate discomfort and self-select not to participate on an outdoor trip. It might also be argued that women survivors feel more comfortable around women and would be over-represented on women's trips. However, almost certainly *every* outdoor trip will have at least one participant who is a survivor.

There is a wide body of literature regarding sexual abuse survivors (Justice, 1976; Armstrong, 1978; Ford & Buck, 1979; Giarretto, 1982; McNaron & Morgan, 1982; Finkelfor, 1983).[1] There is very little written, however, about how survivors experience outdoor living (Mitten, 1986b; Dickie, 1990; Webb, 1990). There is even less written about how male survivors are affected by being in an outdoor environment. While our experience in working with males is more limited, we do believe that some issues are similar while others are not. Because our observations and contacts with women survivors is extensive, we will limit our remarks to women.

In this chapter, we are focusing on women who have been sexually abused as children. Not all survivors will exhibit all or even any of these behaviors, and women who are not survivors will also exhibit these behaviors. Women who are not survivors can have issues of self-perception and difficulties coping with natural elements due to inexperience, lack of self-esteem, or other abusive experiences. In addition, women who have been sexually assaulted as adults may exhibit similar behaviors. These same helping strategies apply. However, the experience of survivors who have been sexually abused as children may tend to be magnified and, therefore, require greater attention.

Leader, Not Therapist

This chapter is not intended to encourage or enable the leader to diagnose, counsel, psychoanalyze, or treat survivors. Our intention is to give information that can help leaders be sensitive to special needs and concerns a survivor may have. If a woman says she does not want to participate in a rain hike or watch a lightning storm, or that she needs to wash her hair, her choices are to be respected.

A word of caution, however. It would be inappropriate for a leader to notice behavioral indicators of sexual abuse and then approach the client and ask her if she is a survivor. A woman's sexual history, including a history of abuse, is personal and it is appropriate for her to share this only if and when she chooses. A leader need not drop hints or fish for this information. If a woman is forced or coerced into sharing intimate information before establishing a trusting relationship, which usually takes more than a few days, it reinforces the abusive pattern of having to give away or having someone take something personal without her consent or without her being ready to give it. In addition, a woman may have no conscious memory of her sexual abuse. In order to survive severe trauma, some survivors "forget" the painful information; they have amnesia (Blume, 1990). Questioning her about sexual abuse or insinuating that she was sexually abused is disrespectful and could be damaging to her healing.

Behavioral Indicators of Sexual Abuse

Being a member of a group can be difficult for a survivor. This can be especially true if anyone reminds her of her family unit. A survivor may distance herself from other group members which can result in unsafe situations. Group members may notice behaviors of the survivor that scare them and may cause them to avoid her or accidentally not give her information. The following behavioral indicators of sexual abuse may be presented by survivors:

- A survivor may act rebellious. Survivors were manipulated and hurt by people who were authority figures whom they were supposed to be able to trust. Therefore, many survivors dislike authority and authority figures.
- Survivors can have trouble expressing their feelings as well as sharing them. They may not trust what they are feeling; therefore, they may not easily

express their fear, anxiety, excitement, or any other emotions. In addition, they may not trust that their feelings will be believed and respected.

- Many survivors have sleeping disorders. These can be exacerbated by sleeping with strangers in the same space, be it in a tent or a cabin. Some survivors were molested in small, enclosed places. A tent can remind her of that space. Many women were molested at night while sleeping. Fears of being abused by the perpetrator while sleeping can be re-stimulated by being in an unfamiliar sleeping space with others. This may be particularly problematic on mixed gender trips.

Assessment by Survivors

Survivors often inaccurately assess their physical abilities, their stamina, what is dangerous, and how to be safe. In general, they tend to overextend or under-challenge themselves. This may stem directly from the effects of the sexual abuse. In order to survive, women had to tune out the pain their bodies were experiencing, to discount what they were feeling, and to act as if they were fine. This is known as dis-associating or disconnecting from the experience. This can become a lifelong pattern. Therefore, some women learn to tolerate high levels of pain without seeming to notice. For example, a woman may overextend herself physically by hiking to complete exhaustion, become dangerously cold before adding clothing, or hike with blisters until they become infected. Conversely, a woman may paddle with minor exertion and feel she is overextending herself

Safety is the primary concern for most outdoor leaders. A leader's understanding of a survivor's experience will influence her safety as well as the group's. If a survivor unknowingly carries a load that is too heavy, back strain may occur. If a survivor is walking on precarious footing and is startled by insects, she might slip. If a survivor doesn't see whitewater as dangerous, she may unwittingly canoe in rapids beyond her ability. If this leads to an accident, the group would have to deal with the situation as illustrated in the following examples:

> At every rest stop on the first day of a backpacking trip, the leader asked each woman if she had hot or sore spots on her feet. Each time, Rosa said her feet had no pain. At the end of the day, the leader noticed Rosa had two medium-sized blisters when she removed her socks. This lack of body awareness and inattention to pain was more than inexperience.
>
> Pearl, a survivor, participated in her first outdoor trip, a week-long backpacking trip. After distributing the group gear, the leader asked who could take a bit more, as there was still some left. Without hesitation, Pearl offered to take the remaining gear. She had already taken some of another participant's gear who was concerned about weight. In addition to not having recognized the limits of her physical stamina, she may have wanted to be more in control. If Pearl carried most of the items, she would have known where they were. If she fixed dinner, she would have known when it was

served and what was in it. This overriding need to control a task was a reaction to having had no control as a child. The abuser/perpetrator was in control of the child's body and, from a child's point of view, her whole world, during the abuse.

Accurately assessing whether an activity or situation is merely fear-producing or truly dangerous and what can be done to be safe is another problematic area for survivors. On a day-trip to practice rock climbing, Kim became panicky about climbing down the rocks, even with rope support. She was convinced it was dangerous. When her leader helped her understand that it was scary but not dangerous, she was able to choose to descend. On another trip, Juanita was in a mountaineering group learning to slide down ice or snow using an ice axe for guidance and braking. Her leader was struck by her absence of fear. She did not appear to enjoy the thrill of the activity; realistically, she simply did not comprehend the dangers. Because survivors were taught, either explicitly or implicitly, to mistrust their feelings and perceptions, their ability to discern realistic levels of pain, fear, and danger have been impaired. In some situations, a woman's fears may be so high that she confuses fear with real danger, or she may be so used to discounting or disassociating with her fear that she does things which are indeed dangerous.

This impaired ability to trust one's perceptions and act on them also extends to setting appropriate boundaries. The essence of sexual abuse is having one's most intimate boundary—the skin on one's body—violated. Survivors, therefore, may feel extremely sensitive or overly casual about nudity. A survivor may be reluctant or embarrassed to undress or change clothes in the presence of other people or to participate in nude swimming or saunas. Some women may feel uncomfortable around women, women and men, or just men.

This lack of clear boundaries extends to emotional and sexual boundaries as well. For example, survivors may say more about themselves than they are truly comfortable revealing to others, or they may engage in sexual activity with which they are uncomfortable. Leaders need to honor the survivor's own sense of boundaries and to help her use them as a guide. In certain instances, it is very important for outdoor leaders to set the example for boundaries rather than following a participant's lead. For example, many survivors have used sex as a way to connect with people or as a way to gain protection. Some habitually sexualize relationships (Blume, 1990). If a leader enters into a sexual relationship with a survivor, even if the survivor initiates the relationship, he/she, in addition to violating the professional client relationship, can perpetuate the cycle of abuse because of the power imbalance—the leader has more power than the participant.

Impact of Natural Elements on Survivors

Interaction with certain natural elements such as flies and mosquitoes, rain and lightning, dirt, and darkness can trigger sexual abuse memories and feelings, or panic. Invasive insects, such as flies and mosquitoes, can remind survivors of their lack of control over their bodies. The following example illustrates this concept:

> On a two-week canoe trip, Sarah would sometimes have to retire to her tent to get away from the bugs. Even though insect repellent kept most of the insects off her body, the buzzing around her was too much. Once while she was rock climbing, large flies landed all over her legs. She felt an immense lack of control and felt the flies were invading her while she was helpless. This incident brought back memories of her sexual abuse experience. She told the leader how uncomfortable she was and was not able to continue. She said it took all of her self-control not to scream, fall off the rock and jump around.

Rain and lightning can also stimulate out-of-control feelings. Rain, like insects, can feel invasive and uncontrollable. Lightning can remind a survivor of "the jolt" her body received in response to being sexually aroused during the abuse or of her world being taken over by a larger force.

Cleanliness is another issue stemming from sexual abuse which is exacerbated on an outdoor trip. Generally, one expects to get dirtier in the wilderness than at home. But for a survivor, this inability to get "really clean" can trigger feelings of shame, feeling dirty, or feeling like "damaged goods," reminiscent of her response to the abuse as a child. Without being able to sustain a certain level of cleanliness, a woman's self-esteem can plummet. This can affect her ability to participate safely on a trip.

Coping with natural elements, which are out of a person's control, can trigger emotional, physical, visual, or other sensual flashbacks. Having a flashback means just that—in a flash, something in the environment catapults a survivor to another time and she acts and feels as though the past is the present. Flashbacks can cause anxiety for a survivor. She may have never experienced them before. Nightmares or uncontrolled screaming can cause embarrassment or terror that lingers into the day.

What to Do?

Recognizing behaviors common to survivors increases an outdoor leader's awareness of the group members. This awareness will help maintain the safety and integrity of the trip. In addition, the practitioner can help survivors learn coping strategies which will help them continue to use the outdoors as a place for nourishment and healing.

As outdoor leaders, there are many practical things we can do or suggest to the participant to do to alleviate some of the stress and reactions survivors may experience in the woods:

1. Maintain a posture of inclusivity. Often a survivor has felt or been excluded. Because of her beliefs or needs around coping with natural elements, other group members may perceive a survivor as odd. Creating an accepting atmosphere where the leader models the survivor's needs as normal and functional helps create a group where there is room for differences. Other group members will most often follow a leader's lead. How the leader treats and behaves toward the survivor affects how other group members will relate to her and each other (Mitten, 1985). Setting a tone of inclusivity at the beginning of the trip can reduce safety concerns during the trip by encouraging everyone to see themselves as part of the group, to take care of themselves, and to be mindful of the well-being of the whole group (Mitten, 1989).

2. Giving concrete tips for self-care not only models healthy outdoor behavior but can also be very reassuring to survivors. Help her to see her body as a source of helpful information. You may help her learn to pace herself and become a safe group member. Helping the participant distinguish between cause and effect in the wilderness gives her a framework in which to make decisions. For example, if a survivor pushes until she is dangerously fatigued, give her specific standards for safe conduct (i.e., when canoeing, canoe for one half-hour and no matter how you are feeling, stop for five minutes and drink at least one cup of water before continuing).

3. If a woman is having trouble sleeping, try to accommodate her as much as possible. Would she be more comfortable with other tentmates? Is there an extra tent in which she can sleep alone? Ask her if she knows specifically what she is afraid of and help her problem-solve. Help her use her imagination. For instance, if she's afraid someone may come into her tent, it might help her to imagine that there is a guard at her tent door. She may be able to position her sleeping bag to minimize her fear. How well a woman sleeps affects both her enjoyment of and safety on the trip. Again, avoid doing therapy about abuse.

4. Avoid pairing women and men as tentmates. A survivor may be very uncomfortable sharing a tent with a man who is a stranger.

5. Help participants find ways to get clean. A solar shower is easy to use to wash hair and get a thorough rinse. Talk about cleanliness early in the trip. Let participants know that their wishes to get clean are important to you, that they are welcome to ask questions and explore more ways to get and feel clean.

6. To increase a sense of control in buggy areas, suggest that participants put on clothes that cover vulnerable parts of their bodies. Encourage use of insect repellents and make sure they bring repellent on day hikes so they are not without it. Bug jackets that repel insects are available from outdoor suppliers.

7. Consider a graduated approach when designing a wilderness experience program for women survivors. For example, the staff at Woodswomen, a service organization in Minnesota, decided on a graduated approach when designing a wilderness experience program for women offenders. Most of the participants in the program were survivors. Their first trip was a short trip of three days. The location was a cabin with an outhouse and a pump for water. This allowed the women the opportunity to ease gently into rugged living. In fact, at the center where the cabin was located, there were also buildings with full baths. During the three days, they made one trip to these facilities for bathing. The women's next trip was a nine-day, wilderness canoe trip. When the women participated on that trip, they were more mentally prepared for the challenge and had time to plan cleanliness strategies.[2]

8. Have a leader available at night in case a woman has an issue about darkness. On a week-long canoe trip, Sue found that going to the outhouse during a dark night felt extremely dangerous to her. She may have been experiencing a flashback. If she does not identify herself as a survivor, calm her fears as you would anyone else who is afraid of the dark. Affirm that being in the dark can be scary and offer to accompany her if she would like that. If she identifies herself as a survivor, remind her that the original, terrifying incident is not happening now. Have her look at her surroundings and tell you what she sees, for instance, tall trees, a blue tent, a purple shirt, and so on. Or ask her to tell you how old she is, what year it is, and where she is. These questions will help her ground herself in current reality.

9. It is not useful to foster an attitude of "pushing through" one's feelings to get to a "better" place. The meaning of being sexually abused is to be pushed physically and emotionally, against one's will, beyond what a person can manage. This approach is dangerous for a survivor and can cause unnecessary stress for other group members as well. In fact, encouraging women to push on, either emotionally or physically, can reinforce women not listening to their bodies and minds.

> One half-hour into a day rock-climbing clinic, Pat told the leader she was going home. The leader, of course, had a pang of disappointment. However, she said to Pat, "I'll walk you to your car." En route, they chatted about the morning and Pat told the leader that she was in therapy for sexual abuse and felt too exposed during the clinic. The leader said she understood, asked Pat if she could call her later that week, and bid her good-bye. That week, the leader called Pat and invited her to join the group on a clinic the next weekend that would have less people. Pat accepted and participated. The following week, Pat attended an intermediate climbing clinic. Again, after a half-hour, she needed to leave. She returned a few weeks later to complete an intermediate clinic. She shared with the leader that by being able to say she felt exposed and needed to leave, then leaving without leader criticism, and being welcomed upon

her return, supported her healing process. Women survivors are often afraid to say they need to leave, or to say no. They are afraid their "no" will be interpreted hostilely and they will be abandoned. When they were small children, this would have threatened their survival. In this case, the value for Pat of saying, "No," leaving, and returning was substantial. The leader gave Pat a gift of knowing that she could set her own limits without being abandoned. In many other instances, it is appropriate for leaders to hear and honor a woman's choice to say "No," or that she needs to stop.

10. As leaders on an outdoor trip, we have a great deal of responsibility, authority, and power. We also have the opportunity to model being sensitive, being noninvasive, and maintaining appropriate emotional and physical boundaries. The power of this modeling is significant, especially for survivors (Mitten, 1986b).

   For example, we can be sure all nude activities are optional. If two leaders are on the trip, one can stay clothed to validate nonparticipation. With an issue as powerful as nudity, it is important for leaders to do more than say nudity is optional. By remaining clothed as a choice, a leader will model that staying clothed is a valid choice. If a leader tells the participants she/he is staying clothed to make it comfortable for others to stay clothed, the power of the modeling is lost.

11. Involving the other group members in a survivor's experience can cause embarrassment for the survivor and model inappropriate boundaries. If questions from other participants arise, answer them frankly and briefly. For example, "Why does Sarah hate flies so much?" Answer, "She doesn't like feeling them on her body." "Why does Sally have to bathe every day?" Answer, "She likes to feel clean."

12. In cases where a survivor discovers her sexual abuse during the trip, suggest further help when she goes home. Refrain from participating in ad hoc "therapy" or making the sexual abuse memories a focus of the trip. However, continue to be available to give practical suggestions that will help increase physical and emotional comfort.

The Healing Power of Nature

The wilderness offers many gifts—spiritual peace, a positive surrender of control, a feeling of connection, and a new sense of empowerment. Seeing others work in harmony with nature and experiencing it herself can help a survivor to gain positive memories through her body, which was often experienced as a source of pain because of the abuse, and to recover a sense of pride and power in herself and her body.

The outdoors is unpredictable and situations such as insects, darkness, lightning, and rain are beyond human control. Because of this, in addition to being part of a new group, issues and reactions regarding control of one's body, for many women, will be on the surface more than in other environments. A survivor can learn practical techniques to more accurately assess objective danger and to take adequate care of her emotional and physical needs. She can experience an authority figure who is kind and understanding and who models appropriate personal boundaries.

Lessons learned during the outdoor trip may be transferred to other parts of her life. The art of problem solving regarding factors such as cleanliness, insect avoidance, and rain tolerance, as well as a myriad of other wilderness experiences, can set examples or guidelines for these women to follow in other situations.

Endnotes

This chapter was originally published in the 1993 *Journal of Experiential Education, 16*(1), 7-12.

[1] In the last five years, the literature on childhood sexual abuse has dramatically expanded. Most bookstores carry clinical treatises, books written by professionals for the general public, and stories by survivors.

[2] Further information about this program can be obtained from Woodswomen, Inc., 25 West Diamond Lake Road, Minneapolis, MN 55419. A handbook describing the program is available for $10. Also available is the publication: *Sexual violence survivors on outdoor programs: A handbook for leaders of outdoor activities.* It is $2.75 for the handbook with a laminated field card.

References

Armstrong, L. (1978). *Kiss daddy goodnight.* New York: Pocket Books.

Blume, E. S. (1990). *Secret survivors.* New York: Wiley Press.

Dickie, J. (1990). *Putting theory into action: An analysis of Woodswomen, a feminist based adventure program.* Unpublished manuscript, Earlham College, Richmond, IN.

Finkelfor, D. (Ed.). (1983). *The dark side of families.* Beverly Hills, CA: Sage.

Ford, S., & Buck, C. (1979). *Betrayal of innocence.* New York: Penguin.

Giarretto, H. (1982). A comprehensive child sexual abuse treatment program. *Child Abuse and Neglect, 6*(3), 263-278.

Justice, R., & Justice, B. (1976). *The abusing family.* New York: Human Science Press.

McNaron, T., & Morgan, Y. (1982). *Voices in the night: Women speak out on incest.* Minneapolis, MN: Cleis Press.

Mitten, D. (1985). A philosophical basis for a women's outdoor adventure program. *Journal of Experiential Education, 8*(2), 20-24.

Mitten, D. (1986a). *Meeting the unknown: Group dynamics in the wilderness.* Minneapolis, MN: Woodswomen.

Mitten, D. (1986b). *Outdoor programming with women who are survivors of domestic violence and rape.* Unpublished manuscript, Association for Experiential Education Conference, CT.

Mitten, D. (1989). Healthy expressions of diversity lead to positive group experiences. *Journal of Experiential Education, 12*(3), 17-22.

Russell, D. (1986). *The secret trauma.* New York: Basic Books.

Webb, B. (1993). The use of a three-day therapeutic wilderness adjunct by the Colorado Outward Bound School with survivors of violence. In M. A. Gass (Ed.), *Adventure therapy: Therapeutic applications of adventure programming,* (pp. 95-102). Dubuque, IA: Kendall/ Hunt.

13

Feminists Challenging Assumptions about Outdoor Leadership

Martha Bell

Some really destructive assumptions operate in groups when stress is involved. People are going to want to silence others. Especially when we are trying to operate in a consensus decision model when underlying power relationships aren't being named. We talk about challenge in Outward Bound, we talk about adventure. That's the greatest adventure: challenging assumptions. Better than challenging lives. 'Cause those assumptions are just like rocks; they're bedrock.[1]

Much of the essence of experiential learning in the outdoors rests on the effective facilitation of personal growth through reflection. As experiential practices have developed, educators have gained unique insight into the experiences and needs of different groups as they synthesise new awareness toward social consciousness, groups of women among others. My interest is not only in women's experiences as participants learning in the outdoors, but also in women as experiential facilitators and instructors. One of the earliest studies of women-only wilderness courses recommended that future research examine the effects of women's outdoor learning on the development of feminist consciousness (Hardin, 1979). Conversely, I believe that it is also important to examine the effects of feminist consciousness on the professional lives of women who lead outdoor experiences.

I write as a feminist, an outdoor facilitator and guide, and now a lecturer and researcher in higher education. Starting from my own experience, I began to pursue the issues raised here when they affected my everyday reality as an instructor; later I gained a language in which to think about them through reading in graduate school in a combination of academic disciplines.[2] In this chapter, I discuss a number of themes which emerged through individual and group interviews with four Canadian women (Bell, 1993). Three women agreed to join me in a qualitative research study, in which I served as participant-researcher, aimed at finding out how our feminist beliefs affect our professional practice, thereby enhancing our collective ability to forge new awareness through personal reflection.

The study[3] indicates that a commitment to feminism in the lives of the women interviewed does affect their daily work as leaders as they do not separate themselves, or their life stories as women, from their practice as instructors. Overall, a commitment to feminism is understood by these women as a process of both learning about ways that they developed a sense of self, capability, and relationships as girls and women, and responding to awareness of how gender continues to organise and inform that identity and their leadership, in perhaps conflicting ways, through intersecting power relations. Gender is the categorical lens through which social relations become viewed and judged as regulating or empowering.

Firstly, therefore, discussing feminism involves context: working from personal histories of difference, determination, and desire, deeply ingrained while sometimes also shared. Identity is shown to be multiple at any one time, such as when a woman is employed to be an instructor and lives in the outdoor program community in which she takes on other leadership positions and has relationships based on diverse affinities and interests. Contexts shift and identities may shift in turn. The relevance to experiential education of the socio-cultural concept of identity as social subjectivities[4] will emerge with the voices of the women who participated in the study.

Secondly, feminist beliefs also involve analysis: thinking about the wider social organisation of oppression as experienced by women and seeing it reproduced in social relations and cultural practices,[5] in outdoor learning groups as much as in other groups in society. The interviews were consciousness raising, a feminist strategy for politicising personal experience, as we became more conscious of our own life stories and the identities they produced. The focus was also on *praxis*, or reflecting on past action in order to theorise to inform future action. As with feminism, praxis also has social change as its goal. Socially meaningful change means identifying and disrupting assumptions about gender difference, group conflict, and social relations in experiential practice inherited from dominant perspectives in outdoor leadership, education, and theories of knowledge. I hope the voices in this study will provoke feminist women to extend their theorising about their own leadership in future group facilitation in the outdoors beyond their individual situation and into a socio-cultural context. In the next section, I introduce readers to the analytical concepts grounding these insights and what they signal for all critical outdoor leaders.

Outdoor Leadership: Gendered Terrain

Imagine a summer camp for girls in which the camp leaders were openly feminist. It does exist. The Iowa Girls' Leadership Camp, according to Deb Jordan (1988), teaches young women leadership values, skills, and knowledge through the outdoors. A diverse group of women, including women of colour, Third World women, and women of European descent are instructors, speakers, and mentors. The young women participants are encouraged to reflect on their lives and goals, growing up as girls in society, and their experiences in their groups in camp. They are encouraged to perceive how the structural influence of gender impacts each of their lives, even in differing ways, and to analyse their experiences as a collective gender group. As an example, "women's and men's roles in society, their relationships . . . in a variety of settings, and the strengths and weaknesses of both genders" are discussed during the camp. The aim is to help "open the eyes and hearts of future leaders to the struggles and needs of oppressed groups," concludes Jordan (1988, p. 32). From personal experience to awareness of oppression to leadership for social change; this is a clear example of experiential learning in action. I immediately want to know more about what motivates the women leaders at this camp. What vision do they have for tomorrow's women leaders? Do they always agree? How do they express differences? How do they apply their feminist beliefs in practice—both as feminist practices and experiential practices in facilitation?

Before turning to questions such as these, I want to emphasize the significance of the notion of social practices. The notion that we each choose certain social roles to adopt and learn is most often applied to explanations of the identities of men and women and their respective preferences for their actions and abilities in the outdoors (e.g., see Jordan, 1992; Nolan & Priest, 1993). This approach, sociologists like Bob Connell (1987) argue, misconstrues biological anatomy of male and female as the source of culturally constituted, or moulded, masculine and feminine behaviours. The so-called natural sex categories are expected to differentiate and naturalise the socially defined gender categories. In contrast, Connell presents gendered behaviour as ideas about gender that are practiced, and he proposes that we see gender identity as a practical accomplishment (Cornell, 1987, p. 76).[6]

The theme for this chapter, then, is that a socio-cultural approach to examining our practice in the outdoors contests the notion that anyone practices leadership—or feminism—as a generic role, abstracted from the cultural context and the influence of social structures. Rather than as single theoretical perspectives, leadership and feminism could productively be explored as sets of varied practices, employed to accomplish their political possibilities self-reflexively. The facilitation of social consciousness in both experiential processes and feminism take each person's and group's own experience as the starting point for unpacking the pack of privilege and social regulation (McIntosh, 1990; Warren & Rheingold, 1993).

Before I proceed with a closer look at what specific feminist beliefs might look like in practice in the outdoors, I want to examine the overriding theoretical perspective about outdoor leadership and group facilitation. Composite theories of outdoor leadership skills, competencies, and style choices articulate them as objective behaviours determined by principles affecting all people equally (e.g., Phipps, 1991; Priest & Chase, 1989; Swiderski, 1987). Theorists propose that all leaders employ objective knowledge and skills requiring rational and logical actions to guarantee the safety of their students. Some detail the procedure for exercising judgment on behalf of others (Ewert, 1988; Priest, 1988; Cain, 1991), a process which is elsewhere simply reduced to "the ability to understand, compare and decide between alternative forces" (Swiderski, 1987, p. 32). The danger of these conceptions of outdoor leadership is that they uncritically conflate authority with forms and degrees of the activity of decision making, that is, making either/or judgments on the basis of mutual exclusion. Hence, ability becomes power in the practice of making judgments and speaking for others. "Astuteness" is thought to determine the ability to make "correct" decisions guaranteeing safe risk taking (Priest & Baillie, 1987), but is astuteness an ability? A trait? What are correct decisions for the girls who have been encouraged to encompass each others' different backgrounds and life experiences in a social analysis at the Iowa Girls' Leadership Camp? How might astuteness allow for decisions to acknowledge cultural diversity? Surely alternate forces are not simply equal in impact, but must be interpreted through cultural lenses as value judgments privileging some at the expense of others.

Thinly veiled is the gendered, race-based organisation of the subjectivity of the leader, such that it is European, able-bodied, autonomous, objective, and rational men who are predisposed to make sound decisions and be natural leaders (Williams, 1993). Deb Jordan (1992) critiques the early trait theories of leadership for establishing the common expectation that good leaders are those who act rationally and objectively, in contrast to women who have historically been labelled irrational, emotional, subjective, and embodied. Although we know many exceptions to the norm, contends Jordan (1992), "many of us maintain a subtle, powerful belief in" it nevertheless (p. 61). Central to this chapter's concerns then, is the question of what moulds and shapes ideas such as astuteness as such powerful, outdoor leadership norms?

In the discussion to follow, four women outdoor leaders speak about their personal experiences. An explanation of the contribution of personal experience to the process of developing sound judgment is the crucial omission in the work of Priest and Chase (1989). While experience is at the centre of Freirian and Deweyan explanations of experiential learning and praxis, once leadership is dissected into its components and disassociated from social contexts, the constitution of the practice is invisible. In order for social change to occur, the cultural constitution of such practices as based in *someone's* lived experience must be made explicit. If decision making is personal, then, as it must be if a leader is to base his or her judgment on an assessment of past experiences, then it must be subjective by definition. Yet, leadership experience is treated in outdoor leadership writing as objective, abstract, and cumulative. Most outdoor leadership theorists ignore the contradiction in the positioning of the subject of the decision making outside the decision made (e.g., Langmuir, 1984; Mortlock, 1984; Priest, 1988; Priest & Chase, 1989). The person responsible is taken for granted as not relevant. The subjectivity of the leader as not relevant to specific situations is accomplished through the practice of abstracting that person with their own personal and social history from the context of the situation and its requisite decision.

A person's experience brings local, contextual, and tacit or embodied knowledge to any situation (Bannerji, 1991, p. 96). However, localised, incomplete, and partial knowledge is judged naive, illegitimate, and not common sense (Foucault, 1980, p. 82). In this context, the notion of experience as constitutive of knowledge is a key site for feminist interventions to highlight differences in women's experiences compared to men's and how knowledge is constructed as a result. Indeed, "the recent feminist movement began with the politics of the personal, challenging the unified, apparently ungendered individual . . . and suggesting that, in its gender blindness, liberal humanism masks structures of male privilege and domination" (Weedon, 1987, p. 41). Universalising masculine traits, such as the exercise of reason, logic, and objectivity as astuteness, and treating feminine traits, such as "nurturing, caring, community and wholeness" as part of the natural "closeness of women and nature," as do Nolan and Priest (1993), perpetuate the dualistic thinking of liberal humanism. Relations of domination continue to privilege the impartial, disembodied practices typified by the masculine outdoor leader.

Women in Outdoor Leadership

Interestingly, some research into women in outdoor leadership does bear out this epistemological critique. Jordan's 1991 study finds that students have role expectations that are gendered and concludes that this gender bias disadvantages women leaders. Attention is also being given to men and women in what is called traditional outdoor leadership to reframe this perspective such that gender identity amongst participants is taken into account by all leaders (Jordan, 1992; Joyce, 1988; Mitten, 1992; Miranda & Yerkes, 1982; Warren, 1990b). New workshops in women's leadership for women in the outdoors have produced models of feminist and interactive leadership (Bialeschki, 1991; Mitten, 1991, 1990, 1986; Warren, 1990a). So far, however, none of these writers calls for a feminist consciousness in all staff. Nevertheless, one such view has emerged within an Outward Bound community, following a study of the theoretical foundations of the Outward Bound movement, and recommending:

> First, that in making explicit the wisdom of its tradition, and in developing the implications for subsequent practice, Outward Bound should ensure that women of the community, past and present, have a voice. Second, that in undertaking critical social analysis, Outward Bound take heed of feminist critiques. Third, and last, that in cultivating the healthy growth and development of its tradition, Outward Bound ask whether it is a hospitable environment for participation of women at all levels of the organization, and if not, what changes might be made to become so. (Vokey, 1987, p. 51)

Perhaps significantly, all four women in my Canadian interviews had worked at the Canadian Outward Bound Wilderness School in their career. Using the interviews to ensure that "women of the community, past and present, have a voice" became important to me. According to a former woman program manager, the School has "made some great strides" toward the practical reality of feminist change since that critical document was published.

> As a community, we have begun some hard work on issues of sexist oppression. We have begun addressing "gender issues" on some courses, dependent largely on instructor capability. There is a strong lesbian community... [and] there are some men who are willing to take some risks in confronting sexism and supporting radical staff members. (Goldman, 1990, p. 21)

Ensuring That Women of the Community Have a Voice

This group of four Canadian women feel that to have a voice means to exercise self-representation from our own knowledge and experience, resisting hegemonic social definitions, such as our "shared cycles" (Nolan & Priest, 1993, p. 14). Terry, Diane, Moon, and I were four white, educated, able-bodied women, two lesbian, one straight, and one transidentified, between the ages of 32 and 37. Two women were in relationships, two women worked full-time, and one owned her own home. One of us had completed a master's degree, while the other three were working toward master's degrees, all in Education Theory at the same graduate school. I participated as a member of the research, including my comments and reflections for textual analysis, in order to preclude any pretext of impartiality. Self-representation to us encompasses talking to co-instructors and co-facilitators about being women in our particular[7] situation and being women leaders, making a plan to deal with gender and other social issues, challenging assumptions about women and social relations, calling inappropriate behaviour, questioning experiences, facilitating space for naming what just happened, learning with and from other women, knowing that how we want to represent ourselves is known—despite opposition, ostracism, and, at times, humiliation. Our collaboration gave us the rare opportunity to compare differences of experience and interpretation. As bell hooks (1988) writes, "to speak as an act of resistance is quite different than ordinary talk, or the personal confession that has no relation to coming into political awareness, to developing critical consciousness" (p. 14).

Practising a Process[8]

Terry's feminism is based on "pretty strong views around what women should be able to do and what women's rights should be." She sees herself as a "really strong, capable woman" and she is concerned that there be a safe and empowering space for other women finding, claiming, and developing their strength. "It's really, really wonderful for me to see women getting in touch with their strength," she explains. She wants them to see that they are not limited by gender roles.

> I think the best example of this was when I worked with a male instructor. We deliberately set out to destroy all those little gender myths . . . he taught cooking, and I taught portaging, and I carried the canoe when we taught portaging, and he carried the packs, and we would trade around each time. . . . And just continually role modelled that strength of women and that nurturing and supporting of men. The group really got into that; most of them identified that as the first time that they'd seen that.

Terry explains the importance of the outdoors as the context for such a practical self-reliance to her feminism. "I just love being up here in this incredibly beautiful wilderness environment. I like to share that with people. That's a real close-to-the-heart thing for me," she says. If a woman wants to experience "the sheer physicalness of it," then she must portage the heavy food packs or canoes for her travel in it. This means relying on her body and her own strength. To Terry, being capable and in control means she is responsible for her own safety. In her relationships with her co-instructors and her students she likes to plan what she will do at all times in a situation, while ensuring safety for others "to try new things" as her primary responsibility. The natural environment draws her to outdoor work even though its unpredictability seems to confront her desire for control.

Diane sees her feminism as reaction to injustice, after watching her mother cope with being virtually an independent parent, with no choice but to accept that responsibility within her marriage. Finding challenges, risks, and self-reliance is how Diane characterises her feminism. It is also part of her adventure base, the reason she instructs in the outdoors. " [I don't] put away my beliefs" during instructing, she says. "If someone's not being heard or issues are not being brought up—it depends on the group—[if there are] dynamics in the group of how women and men relate to each other," she says, "I'll bring it up" as an issue to process. She sees attention to process as the most important aspect of her work at Outward Bound and as a facilitator with college students; it is the foundation to experiential learning, self-understanding, *and* a feminist practice. She points to the politics of voice in exploring her own approach to facilitating change. "First thing is awakening, is awareness and awakening. And then you can name it. And *then* you can go into a process."

"One of the key things of my feminism," says Moon, "is to recognise that all relationships have power . . . I think we learn it as children. We learn who has power and who doesn't, and how to function within all those relationships. We learn it at such a deep level." This awareness has helped her uncover memories of the ways that power dominated her own family relationships, alienating and isolating her as a child. Similar to Diane, she spent her teenage years living on a farm. Being in the outdoors was a way to escape physical cruelty in her home to find solitude and healing. She was the only girl in her family and now feels lucky to have gone to a girls' church camp, where she learned that women could live with a freedom, playfulness, and abandon that her mother had not been able to express. She thinks now that she was affirmed and valued there for the first time in her life. Moon relates feminism to her work as an outdoor instructor in more than one way, but most important is the way it shapes her facilitation.

> When I work with a group and I'm in the out of doors [it's] something that helps me to understand my relationship to these people and the relationships of these people to each other. . . . When the group is bopping along and things are going on, there're some clear indications to me of where people are being silenced or . . . being dominated or dominating. It gives me an opportunity to go in there and challenge some of the assumptions that people are making. So, as an outdoor instructor, feminism is integral to my ability to understand what's going on in a group. . . . Feminism has assisted me in having better working relationships with my peers and in making me a better instructor.

My own articulation of a feminism that informs my instructing goes back to learning from my mother as well. Like Terry and Diane, I spent summers at a remote family cottage where I developed "the skills I needed to swim, paddle, navigate, cook on a fire, and sleep under the stars." From my mother's keen spirit of discovery I learned to cope with unexpected crises, such as coming across rattlesnakes. "There is a history of women who took their freedom in the outdoors for granted on both sides of my family." My paternal grandmother was also a strong figure in the family's century-old lodge in the next bay; she gave me my first fishing rod on my birthday. Being in the outdoors taught me to be active, unself-conscious, independent, and capable. Feminism continues to sustain the connection with other capable women for me. "The outdoors gives me that same feeling of the freedom to be who I am. Travelling and learning with other women re-creates an early affirmation [of freedom and autonomy for me], which does not exist when working with men" in the outdoors. Perhaps it is my independence that has created huge tensions for me in work situations.

> I was being undermined, verbally and interpersonally, by men who were supervisors and co workers . . . in public situations [like] staff meetings. I was being put down. I was . . . sometimes discredited by my male students until I proved myself [physically]. But I [always felt that I] couldn't be too hard back.

Embodying Contradictions

One of the most relevant topics which we discussed in our interviews was the representation of competence and how such competence is embodied in instructors and facilitators, with its connections to strength, technical dexterity, and physical endurance. I present two analyses of our learning here about femininity, strength and power and authority. We see physical ability as linked, for us, to appropriate body use and size, with links to body consciousness, autonomy, self-reliance, and understanding our gendered selves. It became apparent that our bodies, as gendered, were encoded with conflicting meanings in outdoor adventuring, in which it might seem self-evident that the social codes for femininity would have less value. And yet, each of us expressed a self-consciousness linked to our bodies. Terry is a Wen-do instructor,[9] but her worries are that her tall, lithe body may not appear to be capable of doing the work, or inspire confidence. "I am not very big, but I know I'm strong and I'm really proud of that strength." At the same time, she is concerned that perhaps she does not look strong. Although she also hopes that women do not see her as a superwoman (Warren, 1985), or too capable. "I don't know if other people, women in particular, see me as physically strong. I'm not very big, but I know I'm strong. . . . Maybe it's easier for them to say 'oh well, yeah, she can do it, but I can't.'"

Yet a large body, Moon finds, is not allowed value in a woman. She has come to terms with the contexts of preconceived social judgments, in light of what she experiences when she is in the city. "When I go to an Outward Bound meeting or a gathering, I don't look like most of the people there and I'm very self-conscious about that because the context has changed," she says. Students make assumptions about her capabilities and body size.

> I am a big woman. I don't fit the norm of the outdoor wilderness leader because my body shape is different. I carry a lot more weight around. But I also have a powerful body. Learning to love my body is really difficult. My feminism is a kind of resistance, I think, around female sexualization.
>
> What I have to battle with constantly with a group are assumptions on their part that I'm not qualified, because I'm heavy. That "You can't climb. You can't kayak. You're going to be dead weight because you're so big. You're going to slow us down." I have to battle that. So I just quietly go ahead and do what I do and disprove their assumptions about a big woman.
>
> The positive part of it is that I believe that I offer a role model to the students, particularly those students that come that are also big. They see that that's a power, that there are positive things to do and be. I have pride in my body and I use it well. And experience pleasure in it, joy in it. For many students that come that are big, that's not what they experience in their bodies. They experience shame. They experience fear that they're not going to be able to get a climb. I also think too that I role model for those students that are very fat phobic.

Like Moon, I link the affects of my gendered body culture to the context of sexual social relations, that is the sexualisation of the ideal woman in society. It seems like a contradiction to have to be worried about being objectified in the outdoors, when the maternal is the symbolic feminine, and when the skills which I am instructing or facilitating are supposedly generically practiced. Additionally, in contrast to my earlier years, I tend to feel more self-conscious as an adult, even when active and capable in the outdoors. In fact, in one instructing experience, I was told to be more careful about my clothing and energy around men students so that "they don't fall in love with [me]." I reflect on the reason that my shorts and T-shirt would appear to be any different than the running gear of any other woman staff member, and I wonder if "I was colluding in maintaining a heterosexual attractiveness, pursuing a fit and slim body, wanting to appear competent yet accommodating, not wanting to be labelled negative—too critical, too intense, too feminist—and, most of all, wanting to be liked and accepted into the community."

Diane feels that in contrast to her earlier days training as an outdoor instructor, she is now more in touch with her body. She comments on her body, uncomfortable about her "city fat" and body size "at this point," and mentions a recent work situation in corporate adventure training when she felt unusually self-conscious in front of one or two men participants. "What I always want to go back to is that absolute intensity of feeling in my body, and how good I felt," she says, remembering when she was strong, muscular, fit, and could "go anywhere" in the mountains. "Ohhhh yeah! And, you know—you could just *feel* your muscles!"

Feeling afraid while instructing also arose out of our analysis of body size, physical strength, and femininity. Though apparently contradictory, Terry summarises the feeling that haunts many women in the outdoors (see Millard, 1992):

> I really like Moon's analogy of looking over our shoulders all the time. That really hits home . . . I think I *do* look over my shoulder in the outdoors. [She tells a story of a woman who hid in the woods at the rock site until some drunk fishermen left the area.] That is there still. I wish it wasn't there, I wish it wasn't everywhere, and yet that's something that I am really aware of. . . . You know the potential is there. . . . And how is that [managed] when you are leading a group of Junior Girls, for instance, two female instructors and a group of Junior Girls?

The unpredictability of nature and the cultural behaviours which mean that "the potential" for harm to our students or/and ourselves is always there, causing a Wendo instructor to look over her shoulder "all the time," demand constant negotiation for us as women. We experience this in stark contrast to the notion that the outdoors is a place of freedom and autonomy.

Linked to this theme was not just fear of violence, but preparation for confrontation, which could or could not be physical, with men students. Challenges by men to our authority was a topic in each of our transcripts. Again, Terry's comments offer a synopsis:

One of the other issues around being female up here that I've noticed is the testing that goes on when there are two female instructors when there are males in the brigade; particularly, males that either think they're older or see themselves as more proficient in some way. I look pretty young for my age, and so it's not unusual to have a younger male think he's older than I am, and just a lot of subtle testing. In my case, it's certainly never been as extreme as, for instance, sexual harassment, although that's something that I certainly am aware of. It's just one of those nuisance things, in terms of "calling" behaviour. It's like working with adolescents and [saying] "Yes, you really have to do this" and "That's not acceptable." So it's an issue. I go in now expecting it. . . . If it does happen, I'm ready for it, in terms of having some ideas of how I'm going to deal with it. And perhaps my partner and I've talked about that beforehand. In fact, I would think, in most cases we have; [we've] decided how we're going to deal with it.

Conclusion

Miranda and Yerkes (1987) find that 90% of respondents among women leaders in the United States indicate that gender influences their work. The 1987 study finds that women leaders surveyed prefer to use the terms "facilitator" or "guide" rather than leader, which was not a specific issue in my conversations. However, it points to the aspect of the work which underwrites this chapter, which is to disengage the notion of outdoor leadership from an abstraction, a fixed, taken-for-granted disembodied authority. Instead of changing the term for the role of leader, we, the women in this study, change the terms of the relationship which inscribes the role, by whatever term, with codes of power. We set the terms to begin with our personal, partial, and contradictory selves. Moon puts it succinctly: "For me it's a question of how we use our power in relationships and groups in the out of doors or doing adventure education." We can never look at "our power" from a static, fixed and impersonal, that is, objective position, just as we cannot look at our selves from outside ourselves.

American women instructors indicate widely varied interpretations of "strategies to respond to the perceived influence" of gender on their work (Miranda & Yerkes, 1987, p. 19). The brief comments offered here give insight into the complexity of what exactly such strategies must contend with. When we set out to give ourselves "voice" or self-representation, we were attempting to construct ourselves as subjects and found that subjectivity is not necessarily coherent, uncomplicated, or in our own control. At times, the women in the study appear to feel strong and clear, perhaps seeing ourselves as positive, non-traditional role models; at other times, we appear to be hurt by judgments made by students or colleagues when our representations of difference may be understood as personal choice and personal deficit. I hear a woman who is tall and lean worry that she will appear too capable to her students, perhaps inhibiting other women. A Wen-Do instructor, she still worries about travelling the northern fishing routes alone with a group of teenaged girls. I hear a woman who knows she is large and powerful want to convey to others the joys of having pride in one's body, while she contends with students who assume that their instructor is fat and a liability to her group. I hear deeply felt experiences of resistance to norms of passivity and dependence, but also the confusion of finding oneself colluding in the construction of a socially acceptable identity. Decisions such as disclosing our sexual orientation—or even our feminism—in a small community, may not give us any *more* control over our self-representation, and, therefore, they still need to be constantly renegotiated.

It may be that physical capability and strength cannot contribute to deconstructing the many expressions of femininity which cause women to continue "looking over our shoulders all the time . . . in the outdoors," as Moon says. The performance of our skills is in fact a certain disciplining of our bodies in which are embedded the practices that define the competent outdoor instructor, already masculine, Eurocentric, and persuasively proven.

The lived realities of being a woman in the outdoors are expressed in terms of desire for "self": seeing women getting in touch with their strength, questioning what being a woman means, locating her sense of self, and finally "unpacking" her experience. I do not want to risk posing this as a model, an evolutionary design, or even a common aspect to other women's experiences. It emerges in our conversations as a way in which we each come to the practice of "unsettling" our own fixed and certain senses of "self," the practice of feminism. Our aim is always to understand how such shifting social senses of self serve to inhibit our abilities to make the social less limiting for women with whom we work.

Acknowledgements

I want to thank the three women who participated in the Canadian study, and note that they wanted to be known by their own names, not pseudonyms, so as not to make invisible their particular lived realities. I also want to thank the editor and an anonymous reviewer for their insightful and incisive editing of an earlier version of this article.

Endnotes

[1] This is an interview segment that has been edited for clarity for the purposes of this article. The original was recorded for and cited verbatim in an unpublished master's study (Bell, 1993).

[2] These academic disciplines include, first, sociology and cultural studies, second, critical education theory, and third, feminist theory, including epistemology (theory of knowledge) and poststructuralist analyses of identity.

[3] This chapter is not a research report, but rather presents a synthesis of selected themes in relation to current theoretical literature.

[4] By identity, I am not referring to a sense of self as personality, which is more of a psychological construct indicating a unified entity.

[5] Note the use of the terms social and cultural. Social refers to socially endorsed *patterns and routines* that become so embedded in our daily lives that they organise what we do when (such as how we do our banking, participate in rush hour traffic, or undertake pre-season staff training). Social patterns are sometimes called social structures, when they seem so concrete as to give us no option, such as global capitalism or mass media. Social categories are the stratifications which are produced by such structures, such as class, race, gender, and sexuality. Cultural refers to the *ideas* which inform social patterns in specific groups (such as the ideas and rituals which belong to an identity based on ethnicity or an affinity-based subculture). I also use the term sociocultural to refer to acknowledgement that while social structures operate on all of our lives, they do not do so in the same ways, depending on our cultural interpretations and meanings. There will be different cultural meanings about the way that sexual orientation structures social access to outdoor, experiential learning opportunities if one lives in a place in which the gay, lesbian, and bisexual community offering and seeking such experiences is visible or if one lives where members of this community are not visible.

[6] The shortcoming of social role theory is that individual difference is erased as behaviours are seen as immutable, even when it is acknowledged that roles are learned, as demonstrated by Nolan and Priest (1993) in their look at women-only outdoor programs. The solution to role difference is generally a call for androgyny (Knapp, 1985), that is further erasure of difference, which makes it impossible to conceive of social change. How are individual preferences evaluated to be imposed on society's tendencies? There is no adequate explanation for social relations and the structures which operate to privilege dominant interests *despite* our preferences, such as unemployment or homelessness. The promise of the concept of social practices is that it indicates cultural ideas inform skills that must be repeated in order to achieve the desired end, but which can effect different ends if practised differently. If "practice is of the moment" (Cornell, 1987, p. 141), then in the next moment, practices can be altered to accomplish different ends; the examples of fashion, bodily adornment, and depilation come to mind as gendered practices used disparately to convey shifting messages about gender (Bartky, 1990).

[7] While the *specificity of* womanness comes from (rather problematic) notions of a common feminine essence (Spelman, 1988), the *particularity of* a woman's experience locates her knowledge in her personal practices of her gender identity as it might intersect with other important social categories in her life, such as ethnicity, class, sexuality, creed, age, physical challenge, or literacy, among others (Rockhill, 1987a).

[8] The quotes included in the text are from transcripts of individual and group interviews, and are reproduced here verbatim. It is important to note that although discussed as clear topics here, the selected themes presented here were emergent in the research process. The original interview schedule focused on questions of training, certification, professional development, instructor competencies, and future goals. The interviewer did not mention the word feminism until a participant did; the topic was introduced as, "How has being a woman affected your work?"

[9] Wen-do is a form of self-defense for women.

References

Bannerji, H. (1991). But who speaks for us? Experience and agency in conventional feminist paradigms. In H. Bannerji, L. Carty, K. Dehli, S. Heald, & K. McKenna (Eds.), *Unsettling relations: The university as a site of feminist struggles* (pp. 67-107). Toronto: Women's Press.

Bartky, S. L. (1990). *Femininity and domination: Studies in the phenomenology of oppression.* New York: Routledge.

Bell, M. (1993). *Feminist outdoor leadership: Understandings of the complexities of feminist practice as women outdoor leaders.* Unpublished master's thesis, University of Toronto, Toronto, Canada.

Bialeschki, M. D. (1991, February). Women in leadership in the outdoors. Workshop presented to the American Camping Association Conference, Detroit, Michigan, USA.

Cain, K. (1991). Judgment and decision-making ability. In D. Cockrell (Ed.), *The wilderness educator: The Wilderness Education Association curriculum guide* (pp. 13-34). Merrillville, IN: ICS Books.

Connell, R. W. (1987). *Gender & power.* Stanford, CA: Stanford University Press.

Ewert, A. (1988). Decision making in the outdoor pursuits setting. *Journal of Environmental Education, 20*(1), 3-7.

Foucault, M. (1980). *Power/knowledge: Selected interviews and other writings 1972-1977.* New York: Pantheon.

Goldman, R. (1990). *A feminist analysis of the Outward Bound process.* Unpublished manuscript, University of Toronto, Toronto, Canada.

Hardin, J. (1979). *Outdoor/wilderness approaches to psychological education for women: A descriptive study.* Unpublished doctoral dissertation, University of Massachusetts, Amherst, USA. *Dissertation Abstracts International*, 1980, 40(08), Abstract No. 8004934.

hooks, b. (1988). *Talking back: Thinking feminist, thinking black.* Toronto, Canada: Between the Lines.

Jordan, D. (1992). Effective leadership for girls and women in outdoor recreation. *Journal of Physical Education, Recreation & Dance, 63*(2), 61-64.

Jordan, D. (1991). In the eye of the beholder: Perceptions of female and male outdoor leaders. *Leisure Studies, 10*(3), 235-245.

Jordan, D. (1988). To dream the possible dream: A leadership camp for young women in Iowa. *Camping Magazine, 60*(7), 30-32.

Joyce, M. (1988). Rocks & rivers, men & women: Learning from each other at Outward Bound. *Journal of COBWS Education, IV*(1), 22-25.

Knapp, C. E. (1985). Escaping the gender trap: The ultimate challenge for experiential educators. *Journal of Experiential Education, 8*(2), 16-19.

LaBastille, A. (1980). Rebecca Lawton: Crusader for whitewater. In *Women and wilderness* (pp. 224-236). San Francisco, CA: Sierra Club.

Langmuir, E. (1984). *Mountaincraft and leadership.* Edinburgh, Scotland: Scottish Sports Council and MLTB.

McIntosh, P. (1990). White privilege: Unpacking the invisible knapsack. *Independent School.* Winter.

Millard, L. (1992). Fear of falling. In R. da Silva (Ed.), *Leading out: Women climbers reaching for the top* (pp. 257-265). Seattle, WA: Seal Press.

Miranda, W., & Yerkes, R. (1987). Women outdoor leaders today. *Camping Magazine, 59*(4), 16-19.

Miranda, W., & Yerkes, R. (1982). The need for research in outdoor education programs for women. *Journal of Physical Education, Recreation & Dance , 53*(4), 82-85.

Mitten, D. (1992). Empowering girls and women in the outdoors. *Journal of Physical Education, Recreation & Dance , 63*(2), 56-60.

Mitten, D. (1991). Interactive leadership workshop. Presented to Woodswomen Leadership Training. Wilder Forest, Minnesota, USA. September 14-15.

Mitten, D. (1990). Leadership workshop. Presented to Women Outdoors New Zealand. Purangi River, New Zealand. April 3-4.

Mitten, D. (1986). *Meeting the unknown: Group dynamics in the wilderness.* Minneapolis, MN: Woodswomen.

Mortlock, C. (1984). *The adventure alternative.* Milnthorpe, England: Cicerone Press.

Nolan, T., & Priest, S. (1993). Outdoor programmes for women only? *Journal of Adventure Education and Outdoor Leadership, 10*(1), 14-17.

Phipps, M. (1991). Group dynamics in the outdoors: A model for teaching outdoor leaders. In D. Cockrell (Ed.), *The wilderness educator: The Wilderness Education Association curriculum guide* (pp. 35-64). Merrillville, IN: ICS Books.

Priest, S. (1988). The role of judgment, decision making and problem solving for outdoor leaders. *Journal of Experiential Education, 11*(3), 19-26.

Priest, S., & Baillie, R. (1987). Justifying the risk to others: The real razor's edge. *Journal of Experiential Education, 10*(1), 16-22.

Priest, S., & Chase, R. (1989). The conditional theory of outdoor leadership style: An exercise in flexibility. *Journal of Adventure Education, 6*(2), 10-17.

Rockhill, K. (1987a). Literacy as threat/desire: Longing to be SOMEBODY. In J. Gaskell & A. McLaren (Eds.), *Women and education: A Canadian perspective* (pp. 315-331). Calgary, Canada: Detselig.

Rockhill, K. (1987b). The chaos of subjectivity in the ordered halls of academe. *Canadian Women Studies, 8*(4), 12-17.

Spelman, E. V. (1988). *Inessential woman: Problems of exclusion in feminist thought.* Boston, MA: Beacon.

Swiderski, M. (1987). Soft and conceptual skills: The often overlooked components of outdoor leadership. *The Bradford Papers Annual, II*, 29-36.

Vokey, D. (1987). *Outward Bound: In search of foundations.* Unpublished master's thesis, Queen's University, Kingston, Canada.

Warren, K. (1990a). New directions for outdoor leadership: A feminist perspective. Workshop presented to Women Outdoors New Zealand, Christchurch, New Zealand. January 27.

Warren, K. (1990b). Women's outdoor adventures. In J. C. Miles & S. Priest (Eds.), *Adventure education* (pp. 410-417). State College, PA: Venture.

Warren, K. (1985). Women's outdoor adventures: Myth and reality. *Journal of Experiential Education, 8*(2), 10-14.

Warren, K., & Rheingold, A. (1993). Feminist pedagogy and experiential education: A critical look. *Journal of Experiential Education, 16*(3), 25-31.

Weedon, C. (1987). *Feminist practice & poststructuralist theory.* Oxford, England: Basil Blackwell.

Williams, L. (1993). The myths of adventure. *Journal of Adventure Education and Outdoor Leadership, 10*(1), 18.

Caring Voices

*Changes in women's rights change women's moral judgments,
seasoning mercy with justice by enabling women
to consider it moral to care not only for others but for themselves.*

Carol Gilligan

While on professional leave in 1990, I spent a month visiting outdoor experiential education programs in New Zealand. One of my goals was to understand how women outdoor professionals in another country were faring compared to North American women. I ended up meeting, staying with, and sharing stories and adventures with countless dynamic women during my time there.

Early in my trip, I spent a week at the Outdoor Pursuits Centre (OPC), often described to me as the "NOLS of New Zealand." My most poignant memory of the OPC was the huge "Hall of Fame" board prominently displayed in the main lodge. Of the several dozen names painted on the board, all were men. Each day I would read the names, wondering where the women were in the early history of the OPC. Had only men been instrumental in the success of the OPC?[1]

As my journey continued I was to find the answer to that question. I met women who had raised children at the center, caring for their babies so their partners could take time in the field to instruct OPC courses. I got a ride from a woman who spoke of handling logistics for many years so that the coast-to-coast trips, the arduous, long-term wilderness courses that were a hallmark of the OPC, would run smoothly. I stayed with a woman who shared her fond memories of the early days at the OPC, the struggles to buy real dishes so course participants would not have to eat from crude mess kits. Each woman I talked to who had been involved in the OPC spoke proudly of her role in creating an exceptional program and organization, and I knew from the intensity of their stories that the OPC would not be where it is today without their support and hard work.

I was struck by how the role of women in this outdoor organization was based on a caring relationship to others. It was heartwarming to uncover the stories of women who had lovingly shaped the early days of the OPC through their attention to the needs of spouses, children, and students. These women did not do these things because it was morally right; they did them because they cared. Some may consider the transfer of ethics from the domain of rational thought to a domain of caring as a radical idea. Yet it is precisely this infusion of feminist ethics into experiential education that has the potential for transformative social change.

Denise Mitten offers a compelling argument for the consideration of a feminist ethic of caring in experiential education. She postulates that the logical approach commonly used in the field of ethics, with its underlying reliance on principles, does not work for many women based on their experience in the world. Mitten explores an ethic based on relationship rather than reason. Constance Russell and Anne Bell extend the ethic of care to the field of environmental education. They show how educating from an ecofeminist perspective based on a politicized ethic of care can create a new vision of environmental education. In my chapter on the midwife teacher, I detail how experiential educators can assist in the birth of new ideas by guiding the learners while guarding the learning environment. I give specific examples of educational midwifery methods for practitioners to use with students. Finally, Karla Henderson describes spiritual experiences that many women have in their relationships with nature. She asserts that experiential educators must provide opportunities to nurture the human spirit.

The chapters in this section add immeasurably to the discourse about social change in experiential education. By looking at what it means to care—ethically, socially, and spiritually—the authors in this section advance new ideas about how our relationship to others, to ourselves, and to the natural world can transform experiential education as it is now practiced.

Endnote

[1] The OPC is not alone in its underrepresentation of women for recognitions or awards. I have encountered many organizations with a Hall of Fame or Founding Fathers plaque or room. The AEE's Kurt Hahn award, which has been given predominantly to men, is another example.

Reference

Gilligan, C. (1982). *In a different voice.* Cambridge, MA: Harvard University Press.

14

The Value of Feminist Ethics in Experiential Education Teaching and Leadership

Denise Mitten

In this chapter, I will examine what it means to have an ethic and what might be the meaning and the value of feminist ethics in experiential education teaching and leadership. I'd like professionals in experiential education to consider the value of incorporating feminist ethics into their work or to recognize the feminist ethics they do use and perhaps nurture them more. I want to open the door to discussing feminist ethics in experiential education, and I am not assuming in any way that this chapter will be a final answer.

I advocate that practitioners understand and define their personal ethics. Research in psychotherapy about professional client relationships has shown that moral and ethical issues impact professionals' work with clients (Lerman & Porter, 1990). I believe that moral and ethical issues also impact experiential education practitioners' work with clients. Experiential education practitioners' understanding of the implications of ethical decisions they may make in the field will help ensure that their decision making is in the best interest of their clients. By examining the compatibility of their own personal ethics with the ethical foundation of their employing organization, practitioners can also be more clear and confident about their decision making.

I do not underestimate the risk in examining ethics in experiential education. Jasper Hunt (1990), a prominent ethical theorist of experiential education, understands this risk when he observes that "few topics raise emotional hackles like topics involving ethics" (p. 23). Introducing the topic of feminism or feminist theory to the discussion of ethics is likely to elicit added reactions.

Ethics—What Are They?

Most definitions, including Webster's (1969), state that ethics is the philosophical study of morality. When people talk about their moral values, they are talking about their ethics. Noddings (1984) says that to behave ethically is to behave under the guidance of an acceptable and justifiable account of what it means to be moral. Noddings's definition implies an understanding of the question, What does it mean to be moral? Our morals, ethics, and values are typically shaped by our childhood experiences.[1] Noddings (1984) suggests that our ethical responses reflect our memories of both caring and being cared for.

When decisions are based on ethics, morals, or values, they cannot be empirically tested in a scientific manner. For example, the decision to let a youth leave a wilderness course early is an ethical decision. The decision the leader makes may be based on program policy. Program policy comes from the ethical perspective of the people who decided the policy. In this case, it may be policy that all youth complete the course, except in the case of personal health risk. That policy may exist because the organization's staff believes that it is best to finish what one starts, does not want to give refunds, or because the youth would have no other care options.

An example of leaders using their ethics in decision making involves a decision to let the group find a designated camp for the night. Consider a situation where two large men loudly arguing about the route are approached by a much smaller woman, the only one in the group who knows how to use a map and compass, who tries to intervene. The two men then turn their anger toward her, causing her to stop her attempts to help. The leaders can choose to intervene in a variety of ways or to stay out completely. The leaders' actions are guided by their ethics.

There is no way to empirically prove that one course of action is better than another course of action. While we may use empirical data to support our arguments, our responses are based on our ethical beliefs.

The language of ethics is complicated and cumbersome. As in many fields, it is useful to learn and be fluent in this language in order to gain acceptance and credibility. Therefore, I will define some terms that will be useful to this discussion.

- *Summum bonum* is the highest governing value or principle. In ethical decision making using moral reasoning, when deciding an ethical dilemma, one has to be sure to preserve this highest governing value. One example of *summum bonum* is telling the truth at all costs; another example would be saving a life at all costs.
- *Universalizability* is a condition that most ethicists in the dominant culture believe has to be met in order to have an ethic. In the dominant culture, a universalizable ethic means that if under conditions X, you are required to do A, then under conditions similar to X, you and others are also required to do A. In patriarchal ethics, this universality is achieved by having principles. To avoid the problem of humanness, these principles come from without, from a source larger than humans, such as the will of God in the Ten Commandments.
- *Relativism* means that actions may be ethically acceptable in one culture or at one time but not another.

- *Ethical subjectivism* occurs when ethical decisions are based on how a person feels at the moment when they make a decision. Similar circumstances might have different outcomes depending on how the person felt. Ethical subjectivism is avoided by having principles.

Feminist Ethics—What Are They?

A short description of feminist philosophy and its relationship to ethics will lay the groundwork in understanding feminist ethics. A definition of feminism may help set the stage. Lerman and Porter (1990) offer one definition of feminism as "egalitarianism, respect for the individual woman's dignity, and social activism" (p. 5).[2]

Exploration and implementation of feminist ethics has occurred in the field of feminist therapy. Emphasis has been placed on better understanding how the client/therapist relationship can truly benefit the client. Minimizing misuse of power and maintaining the dignity of the individual client is uppermost in feminist therapists' thinking about ethical practice. Feminist therapists believe that "a focus on ethics is a focus on power and how it is used and shared in the process and practices of therapy; it is about the meaning of ethical practice in the relationship of the therapist to her interpersonal world and her intrapsychic reality" (Lerman & Porter, 1990, p. 1). This focus includes recognizing the need for therapists to continually be aware of the power differential between client and therapist so that it will not be abused, and finding ways that the strong can protect the weaker without destroying their sense of dignity in the process.

Other aspects of feminist theory that have been important in shaping feminist ethics for feminist therapists are:

- that women's conflicts, poor self-esteem, and feeling of powerlessness are intimately related to the roles women hold in society
- that self-determination, autonomy, and equal status in society are essential ingredients in promoting women's health
- that the relationship between the therapist and client should promote egalitarianism between the two and foster the client's self-determination and autonomy
- that the feminist therapist be committed to social as well as individual change

(Lerman & Porter, 1990, p. 5)

I will present more information later in this chapter about how relationships are central to feminist ethics. While I do not think that there is one feminist ethic, I will explore the ethic of caring as described by Noddings (1984) as an example of an ethic with feminist considerations.

Ethics in Experiential Education

In his book, *Ethical Issues in Experiential Education*, Jasper Hunt (1990) gives a general perspective on ethical considerations in experiential education. Hunt describes common sources of ethics, using examples of outdoor and wilderness educational situations, to illustrate his points. His discussion of four different approaches to morality helps clarify the kind of thinking that can go into making ethical decisions, and it also introduces a rational ethical methodology. The ethical issues that Hunt raises, still current in experiential education, will come up in the course of most practitioners' work. These include risk-benefit analysis, informed consent, deception, secrecy, captive populations, sexual issues, environmental concerns, individual versus group benefit, students' rights, and paternalism (Hunt, 1990).

Hunt (1990) clearly illustrates that, as practitioners in the field of experiential education,

> We are left with a difficult tension. On the one hand, we must be able to make ethical judgments and on the other hand we are confronted by a subject [ethics] that is elusive by nature. Judgments must be made, yet the criteria and methods by which these judgments are made have never been agreed upon in the history of humankind. (p. 7)

Practitioners of experiential education, often in isolated places, are faced with challenging ethical decisions without having the opportunity to look up the answer in a professional ethics guide or to call another professional to get input and gain perspective.

Hunt (1990) begins his book by saying that "the study of ethics is the study of why one state of affairs is morally better or worse than another state of affairs" (p. 5). The approaches he describes concentrate for the most part on a hierarchical structure of moral reasoning. He focuses on the establishment of principles and that which can be logically derived from them. For ethical guidance, Hunt and many other ethicists in our dominant culture tell people to use principles set forth by Biblical sources, Plato, Aristotle, Kant, and John Stuart Mill. According to these ethicists, using principles keeps ethical decision making rational rather than emotional.

As I carefully read Hunt's book, I noticed that, except for Gilligan's statement that women use a different methodology in coming to ethical conclusions, he did not use the work of any women in his book. In fact, the method of moral reasoning that Hunt uses doesn't fit for me or many women (Gilligan, 1982). As I read Hunt's examples and the descriptions of the thought processes he employs, I realize that I tend to ask different questions, or to see the examples he uses from a very different perspective. His arguments follow a line of thought that leaves out a major issue for me, which is understanding the needs of the individual people I teach and guide in specific situations. This is a concern that is addressed from a feminist perspective.

Feminist Ethics in Experiential Education

As I have mentioned, learning some of the language in the ethics field is useful. However, the accepted language in any field can also be a cloak to keep other perspectives quiet. If a different paradigm does not fit within the accepted language, then that paradigm is often dismissed before it is considered. As I discuss feminist ethics in experiential education, I will use some traditional language of ethics as well as language not often used.

Other authors and ethicists offer different perspectives than the hierarchical picture of moral reasoning (Gilligan, 1982; Noddings, 1985; Lerman & Porter, 1990). Although these different perspectives or paradigms are often described in terms of feminine and masculine—women's ways and men's ways—it does not automatically follow that each individual woman uses a feminist ethic or that each individual man uses a patriarchal form of ethics.

Both Gilligan and Noddings argue that women tend to see ethical questions from a different perspective than reliance on principles. Women can certainly arrange principles hierarchically and derive conclusions logically. However, many women will see this process as peripheral or even alien to many problems of moral action. Women can and do give reasons for their acts, but their reasons, as Gilligan (1982) says, often point to feelings, needs, impressions, and a sense of personal ideals rather than to universal principles and their application. As a result of this approach, women have often been judged inferior to men in the moral domain:

> Faced with a hypothetical moral dilemma, women often ask for more information. We want to know more in order to form a picture more nearly resembling real moral situations. Ideally we need to talk to the participants, to see their eyes and facial expressions, to receive what they are feeling. Moral decisions are, after all, made in real situations; they are qualitatively different from the solution of geometry problems. (Noddings, 1990, p. 3)

Noddings (1984) suggests that the emphasis on a hierarchical picture of moral reasoning, such as using *summum bonum,* "gives ethics a contemporary, mathematical appearance, it also moves discussion beyond the sphere of actual human activity and the feeling that pervades such activity." She notes that:

> Careful philosophers recognize the difference between "pure" or logical reason and "practical" or moral reason. However, ethical argumentation has frequently proceeded as if it were governed by the logical necessity of geometry. One might say that ethics has been discussed largely in the language of the father: in principles and propositions, in terms such as justification, fairness and justice. (p. 1)

A major problem of traditional ethics in our dominant culture is their foundation of unquestioned, tacit principles. Using a patriarchal approach, "for an act to be a good act, it must have been made in accordance with some source of morality that transcends the limitations of a particular person or set of circumstances" (Hunt, 1990, p. 10). This rule often implies that the rules set forth by God in a patriarchal religion must be followed. If cultures use principles, then behavior is judged on the basis of how well people follow the rules, not on how they meet others morally. So, following rules takes on a higher degree of importance than does how people are actually treated. For example, if a rule states that the group members are to establish their own internal social order, and I see a person being harassed by another group member, as an instructor, do I intervene or do I let the group members work with the situation? One might say that I can address the harassment in a debriefing. If I do that, I am still allowing the harassment to take place. From what I know about people, I feel certain that it is not in a person's best interest to experience harassment without intervention, nor is it of value for others to witness harassment, even if it is addressed in a debriefing.

Hunt says that principles are required so that emotions are not used to settle ethical conflicts. However, principles, spoken or unspoken, can serve to separate human beings. Relying on principles for decision making enables people to treat other people differently, and can even lead to use of violence. Using an ethic based on hierarchical principles for moral guidance virtually ensures that groups will argue and fight to prove which principles are the right ones. For example, the Judeo-Christian ethic guides many people and cultures. Among groups that follow the Judeo-Christian ethic, different interpretations exist of what are the true guiding principles. Hence, many people have used ethical principles to justify war and genocide.

> One of the saddest features of the fighting, killing, and vandalism is that these deeds are so often done in the name of principle. When we establish a principle forbidding killing, we also establish principles describing the exceptions to the first principle. Supposing then, that we are moral (we are principled, are we not?), we may tear into others whose beliefs or behaviors differ from ours with the promise of ultimate vindication. This approach through law and principle is not the approach of the mother. It is the approach of the detached one, the father. (Noddings, 1984, p. 2)

Proponents of principles may deny the relativism of moral beliefs, yet principles change as people grow and learn. Professionals in the field of experiential education are inevitably engaged in criticizing and reconstructing our ethical principles in light of new experience. Many professionals in the field of experiential education use some guiding principles that differ from those they used a few years ago. One such shift in position pertains to participants' safety. For example, many practitioners now extend the concept of physical safety to emotional safety.[3] A more dramatic shift in principle took place in a program whose *summum bonum* or highest governing value was a particular educational goal. The change, which consisted of the establishing of a written policy that fatality on a trip is unacceptable, means that students' survival is now the highest governing principle. Therefore, the goal is to keep students alive, no matter at what cost to the educational goal.

My own career in experiential education began as a counselor at a Girl Scout camp. I realize now that there were feminist components in the organization's ethics and, in retrospect, I appreciate my exposure to them. When I worked for other programs, which were originally developed to teach boys to become better men, I realized that I looked at my practice differently than the male instructors did. I did not understand how they could do some of the things they did and they did not understand my questioning. For example, one program in the early 1970s included a component requiring the students to shoot a tied lamb and then butcher and eat it. I was adamant that the students would have a choice about whether they participated in any part of this activity. Offering a choice was in conflict with the program goal of the students learning experientially about where the meat they ate came from.

This example illustrates another important shift in experiential education thinking, that of "challenge by choice." Today, few organizations include killing mammals in their program and many programs profess a commitment to "challenge by choice." Using the program component of "challenge by choice," accomplishments for people become personal and contextual. This is a shift in thinking that the goal or principle is to "finish" the climb or to "finish" the ropes course in order to be successful. Increasing numbers of women leaders may have helped influence these changes.

The example also illustrates an ethical dilemma of *summum bonum*, or using the highest governing value or principle for a basis of decision making. Is it more important to teach where meat comes from, or to respect a person's choice not to kill animals? These are conflicting highest principles. I, as an instructor, and the program developers had different highest governing values. Or, more accurately, because I had a feminist ethic, I came from a totally different perspective.

Characteristics of a Feminist Ethic of Caring

I believe that a feminist ethic in experiential education would be an ethic based on relationship and that relationship is based on caring. Noddings (1984) calls this an ethic of caring. In an ethic of caring, one responds to another out of love or natural inclination. Ethical caring is more than natural caring, though. One also learns to care as well as learns to be cared for. Therefore, a caring ethic is reflective of one's caring experiences, both natural and learned. However, ethical caring is dependent on, not superior to, natural caring. An ethic built on caring is characteristically and essentially feminine—which is not to say that it cannot be practiced by men. An ethic of caring arises out of women's experience as women, just as a logical approach to ethical problems arises from the traditional masculine experience. This feminine approach is an alternative approach to matters of morality as prescribed by the traditional logical approach (Noddings, 1984).

In an ethic of caring, one steps into a world of relationship. While this is a feeling mode, it is not necessarily an emotional mode. It is a receptive mode where one is able to receive what-is-there as nearly as possible and without evaluation or assessment. Much of what goes on in a caring relationship is rational and thought out; however, the bottom line is that caring is fundamentally not rational. At the heart of this ethic is the maintenance of the caring relationship.

Describing what caring means in this sense is integral to understanding. Caring involves stepping out of one's own personal frame of reference into the other's, and it is characterized by a move away from self. One makes an internal commitment to promote another's well-being, and does this by learning about and understanding the other person.[4] In an ethic of caring, respect for diversity—including diversity of experiences—is implicit. Intimacy is achieved without annihilating differences. Noddings (1984) also says that since people are so different, there is no simple formula that describes what to teach our children about caring in order to care meaningfully for other people.

Another feminist therapist, Valle Kunnha (1990), affirms the need to understand others as well as to understand oppression, and she asserts that "discussion and development of the philosophy and practice of feminist therapy principles must directly address the concept of an integrated analysis of oppression" (p. 30). She argues that in order to be feminist, an ethic must acknowledge the interface of sexism with other forms of oppression such as age, gender, race, socioeconomic class, and affectional preference, and that the true testimony to ethical beliefs is ethical *action* based on those beliefs.

True caring and understanding of others can add in their personal empowerment. Using a feminist ethic in a therapeutic setting, Smith and Douglas (1990) describe empowerment as the process by which clients are encouraged to make their own decisions, honor their own feelings, and choose their own actions (p. 43). They see empowerment as an ethical imperative. Noddings (1984) agrees, though she makes an important distinction between promoting another's well-being and helping another grow and actualize. She takes issue with Milton Mayeroff's (1971) statement that "to care for another person, in the most significant sense, is to help him [sic] grow and actualize himself [sic]" (p. 1). Noddings says Mayeroff's definition misses the caring connection. She believes that making the other person's growth the most significant part of caring turns caring into a form of husbandry, rather than a compassionate act of being with another person. When cared about, people may grow and actualize, if they choose to. If a practitioner's belief is that the participant has to grow and change for the process of experiential education to be successful, then the practitioner has shifted from being present in the moment with the participant to being paternalistic. If practitioners have the participants' growth and actualization as their goal, then the participant's ability to choose growth and actualization has been undermined.

Practitioners in experiential education often want participants to achieve some level of actualization or to complete challenges. Practitioners interested in an ethic of care will avoid focusing too much on their own agenda for achievement. Doing so could be very uncaring, especially if the agenda is not appropriate for the other person or if the other person is not given the opportunity to find it in her or his own way, on her or his own timing. Being responsible to a participant requires that the person caring, the leader, must monitor her or his own self-interests while operating in the context of the relationship (Peterson, 1992). Professionals, using an ethic of caring, shape what they have to offer to fit the individual participant.

In feminist ethics, one is not guided by a god or principles outside oneself, but instead, by one's internal source of what is known to be true. The uniqueness of human encounters is thus preserved, because decisions are based on the subjective experience of those involved. In an ethic of caring, each person's picture of what it means to be a caring person guides her or his ethical decision making. The decisions people make depend on the nature and strength of their picture of their ideal. How "good" people perceive themselves to be is partly a function of esteem and partly a function of how others respond to and receive them. These others include parents, teachers, outdoor leaders, partners, friends, and the like. For example, if a young child learns that her parents love her unconditionally and have structured behavioral expectations of her, then that child will learn that a caring person loves unconditionally and has certain expectations of others' behaviors. Bronfenbrenner (1978) reports that children engaged in relationships based on an ethic of caring gain competence and flourish. They become able to master situations of greater and greater complexity through their cooperative participation with adults. The acceptance of the adult encourages the child to try. Likewise, in experiential education, it is important that participants are welcome, and that the participants believe they are seen by leaders as contributing people. If participants are in caring relationships with leaders, it follows then that the participants trust the leaders. Due to this trust, participants will often respond with interest to challenges offered by the leaders.

While an ethic of caring does not embody a set of absolute guiding moral principles, there is a universal aspect to the ethic of caring. This universal concept is that the caring attitude—being able to be cared for and being able to care about—is potentially accessible to everyone (Noddings, 1984). The caring attitude remains over time for all humans.[5]

The fundamental universality in the ethic of caring precludes relativism and subjectivism. In an ethic of caring, actions are contextual; however, an ethic constructed on caring is not a form of ethical subjectivism. Caring actions, while predictable in a global sense, will be unpredictable in detail. Ralph Waldo Emerson (1903) describes this as "the sort of behavior that is conditioned not by a host of narrow and rigidly defined principles but by a broad and loosely defined ethic that molds itself in situations and has a proper regard for human affections, weaknesses, and anxieties" (p. 45).

In an ethic of caring, the emphasis is not on the consequences of our acts, although these are not irrelevant, but rather on the pre-act consciousness of the one responsible. This is where morality is expressed. There are no principles or prescriptions to behavior, yet this ethic is not arbitrary and capricious. This is because actions are guided by the pre-act consciousness of the responsible ones. In experiential education this means that practitioners should strive to be conscious and deliberate about their behavior while remaining in caring relationships with their participants. Therefore, the actions of caring will be varied rather than rule-bound.

Lerman and Porter (1990) maintain the importance of pre-act consciousness and proactive behavior in feminist ethics. They are concerned that traditional ethical codes dating back to Hippocrates do not encourage positive action. They observe that most ethical codes are reactive rather than proactive in that the codes list the lowest common denominator of acceptable behaviors, rather than establish standards that establish and promote ethical behavior that reaches toward the optimum.

The internal guidance that shapes an ethic of caring is similar to what feminist psychologist Jean Shinoda Bolen (in Lee, 1994) describes as women learning to trust what women know and to trust that women know something about themselves. She suggests that living in a patriarchal world has shaped and limited women's perceptions of themselves, their self-esteem, and their actual potential. An essential feature of having access to one's internal guidance is to be able to have the space, freedom, and support to define one's experience and realize that "I am my own best expert."[6] As more women realize that they are their own best experts, the ethic of caring may become more pervasive in the dominant culture, to the point of becoming the norm for how people relate to each other in an ethical way.

Implications for Experiential Education Programming

Development of an ethical framework to use in experiential education programming is an important part of the work of experiential education professionals. Examining ethics helps practitioners become more perceptive and sensitive leaders. It helps practitioners better understand their impact on the people they serve. In fact, practitioners may find that as they examine experiential education under the guidance of an ethic of caring, they will see that the greatest obligation of experiential education educators is to nurture an ethical ideal of caring in students. If practitioners accept this even to a small degree, I then suggest they look at the congruency between the experiential education programming they are using and an ethic of caring. As practitioners look at certain program areas, it may be tempting to say, "Oh, yes, I do that." I am asking them to look deeply, to see if they are operating from their heart in a receptive mode. I am asking practitioners to be able to walk our talk.

Already an ethic of caring has guided some leaders in experiential education as they develop their programming components (Mitten, 1986; Lehmann, 1991; Warren, 1993). I mentioned earlier that one development in experiential education programming has been the concept that participants learn better if, in addition to being physically safe, they also feel emotionally safe. This concept has been extended by some programs to include a framework that helps participants feel spiritually safe as well. For many women's programs, this concept was a cornerstone from their conception. It is the leaders' job in their relationships with participants to create this safety framework.

A leader's ability to develop and maintain ethical caring relationships and to have this as the driving force behind programming is a crucial piece in the success of experiential education experience. Hardin's (1979) ground-breaking research on participants' outcomes on outdoor education courses showed that because participants look to leaders for direction and protection, the impact of the leaders' behavior on participants is powerful. Participants want to be in a caring relationship with the leaders. This is why leaders' goals and assumptions influence the experiences of the course participants so strongly.

While leaders usually cannot choose their participants, leaders can be prepared to meet their participants in a caring relationship. However, if the caring relationship is missing, the one who is supposed to benefit from caretaking may feel like an object. Participants become "cases" instead of people. In our culture, it is likely that most people have at some time experienced being treated like a "case" or object. To be talked at by people for whom we do not exist, to be treated as types instead of individuals, or to have strategies exercised on us, objectifies us (Noddings, 1984).

Practitioners in experiential education can also borrow from the work done by feminist therapists in the area of power. Feminist therapists have gone from thinking that they can erase power differences to acknowledging that they have to deal with them responsibly (Lerman & Porter, 1990). I think the same is true for many experiential education practitioners. It is important to understand that participants are dependent on leaders not only for the social needs of being welcomed and cared for but also for the physical needs of how to tie into a climb or where and how to make camp and food, for example. These needs are often viewed by participants as crucial to their survival. Traditionally, because of the nature of experiential education and the typically informal settings in which experiential educators work, including being outdoors and camping, the power difference between practitioners and participants has sometimes been minimized. Additionally, some of the participants are professionals, including doctors, lawyers, teachers, and such, some participants may have a significantly higher income than the experiential educators, and some youth participants may appear bold and worldly, again making it possible for practitioners to overlook the power differences between leaders and participants. However, most participants coming to an experiential education situation will come with increased feelings of insecurity which can accentuate the power difference that already exists between leaders and participants. In dependent relationships using an ethic of caring, the greater responsibility belongs to the leader. This includes maintaining what Peterson (1992) refers to as a professional boundary. When leaders maintain this professional boundary, participants are better able to attend to their own learning. If the boundary is blurred, participants may become the ones who are caring instead of the ones cared for. A blurred boundary may cause participants to try to do what they believe the leaders want and thus are distracted from their own learning.

The test of the leaders' caring is not wholly in how things turn out; the test lies primarily in how fully, in their actions and decisions, the leaders considered the participants' needs as well as all of the circumstances of the situation, including the leaders' personal beliefs and agendas (Noddings, 1984). The people whom practitioners teach are under their support, not their judgment. In an ethic of caring, judgment is replaced by acceptance and support.

Summary

Somewhere along my career, I realized that the difference between how I used certain components of experiential education and how some others used certain components of experiential education was a fundamental ethical difference. It was not just a difference in principles but a complete paradigm difference. At first, I attempted to understand, explain, and justify these differences I felt and saw; I could not satisfactorily do this. Later I learned to trust my internal knowledge, and for that I am grateful because it is from this place that I have learned more about an ethic of caring. I have decided that human love and caring are enough on which to base an ethic.

Nodding (1984) postulates that ethics in our dominant society are guided by Logos, the masculine spirit, whereas the more natural and perhaps stronger approach would be through Eros, the feminine spirit. I encourage practitioners in experiential education to look closely at this feminine spirit in both research and practice. Practitioners in experiential education care passionately about their participants and work. This commitment to care is the guide to an ethical ideal.

Endnotes

[1] Hunt and Noddings suggest that the terms "ethical" and "moral" can be used interchangeably and I agree with this clarification.

[2] I encourage readers not to misinterpret this statement. By having respect for the individual woman's dignity, it does not mean disrespect or no respect for anyone else's dignity.

[3] Helping participants to feel emotionally as well as physically safe on outdoor trips was a component in many women's programs since the 1970s. A future shift in this component may be to want students to be physically, emotionally, and spiritually safe on programs.

[4] An important component to the ethic of caring is practitioners' caring about themselves. Practitioners must understand what it means to be cared for and must also care for themselves before they can care for others.

[5] This is not to say that different cultures may not have different expressions of caring. These, too, are respected, as are cultures that may not ascribe to an ethic of caring.

[6] Jean Shinoda Bolen is probably most known for her book, *Goddess in Everywoman*, published in 1984. Since then, she has written a sequel equally important for the men's movement, called *God in Every Man*. She has also written *Ring of Power* and *Crossing to Avalon*.

References

Bronfenbrenner, U. (1978). Who needs parent education? *Teacher College Record, 79*, 773-774.

Emerson, R. (1903). Self-reliance. In *Essays*, (pp. 45-90). First Series Boston and New York: Houghton Mifflin.

Gilligan, C. (1982). *In a different voice*. Cambridge, MA: Harvard University Press.

Hardin, J. (1979). Outdoor/wilderness approaches to psychological education for women: A descriptive study. (Doctoral dissertation, University of Massachusetts). *Dissertation Abstracts International, 40*(8), 4466-A.

Hunt, J. (1990). *Ethical issues in experiential education*. Dubuque, IA: Kendall/Hunt.

Kanuha, V. (1990). The need for an integrated analysis of oppression in feminist therapy ethics. In H. Lerman & N. Porter (Eds.), *Feminist ethics in psychotherapy*. New York: Springer Publishing.

Lee, V. (1994). The eternal quest for the grail: An interview with Jean Shinoda Bolen. *Common Ground, 81*, 148-159,169.

Lehman, K. (1991). *Integrating ethics and leadership: A journey with Woodswomen*. Master's thesis, College of St. Catherine, St. Paul, MN.

Lerman, H., & Porter, N. (Eds.). (1990). *Feminist ethics in psychotherapy*. New York: Springer Publishing.

Mayeroff, M. (1971). *On caring*. New York: Harper & Row.

Mitten, D. (1986). Women's outdoor programs need a different philosophy. *The Bulletin of the Association of College Unions-International, 54*(5).

Noddings, N. (1984). *Caring: A feminine approach to ethics and moral education*. Berkeley, CA: University of California Press.

Peterson, M. (1992). *At personal risk*. New York: W. W. Norton.

Smith, A., & Douglas, M. (1990). Empowerment as an ethical imperative. In H. Lerman & N. Porter (Eds.), *Feminist ethics in psychotherapy*. New York: Springer Publishing.

Thatcher, V. (1969). *The new Webster encyclopedic dictionary of the English language*. Chicago, IL: Consolidated Book Publishers.

Warren, K. (1993). The midwife teacher: Engaging students in the experiential education process. *Journal of Experiential Education, 16*(1), 33-38.

15

A Politicized Ethic of Care: Environmental Education from an Ecofeminist Perspective

Constance L. Russell and Anne C. Bell

As doctoral students, environmental educators, and nature advocates, we are often torn between the highly abstract, cerebral requirements of academia and the immediate, emotionally charged demands of teaching and activism. Although not entirely or necessarily distinct, these realms of activity do not meet to challenge and enrich each other as often as they should. In our desire to bring them together, we find inspiration in Carol Gilligan's (1982) notion of an "ethic of care." It is an idea central to much North American ecofeminist theory, and in its focus on contexts, relationships, and felt sense of need and responsibility, it bears great promise, we believe, for rethinking approaches to environmental education. In this chapter, we briefly introduce ecofeminism and describe how an ecofeminist ethic informs our teaching and learning.

Ecofeminism: An Introduction

Ecofeminism is a theory and a movement which makes explicit the links between the oppression of women and the oppression of nature in patriarchal culture; an ethical position informed by ecofeminist thought and activism is one which resists these oppressions. Exactly what ecofeminism means, however, is debated. Many different interpretations of ecofeminism exist and, as Linda Vance (1993) asserts, each is "rooted in a particular intersection of race, class, geography, and conceptual orientation" (pp. 125-126). This diversity also reflects the multiple points from which ecofeminists have entered the movement. These include both academic and activist involvement in animal liberation, environmentalism, international development, peace activism, biotechnology, and genetic engineering, to name but a few.

Our particular "take" on ecofeminism resembles most closely that which Carolyn Merchant (1990) has called socialist ecofeminism. According to her typology, socialist ecofeminists advocate a reassessment of cultural and historical attitudes toward nature and consider an analysis of the systemic oppression of women and nature essential to social transformation. Through our involvement in conservation and animal welfare issues, we have become keenly aware of the need for such an analysis. In practice, this has meant coming to terms with a number of cherished and widespread beliefs. Central is the anthropocentric (human-centred) assumption that humans are not only different from but superior to the rest of nature, and, therefore, can and ought to dominate.

A strong influence in ecofeminism has been deep ecology, a primarily academic movement which posits anthropocentrism as the root cause of the environmental crisis. The pervasive belief that nature is solely a resource for human use, according to deep ecologists, has led to exploitive and destructive relationships with the non-human. Unlike deep ecologists, however, many ecofeminists give equal if not greater importance in their analyses to androcentrism (male-centredness) and suggest that it is primarily men, not women, who have contributed to environmental degradation. Ecofeminists are critical of deep ecology's masculinist bias and of its failure to address issues of gender. Janis Birkeland (1993) writes, for example, that it is "abstract, aloof, impersonal, and gender-blind, and it ignores power" (p. 29). She dismisses deep ecology's focus on anthropocentrism on the grounds that "our gendered behavioural programming runs far deeper, and it is much harder to change than are cerebral concepts such as anthropocentrism" (p. 43).

Concerns about Anthropocentrism

While we recognize the need to address these criticisms, in our own work we share deep ecology's preoccupation with anthropocentrism. In our experience, anthropocentrism is anything but a merely cerebral concept. Indeed, it is a bias so deeply ingrained and so consistently acted upon in Western societies that, for the most part, it passes entirely unnoticed, or, when acknowledged, is simply regarded as "natural." In schools, for example, anthropocentrism is manifest in the fact that the nonhuman rarely figures except as a backdrop to human affairs (or worse, as an object for dissection or other experiments). The implications of what is taught and learned about living, breathing, sensing nonhuman beings are never examined.

Even in forums where critical pedagogy[1] is the order of the day, challenges to human-centred teaching practices are seldom articulated; and when they are, they are often vehemently resisted. For example, while fellow graduate students have been more than willing to probe the classist, racist, and sexist underpinnings of their methods and beliefs about education, most are, at best, only politely tolerant of our concerns about anthropocentrism. At times, when we have attempted to express them, we have been accused of self-righteously hijacking the class agenda. We feel caught in a bind in this regard: when the agenda itself is so strikingly anthropocentric, how does one raise these issues without deviating from the matters at hand?

In allying ourselves with ecofeminism, we are reluctant to enter chicken-or-egg deliberations about which comes first, androcentrism or anthropocentrism, or for that matter, racism, classism, or heterosexism. Instead, we agree with those ecofeminists who suggest that such either/or thinking be avoided. This means that while the two of us may focus our efforts in one direction, we need to be cognizant of different but equally pressing concerns. Inevitably, forms of oppression intersect, overlap, and feed on each other. They share a common logic. Consequently, it is important, as Val Plumwood (1991) maintains, that ecofeminists aim not to "absorb or sacrifice" each other's critiques, but to "deepen and enrich" them (p. 22). Indeed, ecofeminists are better able to resist the colonizing and homogenizing projects of capitalism and patriarchy as part of a solidarity movement that honours a diversity of perspectives (Shiva, 1993a). It is precisely in our differences that we find comfort and strength.

Certainly feminism's "critical bite" has much to offer deep ecology. As Karen J. Warren (1990) points out:

> [The label *feminist*] serves as an important reminder that in contemporary sex-gendered, raced, classed, and naturist [i.e., anthropocentic] culture, an unlabelled position functions as a privileged and "unmarked" position. That is, without the addition of the word *feminist*, one presents environmental ethics as if it has no bias, including male-gender bias, which is just what ecofeminists deny: failure to notice the connections between the twin oppressions of women and nature *is* male-gender bias. (p. 144)

Understanding Ways of Knowing

Coming to grips with such underlying biases has been and continues to be a challenge for us. We have come to realize, for example, that it is no mere coincidence that men tend to hold the positions of power in environmental and animal welfare circles (Hessing, 1993; Simmons, 1992; Vance, 1993). We have also learned to identify as fundamentally patriarchal the prevailing arguments that can be brought to bear in the defense of nature. Within the conservation movement, for instance, advocacy increasingly takes the form of environmental assessments, cost-benefit analyses, minimum viable population estimates, G.I.S. mapping, and so on. The knowledge that counts, in other words, is based in science and economics. It is assumed to be quantifiable and objective, and, therefore, best able to influence rational decision-makers. In contrast, knowledge which is admittedly partial, impassioned, and subjective is deemed suitable primarily for swaying the uninformed public and for soliciting funds. In Plumwood's (1991) opinion, the privileging of rationalism within environmental discourse is evidence of a patriarchal bias that relies on the historical dualization of reason and emotion which parallels the dualization of masculine and feminine as well as culture and nature (p. 5).

In thus linking patriarchy to the privileging of science and economics, our intent is neither to blame the men or women who use such arguments, nor to suggest that abstraction, quantification, and reason are somehow foreign to "women's ways of knowing." First, most conservationists of our acquaintance, motivated by love and deep concern for the natural world, use whatever means are available to them to sway the powers that be. In their desperate bids to dismantle the Master's house, they wittingly or unwittingly resort to the Master's tools (Lorde, 1984); whether they thus choose wisely is an open question.

Second, in qualifying ways of knowing as "masculine" or "feminine," we do not wish to imply that they are universal or biologically determined. Carol Gilligan's research demonstrated that, in current North American society, males tend to make moral decisions based on abstract reasoning about an ethic of justice, whereas females' decisions tend to be more contextual and based on an ethic of care. Nevertheless, as Birkeland (1993, pp. 22-23) points out, men and women have the capacity to choose between values and behaviour patterns. Just as some women exhibit more "masculine" traits, likewise many men are openly caring, gentle, and nondominating. We believe that nurture, not nature, is the deciding factor.

Our quarrel is not with men or even with reason per se, but rather with the unwarranted pretence that logic and abstractions are a means to universal and objective knowledge, and that they therefore deserve to be privileged at the expense of other ways of knowing. We are not advocating the abolition of reason; rational arguments have their place. Reliance on this approach alone, however, is insufficient.

A Politicized Ethic of Care

Our purpose here, then, is to advocate instead a pedagogy which is rooted in a politicized ethic of care. Deane Curtin (1991) first coined the phrase and suggested that the addition of a "radical political agenda" to Gilligan's ethic of care was essential to the development of an ecofeminist ethic (p. 66). Otherwise, caring could become localized in scope and we might, for example, "care for the homeless only if our daughter or son happens to be homeless" (p. 66), without examining the structures that contribute to the problem and our own role in perpetuating these structures. For Curtin, then, it is important to distinguish between caring *about* versus caring *for*. In other words, it is often much easier to proclaim how one cares *about* an issue like the homeless; to move toward what Curtin characterizes as caring *for* requires that one not only become actively involved in a local manifestation of a particular problem, but that one also explore the complex sociopolitical contexts in which the problem is enmeshed.

In our own practice, educating from an ecofeminist perspective based in a politicized ethic of care means that we have a dual purpose: helping students identify and participate in issues that are locally important and personally meaningful while ensuring that they make connections between these issues and the "big picture." We also attempt to provide opportunities for students to develop relationships with, for example, the river that runs through their neighbourhood or the toad that lives in their backyard; we believe that caring for specific subjects often encourages activism aimed at ensuring that these new (or old) friends continue to prosper (Quinn, 1995).

Annette Greenall Gough (1990) makes a similar distinction based on prepositions when discussing approaches to environmental education: One can teach *about* the environment, *in* the environment, *for* the environment, or *with* the environment. Teaching *about* the environment typically takes place in classrooms where interactions with nonhuman nature are mediated through books, theories, and laboratory equipment. Such mainstream methods, we feel, are part of the problem. For example, we both completed a Master in Environmental Studies, where we learned about abstract ecological principles and conservation issues primarily within the confines of the built environment; had we not ourselves emphasized field work in independent studies and extracurricular activities, we could easily have graduated with minimal experience with the very creatures and communities we were being taught how to protect.

In contrast, teaching *in* the environment represents an implicit challenge to the widespread belief that "education is solely an indoor activity" (Orr, 1992, p. 87). Many of the traditional disciplines can be enriched by going outside. Possibilities include pond and snow studies in biology; field trips to local eskers and moraines in geography; walks through the community to determine the influence of natural areas in human settlement patterns for history class; and poetry readings while enjoying direct sensory access to the skies, trees, rivers, and wildlife that have inspired so many writers. While mere change of locale could constitute teaching *in* the environment, ideally the point is to create a learning experience where the subject matter is tangible and situated in time and place.

Greenall Gough suggests, however, that the concept can be pushed further to include teaching *in* the environment while actually teaching *about* environmental issues. The difference, essentially, lies in the attention brought to problems as opposed to mere facts; implicitly, when teaching *about* the environment, knowledge is understood to be for something other than its own sake. Learning *about* the environment *in* the environment can be a powerful experience indeed. It is one thing, for example, to read books and attend lectures about deforestation in the tropics. It is quite another to visit, as we both did during a field course, the Tabasco region in Mexico where the last few acres of uncut forest are cordoned off for protection, and where the rest of the landscape looks just like home—fields and pastures, dotted with the same cattle and the same tractors, with tiny woodlots at the sides or back of the farms. Indeed, what struck us most about that experience was the realization that the razing of forests we so feared and condemned in the tropics had already taken place in southern Ontario. It was an unforgettable lesson—one which has forever coloured our understanding not only of deforestation but also of who we are and where we live.

Teaching *for* the environment, as the preposition suggests, is more explicitly political and perhaps for this reason, relatively rare. Of course, what is often overlooked is that *all* education is political. For us, then, one of the greatest benefits of teaching *for* the environment is that it creates a space within which to draw attention to the politics implicit in all curriculum. If we choose, for example, to stress the "man versus nature" theme in Canadian literature, that choice is political. If we teach the principles of resource management without questioning the human/nature relationships implied by those very words, that choice is political, too. Teaching *for* the environment is deemed to be more political only because it openly challenges the biases of mainstream industrial society which normally pass unnoticed.

In teaching *for* the environment, we aim to help students understand the cultural and historical specificity of various attitudes and behaviours toward the nonhuman. It is not a case of indoctrinating students; quite the contrary, it requires bringing to their attention choices and possibilities which are otherwise hidden. At a recent workshop, for instance, where we introduced environmental activism as a topic for discussion, our goal was to help students identify the types of actions that they considered effective and with which they personally felt comfortable. Taking inspiration from an activity suggested to us by David Selby (1994), called, "Where do you draw the line?" (p. 16), we presented students with a variety of statements which they were to arrange and rank as "acceptable" or "unacceptable" (terms which the students themselves were left to define). The statements given out ranged from signing a petition, to writing letters of protest, to participating in a restoration project, to breaking into a laboratory to steal files. Students deliberated on their own for a few minutes, then shared their thoughts with a partner and, finally, with the entire class. In this way, they were able to reflect on the forms of activism most suited to their interests, personality, and code of ethics, and, at the same time, to understand that others might choose differently, and why.[2]

The last category, teaching *with* the environment, is also rare. According to Greenall Gough, teaching *with* implies fostering deep personal connections between the students and their particular life contexts. A good place to start is with the students themselves—with the ways in which they, as natural entities, respond, for instance, to light, heat, smells, sounds, and so on. Too seldom are we invited to pay attention in this way to our embodied connections with the rest of nature and, consequently, as Susan Griffin (1989) maintains, we tend to ignore "the evidence of our own experience" (p. 7). One of our goals as environmental educators is to challenge such devaluation of embodied knowledge and to celebrate with students the fact that we are living, breathing creatures with profound ties to the natural world.

To do so often means simply getting outside where opportunities arise or are created to engage with and wonder at the miraculous workings of life. For example, there is nothing quite like accompanying a bunch of rowdy teenagers on an "owl prowl." En route along a dark path in the woods, much giggling, guffawing, and general silliness occur until that first owl is enticed in by the imitations of its call; the ensuing silence is magical as each student strains to hear the hoots and squints in the darkness for a fleeting glimpse. Time stands still.

By fostering this sense of wonder, we can begin to develop an understanding for and appreciation of our connectedness to our home place. Thus, even when dealing with abstract concepts like extinction and extirpation, students are more likely to situate their knowledge in the experiences of their own lives. For example, we recently accompanied students from London, Ontario, on a hike to the Thames River which flows through their city. London is located at the northernmost limit of the eastern deciduous forest which in Ontario is known as "Carolinian Canada." Many non-human residents are unique to this part of the country, one being the hackberry tree whose bark is distinguished by thick, wavy, protruding ridges. Having students touch the bark, take notice of it, and then reflect on the challenges facing species trying to survive in this heavily developed part of Canada made the ensuing discussion on conservation and ecological restoration that much more compelling. We concur with Plumwood (1991) when she writes:

> Special relationship with, care for, or empathy with particular aspects of nature as experiences rather than with nature as abstraction are essential to provide a depth and type of concern that is not otherwise possible. Care and responsibility for particular animals, trees, and rivers that are known well, loved, and appropriately connected to the self are an important basis for acquiring a wider, more generalized concern. (p. 7)

Donna Haraway (1988) maintains that "situated knowledges are about communities, not about isolated individuals" (p. 590). And it is communities which are the basis of much ecofeminist activism (Salleh, 1993). Indeed, Vandana Shiva (1993b) asserts that much of what has been labelled environmentalism could just as easily be called activism for community (p. 99).

Working from the standpoint of a politicized ethic of care which includes both the human and nonhuman is a good place from which to start acknowledging and nurturing connections to community. Since encouraging relationships with life other than human is much neglected in mainstream education, it is here that we have chosen to turn much of our attention. Nature experience and natural history are essential in that regard. Unfortunately, natural history has fallen somewhat out of favour in environmental education circles, probably, as Mike Weilbacher (1993) has suggested, as a result of it having the lifeblood drained from it by practitioners who equated it with the memorization of the "encyclopedia of ecological esoterica" (pp. 5-6).

Nevertheless, natural history has an important role to play in learning with and teaching with nature and understanding what is happening in our own neighbourhoods. The "environment" is not somewhere out there, far away; it is part of our lives in an immediate and tangible way. Natural history, from this perspective, involves learning about the needs, quirks, and life histories of nonhuman members of the natural communities of which we are a part. It is about understanding the intimate relationship, for example, between monarch butterflies and milkweed and marvelling at the monarch's astonishing migratory feats. And it is the surprise of an explosive shower of seeds upon handling the ripe pods of a touch-me-not. Natural history is about the delight and satisfaction which come from close observation of and acquaintance with our many nonhuman neighbours throughout the seasons. It works against the sheer and willful inattention to the world around us which, as Mary Midgley (1989) points out, underlies many of the environmental problems we now face.

This customary inattention, alas, detracts from even the best-intentioned undertakings of environmental educators. For example, two different school boards with whom we have worked have actively promoted tree planting. Even though the initiative stemmed from an admirable idea, they were botched, in our opinion, by the fact that the saplings distributed and planted were non-indigenous Norway spruce. The cardinal rule of ecological restoration, which is to plant native species, was ignored. As a result, instead of learning about the importance of species that co-evolved within a natural community, students experienced first and foremost an exercise in hard physical labour unrelated to the broader environmental picture.

It is not enough simply to plant trees. It is not enough simply to have experiences, as John Dewey (1938) pointed out long ago. The contexts of our endeavours—not only ecological, but also cultural, political, and, of course, pedagogical—must be taken into account. To do so, we advocate starting where students are and from there, helping them discover and work toward building healthy relationships with their local communities—human and nonhuman. Moving beyond the lived experience of students to bring into consideration larger, even global, issues is the next essential step. The trick becomes entertaining a variety of concerns while avoiding the pitfalls of either reducing environmental education to "personal toilet training" (Gough, 1990, p. 66), or creating "ecologically concerned citizens who, armed with ecological myths, are willing to fight against environmental misdeeds of others but lack the knowledge and conviction of their own role in the environmental problems" (Gigliotti, 1990, p. 9). If environmental education is to be truly transformative, connections must be fostered in such a way that students have both the desire and the ability to become actively involved. Teaching from an ecofeminist perspective with the goal of developing in students a politicized ethic of care is, in our opinion, a sound beginning.

Endnotes

[1] Critical pedagogy is not easily defined since proponents take inspiration from a diverse range of critical theory. Nonetheless, Weiler (1992) has suggested that a common focal point is the critical examination of existing structures which "challenge dominant understandings

about education and schooling" (p. 5). Education which specifically addresses racism, classism, sexism, and heterosexism is an example of this type of approach.

[2] We do *not* advocate illegal activities in the classroom, but use examples of such activism to demonstrate what others have done; in our experience, most of the students are well aware of these activities because they are highly publicized and already have strong feelings about their appropriateness.

References

Birkeland, J. (1993). Ecofeminism: Linking theory and practice. In G. Gaard (Ed.), *Ecofeminism: Women, animals, nature*. Philadelphia, PA: Temple University Press.

Curtin, D. (1991). Toward an ecological ethic of care. *Hypatia, 6*(1), 60-74.

Dewey, J. (1938). *Experience and education*. New York: Collier.

Gigliotti, L. M. (1990). Environmental education: What went wrong? What can be done? *Journal of Environmental Education, 22*(1), 9-12.

Gilligan, C. (1982). *In a different voice*. Cambridge, MA: Harvard University Press.

Gough, N. (1990). Renewing our mythic links with nature: Some arts of becoming ecopolitical in curriculum work. *Curriculum Perspectives, 10*(2), 66-69.

Greenall Gough, A. (1990). Red and green: Two case studies in learning through ecopolitical action. *Curriculum Perspectives, 10*(2), 60-65.

Griffin, S. (1989). Split culture. In J. Plant (Ed.), *Healing the wounds: The promise of ecofeminism*. Philadelphia, PA: New Society Publishers.

Haraway, D. (1988). Situated knowledges: The privilege of partial perspectives. *Feminist Studies, 14*, 575-599.

Hessing, M. (1993). Women and sustainability: Ecofeminist perspectives. *Alternatives, 19*(4), 14-21.

Lorde, A. (1984). The Master's tools will never dismantle the Master's house. In *Sister outsider: Essays and speeches*. Trumansberg, NY: Crossing Press.

Merchant, C. (1990). Ecofeminism and feminist theory. In I. Diamond & G. F. Orenstein (Eds.), *Reweaving the world: The emergence of ecofeminism*. San Francisco, CA: Sierra Club.

Midgley, M. (1989). *Wisdom, information and wonder: What is knowledge for?* New York: Routledge.

Orr, D. W. (1992). *Ecological literacy: Education and the transition to a postmodern world*. Albany, NY: SUNY.

Plumwood, V. (1991). Nature, self, and gender: Feminism, environmental philosophy, and the critique of rationalism. *Hypatia, 6*(1), 3-27.

Quinn, M. (1995). Knowing your friends. *Pathways: Ontario Journal of Outdoor Education, 7*(6), 5-8.

Salleh, A. (1993). Class, race, and gender discourse in the ecofeminism/deep ecology debate. *Environmental Ethics, 15*, 225-244.

Selby, D. (1994). Humane education: The Ultima Thule of global education. *Green Teacher, 39*, 9-17.

Shiva, V. (1993a). *Monocultures of the mind: Perspectives on biodiversity and biotechnology*. New Jersey: Zed Books.

Shiva, V. (1993b). Homeless in the "global village." In M. Mies & V. Shiva (Eds.), *Ecofeminism*. New Jersey: Zed Books.

Simmons, P. (1992). The challenge of feminism. *The Ecologist, 22*(1), 2-3.

Vance, L. (1993). Ecofeminism and the politics of reality. In G. Gaard (Ed.), *Ecofeminism: Women, animals, nature.* Philadelphia, PA: Temple University Press.

Warren, K. J. (1990). The power and the promise of ecological feminism. *Environmental Ethics, 12,* 125-146.

Weilbacher, M. (1993). The renaissance of the naturalist. *Journal of Environmental Education, 25*(1), 4-7.

Weiler, K. (1992). Introduction. In K. Weiler & C. Mitchell (Eds.), *What schools can do: Critical pedagogy and practice.* Albany, NY: SUNY.

16

The Midwife Teacher: Engaging Students in the Experiential Education Process

Karen Warren

Uncritical advocates of experiential education might say that students are so naturally impelled into an absorbing experience that it just cannot help being richly educational. Yet, is creating a dramatic unknown enough to engage tentative participants in activities? I suggest that the skilled experiential educator must do more than create an activity and hope that students will embrace it with willingness. A major role of the teacher in the experiential education process is to provide a safe space for learning to occur and to encourage students to recognize the opportunities for growth available to them. How to create both safe and educationally nurturing programs is the focus of this chapter.

Teacher as Midwife

> Midwife teachers are the opposite of banker teachers. While the bankers deposit knowledge in the learner's head, the midwives draw it out. They assist the students in giving birth to their own ideas, in making their own tacit knowledge explicit and elaborating it. (Belenky, Clinchy, Goldberger, & Tarule, 1986, p. 217)

The experiential educator as midwife is a useful metaphor in describing how to engage students. This idea is based on the notion that the group or class collectively holds all the information, experience, or knowledge necessary for learning to occur. The role of the midwife instructor is similar to the traditional midwife, whose job is to guide and to guard birth (Willis, 1991). She/he assists in the birth of new ideas by: 1) drawing from the resources of the group of learners (*guiding*), and 2) securing the safety of the learning environment (*guarding*) (see Table 1).

While I have used a midwife teaching style to work with college students in experiential classroom settings or Hampshire College and Lesley College's National

Audubon Expedition Institute, applications of these ideas are possible with other student populations or in other classroom, outdoor, or community situations.

When acting as a midwife, the teacher creates a safe learning atmosphere, both physically and psychologically, where learners are not afraid to take risks. A student in an educationally safe space more fully bonds with the group, maintains self-esteem, and embraces all learning potentials. As Rogers (1969) points out, learning that is perceived as threatening is much more easily assimilated when the environment is safe.

Table 1
Parallels Between the Traditional Midwife and the Teacher Midwife

Traditional Midwife*	Experiential Educator Midwife
1. Provides a quality of care and uses available resources effectively	1. Manages logistics
2. Guards the birth environment	2. Guards the learning environment by using ground rules and naming fears
3. Displays an attitude of undiscriminating nurturance	3. Serves as nurturer
4. Does not place instruments between herself and the mother and baby	4. Establishes an accessible relationship with students
5. Is able to see the whole picture of the woman and child	5. Acknowledges commonalities and recognizes differences
6. Remains an apprentice to the birth process with a capability to cycle, change, and grow	6. Remains a learner/participant
7. Believes that women and babies are the true experts in giving birth and being born	7. Creates student-centered learning by using dialogic teaching, student decision making and real choices
8. Is not afraid of death, rather sees it as a natural process	8. Assists with closure

*(Adapted from Willis, 1991, and Solomon & McLean, 1991)

Methods of Educational Midwifery

The traditional midwife guides the pregnant woman along the journey toward birth, stepping aside when the mother's ability to give birth naturally occurs. The teacher midwife steps aside when the student is engaged in the learning process, yet continues to guard the learning environment to allow a blossoming of the student's curiosity and quest for knowledge. In a sense, the teacher vacillates between guiding the students to solve the barriers to learning they often encounter, and guarding the intensity and safety of their engagement.

Based on definition, the traditional midwife is with the mother and child at birth (Kramarae & Treichler, 1991); accordingly, the midwife experiential educator is with the student in their learning cycle—guiding and nurturing the experience from whatever role seems necessary at the time.

The following eight responsibilities are essential for teachers who hope to utilize methods of educational midwifery in experiential education settings.

1. Manage logistics

It is the job of the midwife teacher to handle logistics, to allow students full attention to the lessons possible in the situation. Shoddy logistical management often gives rise to focus on minutiae rather than substantive experiential learning. For example, if the experience I have chosen is a blindfold walk in a local woods to build group unity and awareness, certain logistical supports will enhance the event. If I ignore the transportation arrangements, forget the blindfolds, get lost because I'm not familiar with the environment, or neglect to tell the students what to wear, then I am detracting from the intended experience. Of course, I could use the "teachable moment" to transform my mistakes into something educational (i.e., that getting lost shows students' self-reliance). However, the original goals of the activity have been compromised. The activity had been chosen to glean results from the original intention of the experience, not its serendipitous transformation.

Equipment that doesn't work, areas that are unfamiliar to the instructor, and lack of suitable contingency plans all impede the smooth development of a learning experience. Experiential education has enough distracting moments without neglected logistical details adding to the chaos. Time is valuable in teaching; therefore, having the props, as well as a finely crafted progression of presentation, is imperative.

2. Guard the initial learning environment

The creation of safe space in teaching geared to using experiences cannot be underestimated. Both physical and emotional safety are imperative; they also don't just happen. In fact, they are often overlooked due to what I call the tyranny of experience. Often in their belief in the value of the activity and the subsequent follow-up, instructors bypass the initial psychological safety building in an effort to get right to the heart of the experience. Such instructors have students out swinging in the treetops before they are even comfortable in a group of their own peers.

Taking small incremental steps in culturing safe space pays tremendous dividends later on in the experience. Illustrative of this concept is a statement a student once made after a particularly intense class. She said that when there were unknowns in class, she did what was most familiar to her, but when she felt comfortable, she was able to branch into the unknown. She could risk only when she was emotionally protected.

Sometimes I'm tempted to pass over steps in the development of a safe space because it appears that the students are already at ease. I remind myself that adaptation to a situation is not the same as true engagement; and the appearance of comfort displayed by the group should be tempered by an awareness that, in our culture, people are often not taught to be responsible for their emotional safety.

The following methods are ways for an instructor to set the stage for enhanced student engagement in an experience. They are hallmarks of an educational midwifery process that values a psychological safety net.

a. Ground rule setting

Ground rules, or ways of relating to each other in class, provide a consistent set of operational standards for the learning community. Students help set these standards and are responsible for ensuring that they are upheld. I usually start a course by facilitating a brainstorm of the ground rules, so students have an initial sense of security they can control (see Table 2). An immense degree of trust and potential for risk taking emerges when the students voice to their peers how they envision the class can be made safer for them.

Table 2
Examples of Ground Rules Set by Students

- Confidentiality—whatever is said in the group stays within the membership.
- Each person has the freedom to say no or to pass.
- There is no right answer or way of doing something.
- Everything is negotiable.
- Use communication enhancers:
  - Allow people to say complete sentences without interruption.
  - Leave a pause after someone speaks to allow less vocal people a chance to enter the conversation.
  - Allow brief moments of silence to assimilate what a person has said.
- Use inclusive language whenever possible.
- Each person's experience is valid—you don't have to be politically correct.
- Disallow "put downs."
- Respect people's different backgrounds and learning styles.
- It's okay to listen and not have to talk.
- Speak only for yourself—use "I" statements.
- Stick to commitments made.
- Respect people's ideas and where they are on the "path."
- Both feelings and logical ideas are important.
- Be honest to both self and others.

---

b. Naming of fears

Each student carries to an experience a certain hesitancy which they sometimes are not able to share with the rest of the group. A common assumption, that if fears are ignored they will be dispelled, can invalidate the students' experience. Bringing fears to the awareness of the entire group is a method for diffusing their impact and an opportunity for the group to problem-solve solutions before they potentially occur.

At Hampshire College, we often use a game called "Fear in a Hat." Group members anonymously write a fear they have about the impending experience on a slip of paper which goes into a hat. A fear is then drawn from the hat by each student, who makes sure not to choose his/her own. Each person in succession then acts out the fear as if it were their own, ad libbing to clarify and truly "own" the fear. Other group members offer support for the person's fear and suggest ways to resolve it. The advantage of this exercise is that it allows people to voice fears anonymously and experience a compassionate response from the group. Many times the fears in the hat are similar and students express relief that others in the group share their apprehension.

3. Serve as Nurturer

Students come to classes with years of very intense schooling in ways that are far from experiential. They are bursting with hopes of an educational panacea, yet at the same time, they are caught by routinized constructs of learning. They are ineffective and clumsy in their attempts to question and dismantle stilted educational methods because they have been trained so well in what to expect from a class. They have been indoctrinated in what to give and receive, while being mystified about how much they can claim of their own learning and how much they must wait to be fed. Therefore, the teacher's first challenge is to deprogram the students' dependence on spooned learning and to inspire curiosity.

Many times I see experiential educators who are wary of structuring an experience, believing that rigidity and loss of creativity might result. Yet if structure is reframed as nurturing and respectful guidance, its value is obvious. Dewey (1938) maintains that guidance given by the teacher is an aid to freedom, not a restriction. So at those times when I expect the students to dive right into an exciting activity, yet they seem to be holding back, I should consider that they might need a compassionate boost.

The Foxfire program is an excellent example of this concept of educational midwifery. When the Foxfire staff started using cultural journalism, they didn't just cast students out into the mountains of Georgia to find a good story. Teachers nurtured students by instilling confidence and, with student input, set up a structured experience (Wigginton, 1986). Conducting an interview and writing a proper sentence were just a few of the skills students were taught to guide their endeavors. Foxfire teachers took the background and heritage students brought to the program and cultivated it to draw forth new skills and knowledge.

4. Establish Relationship

As any effective speaker knows, establishing a relationship with the audience is the foundation of a successful speech. The midwife teacher strives in the same vein to convey a sense of connection with the class so that trust and relationship sustain the budding learning collaboration. Because relevance of knowledge occurs when we can understand something in relationship to ourselves or the world, the model that the midwife teacher creates in building relationship is integral to constructing knowledge. Being vulnerable and accessible are primary avenues for the teacher to build relationship.

Analogous to the midwife, who places no instruments between herself and the mother and baby, is the midwife teacher who demonstrates no excessive reliance on power between themselves and the student. Their relationship is symbiotic with learning flowing in both directions. Power entrusted to the teacher in a midwifery model of education is based on "the concept of power as energy, capacity and potential rather than as domination" (Shrewsbury, 1987, p. 8).

5. Acknowledge Commonalities and Recognize Differences

When beginning a group experience, students need to feel that there are others like them ready to embark on the journey. Feeling alone is not conducive to engagement in an activity. Consequently, the midwife instructor's attention to discerning commonalities takes priority in the initial stages of the group. This is consistent with many group theorists' (Jensen, 1979; Weber, 1982) ideas about the cycle of group process.

"Common Ground" is a great exercise to achieve recognition of things potentially shared by group members. The group stands in a circle with one person in the center who invites anyone who, for example, was born on the East Coast, or likes avocados, or plays the guitar, etc., to come into the circle and share common ground. After a moment of acknowledgment, the game continues with a new person stepping to the center and announcing the next commonality. Students begin to recognize their connections with other group members and use the feelings of belonging as support to take risks in new situations.

As with commonalities, when teachers ignore diversity, they lose a vital opportunity to promote a climate of psychological safety in their classes. If students are assimilated into a narrowly defined view of identity (i.e., the dominant social paradigm), teachers disallow students who are different to occupy a central place in the learning community. Some differences are obvious, but others are hidden, in part, due to the melting pot mentality of many societies. It might be useful for teachers to consider that the composition of any group they work with might include students who have physical and learning disabilities, who are survivors of physical or sexual violence, who are gay/lesbian, whose subordinate religious or ethnic identity is not immediately obvious, or who have contact with some form of drug or alcohol abuse. Good midwife teachers cannot afford to imagine their classes as homogeneous units where they teach to a presumed common denominator.

After I've established some initial commonalities, I usually proceed with a "diversity rap." I name the significant differences that may be present in any group and state that each student brings the gift of their unique experience even if that difference is considered silent or taboo in this society. I don't single out or ask people to reveal any secrets, but I do acknowledge that we are vulnerable and have parts of ourselves that are difficult to share. I've had students tell me later on that the unconditional acceptance they experienced early in the group solidified their ability to participate as themselves.

6. Remain a Learner/Participant

Experiential education should not be something we do to our students. Passion must not be passé in teaching. Students benefit when they know what raises the teacher's creative energy level. Beidler (1986) suggests the best way to learn a new subject is to teach it.

The midwife experiential educator sees students as her/his primary teachers and listens to the students in order to retrieve the information essential to strengthen the teacher/learner synergy in the learning process.

While I'm not supposing that teachers will engage in each activity in the same manner as the students, teachers who model the joys and challenges of their own learning process can help students become comfortable with learning experientially. So if educators require students to read journal reflections, they should be prepared to share their own. If they use initiatives to build group unity, they should do the Trust Falls right along with the students.

7. Create Student-Centered Learning Experiences

Student-centered learning is essential to keep students passionately involved in the experiential education process. Students plunged into an experiential learning situation do not necessarily embrace a student-centered existence; it is through the conscious intention and skilled educational invitation of the midwife teacher that a student-centered milieu is created. Teachers, by virtue of their granted power of position, are continually engaged in guiding students to claim their own education (Rich, 1979). Similar to the traditional midwife who believes that the woman and baby innately understand birth, the midwife teacher respects the student's ability to discern a responsible learning path. Therefore, acting as a resource and facilitator of the student's chosen path is the role of the midwife teacher. Student responsibility for curriculum development is one way to achieve this (Warren, 1988), but there are other methods as well.

a. Dialogic teaching

The use of a dialogic technique, suggested by Freire (1984), is an excellent tool for the experiential educator. The teacher strives to engage the students by posing questions or problems to be solved, then cultures an interactive discussion rich in critical thinking. The goal is to decrease teacher "air time" and promote student involvement. As Shor (1986) points out, "dialogue is the art of intervention and the art of restraint, so that the verbal facility of a trained intellectual (the teacher) does not silence the verbal styles of unscholarly students" (p. 420). How experiential learning situations are processed could certainly be enhanced by the dialogic method. A midwife experiential educator can guide the reflection sessions by instigating a dialogue that builds on students' reactions to an experience, and then encourage students to engage in dialogic processing with each other.

b. Student-centered decision making

There are many decisions that teachers make out of habit that can be the domain of the learners. Everything, from when to take a break to what to learn, can be the responsibility of the students to decide in a course taught with attention to educational midwifery.

The midwife teacher guides the students by teaching them how to make decisions consensually, by assisting with the development of new roles in the use of consensus, and by pointing out where other forms of decision making might be better employed (Warren & Tippett, 1988). They guard the students' newborn flash of power to determine their own destiny by firmly facilitating through the problem parts in early attempts to reach consensus. The teacher does this by protecting the consensual process from being subtly subverted or railroaded, and by picking up advocacy roles the group forgets to assume.

c. Real choices

Student choice is at the heart of student-empowered learning. Pioneered by women's programs, the "okay to pass" option in an activity has gained popularity over the "only failure is not to try" philosophy that has been the foundation of many adventure-based programs in the past. This trend evolved as program staff started to realize that empowerment came more from choice than subtle coercion. Certainly work by Hunt (1990) on ethical considerations of experiential education advanced the notion that a participant's informed consent extended to all elements of experiential programming.

I remember the days in outdoor adventure programs when pressuring students off rappels or onto ropes courses because it was "good for them" was the norm. Students either caved in to the peer pressure or abdicated their power to the instructor's "Trust me." Fortunately, professional leaders have come to realize that giving learners the power to determine what will enhance their experience is an avenue of real growth. Students must have the ability to say "No" before they can ever strongly affirm a "Yes."

The midwife teacher fosters student choices that can be supported no matter which they choose. They work to remove the subtle consequences and implications of failure that exist when a student says "No" to an experience.

8. Assist with Closure

The teacher midwife's role in a group which is ending is to provide guidance that will ease the transition. Closure is difficult for students; it brings up other endings in their lives that might not have been satisfactorily resolved. Students have not been taught in our society to productively reconcile losses such as death, divorce, and the breakup of friendships, so these losses have echoes haunting the closing of every group (Tippett, 1988).

Teacher-assisted endings are critical. There is a psychological satisfaction in tying things up, in reaching conclusions, in making connections between things learned. Sloppy closure robs importance from what might have been a poignant experience. The teacher assists with termination primarily by providing a safe space for feelings to exit. It helps to inform groups that intense emotions will arise, that tasks will take longer, and that expectations individuals have of themselves and others may need to be temporarily scaled down. It behooves the instructor to provide more structure than might be apparent at this stage of group development, mainly because the group is so engaged in feelings of mourning and transformation that group members don't have the same ability to attend to group needs that they had earlier in their process. Their detachment is the challenge confronted by the midwife teacher who attempts to deliver them safely to the next life experience by effectively facilitating the closure of the present experience.

The following are closure ideas I have used in teaching situations:

- Set a distinct time for closure with the group. It may be difficult but attempt to find some time when everyone can be present. Be clear about the starting and ending time of the closing session. People leaving early profoundly discounts the value of designated closure, so it is important to get each group member to agree to a workable ending time.
- Have a ceremony. Graduations are one possibility. Rituals are another. In a Hampshire College Outdoor Leadership class, I copied quotes from Heider's (1986) *The Tao of Leadership* onto certificates that I presented as part of an ending ritual. Each quote represented the path I saw the student taking in becoming an outdoor leader.
- Have a give-away where students present gifts to each other to symbolize the connections they have developed with other group members. I had one class in which the students drew names and each brought their person something they had made which represented what that person had contributed to the group.
- Use affirmations, either written or verbal, as ways of ending. The midwife teacher should set the tone appropriate to the level of the group. On some outdoor trips I've led, the group ends by writing affirmations of each person that they gain support from in starting the next chapter of their life.
- Make time for evaluation. Creative evaluation allows students to synthesize meaning from their experience. It also indicates that their opinion is valued. I make it a point to let students know I prize the constructive feedback they give me.
- Pay attention to the value of metaphoric transitions. Students from a National Audubon Expedition Institute course I taught designed a group project where they elaborately drew their semester together on a huge piece

of paper and then convened outside to burn their collaborative work. Students took ashes away with them to symbolize the ending of their group as well as the transformative beginning of new opportunities.

Conclusion

An experiential educator has many opportunities to entice a student into learning activities. The attention given to promoting engagement enriches the ultimate learning of the student. Ignoring the element of emotional safety may cause incomplete immersion in an experience and an eventual loss of learning potential.

Most of the methods of engagement detailed in this chapter can be construed as simply good teaching, not just effective experiential education. Yet since the power of experience intensifies with the degree of involvement of the learner, methods to create more profound immersion levels can particularly benefit experiential educators.

Exploring the metaphor of the teacher as a midwife who guides and guards the learning environment may assist experiential educators in developing means to amplify learning. As it is based on a foundation of respect for what the student brings to any experience, like traditional midwifery, this style can be seen as holistic and empowering.

Endnote

This chapter was originally published in the 1993 *Journal of Experiential Education*, *16*(1), 33-38.

References

Beidler, P. (1986). A turn down the harbor. In R. Kraft & J. Kielsmeier (Eds.), *Experiential education and the schools* (pp. 118-126). Boulder, CO: Association for Experiential Education.

Belenky, M. F., Clinchy, B. M., Goldberger, N. R., & Tarule, J. M. (1986). *Women's ways of knowing*. New York: Basic Books.

Dewey, J. (1938). *Experience and education*. New York: Collier.

Freire, P. (1984). *Pedagogy of the oppressed*. New York: Continuum.

Heider, J. (1986). *The tao of leadership*. New York: Bantam.

Horwood, B. (1986). Are good teachers born or made?: A Canadian attempt at teacher midwifery. In R. Kraft & J. Kielsmeier (Eds.), *Experiential education and the schools* (pp. 331-333). Boulder, CO: Association for Experiential Education.

Hunt, J. (1990). *Ethical issues in experiential education*. Dubuque, IA: Kendall/Hunt.

Jensen, M. (1979). Application of small group theory to adventure programs. *Journal of Experiential Education*, *2*(2), 39-42.

Kramarae, C., & Treichler, P. (1991). *Feminist dictionary*. Champaign, IL: University of Illinois Press.

Lazarus, R. S., & Launier, R. (1978). Stress-related transactions between person and environment. *Perspectives in Interactional Psychology*, 287-327.

Rich, A. (1979). *On lies, secrets, and silence.* New York: W. W. Norton.

Rogers, C. (1969). *Freedom to learn.* Columbus, OH: Charles E. Merrill.

Shor, I. (1986). Equality is excellence: Transforming teacher education and the learning process. *Harvard Educational Review, 56*(4), 406-422.

Shrewsbury, C. (1987). What is feminist pedagogy? *Women's Studies Quarterly, XV*(3 & 4), 6-14.

Solomon, N. K., & McLean, M. (1991). The traditional midwife. *Midwifery Today, 19,* 30-32.

Tippett, S. (1988). *Small group development.* Unpublished manuscript.

Warren, K. (1988). The student directed classroom: A model for teaching experiential education theory. *Journal of Experiential Education, 11*(1), 4-9.

Warren, K., & Tippett, S. (1988). Teaching consensus decision making. *Journal of Experiential Education, 11*(3), 38-39.

Weber, R. (1982). The group: A cycle from birth to death. In *NLT reading book for human relations training.* National Training Laboratories Institute.

Wigginton, E. (1985). *Sometimes a shining moment: The Foxfire experience.* New York: Anchor Press/Doubleday.

Willis, S. (1991). The traditional midwife. *Midwifery Today, 19,* 28-30.

17

Women and the Outdoors: Toward Spiritual Empowerment

Karla A. Henderson

Many people today feel a spiritual impoverishment. Some women and men are out of touch with the aspects that money cannot buy, such as their way of being in the world. Spiritual enrichment is difficult with the pressure to consume and behave in a world that has often alienated us, as women, from experiencing ourselves in the natural world. When driven by external factors rather than internal beliefs and values, life has little meaning. Perhaps these reasons explain why many women today are seeking to find a spiritual inclusion through their involvement in the natural world. Sometimes it means planning a weekend get-away; other times it means stopping for a minute and watching the birds at a feeder or the squirrels play in the backyard. Many of us seek empowerment in our experiences in the outdoors.

I would like to describe the spiritual experiences that many women have had in their relationships with nature. I am not suggesting that men do not have similar experiences, but I want to examine how women living in a gendered society have realized spiritual empowerment through their inclusion in the natural world. I will examine some of the pervasive meanings that are associated with women as they have found spiritual empowerment through the outdoors. I will also examine specifically women's connections with the outdoors, women's experience with earth religions, ecofeminism and outdoor activism, and the implications of spirituality for outdoor experiential education. I am writing from my own experience, but I draw on the personal conversations with and the writings of other women who have described the significance of the outdoors and their spirituality. Susan Griffin (1978) summed up my feelings more poetically when she wrote:

> We know ourselves to be made from this earth. We know this earth is made from our bodies. For we see ourselves. And we are nature. We are nature seeing nature. We are nature with a concept of nature . . . all that I know

193

speaks to me through this earth and I long to tell you, you who are earth too, and listen as *we speak to each other of what we know: the light is in us.* (Prologue)

Defining and Finding Spirituality

For me, spirituality is manifested in relationships—with a higher being or beings, with one another, with nature, and within ourselves. A quest for self-knowledge and meaning in life results in feelings of inclusion. Through spirituality, I recognize a power greater than myself and a connectedness to others. I often find proof of a power greater than me through the awesome majesty of nature. This spirituality involves a sense of mystery about the world that exceeds my analysis or understanding. Spirituality is like the wind or one's breathing—you can't see it but you can feel it and be moved by it. No one single viewpoint about spirituality exists, but the door is open for many ways to experience spirituality as linked to women's involvement in the outdoors.

A variety of interpretations about spirituality and the outdoors occur. These interpretations are not due to biology, but are created culturally within a patriarchal society. For example, almost all women are socialized toward the view that "man" has dominion over nature; some women have resisted this socialization by becoming environmentally active, espousing a philosophy of ecofeminism, and developing a spirituality based on intuitive values and a relationship with nature. Other women have sought to define themselves by the activities they undertake in the outdoors. Many women, however, have described spirituality and the natural world by noting the concern for caring not controlling, harmony not mastery, humility not arrogance, and appreciation not acquisitiveness (e.g., Anderson, 1991; Merchant, 1990).

Many females have trouble speaking about the spirituality surrounding their attitudes and experiences in the outdoors because they have not had a chance to articulate these experiences. Naming or describing experiences is a power that shapes the reality, interests, and goals of the one doing the naming (Gray, 1988). Thus, when women are given an opportunity to articulate their experiences by sharing with others through written or spoken words, their experiences are made visible and they become empowered. Many women are seeking opportunities to name and talk about their experiences with nature. One of the reasons why *Women Who Run with the Wolves* (Estes, 1992), a book about myths and stories of the wild woman archetype, is so popular may be that for many women these stories represent what they have been unable to articulate in the past because of the invisibility of their voices.

Women have always been a part of (not apart from) nature and involved with the outdoors, but their efforts often have been invisible. For example, some of the early exploration of the American west and the Canadian Rockies was done by women. Outdoor activities for females at this time were spearheaded by middle- and upper-class women determined to break from their gendered roles. Women found the values of activities such as mountaineering, canoeing, and exploring to symbolically represent freedom from traditional Victorian roles and a move toward independence and equality (Bialeschki, 1990). Women commonly participated in outdoor activities, but were often obscured in the literature by the exploits of male colleagues, by their relegation to a helpmate role, or by the achievements being questioned or trivialized (LaBastille, 1980; Lynch, 1987). For example, a 1905 ascent of Mt. Ranier had 112 ascent members—46 of whom were women (Kaufman, 1986). One year after the Alpine Club of Canada was formed in 1906, a third of its members were women and within a decade, that percentage had risen to nearly half (Smith, 1989). Historically, women have been invisible in outdoor pursuits and inaccurately depicted because of the incompatibility between traditional perceptions about women's roles and their participation in outdoor activities. Their stories, further, have not been told in the same way that men's stories have been told. This exclusion of women's voices in the outdoors historically, and today, has resulted in a continuing circle of exclusion in other aspects of life.

Sharing and empowerment, however, are more than simply talking or writing historically about the importance of outdoor experiences for women. They involve living our personal lives and talking "from" the experiences and connections that we have with the outdoors, with one another, and/or with higher beings. Empowerment involves getting in touch with the feelings that emerge about meaningful outdoor encounters and how they influence each of us every day of our lives as well as how these experiences influence other women. To realize that many of us have these "peak" and these "day to day" experiences related to our connections to nature is empowering. An understanding of their spiritual value helps us to develop strategies to make experiences with nature an important aspect of our lives.

Clarissa Pinkola Estes (1992) recently illustrated popular views about the relationship and connection between nature and women. She suggested that many women see the world through eyes that focus on aspects of the environment:

> For some women, this vitalizing "taste of the wild" . . . comes through the vision; through sights of great beauty. I have felt her when I see what we call in the woodlands a Jesus-God sunset. I have felt her move in me from seeing the fishermen come up from the lake at dusk with lanterns lit, and also from seeing my newborn baby's toes all lined up like a row of sweet corn. We see her where we see her, which is everywhere. (p. 7)

The Connections between Spirituality and the Outdoors for Women

Many spiritual connections exist between women and the outdoors. Some researchers suggest that female ways of being may result in different experiences for females than males (e.g., Belenky, Clinchy, Goldberger, & Tarule, 1986; Gilligan, 1982). The reasons for some of these differences may be linked to the biological aspects of women's lives with monthly cycles and the ability to reproduce. In addition, culturally women's ways of being are associated with relationships and connections rather than with justice and rights; thus, women more often than men, are attuned to voices of nature and moments of mystical union in the outdoors as authors such as Estes (1992), Griffin (1978), and Gray (1988) have suggested. Further, Ynestra King (1991) suggested that by virtue of their close relationship to nature, women are more likely than men to care about nature and do something about their caring.

The connections between women and the outdoors are depicted in several ways. Clare Simpson (1991), for example, described the journey and not the quest, that epitomizes outdoor trips for a majority of women. She suggested that women do not participate in outdoor experiences for the goal or product (i.e., to climb a mountain) but because of the process of challenging and experiencing themselves in and connected to the natural world. This excerpt from the poem "Fire" by Joy Harjo (1978), a Creek Indian, describes in another way this journey of connection and inclusion:

> *a woman can't survive*
> *by her own breath*
> > *alone*
> *she must know*
> *the voices of mountains*
> *she must recognize*
> *the foreverness of blue sky*
> *she must flow*
> *with the elusive*
> *bodies*
> *of night wind women*
> *who will take her into*
> *her own self*

Outdoor experiences for women may also be the response of some women to resisting gender expectations so they can get in touch with their "true" self. Many of us spend our lives taking care of others; going to the outdoors offers an opportunity to remove those ascribed roles and find the "wild" self that sometimes is covered up with gender expectations. In research about women's involvement in outdoor recreation activities, Rita Yerkes and Wilma Miranda (1985) suggested that many women have found the value, both consciously and unconsciously, of shedding socially assigned roles and finding a spiritual self in experiences with nature. In nature, conformity to traditional female roles is not required. In the outdoors, women often discover aspects of themselves that they did not know existed prior to challenging themselves in this environment. Further, as Barbara McDonald and Richard Schreyer (1991) suggested, many people may not be consciously seeking a spiritual experience, but may encounter it unintentionally. Martha Reben (1963) described her experience in this way:

> I sat alone before my campfire one evening, watching as the sunset colors deepened to purple, the sky slowly darkened, and the stars came out. . . . All at once, the silence and the solitude were touched by wild music, thin as air, the faraway gabbling of geese flying at night. Presently I caught sight of them as they streamed across the face of the moon. . . . and suddenly I saw in one of those rare moments of insight, what it means to be wild and free . . . a forgotten freedom we must all once have shared with other wild things, which only they and the wilderness can still recall to us, so that life becomes again, for a time, the wonderful, sometimes frightening, but fiercely joyous adventure it was intended to be. ("Night Song")

Through a number of years of leading trips for Woodswomen, a well-known, Midwestern-based, outdoor organization, Denise Mitten (1992) concluded that concern for connections with nature, as well as with others, through group-centered values is a common description of female ways of being in the outdoors. On one level, the outdoors can provide an escape from roles and responsibilities. It has also provided me, for example, with a way to become more in touch with the importance of others in my life. By sharing outdoor experiences and learning with others who have similar values, I validate my own feelings. The creation of connections for women through the outdoors reinforces the spirituality of caring for self, for others, and for the natural world.

Several contradictions about the connections between females and the outdoors are also worth mentioning. For example, although women are attuned to nature, they are also conditioned to fear it. "Goldilocks and the Three Bears" and "Red Riding Hood" with the Big Bad Wolf are children's stories that socialize a negative and sometimes frightful message about girls and nature. The fears generated in women due to the socialization from these stories, as well as the rising violence in society, may constrain the possible positive values that might be associated with the outdoors. In addition, although the perception exists of the earth as mother, the woman as wild and untamable also comes forward. Although time and space do not allow for a complete analysis of these contradictions, Carolyn Merchant (1980) has written eloquently about them in her book, *The Death of Nature*. The empowering potential must be acknowledged in understanding women's connections with the natural world.

Women's Spirituality and Earth Religions

Some women find spiritual empowerment through alternative perspectives related to encounters with nature. Elizabeth Gray (1988) suggested that most women are concerned with the welfare of the planet. Although the Judeo-Christian ethic works well for some people, much can be learned from other perspectives that include aspects of the natural world. Some "new age" philosophies, Eastern religions, and Native American spiritualities are closely tied to the outdoors and relationships between people. Eastern religions, for example, offer philosophies that promote self-restraint and moderation with a realization that our world has limits and that we are all in this "limited" world together (Dustin, 1984). Similarly, Native American spirituality, although as varied as are native peoples, shares a common world view of cosmic harmony, an emphasis on experiencing powers and visions directly, and the importance of the life-and-death cycle.

Women's values about nature have also resulted in the emergence of spirituality and religions associated with female ways of being and the earth. Religious beliefs intersect with spirituality and environmental ethics in Goddess and earth religions. According to Starhawk (1982), the rebirth of earth religions, which are not solely the property of females but are attractive to many women who can no longer relate to popular religions, "is a part of a broad movement that challenges domination—that seeks to connect with the root, the heart, the sources of life by changing our present relationships" (p. xiii). These religions often have evolved because of some women's desires to name their experiences in a different way and to reconnect with the ancient earth that existed before patriarchy dominated.

The Mother Goddess, as one image of women's spirituality, is fundamentally the work of creation. Goddess religions stress female symbolism and immanence (i.e., operating within, living, present through the universe). To honor the Goddess, or Goddesses, is to honor traditional female attributes. These religions make the role of women important and stress community, interdependence, and mutual aid. Goddess followers believe that divine foundations of reality do not force us to deny our bodies and our material existence. They accept the naturalness and goodness of things—to see all humans and animals, plants, stars, and rocks as brothers and sisters (Ruether, 1983). In Goddess religions, as well as other forms of women's spirituality, communitarian and ecological values are expressed throughout the ideology.

One example of a religion emanating from early Goddess worship is called Witchcraft, Wicca, or the Craft. The myths and symbols are drawn from women-valuing, matristic, Goddess-centered cultures that underlay the beginnings of civilizations. This religion connects with the Goddess who is immanent in nature and is akin to some aspects of Native American and African religions. The focus is to bring human community into harmony with nature. The idea is to rectify personal style along with the struggle against "pollution of patriarchy" (Ruether, 1983). These religions are frequently female-dominant, but many include men.

The involvement of women in alternative experiences that focus on inclusion with nature is an important expression of spirituality for some women. I am not suggesting that women must go outside popular religions or drive a wedge between themselves and men to pursue spirituality in the outdoors. Women's spirituality reflected in these alternative perspectives, however, has connected and reinforced female values with nature as an emphasis that is not commonplace in most mainstream religions. These evolving Goddess and earth religions have offered a way for some women to connect directly and indirectly with their spirituality through the outdoors.

Ecofeminism and Outdoor Activism

Some women have chosen to activate their spirituality with nature by becoming involved in ecofeminist and outdoor activism issues. Many women who care about the outdoors believe that something must be done to save the earth and that female ways of being provide one such model. Ecofeminism provides a philosophical framework and a praxis that some women who care about the outdoors have found useful. Ecofeminism describes "how an understanding of human liberation (feminism) and a concern for interdependence and relationships between humans and nonhumans (ecology) can provide a personal philosophy for both males and females" (Henderson & Bialeschki, 1990-91, p. 1).

Ecofeminism is not a monolithic, homogeneous ideology. It is an attempt to reweave new stories that acknowledge and value the biological and cultural diversity that sanctions all life (Diamond & Orenstein, 1990). The ecofeminist views share a common commitment to making visible the ways that women and nonhuman nature are dominated under patriarchy. In essence, the emerging values of ecofeminism suggest that everything that happens in the natural world should focus on respect for, and the diversity of, human beings as well as the life enhancement of all environments. Although ecofeminists may have many approaches, the philosophy underlines that any form of oppression, such as sexism or racism, is hurtful and exclusive. Ecofeminism as a basis for praxis has helped many women lay a foundation for their outdoor activism.

Many of the environmental projects today are a result of the efforts of women who have taken their spirituality and connection with nature one step further into social action. One of the classic examples is Chipko, the tree-hugging movement. In 1973, manufacturers arrived in a small village in India to oversee the felling of trees. By this time, much of India was deforested and villagers were aware of the consequences including massive flooding and soil erosion. The villagers proceeded with a non-violent protest by walking in a procession, beating drums, and singing songs until they got to the trees. They hugged the trees so that they could not be felled and the manufacturers retreated. This same approach occurred other times and although men were involved, it was the women who were most active and sometimes even fought their husbands and families to save the trees. The tree-hugging movement also empowered women to address other environmental issues (Gooding-Ray, 1994).

As Mary Faeth Chenery (1984) has suggested, "spirituality and philosophical centering is empty, in the long run, if it is not accompanied by action. Action arises from personal empowerment—the belief that individual action can have a tangible effect in the world" (p. 23). To allow, encourage, and focus on spiritual commitment as an essential, and perhaps imperative value of women's outdoor experiences, often results in outdoor activism.

Implications for Outdoor Experiential Education

Outdoor connections, earth religions, and ecofeminism are some of the ways that women become spiritually empowered. For many women, the outdoors underlines values such as caring, concern for future generations, protectiveness and responsibility toward lives besides our own, gentleness, tenderness, patience, sensitivity, nurturance, reverence for life, aesthetic intuition, and receptivity (Anderson, 1991). These values can become the cornerstone for experiential activities in the outdoors. As females who have been empowered by the outdoors, it is our ethical responsibility to reinforce and nurture the values of spirituality through outdoor experiences for girls and women. No one best way exists to promote the meanings of spirituality for females in the outdoors, but the tenets of ecofeminism, earth religions, and connections may be incorporated into the philosophy and development of experiential outdoor programs for girls and women.

Although many benefits result from the inclusion of spiritual dimensions in outdoor experiential education for females, we must be careful not to essentialize the experience of women in the outdoors. Women's experiences in the outdoors are no better or worse than men's, just different. Further, women coming from varying backgrounds may experience the spirituality that emanates through the outdoors in different ways. In general, however, opportunities for girls and women to experience nature and outdoor pursuits can result in a sense of personal and social empowerment and the learning of respect and restraint in the natural world. Spiritual empowerment, rather than impoverishment, results when we overcome a gendered society that tends to alienate women from experiencing the natural world from a variety of perspectives.

Women owe it to themselves to explore the meaning of spirituality and the outdoors. Experiential education leaders/teachers must advocate and provide opportunities to nurture the human spirit. Nurturing the human spirit will require the concerted efforts of each one of us helping ourselves and each other to more fully appreciate and experience the natural world. The potential for spiritual growth and the sense of finding meaning and purpose in life through outdoor experiences are needed now more than ever. Each woman who appreciates nature and/or who goes to the outdoors will need a vision that the spiritual aspects of natural experiences are empowering and that spirituality through the outdoors can lead to a better quality of life. In conclusion, Mary Faeth Chenery (1984) has offered a vision that can guide female leaders/teachers, as well as students, in these endeavors:

> We should without apology be able to imagine pursuing happiness and to imagine more people feeling strong, experiencing joy often, having more friends, stopping longer and noticing the incredible beauty of the autumn

colors, expressing themselves more creatively, and supporting a caring community. (p. 22)

Acknowledgments

I wish to thank the women in the Orange County Women's Center Nonfiction Writing Group for the comments and encouragement given during the writing of this chapter. I also wish to thank all the women who have written about the outdoors who have provided inspiration and food for my own spiritual development over the past several decades.

References

Anderson, L. (1991). *Sisters of the earth.* New York: Vintage Books.

Belenky, M. F., Clinchy, V. M., Goldberger, N. R., & Tarule, J. M. (1986). *Women's ways of knowing.* New York: Basic Books.

Bialeschki, M. D. (1990). The feminist movement and women's participation in physical recreation. *Journal of Physical Education, Recreation and Dance, 61*(1), 44-47.

Chenery, M. F. (1984). Nurturing the human spirit in camping. Occasional Paper, Fund for Advancement of Camping, appearing in *Camping Magazine, 57*(1), 21-28.

Diamond, I., & Orenstein, G. F. (Eds.). (1990). *Reweaving the world.* San Francisco, CA: Sierra Club.

Dustin, D. L. (1984, March). Recreational limits in a world of ethics. *Parks & Recreation*, pp. 48-51, 70.

Estes, C. P. (1992). *Women who run with the wolves.* New York: Ballantine.

Gilligan, C. (1982). *In a different voice.* Cambridge, MA: Harvard University Press.

Gooding-Ray, T. N. (1994). *Towards an ecofeminist praxis.* Unpublished honors thesis, University of North Carolina at Chapel Hill.

Gray, E. D. (Ed.). (1988). *Sacred dimensions of women's experience.* Wellesley, MA: Roundtable Press.

Griffin, S. (1978). *Woman and nature: The roaring inside her.* New York: Harper & Row.

Harjo, J. (1978). *What moon drove me to this?* Berkeley, CA: I. Reed Books.

Henderson, K. A., & Bialeschki, M. D. (1990-91). Ecofeminism: Recreation as if nature and woman mattered. *Leisure Information Quarterly, 17*(1), 1-5.

Kaufman, P. W. (1986). Early women claim parklands for adventure and aspiration. *Courier, 31*(10), 16-18.

King, Y. J. H. (1991). Caring about nature: Feminist ethics and the environment. *Hypatia, 6*(1), 75-89.

LaBastille, A. (1980). *Women and wilderness.* San Francisco, CA: Sierra Club.

Lynch, P. (1987). Scaling the heights: They called it 'an easy day for a lady.' *New Zealand Women's Studies Journal, 3*(1), 59-73.

McDonald, B. L., & Schreyer, R. (1991). Spiritual benefits of leisure participation and leisure settings. In B. L. Driver, P. J. Brown, & G. L. Peterson (Eds.), *Benefits of leisure* (pp. 179-194). State College, PA: Venture Publishing.

Merchant, C. (1980). *The death of nature: Women, ecology, and the scientific revolution.* San Francisco, CA: Harper & Row.

Merchant, C. (1990). Ecofeminism and feminist thought. In I. Diamond & G. F. Orenstein (Eds.), *Reweaving the world* (pp. 100-105). San Francisco, CA: Sierra Club.

Mitten, D. (1992). Empowering girls and women in the outdoors. *Journal of Physical Education, Recreation and Dance, 63*(2), 56-60.

Reben, M. (1963). *A sharing of joy.* New York: Harcourt, Brace & World.

Ruether, R. R. (1983). Sexism, religion, and the social and spiritual liberation of women today. In C. C. Gould (Ed.), *Beyond domination: New perspectives on women and philosophy* (pp. 107-122). Totowa, NJ: Rowman and Allanheld.

Simpson, C. (1991, July) *Women outdoors: New Zealand study.* Paper presented to the World Leisure and Recreation Association, Sydney, Australia.

Smith, C. (1989). *Off the beaten track: Women adventurers and mountaineers in western Canada.* Jasper, Alberta: Coyote Books.

Starhawk. (1982). *Dreaming the dark: Magic, sex, & politics.* Boston: Beacon Press.

Yerkes, R., & Miranda, W. (1985). Women outdoors: Who are they? *Parks & Recreation, 20*(3), 48-51, 95.

Voices of Resistance

*When I dare to be powerful—
to use my strength in the service of my vision,
then it becomes less and less important
whether I am afraid.*

Audre Lorde

I remember how my heart raced when I first read the small sign posted in the women's bathroom at the 1983 Association for Experiential Education Conference in Lake Geneva, Wisconsin. The sign invited lesbians who worked in the outdoor experiential education field to gather to share experiences and ideas of how to deal with the challenges. Meet at the picnic table by the lake after the major speaker, the sign said. I was interested but terrified, my internalized homophobia was working overtime. As a lesbian who had struggled for some time with my own invisibility and the silence in the field, I was excited to talk with other lesbians who shared the same struggles. At the time, there were no visible lesbian role models in the outdoor field, and the horror stories that circulated about the risks of "coming out" in the prominent adventure-based programs had successfully silenced any chance for sharing between women about this important issue.

There were six of us sitting in the dark that night at a picnic table a very long distance from the main conference site. I don't remember what we said, only how I felt so empowered that we had gathered in resistance to the factors that strive to silence and separate us. Walking back, I thought about my lesbian sisters who had wanted to be at that picnic table, but for whom it was still too risky and unsafe to break the silence. I vowed to be a voice of resistance.

We have come quite a way since that night. There is a Lesbian, Gay, Bisexual, and Allies Special Interest Group in AEE. The passage of the anti-gay Amendment 2 in Colorado forced the AEE Board and membership to take a hard look at their support of the human rights of gays and lesbians in experiential education. Karen Thompson, a lesbian activist, has been a major speaker at the AEE International Conferences. "Sexual orientation" has been added to many diversity statements of experiential education programs.

I am acutely aware that many of these advances, as well as others to right injustices for all people, occurred because the voices of resistance refused to be silenced. Not taking a stand on issues of oppression is really taking a stand for the status quo. And, if we are to speak boldly of the true experience of women in experiential education, it must be noted that the voices of resistance are often set against a backdrop of oppression, backlash, marginalization, and silencing.

A challenge for experiential education programs is to confront difficult issues directly. The chapters in this section strive to demystify some of the perplexing ways that sexism subtly works to keep women "in their place," and they offer important advice for practitioners and program directors who are ready to "walk their talk" in addressing these vital concerns. Deb Jordan's chapter on language makes a case for the use of gender-neutral language in experiential education. She suggests that the persistent use of the terms "hard " and "soft" skills is sexist and urges outdoor professionals to find alternatives. T.A. Loeffler identifies the tremendous potential of sexual harassment to adversely affect the experience of women and girls in experiential education programs. Her examples of sexual harassment in outdoor settings give clarity to both those confronted with sexual harassment and those committed to eradicating it from their programs. Nina Roberts critiques the generic adventure experience of women by pointing out that it is almost exclusively focused on white women's experience. She notes the absence of the voices of women of color from programs and research in experiential education and calls for us to resist looking solely through a Euro-American lens at the experience of women and girls in outdoor adventure and recreational pursuits. Finally, Mary McClintock identifies lesbian baiting as the labeling of individual women or groups of women as lesbians in order to discredit them or pressure them to conform to traditional gender expectations. She shows how lesbian baiting, which is a by-product of the intersection of sexism and homophobia, is harmful to all women.

These chapters identify ideas about how to proactively halt the discrimination faced by women and girls; however, it is up to experiential educators interested in equity and inclusivity to take the vow to raise their own voices of resistance. Only by speaking out against situations that disadvantage women and girls and relegate them to something less than their full potential, can change occur.

Reference

Lorde, A. (1984). *Sister outsider*. Freedom, CA: The Crossing Press.

18

Snips and Snails and Puppy Dog Tails . . . The Use of Gender-Free Language in Experiential Education

Deb Jordan

"What are little boys made of? Snips and snails and puppy dog tails. . . ." "What are little girls made of? Sugar and spice and everything nice. . . ." These childhood singsongs portray subtle attitudes and expectations of the roles for women and men in today's world. Research has shown that these gender-role stereotypes have changed little over the years; women are still viewed as soft and yielding while men are seen as strong and assertive (Werner & LaRussa, 1985).

Through television shows and commercials, magazine advertisements, and radio voice-overs, the media continually depicts women and men in traditional social roles: women are wives, mothers, and helpers; men are money earners supporting women and children. Gender influences also are depicted in our nonverbal, verbal, and written communications. Women tend to take up less physical space with their bodies and gestures, men talk and interrupt conversations more, and written language is filled with generic [sic] male pronouns. This chapter will help you rediscover the implications for use of gender-identified language and behaviors in experiential education.

Change is Slow

While there certainly has been a move toward gender-neutral language in general, and in the field of experiential education in particular (admonitions from journals such as this for use of inclusive language), there also has been resistance (Shivers's exclusive use of the male pronoun in a recreation leadership text published as recently as 1986; Shivers, 1986). Newspapers, news magazines (*Time*, January 1989), and news shows continue to use "he" and "man" as generic, gender-neutral terms, even though research has shown that these terms are not perceived as being gender neutral. Miller and Swift (1988) have demonstrated that "he" and "man" conjure up images of male persons to the exclusion of female persons.

Persistent use of these gender-specific terms will continue to reinforce the notion that being male is better (Connell, 1987).

In experiential education, we are all guilty of some gender bias. Most of us were socialized in a society that is heavily male oriented. Although we may have been exposed to nontraditional family models, the media, schools, and religious institutions inundate us with pro-male messages. As long as the overriding message is that boys are better than girls, we are in a sense trapped. Intellectualizing, while a necessary beginning to breaking free of these inhibiting attitudes, does not totally eradicate the lessons of youth.

The theory of expectation states, and gender-role theories tell us, that high power, high potency, and high status are attributed to those things we value. In our society, the male sex is more highly valued; therefore, those characteristics and materials associated with the male gender are more highly valued. The female gender is accorded low value, low legitimacy, and low status; therefore, those items and characteristics associated with females are attributed little or no respect (Berger & Zelditch, 1985; Eagly, 1987). We can make similar comments about differences in ages, races, and any other categories we establish.

While conscious efforts are being made to reduce gender bias and lessen these misattributions of status, change is slow. As a group, experiential educators and outdoor professionals appear to make a sincere effort to minimize gender bias in the field. They appear to be open to new ideas, support participation by both sexes, and encourage skilled individuals to develop personal skills to their full potential. There is, however, one very prevalent example of gender bias that pervades the field of experiential education: the use of gender-identified language and terminology.

The Bias in Language

In examining the impact of sexism in language, we need to look at the three functions of language bias. Sexism may ignore one gender, define the genders, and/or depreciate a gender (Pearson, 1985). Ignoring one gender is accomplished through the use of so-called "generic" terms. This includes the use of the masculine pronoun in describing both sexes (i.e., man for both female and male persons) and in the use of such terms as chairman, man-hours, mankind, and two-man tent. This function serves to make the female gender invisible, and in reality is not inclusive.

Sexist word usage also may define a sex in relation to something else. An example of this would be the lumping together of "women and children" in the same phrase. This type of definition effectively reduces women to the level of children: having few rights, having little world experience and maturity, and needing care.

Another example of defining a sex in relation to something else, thereby reducing its value and power, is when people refer to adult females as girls (or ladies) and males as men. I often spend time in my classes discussing "words that go together." Those words include girls and boys, women and men, ladies and gentlemen.

While listeners have little difficulty in seeing the problem with using "girls and men" in a phrase together, they can't seem to see a problem with using the term "ladies and men." The problem, of course, is in the connotation of the words. Females well know the differences: remember when you were a child and your mother scolded you to sit or walk "like a lady"? Not once have I ever heard of anyone being scolded to walk "like a woman." I dare say a child never would have known what that meant. There is power in the word "woman," and I believe that's why most participants balk so strongly at the word. To facilitate every participant to reach their full potential, we should allow them equal access to the power of words.

A gender may also be defined in terms of relationships in ordering of words. Thorne and Henley (1975) suggest that consistently utilized word-order is similar to ranking by importance and status. The accepted ordering of "men and women" in a phrase, rather than "women and men," indicates power and dominance of the former over the latter. Similar ordering of the terms "hard skills and soft skills" rather than "soft skills and hard skills" also illustrates a type of ranking, whereby hard skills are given more importance and status than soft skills.

Depreciation of a gender occurs when adjectives discredit one gender. "Dumb jock" as a referent to male athletes identifies them as wholly physical beings with little or no mental capabilities. Similarly, as a term, "women's work" is often used disparagingly. Adjectives to describe work that women do include such words as nice and pretty, while the same work attributed to men is described as masterful and brilliant (Sargent, 1984). Another example of the negative use of adjectives is found in the connotations of adjectives used to describe similar women and men. While assertiveness and a sharp mind are desired management and leadership skills, those traits manifested by females often result in characterizations of bitchy, aggressive, aloof, and cold. Those same behaviors exhibited by a male, however, are considered assertive, indicative of having a keen mind, and demonstrating competence (Sargent, 1984).

Hard Skills/Soft Skills: The Power of Gender Bias

In addition to the implication of ordering, the generally accepted terms, hard skills and soft skills, can also depreciate the female gender and its contribution to the field of experiential education due to the phallocentric nature of the words. Hard skills and soft skills generally have been recognized as two types of skills in the practice of outdoor leadership. Hard skills are those that encompass such things as logistics, planning, and technical skill development; soft skills are those that involve human relations, communications, and social skills (Swiderski, 1987). For a long time, hard skills were the more highly valued of the two (Swiderski, 1987). Technical skills were those competencies people bragged about (and some still do), and at which people trained long and hard to become the best. Interpersonal skills, on the other hand, just sort of "happened" as the experience evolved. There was little or no formal training in interpersonal skills since it was assumed that everyone could successfully work with people. After all, people practice social skills in everyday living.

Recently, however, it has been recognized that both interpersonal and technical skills play an equally important role in experiential education. In training sessions, journal articles, and conference programs, more and more attention is being given to such skills as processing, debriefing, conflict management, and group dynamics. Currently, the development of people skills is being stressed as heavily as activity skills in many experiential programs. If, as a profession, experiential education truly believes that interpersonal skills are as valuable as technical skills, this is the time to alter our language to agree with those beliefs.

There have been assertions that terminology is a matter of personal, semantic preference and that the use of "hard and soft" or "technical and interpersonal" as skill descriptors is not a matter worthy of examination. After all, these terms have the same meanings and everybody understands the lingo, right? A word is a word is a word, so to speak. The importance of semantics in the understanding and full acceptance of one aspect of experiential education, however, has been long overlooked. Word choice can alter meanings, result in misunderstandings, and provide only partial information (Pearson, 1985).

Gender-identified language often obscures the contributions and existence of the disregarded gender; it presents imprecise and half-true information. If we always talk in terms of one grouping of people (i.e., male people), we effectively negate the contributions of the other grouping (i.e., female people). Pearson (1985) states that language shapes the way we perceive reality; therefore, if we continue to promote one sex over the other in the course of everyday language, we will continue to define reality in terms of that one gender. This would perpetuate a pro-male bias in an already-biased society and essentially maintain female oppression.

The choice of hard and soft as accepted synonyms for technical and interpersonal functions tends to slight the female gender, define the importance and status of maleness and femaleness in experiential education, and depreciate the contributions of female leaders and participants. These terms are laden with subtle messages about valuing, status, and acceptance of women and men in this field. Much more accurate descriptors of these skill areas, which are also gender-free descriptors, are interpersonal and technical skills.

The concern with gender-identified language (i.e., hard and soft as descriptors, use of "man" as in two-man tent, etc.) is with the images and expectations conjured up by that particular word usage. As mentioned earlier, research has indicated that when exposed to "he" and "man," respondents imagined male persons, not female and male persons. Examining the impact of hard and soft as skill descriptors illustrates the gender-identifying qualities of the terms. *Webster's New World Dictionary* (1978) defines hard as "having firm muscles; vigorous and robust," while soft is defined as "giving way easily under pressure." Comparatively, masculine and feminine as terms indicating characteristics attributed to males and females are also related to the connotations for hard and soft. Masculine is defined as "having qualities regarded as characteristic of men and boys, as strength, vigor, etc." (snips and snails and puppy dog tails ...). Feminine is defined as "having qualities regarded as characteristic of women and girls, as gentleness, delicacy, etc." (sugar and spice and every thing nice ...). Males are perceived as being hard in musculature and emotionally and mentally tough, while females are perceived as physically soft and emotionally and mentally delicate.

A distinct relationship between the meanings of male, masculine, and hard exists; hard may be characterized as being masculine and, therefore, attributed to men or boys. Since the male sex is more highly valued and attributed more status than the female sex, it is easy to see why, in the past, hard skills have been more highly valued—they are masculine, and according to social norms, masculine is the way to be.

Definitions of feminine and soft reveal a similar connection. The term "feminine" elicits an image of gentleness and delicacy—one may certainly argue that it also portrays softness and giving way under pressure. Most would agree that society does not view softness with much respect. One who is considered soft often is denigrated by being referred to as a wimp, pansy, or softhearted. In the out-of-doors and in many business situations, being soft or giving way under pressure is a highly undesirable trait. A leader who is able to make sound decisions without being unnecessarily swayed by popular thought is preferred over the leader whose decisions can be influenced by the most vocal group members.

By their very definitions, the use of the terms "hard skills" and "soft skills" makes a statement about underlying beliefs of femaleness and maleness in outdoor skill development. Although we verbalize the importance of interpersonal skills in experiential education, we will continue to deny the essence of that in our choice of terminology if we persist in using gender-identified language. The order of wording in written and spoken language is also a subtle manifestation of sexism. Why and how has it come about that we should always speak of hard (or technical) skills before soft (or interpersonal) skills?

It has been suggested that hard and soft as descriptors are evidence of a phallocentric history (Wilkinson, 1986). Experiential education has this history in that, traditionally, it has been a male domain where males are the doers. Perhaps we should change the linguistic approach to a more vaginocentric stance by utilizing "dry" and "wet" as adjectives. While it might take some getting used to, wet and dry make just as much sense in describing interpersonal and technical skills as do soft and hard. In fact, dry actually may be more accurate than hard. *Webster's New World Dictionary* (1978) defines dry as "having no personal bias or emotional concern." Technical skills are those very skills that (generally speaking) can be reduced to objective, tangible tasks and knowledge. The phrase "cut and dried" is an apt representation of skills that are supposed to be logical and relatively emotion-free. As an antonym, wet could be utilized adequately to characterize interpersonal skills.

Words to Actions

Why all this fuss about semantics? Because, as noted by Spender (1980, as cited by Miller & Swift, 1988):

> For women to become visible, it is necessary that they become linguistically visible. . . . New symbols will need to be created and old symbols will need to be recycled and invested with new images if the male hold of language is to be broken.

In addition to linguistics, behaviors are prime areas for discovery of subtle sexism. Leaders and teachers in experiential education need to examine behaviors, not only between themselves and participants, but also between and among participants. Leaders should be aware of how they address participants—who is referred to by name most often, boys or girls? Calling male participants by their names more frequently than females (which, by the way, is quite common) has the impact of legitimizing males, while negating females.

Praising males for their competence (Good decision! Nicely done!), while praising females for their appearance and domestic abilities (Great dinner! Pretty outfit!) is another insidious example of sexism. Related to this is the way we handle someone who is having difficulty with a given task—let's say using a compass. Study the way you (as the leader) handle the difficulties experienced by female and male participants. Telling a female participant to "not worry, girls are never very good at compass work anyhow," or, even more subtly, giving up on even helping her, can imply to that female that she doesn't have the inherent abilities to succeed. Yet challenging a boy with the same problem, "Come on, try again, you can do it," and letting him struggle through the course acts as a cue that expectations are different for him (he will succeed) because his inherent abilities are different.

Tolerating a wider latitude of behaviors from male participants than female participants is another way sexism from leaders/teachers rears its ugly head. Easily seen in structured classrooms, rowdy and loud behavior from boys is tolerated much more readily than rowdy or loud behavior from girls. This includes talking out of turn, cutting in lines, physical positioning, and working with other students. Until we get a handle on how attitudes are being manifested through language and behaviors in experiential settings, this subtle sexism will continue.

Leaders also need to monitor intergroup behaviors and word usage to facilitate a gender-neutral environment. It is very common for participants in mixed-sex groups to fall into those roles which are most comfortable, yet those roles have been accepted based on heavy, but subtle, social pressure. Leaders need to keep an eye on participants who short themselves by buying into a restrictive belief system and on participants who short others by limiting their experience. The ever-helpful male who always lifts heavy objects, the female who always calls for help before fully assessing her own capabilities, the participant who puts down another because they dared to step outside the bounds of socially accepted roles, these are individuals who, while perhaps under the guise of cooperation and courtesy, restrict another's experience.

Steps Toward Equality

Now is the time for all of us in experiential education to share in the effort to make women visible, to further reduce sexism in the field, and to use terminology and behaviors that accurately reflect the nature of described skills. We can do this by referring to the specific bodies of knowledge with appropriate adjectives (i.e., interpersonal and technical). In written and spoken language, we should continue to encourage and utilize gender-free and gender-neutral terms such as two-*person* tent and chair*person*. Fully value both sexes by using and encouraging the use of "words that go together." It is also appropriate to encourage the reordering of terms. When discussing the sexes, discuss women and men rather than men and women; when discussing skills, discuss interpersonal and technical skills rather than the reverse.

When examining behaviors with participants, investigate how you use names of participants, what types of behaviors you tolerate from whom, and how you react to difficulties experienced by females and males. Investigate how participants relate to one another; try to isolate and deal with those behaviors encouraged by sexist thinking and attitudes. Listen to the group talk. How do individuals refer to one another? What are the underlying expectations as seen through behaviors and word usage? As a profession, we can continue to respect all persons and their individual abilities by permitting and openly supporting cross-gender skill and social development.

Endnote

This chapter was originally published in the 1990 *Journal of Experiential Education*, *13*(2), 45-49.

References

Berger, J., & Zelditch, M. (Eds.). (1985). *Status, rewards, and influence.* San Francisco, CA: Jossey-Bass.

Connell, R. (1987). *Gender and power.* Stanford, CA: Stanford University Press.

Eagly, A. (1987). *Sex differences in social behavior: A social role interpretation.* Hillsdale, NJ: Lawrence Erlbaum Associates.

Miller, C., & Swift, K. (1988). *The handbook of nonsexist writing* (2nd ed.). New York: Harper & Row.

Pearson, J. (1985). *Gender and communication.* Dubuque, IA: Wm. C. Brown Publisher.

Sargent, A. (1984). *Beyond sex roles* (2nd ed.). New York: West.

Shivers, J. (1986). *Recreational leadership. Group dynamics and interpersonal behavior.* Princeton, NJ: Princeton Book Co.

Swiderski, L. (1987). Soft and conceptual skills: The often overlooked components of outdoor leadership. *The Bradford Papers Annual, 2,* 29-36.

Thorne, B., & Henley, N. (1975). *Language and sex: Difference and dominance.* Rowley, MA: Newbury House.

Time (1989, January 2). Planet of the year: Endangered earth. *Time Magazine.*

Webster's New World Dictionary (2nd concise ed.). (1978). New York: Avenel Books.

Werner & LaRussa. (1985). Persistence and change in sex-role stereotypes. *Sex Roles, 12*(9/10), 1089-1100.

Wilkinson, S. (1986). Sighting possibilities: Diversity and commonality in feminist research. In S. Wilkinson (Ed.), *Feminist social psychology.* Philadelphia, PA: Open University Press.

19

Sexual Harassment and Experiential Education Programs: A Closer Look

T.A. Loeffler

This chapter will examine the influence of sexual harassment on experiential education programs. Sexual harassment was brought to the forefront of public attention by the confirmation hearings of Clarence Thomas. People across the United States and around the world watched the Senate hearings live on television. With her testimony, Anita Hill launched the country on an intensive examination of the nature of the relations between women and men. Despite this period of intense scrutiny, experiential educators have just begun to examine the effects of sexual harassment on their staff, participants, and programs.

Sexual harassment has enormous potential to influence the experiences of both participants and staff in experiential education programs because of the intense, physical, 24-hour-a-day, remote nature of many programs. In a recent study (Loeffler, 1995), female outdoor leaders were asked if they had experienced sexual harassment in their outdoor leadership careers; 52% of the women in the interview sample said they had. Other than Loeffler's study, research has yet to be done on the occurrence rates of sexual harassment in experiential education programs.

Extensive research has been completed in academic and workplace settings. One study found that 30% of undergraduate women were sexually harassed during their college experience by an instructor (Dziech & Weiner, 1984), and another study found that 78% of undergraduate women had been sexually harassed by their peers (Paludi & Barickman, 1991). In the largest sexual harassment study done to date, it was found that 42% of 10,644 women had experienced sexual harassment in the workplace (United States Merit Systems Protection Board, 1991). Given the findings of these and other studies, sexual harassment is a pervasive problem in both academic and workplace settings. Because of the extent of the problem in other settings, it can be concluded that sexual harassment takes place in experiential education settings and that it is imperative that experiential education program staff take proactive steps to prevent its occurrence.

Definitions of Sexual Harassment

Since 1964, government regulations in the United States have prohibited sexual harassment and the legal system has determined that sexual harassment is illegal in employment settings and educational institutions. Workplace sexual harassment is prohibited as a form of sexual discrimination under Title VII of the 1964 Civil Rights Act. Federal Title IX of the Education Amendments of 1972 prohibits sexual harassment in educational settings that receive federal funding.

Several definitions of sexual harassment have evolved from the legal, educational, and psychological literature. Table 1 summarizes some of these definitions.

Table 1
Summary of Sexual Harassment Definitions

Equal Employment Opportunity Commission
Unwelcome sexual advances, requests for sexual favors, and other verbal or physical conduct of a sexual nature constitute sexual harassment when (1) submission to such conduct is made either explicitly a term or condition of an individuals' employment; (2) submission to, or a rejection of, such conduct by an individual is used as the basis for employment decisions affecting such individual; or (3) such contact has the purpose or effect of substantially interfering with an individual's work performance or creating an intimidating, hostile, or offensive working environment.

National Advisory Council on Women's Education Programs
Academic sexual harassment is the use of authority to emphasize the sexuality or sexual identity of the student in a manner which prevents or impairs that student's full enjoyment of educational benefits, climate, or opportunities.

McKinnon (1979)
Sexual harassment . . . refers to the unwanted imposition of sexual requirements in the context of a relationship of unequal power. Central to this concept is the use of power derived from one social sphere to lever benefits or impose deprivations in another. . . . When one is sexual, the other material, the cumulative sanction is particularly potent.

Fitzgerald (1990)
Sexual harassment consists of the sexualization of an instrumental relationship through the introduction or imposition of sexist or sexual remarks, requests, or requirements, in the context of a formal power differential. Harassment can occur where no such formal power differential exists, if the behavior is unwanted by, or offensive to, the woman. Instances of harassment can be classified into the following continuum; gender harassment, seductive behavior, solicitation of sexual activity by promise of reward or threat of punishment, and sexual imposition or assault.

When a formal power differential exists, all sexist or sexual behavior is seen as harassment, since the woman is not considered to be in a position to object, resist, or give fully free consent; when no such power differential exists, it is the recipient's experience and perception of the behavior as offensive that constitutes the defining factor.

(Paludi & Barickman, 1991, p.3)

Paludi and Barickman (1991) suggest that "definitions of sexual harassment are important because they educate . . . and promote discussion and conscientious evaluation of these experiences" (p. 2). Definitions also help the person who has experienced sexual harassment recognize and identify it for what it is and, therefore, begin to heal from it. Fitzgerald et al. (1988) found that many women who experience relatively blatant sexual harassment fail to label it as such.

The Effects of Sexual Harassment

Sexual harassment can be devastating and have tremendous impact on the emotional well-being, physical health, and vocational success of those who experience it (Paludi & Barickman, 1991). Dziech and Weiner (1984) found that it causes students to relinquish work, educational advancement, and career opportunities. Research indicates that 21%-82% of women who have been sexually harassed report a deterioration of their emotional and/or physical condition (Koss, 1990). The emotional and physical effects of sexual harassment are similar to rape and incest and meet the diagnostic criteria for post-traumatic stress disorder (Koss, 1990). Shullman (cited in Paludi & Barickman, 1991) developed the label "Sexual Harassment Trauma Syndrome" to describe the constellation of effects surrounding sexual harassment which are listed in Table 2.

Table 2
Sexual Harassment Trauma Syndrome

Emotional Reactions
Anxiety
Shock, Denial
Anger, Fear
Insecurity, Betrayal
Humiliation
Confusion
Self-consciousness
Shame
Powerlessness
Guilt
Isolation
Frustration

Physical Reactions
Headaches
Sleep disturbances
Lethargy
Gastrointestinal distress
Hypervigilance
Dermatological reactions
Weight fluctuations
Nightmares
Phobias, Panic reactions
Genitourinary distress
Respiratory problems
Substance abuse

Changes in Self-Perception
Negative self-esteem
Lack of competency
Lack of control
Isolation
Hopelessness
Powerlessness

Social, Interpersonal, and Sexual Effects
Withdrawal
Self-preoccupation
Lack of trust
Lack of focus
Fear of new people, situations
Changes in social network patterns
Negative attitudes & behavior in sexual relationships
Sexual disorders associated with stress & trauma
Changes in dress or physical appearance

Career Effects
Changes in study and work habits
Loss of job or promotion
Unfavorable performance evaluations
Drop in academic or work performance because of stress
Lower grades as punishment for reporting sexual harassment or for noncompliance with sexual advances
Absenteeism
Withdrawal from work and school
Changes in career goals

(Paludi & Barickman, 1991, p. 29)

Examples of Sexual Harassment in Outdoor Programs

Returning to the realm of experiential education, the Equal Employment Opportunity Commission definition of sexual harassment is divided into its three parts (Paludi & Barickman,1991), and examples from adventure programs are provided to illustrate the range of behavior that may constitute sexual harassment. The examples were adapted from a University of Minnesota Sexual Harassment pamphlet.

Part One of the Definition: Certain behavior constitutes sexual harassment when "submission to such conduct is made either explicitly or implicitly a term or condition of an individual's employment or academic advancements":

1. Leslie was attending a multi-activity, semester-length, outdoor instructor course. Leslie was very impressed by the interest one of her instructors, a famous mountaineer, showed in her during the course. Because of his encouragement, she chose to specialize in mountaineering. Later, she realized that his interest had only been sexual. She was astonished and angry. She felt humiliated and foolish for having believed he respected her outdoor work. She never finished her instructors' course and has taken a job in another profession.

2. Tony, an instructor for an adventure program, likes to joke with his students. He often uses sexual innuendo and imagery as the basis for his humor. One day, as a joke, he suggests that the better looking a women is, the more help (sexual and otherwise) she will get from him. Sandra is an attractive student on Tony's programs who needs extra help with foot care since she has diabetes. She is deeply offended and scared by Tony's attitude and tries to stay far away from him. After a long hike, Sandra notices that she has a blister on her foot but she feels too uncomfortable to seek out Tony's help and as a result develops a foot ulcer and needs to be evacuated.

3. Since the first week of the outdoor semester program, Michael has been uncomfortable with how one of the male instructors has been looking at him. Now Michael must see the instructor about his lesson plan for the next day. The instructor told Michael that the only time he could meet with him was at his tent that evening.

Part Two of the Definition: Certain behavior constitutes sexual harassment when "submission to or rejection of such conduct by an individual is used as the basis for employment decisions or academic decisions affecting such individual":

1. Mary is an assistant instructor completing her second course at the adventure education program. The chief instructor on her course has been confiding details of his personal life to her and recently has begun pressuring her for sex. When she refuses, he threatens that she will not get a good evaluation and she will not be promoted to instructor. She feels nobody would believe her if she complained because of his status at the program.

2. Jill is recently laid off as administrative assistant for a large outdoor program. She had been involved with her boss for several months, but broke off the relationship before she got the layoff notice. She is told the layoff was due to budget cuts, but Jill handled the budget and knows that this was not the reason.

3. Connie is a student in an outdoor leadership development program. Her instructor invites her to share a hotel room the night after the course ends. When she refuses, he accuses her of being immature. He tells her she probably couldn't handle the demands of outdoor leadership.

Part Three of the Definition: Certain behavior constitutes sexual harassment when "such conduct has the purpose or effect of unreasonably interfering with an individual's work or academic performance or creating an intimidating, hostile, or offensive working or academic environment":

1. Tanya depends on her part-time job in the gear room to help pay for her tuition for a semester-length adventure program. One Saturday, while she was alone with her boss, he touched her leg in a way that made her uncomfortable. She moved away from him and went about her tasks of the day. Another time while Tanya was cleaning the stoves, her boss came up behind her and started to rub her neck. She asked him to stop and he said, "I was only trying to be friendly." His advances continued and Tanya became so uncomfortable she quit her job in the gear room. Unable to find another job, she couldn't pay the tuition and had to drop out of the adventure program.

2. On the first day of the rafting trip, the guide asked students to fill out a survey about themselves. The survey asked about their rafting experience, their food preferences, and their health. One of the questions asked was whether the students liked recreational sex. Another of the questions asked if the students were on birth control.

3. Students in a mountaineering course know their instructor is in a sexual relationship with one of their coursemates. Although the instructor and the student try to be discreet about their relationship, the other students notice the special attention their coursemate receives. They feel their coursemate has an unfair advantage and they resent it.

As noted in Fitzgerald's (1990) definition, sexual harassment can occur in instances in which a formal power difference does not exist. Peer harassment is the term used to describe the sexual harassment that occurs between two students, two employees, or two colleagues when an institutional power difference does not exist (Paludi & Barickman, 1991). Group harassment is the term used to describe the sexual harassment that occurs when a single person is harassed by a group of peers. The following examples, from the author's experience, illuminate how peer and group harassment may occur in adventure programs:

1.   Shelly, a student in a mountain search and rescue course, is struggling to set up the knots and carabiner arrangement of a lowering system. A fellow student says, "Women just can't understand mechanical things" and grabs the carabiners out of Shelly's hand and proceeds to set up the system. Shelly begins to doubt her ability and hesitates to volunteer again to set up the lowering system. As a result, she never learns the system and fails the course.

2.   Judy is a newly hired ropes course instructor. Her co-workers regularly leave pornographic pictures where she will find them. She dreads going to work and is finding it harder and harder to keep herself motivated because of the situation.

3.   Some rock-climbing students are traveling to the climbing area on the program bus. A male student tells a story of a woman climber who had large breasts. He says he'd "sure like to climb those mountains" and gestures suggestively at the female student sitting beside him.

4.   Molly is the only female student on a mountaineering course. The group gets stuck in a mountain hut for six days because of white-out conditions. One day, Molly's fellow students decide she needs to become one of the guys and they pin her down and cut her hair.

5.   Maria, a student on a one-month backpacking course, mentions missing her partner, Joan, back home during a debrief. Her fellow students begin to make excuses not to sleep in her tent. Maria finds rocks hidden in her backpack.

Sexual Harassment and Participant Safety

Experiential education programs advertise many benefits for their participants. A recent Colorado Outward Bound School catalog (1992) states that its "courses are designed to offer experiences, both strenuous and bold which demand an increase in initiative, self-confidence, personal responsibility, leadership, fitness, teamwork and commitment to others." Outdoor programs often place people in a physically and/or psychologically demanding and stressful environment to facilitate building of trust, self-confidence, and acceptance of personal responsibility (Durian, Owens, & Owen, 1980). This list of intended benefits differs greatly from the effects on participants if they are subjected to sexual harassment. According to John Dewey, a proponent of experiential education, the goals and objectives of our educational programs must be reflected in our educational means (McDermott, 1981). Hunt (1990) coined the phrase "valuational schizophrenia" to describe the results "if the ends of a program and the means that the program uses are disjunctive" (p. 29). If experiential education programs do not proactively address sexual harassment in all its forms, they will suffer from valuational schizophrenia because the damaging effects of sexual harassment are in severe contrast with the goals of most programs. Experiential education program participants can never reach their full psychological and physical potential if sexual harassment occurs.

Along with the serious emotional, health, and vocational effects, sexual harassment may affect the physical safety of outdoor education program participants. Adventure programs often take place in remote locations. This remoteness may make the escape from a sexually harassing situation difficult, expensive, or impossible. As well, persons experiencing sexual harassment may be dependent on their instructors for navigation, backcountry travel, or belaying. Imagine the psychological trauma of having the person who sexually harassed you yesterday, be responsible for your life and safety the next day. Students like Sandra and Shelly, mentioned in the previous examples, may be in safety-compromised situations because instructional help and guidance is not available to them because of sexual harassment. Shelly could fall because she wasn't given the opportunity to learn the lowering system and Sandra suffered a severe foot injury because it was not safe for her to approach her instructor for assistance. If an experiential educator is being sexually harassed by her/his co-workers, her/his judgment may be impeded and this could affect the safety of the students.

One area of outdoor programs that has been a serious point of contention has been "consensual" relationships between outdoor instructors and adult students. In years past, in some outdoor programs, it was considered a "job perk" for male instructors to choose a female student to have sex with while on the course. The male instructors gave the rationale that they were away from their usual sexual outlets and needed relief (Hunt, 1990). An article entitled "The Stone Syndrome or Skin in the Adventure Trade" in *Rock and Ice* magazine demonstrates this attitude is still prevalent (Bangs, 1988). The author, an adventure travel company owner, sees nothing wrong with guides having sexual relationships with clients. In fact, he almost glorifies the practice. Bangs quotes a male guide who says, "I don't want to make like all our guides are gigolos. This is not a stud service. On the other hand, I've had an affair on almost every tour I've guided" (p. 19). Bangs quotes another guide who acknowledges the fundamental power difference that exists between outdoor leaders and participants:

> It has to do with control. Somewhere along the way most people realize they're not in control of their environment, or their lives. And neither are the people around them. There's something very alluring about the appearance of control, self-reliance, and power, and adventure guides seem to have it. We really know our jobs well. Fortune 500 presidents, celebrities, politicians join our trips, and they look to us for all the answers: how to set up the tent, where to go to the bathroom. They can't call their secretaries or an ambulance so they become very dependent on their guides. And it's a huge dependency. The guides feed them, administer first aid, tell them when it's time to eat, when to sleep. We appear to control the group, and the elements. "Is it going to rain tonight?" "Fuck yes!" and it will. (p. 18)

Later in the article, the same guide is quoted as saying, "Male guides have more of a romantic life in terms of numbers than probably anyone. They live a life that could only be imitated by a playboy millionaire" (p. 19). Hunt (1990), one of the eminent ethicists of experiential education, considers student/teacher and client/guide sexual relationships to be unethical in the extreme because such a relationship violates the fundamental nature of the teaching affiliation.

According to Fitzgerald (1990), "When a formal power differential exists, all sexist or sexual behavior is seen as harassment, since the person is not considered to be in a position to object, resist, or give fully free consent" (p. 38). By this definition, there cannot be a consensual relationship when a power differential exists between individuals. As so aptly put by the guide above, there is a fundamental power differential between outdoor adventure leaders and participants. To conclude, within the confines of these so-called "consensual" sexual relationships, sexual harassment occurs.

Fraternal Bonding

The theory of fraternal bonding offers a possible explanation of why sexual harassment may occur in outdoor adventure programs. Lyman (1987) suggests that men use shared experience, fun, and humor as the base for fraternal bonding. Curry (1991) defines "the fraternal bond as a force, link, or affectionate tie that unites men" (p. 119). In addition, Lyman (1987) found "the humor of male bonding relationships generally sexually aggressive, and frequently consist of sexist or racist jokes" (p. 151). Fine (1987) reports that "women who wish to be part of a male-dominated group typically must accept patterns of male bonding . . . and be willing to engage in coarse joking and teasing" (p. 131). This coarse joking can frequently be defined as sexual harassment and may create an intimidating, hostile, or offensive working or learning environment.

In some settings, outdoor adventure programs are male-dominated and filled with sexual joking. Examples of this joking are found in published rock-climbing guides (Harlin, 1986; Steiger, 1985; Waugh, 1982; Webster, 1987). Rock-climbing guides provide maps and route information for particular rock-climbing areas. The person(s) who make the first ascent of a rock climb have the honor of naming it. Table 3 lists the sex-related names of rock climbs found in four climbing guides representing various locations around the United States. From the first-ascent information provided in the climbing guides, it was determined that these climbs were all named by men. These names exemplify how fraternal bonding through joking can occur in an adventure setting.

In terms of women's safety, this joking is no laughing matter. Curry (1991), in a study of fraternal bonding in the locker room, found that in order to affirm their masculinity, men engaged in conversations that treated "women as objects, encouraged sexist attitudes toward women, and in its extreme, promoted rape culture"

(p. 119). Intensive fraternal bonding in all-male groups or male-dominated groups may create an environment that leads to violence against women. An example of this is when members of a sports team gang-rape together (Sanday, 1990). According to Melnick (1992), gang rape is associated with small, all-male groups of tightly knit members who frequently live and eat together. In these situations, group loyalty "is often so strong that sometimes it can override personal integrity" (p. 32).

Table 3
The Sex-Related Names of Rock-climbing Routes

Names Referring to Female Anatomy
Big Breasted Bikers
Throbbing Labias
Magnolia Thunder Pussy
Here Come the Jugs

Names Referring to Male Anatomy
Dildoe Pinnacle
The Phallus
Family Jewels
Handsome and Well-Hung

Names That Degrade Women
Bitch
Topless Tellers
Crazy Woman Driver
Happy Hooker

Names that Degrade Gay People
Ethics are for Faggots
Homosexual Armadillo
Flirting with Dikes
Revolt of the Dike Brigade

Names About Sexual Violence
Cornholer's Incest
Gang Bang
Double Ganger
Slam Bam Book Jam
Matricide
Jack the Ripper
Slammer Jam
Assault and Battery
Psycho Killer

Names About Sex
Foreplay
For Sexual Favors
Ménage à trois
Orgasm
Celibate Mallard
Swinging Hips

(Harlin, 1986; Steiger, 1985; Waugh, 1982; Webster, 1987)

Proactive Strategies

When sexual harassment occurs, it exposes participants and staff to increased physical and emotional risks. It is imperative that experiential education programs take an active stance in preventing and interrupting sexual harassment. Experiential education programs need to have a sexual harassment policy which is distributed to all staff and students. This policy should include both a theoretical definition of sexual harassment and examples of behaviors that could constitute sexual harassment. This definition and examples need to cover the behavior of staff and students. The policy should also list the procedures for reporting a sexual harassment complaint and should be relatively easy to execute so they are not a barrier or obstacle to reporting sexual harassment.

With these policies and procedures in place, both staff and students need to be educated about sexual harassment. The sexual harassment policies should be included in the staff manual. During staff training, it is important to review the sexual harassment policy and reporting procedures, ensure staff understand what sexual harassment is and that it will not be tolerated, and provide training for staff in interrupting peer and group harassment.

Along with the above training, staff members need to be instructed to use nonsexist and nonsexual teaching language and style. Paludi and Barickman (1991) suggest a number of techniques:

- When making general statements about women (or any other group), ensure they are based on accurate information. Universal generalizations about any social group, such as "Women can't do technical things like anchor systems," are likely, at best, to represent uncritical oversimplifications of selected norms.

- Avoid humor or gratuitous remarks that demean or belittle people because of gender or sexual orientation, just as you would avoid remarks that demean people because of their race, religion, or disability. Respect the dignity of all people.

- Avoid using generic masculine terms to refer to people of both sexes, such as "You guys," "manpower," and "two-man tents."

- When using illustrative examples, avoid stereotypes, such as making all authority figures men and all subordinates women.

- Try to monitor your behavior toward men and women participants. Ask, for example: Do you give more time to men than to women participants? Do you treat men more seriously than women participants? Are you less attentive to women participants' questions and concerns? Do you assume a heterosexual model when referring to human behavior?

- When assigning participants to temporary leadership or teaching roles, ensure balanced gender representation.

- Encourage participants to go beyond traditional gender roles when participating in program activities.

The use of these techniques creates a learning environment that is inclusive, empowering, and nonconducive to sexual harassment.

With this training, expect that staff should be able to educate participants about sexual harassment. Participants could receive a brochure outlining the sexual harassment policy and procedures with the information sent to them after registration or when they first arrive at the program. During the first safety briefing, the policy and procedures need to be reviewed to ensure participants understand them.

It is important for adventure educators to consider the dynamics of sexual harassment when forming groups. If possible, if the groups are to be coed, women should be placed in equal numbers to men. One outdoor organization is known for splitting its women students apart from each other. This results in women being placed in groups where they are outnumbered greatly by men. This practice may increase the opportunity for sexual harassment to occur.

Finally, sexual harassment takes place within a climate of secrecy, intimidation, and coercion. If a student or staff member finds herself in a remote wilderness location within this type of damaging climate, it may be impossible for her to enact the sexual harassment reporting procedures. For this reason, it is important that on long, field-based courses there be a mechanism for staff and students to communicate with someone outside of the immediate situation, such as the program director, if necessary. These mechanisms could include radio contact, written contact, or field visits by the program director. These measures would prevent someone from being trapped in a sexually harassing situation because of dependence on an instructor or co-staff member. The program evaluation forms should have questions asking if sexually harassing behavior occurred during the course to give participants and staff another opportunity to report it. It is important to provide many reporting methods because of the intimidating atmosphere that may surround sexual harassment.

Conclusion

The effects of sexual harassment conflict greatly with the benefits of participating in an experiential education program. Experiential education programs need to recognize that sexual harassment occurs and take proactive measures to prevent and interrupt it. These measures will make adventure programs more accessible, empowering, and safe for both women and men.

Additionally, further research is needed to determine the occurrence rates and circumstances of sexual harassment in experiential education programs. This information will assist experiential education programs in the continuing process of assessing their programs, educating their participants, and eradicating sexual harassment.

References

Bangs, R. (1988). The stone syndrome or a bird in the hand is worth two in the bush or skin in the adventure trade. *Rock and Ice*, pp. 16-19.

Colorado Outward Bound School. (1992). *Program catalog*. Denver, CO: Author.

Curry, T. (1991). Fraternal bonding in the locker room: A profeminist analysis of talk about competition and women. *Sociology of Sport Journal, 8,* 119-135.

Dziech, B., & Weiner, L. (1984). *The lecherous professor*. Boston, MA: Beacon Press.

Fine G. (1987). One of the boys: Women in male-dominated settings. In M. Kimmel (Ed.), *Changing men* (pp. 131-147). Newbury Park, CA: Sage.

Fitzgerald, L. (1990). Sexual harassment: The definition and measurement of a construct. In M. Paludi (Ed.), *Ivory power: Sexual harassment on campus*. Albany, NY: SUNY Press.

Fitzgerald, L., Shullman, S., Bailey, N., Richards, M., Swecker, J., Gold, Y., Ormerod, M., & Weitzman, L. (1988). The incidence and dimensions of sexual harassment in academia and the workplace. *Journal of Vocational Behavior, 32*, 152-175.

Harlin, J., III. (1986). *The climber's guide to North America—East Coast rock climbs*. Denver, CO: Chockstone Press.

Hunt, J. (1990). *Ethical issues in experiential education*. Dubuque, IA: Kendall/Hunt.

Koss, M. (1990). Changed lives: The psychological impact of sexual harassment. In M. Paludi (Ed.), *Ivory power. Sexual harassment on campus* (pp. 73-92). Albany, NY: SUNY Press.

Loeffler, T. (1995). *Factors that influence women's career development in outdoor leadership*. Unpublished doctoral dissertation, University of Minnesota, Minneapolis, MN.

Lyman, P. (1987). The fraternal bond as a joking relationship. In M. Kimmel (Ed.), *Changing men* (pp. 148-163). Newbury Park, CA: Sage.

McDermott, J. (Ed.). (1981). *The philosophy of John Dewey*. Chicago: University of Chicago Press.

Melnick, M. (1992). Male athletes and sexual assault. *Journal of Physical Education, Recreation and Dance, 63*(5), 32-35.

Paludi, M., & Barickman, R. (1991). *Academic and workplace sexual harassment: A resource manual*. Albany, NY: SUNY Press.

Sanday, P. (1990). *Fraternal gang rapes: Sex, brotherhood, and privilege on campus*. New York: New York University Press.

Steiger, J. (1985). *Climber's guide to Sabino Canyon and Mount Lemmon Highway*. Glendale, AZ: Polar Designs Publication.

United States Merit Systems Protection Board. (1981). *Sexual harassment in the federal workplace: Is it a problem?* Washington, DC: U.S. Government Printing Office.

Waugh, J. (1982). *A topo guide to Granite Mountain*. Glendale, AZ: Polar Designs Publication.

Webster, E. (1987). *Rockclimbs in the White Mountains of New Hampshire* (2nd ed.). Eldorado Springs, CO: Mountain Imagery.

20

Women of Color in Experiential Education: Crossing Cultural Boundaries

Nina Roberts

An Overview

There is a need to be expansive in our thinking about the outdoor experience of diverse people in this society. Race and ethnic relations have been greatly shaped by historical perspectives, political correctness, social construction, cultural ideologies, and power structure. The intent of this chapter is to describe a connection of race and ethnicity to women's involvement in experiential education and recreation in the outdoors. Incorporating what has been found in the literature, I will discuss issues of empowerment, difference, socialization, spirituality, and leadership. It is well known that people of color, as both participants and leaders, make up a very small percentage of those involved in experiential education. Any research directed at why this is so will require a radical expansion of our usual categories of analysis.

Discussion of the outdoor adventure experiences of women in particular, quite often neglects experiences of women of color. Little is known about *how* ethnic background affects the quality and quantity of their experiences in the outdoors. It is therefore critical to understand not only the outdoor experience of all women, but to acknowledge and ascertain how race and ethnic relations shape each of us individually as well.

Just as we (as professionals) cannot make generalizations about all women as a single group, we also cannot make generalizations about women of color, since this group includes women from numerous racial, ethnic, and national origin backgrounds. Subsequently, although people of color are not a minority on a global scale, this chapter refers to the dominant culture as it relates to European Americans within U.S. society. Aguilar and Washington (1990) differentiate the terms *people of color*, *race*, and *ethnicity* as follows:

The term people of color is used to refer to ethnic and racial groups that have previously been referred to as minorities. Race is used to refer to color (i.e., black, white, red, yellow) and makes distinctions primarily on physical characteristics. Ethnicity refers to affiliation with a social group due to heritage or nationality. (p. 50)

Aguilar and Washington (1990) state that "while ethnicity is often ascribed by others, we should consider that not everyone chooses to embrace their ethnic backgrounds. Thus, one may choose to identify or reject her/his ethnicity. Race, however, does not generally allow the same flexibility" (p. 50). Additionally, rather than maintain distinct social, economic, and political conventions, some ethnic groups experience a cultural assimilation into mainstream society. How, then, can minority groups have cross-cultural experience without losing traditional cultural values?

Socialization Research

Socialization experiences research primarily involves looking at the socioeconomic conditions of women of color (Baca-Zinn & Thornton-Dill, 1994; Floyd & Gramann, 1993). Where minority women are situated on the continuum of the economic ladder really conditions the quality and quantity of the experience they have. However, it is the cultural variables (e.g., language, traditions, values), rather than the socioeconomic factors, which are more important in understanding and explaining differences in participation patterns (Floyd & Gramann, 1993). Through my research, I've learned that the socialization of women of color pertaining to participation in outdoor recreational activities has been different from that of European American women. Social forces of race often affect the outdoor experiences of women of color. Combined with other social forces that affect all women (i.e., gender, class, sexual orientation, employment) are conditions such as lack of funds, lack of knowledge or understanding, and strong feelings of distrust for others (Hall, in Ashley, 1990), that have been more of a barrier for women of color than for European American women.

Women of color may not be aware of the opportunities often because certain activities have not been considered socially acceptable forms of recreation (Carr & Williams, 1993; Roberts & Drogin, 1993; Washington, 1990). For instance, while a European American woman might enjoy wilderness backpacking, an African American might prefer a walk in the park because she feels more comfortable in close proximity to a more "civilized" environment (i.e., large number of people and provision of facilities).

Further, to ignore the racial and gender classifications, is to ignore realities of multiple social identities. Women of color are aware that participation in outdoor adventures has traditionally been primarily stereotyped as a white, male activity. Although difficult to ascertain, the socialization of women of color, in general, has been exclusive of opportunities for outdoor adventure experience. For instance, it is essential for white women and women of color to know that women in general are going against the stereotype of outdoor activities as a male domain. However, while white women are going against the concept of gender, women of color additionally confront the domain of race.

Constraints to Participation

While research about the experience of women and the experience of people of color exists, the full range of opportunities and experience for women of color in experiential education has yet to be addressed. Various limiting factors may affect participation. Media images and marketing for experiential programs, for instance, quite often omit women of color. A cultural lag exists between the media's presentation of women of diverse ethnic backgrounds and their changing rate of participation in outdoor activities.

The few images which portray women as attractive, glamorous, and possessing strong European features may discourage women of color. That is, the message received in such instances is that attractiveness, success, and popularity are basically unattainable for females of color (Boyd, 1990). Furthermore, Kane and Parks (1990), from their examination of *Sports Illustrated*, indicate that males receive significantly more comments than females. Findings from this study suggest that men's sports are more important than women's sports due to the dominant ratings and greater coverage in all aspects, including athletic ability. "If women internalize this message, they may believe that their abilities as serious athletes are not valued" (p. 47).

Given the power of the media to influence one's behavior, it becomes difficult to make participation decisions also based on photographs in brochures, for instance, if none depict women of color. "If there are no women like me in these pictures of outdoor activities, why should I participate?" is a question sometimes asked (Roberts, 1992).

Bialeschki and Henderson (1993) have been in the forefront of research pertaining to women in recreation, outdoor pursuits, and the constraints to participation which they face. Although living in a more progressive society where women's roles have changed drastically during the last 50 years, the constraints on women's involvement in outdoor activities persists and is undeniably linked to issues of gender. "Some women may not participate in certain activities because of the perceived gender appropriateness of them. In other cases, the roles expected of women will result in their being directed into particular roles" (p. 38). It is important to note that Bialeschki and Henderson's investigation of women's participation in the outdoors has focused on European American women. Not to say their discourse ignores women of color, but it's no different than other researchers' analyses of people of color in the outdoors—which is quite minimal. A significant point I want to note is that participation for women of color has limitations in the greater society as well. Baca-Zinn and Thornton-Dill (1994) suggest that restricted participation in social institutions and structured placement in roles with limited opportunities are distinct constraining factors in the lives of women of color. Racial oppression and class domination create barriers, limit possibilities, and constrain choices (p. 5).

Other constraints which Bialeschki and Henderson (1993) discuss include women's socialization into an ethic of care (placing others' needs before their own), safety issues (physical and psychological), and lack of skills and opportunities (i.e., continuum of choices limited by time and money). For women of color, added stresses of either noticeable or covert prejudice and marginality accentuate any injustice, or inequality, that they may experience (Baca-Zinn & Thornton-Dill, 1994; Locke, 1992; Albrecht & Brewer, 1990).

Defining the Cultural Experience as Related to the Outdoors

How and why have the outdoor experiences of culturally different groups and subgroups been similar to and different from one another? How and why have the outdoor experiences of culturally different groups been similar to and different from the dominant culture? To better understand a particular cultural group, it is important to not only study information about the specific groups, but to also foster an appreciation of the wide diversity of individual experience.

Further, to understand the "myth of the model minority" is to understand "privilege." That is, some members of a minority group accept cultural patterns of the dominant group (acculturation) and sacrifice the traditional values and customs of their own culture. This is a way of achieving recognition so as not to "make waves" (which historically has led to lynching or other acts of violence toward ethnic minorities). Often these myths are rooted in political and/or religious ideology.

African American Women

For African American women, constraints to participation are similar to those discussed by Bialeschki and Henderson (1993) (i.e., time, money, family responsibility, lack of opportunity), yet may be accentuated based on their cultural context. For instance, in the African American community, an inescapable aspect of socialization and nurturing is to prepare the family for survival and protect them from an environment that is covertly, if not overtly, hostile, racist, and discriminatory. "The likelihood of major progress in eliminating racism is remote" (Locke, 1992, p. 21). For many African American women, outdoor programs are too threatening and they struggle with a fear of failure or uncertainty. Reasons for this range from lack of knowledge, low self-esteem due to fear of judgment by white people, to the dominance of white people as primary participants in outdoor-based programs. Support and participation by others from a similar culture or minority support system may ameliorate the problem of safety (Roberts & Drogin, 1993). A history of segregation and discrimination against African Americans has separated them from the dominant culture (Locke, 1992; Donald & Rattansi, 1992). This isolation has created a lack of exposure and inability to gain valuable skills in experiential education.

Roberts and Drogin (1993) looked at factors affecting participation in outdoor recreation activities of African American women. Primarily based on interviews, their conclusions were quite similar to Ashley's concepts developed from the study conducted by Hall (in Ashley, 1990). That is, nonparticipation can be attributed to perceptions of race and gender (e.g., socialization and "appropriateness" of activities), lack of role models, lack of exposure, difficulty accessing wilderness from urban areas, and, in some instances, economic conditions.

Native American Women

Ceremonies, rituals, and traditions for Native American women provide a spiritual ethic of care that is rich in nonverbal language. Learning in Native culture is often based on listening, watching others, and experience. Forced from their sacred and valuable lands, Native Americans were stripped of their cultural identity and relegated to property unwanted by white people (Locke, 1992). A culture which passes on traditions and customs through oral myths and legends, Native Americans both live and learn holistically (p. 51). They believe, for instance, that children should be allowed to make mistakes and learn the natural consequences of their mistakes. They develop an inner motivation to learn by seeking out knowledge of human experience (More, 1987).

The Native American family structure and dynamics assert that the female is responsible for and performs the duties necessary to preserve the "social organization." Unlike the dominant culture, Native Americans traditionally trace their family history through matrilinear descent. The primary constraint to participation in experiential programs or activities is the dominant culture "forcing Native Americans to live a difficult and impoverished existence" (Locke, p. 48). It was the taking of this land—occupied by Native Americans—by the dominant white culture which sent a message that the Native American culture was inferior (Locke, 1992; More, 1987). The land that many European Americans take for granted as a means to fulfill outdoor experiences may have sacred and spiritual power to Native Americans.

One of the goals of outdoor adventure is to feel the experience, explore the natural environment, and draw valid and meaningful conclusions based on these personal experiences. Subsequently, as each individual is a product of their cultural environment, it can be learned from Native American culture that respect for nature magnifies a self-discovery not obtained in any other surroundings. The focus of experiential activities is often individual self-exploration and discovery, and instilling an appreciation for the natural world. Such programs are truly complementary to Native American values.

So why are there so few Native American women participating in structured outdoor programs? As stated by Luther Standing Bear, Oglala Sioux Chief, "The American Indian is of the soil, whether it be the region of forests, plains, pueblos, or mesas. He [sic] fits into the landscape . . . he [sic] once grew as naturally as the wild sunflowers; he [sic] belongs just as the buffalo belonged . . ." (Aaron & Borgenicht, 1993). In essence, the message is that "structure" reduces what is a viable part of life to begin with. Subsequently, from an early age, Native Americans know who they are and what their heritage is. Being proud to be related to the land is part of the traditional culture. Hepsi Barnett, an Osage Indian, proclaims that Native people could never imagine paying money to go and be out on the land. "In many parts of the country they are already living on the land; it is an everyday thing for them" (personal communication, January 1995). For Native people, the earth and their minds are one; the measure of the land and the measure of their bodies are the same. Why place "structure" to that which is already known and practiced?

Asian American Women

In Asian American culture, women tend to be dependent, conforming, obedient to men, inhibited and reserved, less ready to express impulses, and less assertive (Sue, 1981). Women from this culture emphasize suppression of strong feelings and stress family as well as community over the individual. Unlike the dominant culture, according to Locke (1992), Asian American women approach time in an unhurried, flexible manner; additionally, moral virtue and showing respect for the elderly is essential. In the area of social relations, the avoidance of conflict and instilling harmony is valued in the Asian American culture (Locke, 1992).

Historically, Asians have been unwilling victims of derogatory stereotyping throughout the United States (Sue, 1981). The first immigrants were all males because the only females allowed to immigrate were prostitutes. The "success" of Asian immigrants can be attributed, in part, to their emphasis on education and a very strong system of discipline (Sue, 1981; Locke, 1992). Locke (1992) characterized their success based on a continuation of racist and prejudiced thinking by the dominant U.S. culture. In other words, because Asian Americans were socially isolated, this provided the ingredients for them to adjust to inherent problems within the dominant culture (e.g., ". . . the Chinese Exclusion Act of 1882 [was] the only federal statute to deny citizenship to an entire people because they were considered undesirable" p. 87). This isolation manifests itself by indicating to individuals in the Asian culture that they can succeed if they work hard enough; therefore, if one does not succeed, it is not because of forces operating in society, but because of other factors such as racial inferiority (Locke, 1992).

Many Asian American women devote themselves to raising their children while experiencing a strong push for them to excel academically. Watanabe (1973) describes the family system as patriarchal; authority of the father remains unquestioned. Subservience to males is the female's role in the family, along with performing domestic duties.

Culturally, Asian Americans place an emphasis on nonverbal communication and the use of silence as a safe response to uncertain situations (Locke, 1992, p. 74). All of these points concerning Asian Americans, in general, may be applicable to any variety of subcultures (e.g., Chinese, Japanese, Korean, or Vietnamese). Implications for experiential learning may relate to pursuing a course of cultural enrichment, rather than cultural change. For example, providing a nonthreatening group climate to encourage more verbal participation (i.e., language barriers often cause discomfort and a difficulty with communication) may enhance the experience. Because women and girls are under very strict supervision by male family members, opportunities for increasing confidence and independence through experiential programs is great. Adventure activities may provide an avenue for self-expression otherwise suppressed in their culture.

Mexican American Women

The Hispanic population is growing steadily, and it is quickly becoming the largest minority group in the United States. Mexican Americans (a cultural mix of Spanish, Indian, and American) account for 60% of the Hispanic population (Locke, 1992; Donald & Rattansi, 1992). Historically, many Mexicans fought with the Americans in order to acquire the independent state of Texas, only to find themselves as foreigners; the Mexican government relinquished the Southwestern territories to the United States under the Treaty of Guadalupe Hidalgo (Locke, 1992). Hence, immigrating from Mexico to the U.S. was based on a strong desire for change and opportunity.

By "standards" of the dominant culture, Mexican Americans have experienced little social progress; additionally, they are markedly behind other cultures in the total amount of education, occupations, income, housing, political representation, and professional identification (Locke, 1992). Many newly emerging Mexican American organizations have been formed to demand social and political equality.

During adolescence, a female remains closer to home than males and is protected and guarded whenever she comes in contact with individuals beyond her family (Mirande, 1985). Mirande (1985) contends that based on relationships with her mother and other female relatives, the Mexican American female is prepared for the role of wife and mother. Conversely, a male is given freedom to come and go as he chooses and is encouraged to obtain "worldly" knowledge and experience in order to prepare for his role as husband and father.

While individuals of the dominant culture are taught to value being open, frank, and direct, the traditional Mexican American approach uses a diplomatic and tactful means of communicating with other people (Mirande, 1985; Locke, 1992). However, interesting and often-misunderstood values and attitudes relate to this manner of expression. For instance, Mexican Americans aim to be "elaborate and indirect" because their goal is to make the personal relationship at least appear to be harmonious in order to show some respect for the other's individuality. "To the Mexican American, direct argument or contradiction appears to be rude and disrespectful" (Locke, 1992, p. 40). Superficially, there may be some agreement, yet their manner of expression dictates they ought not reveal true feelings openly unless the two people know each other well, and if there is sufficient time to express differences with tact.

Implications for experiential education may be expressed through the development of relationships. Proudman (1992) described the experiential process as a series of relationships: the learner to self, the learner to teacher, and the learner to the learning environment. His discussion of the variables involved included the importance of responsibility for self-growth, defining boundaries, and understanding different learning experiences and varying reactions individuals have to the same learning environment.

Pertaining to outdoor recreation as the experiential learning medium, Mexican Americans tend to participate in large groups and with extended families. Floyd and Gramann (1993) conducted an analysis of outdoor recreation patterns of Mexican Americans and concluded that the effects of acculturation, the process of a minority group acquiring the cultural characteristics of the dominant group (p. 8), were primarily expressed in which types of activities were chosen versus which outdoor areas were visited. For example, fishing, tent camping, and off-road vehicle use were activities highly valued; whether they occurred adjacent to a local river or within a national forest was secondary to the opportunity itself. Additionally, it was demonstrated that assuming all ethnic groups are culturally homogeneous is a fallacy (i.e., U.S.-born Mexican American, born in Mexico, parents born in Mexico, Spanish influence). Just as there is no one Anglo type, there is no one Mexican family type.

What role do variables such as socioeconomic status, social class, race, and gender play in the outdoor recreation activities in which Mexican American females become involved? I have found no supporting research which has broken down the variables by gender. We must employ new methods of investigation and examine the various social and cultural variables influencing socialization of Mexican American women into adventure education. Although, within their culture, Mexican American women are supposed to be completely devoted to the men and serve their every need, they also ought to be provided an opportunity to take initiative, increase decision-making skills, and participate in self-directed learning activities in outdoor-based programs.

Perceptions of Participation: Three Case Studies

Roberts (1992) elicited perspectives on leadership, gender issues, experiences of outdoor adventure participation (with friends, with organized groups, or solo) from several women of color. Because of their unique backgrounds and various regional representations, three women were selected as case studies to provide personal perspectives for this chapter (i.e., African American, Chinese American, and Chicana with Navajo ancestry). They speak from their experiences as women of color in a field that has historically not heard their voices.

In order to convey the detail of these personal accounts, while including a brief background but not revealing the actual names of these women, fictitious names have been used to profile their experiences. The African American woman will be known as "Angela." She's a 31-year-old counselor and teaching aide from Arkansas. Her interests include reading poetry and short stories and travel. The Chinese American woman, who shall be called "Suyuan," is a 50-year-old teacher from Baltimore, Maryland. She enjoys woodworking, sports, crafts, and travel in the outdoors.

Lastly, "Evelyn" is a 33-year-old program coordinator working for a Native American youth program in New Mexico. She is a Chicana woman with Navajo ancestry. Her interests include a variety of cultural activities, outdoor activities, reading, and cooking.

Leadership

These women felt that encouraging more women of color to be role models, restructuring of internships to include distinct mentoring relationships, and greater involvement of the school system (e.g., career days that highlight opportunities for women of color to pursue nontraditional fields) might contribute to a change in participation rates and add to a greater racial and ethnic diversity in professional leadership.

The outdoor experiential education movement has only just begun to provide an avenue of leadership opportunities for minorities. For women of color, the interest in programming, supervising, and directing outdoor activities is growing. These opportunities may be more community-based and centered in areas where people of color live (Roberts, 1992). An important aspect shared by the women in these case studies is for professionals to remember that the outdoors has become one of the *many* ways for women to find self-fulfillment. Professionals in the field should provide encouragement, but should also be reminded that not all women share the same passions in life.

Empowerment

Denise Mitten (1992), who has worked with women's groups for over 15 years, confirms that women have attributed life changes and positive experiences to their participation in outdoor trips. Personal benefits regarding empowerment and self-esteem are overwhelmingly expressed. Angela and Evelyn were in accord that participation in outdoor activities builds confidence and offers challenges not available anywhere else. Such opportunity, they agreed, provides a spirituality and personal time for "getting in balance" with themselves. On the other hand, Suyuan did not feel that the outdoors empowers women in particular and that the same empowerment (i.e., meeting physical and/or mental demands that one thought were too much) is the same empowerment that applies to anyone. She also expressed difficulty in seeing why women of color need to be "so strongly separated" from the rest of the population.

Evelyn and Angela described their source of energy and personal empowerment as it related to knowledge of their heritage, family, religion, and an array of multicultural experiences. Additional comments ranged from finding a strong foundation and gaining strength and mutual support of women within a community, to enjoying the simple pleasures of nature. Although Suyuan felt that some ethnic cultures have rituals and customs that can be a powerful means of sharing and celebrating, she believes that what empowers women of color should be the same as that which empowers anyone else; that is, "a sense of self and mission, a belief in oneself and a trust in the goodness of what lies ahead." Her own creativity and ideas give her energy along with the excitement that comes from thinking about the adventure of trying something new.

Feminist Theory and the Structure of Power

Perspectives differ in terms of feminism, leadership, and power. Based on the work of Starhawk, Albrecht and Brewer (1990) assert that when many feminists speak of power, it is often *power-with*, rather than *power-over*. And, access to social power is a privilege. The element of privilege is significant in that it may be different based on gender, class, education, ability, etc. This is a multifaceted concept which must be recognized. Power differences between groups, and within groups, when crossing cultural boundaries and creating alliances, are also important. White people, men, and middle- and upper-class people monopolize a disproportionate amount of power in a society divided along race, class, and gender lines (p. 5). The issue for women's alliances is to recognize power differences and positions of privilege, and to create bridges to link these differences.

The implications of this power structure upon women's leadership models is dramatic. Albrecht and Brewer (1990) looked at how women have developed alternative leadership strategies and whether these strategies have worked toward the building of alliances among women. In the context of building alliances, the essays in their book support the fact that in order to effect change at various levels, each woman must risk using her own personal power (p. 6). Not only must women take responsibility for breaking down their own barriers of internalized oppression and internalized domination, they must also come to understand that the cultural, racial, class, generational, sexual, ethnic, and religious diversities among them are what create different leadership styles. Internalized dominance for white women may pertain to race; yet for women of color, it is racism. To successfully cross these boundaries, individuals must listen and respect each other and learn about differences. Subsequently, differences should not be viewed as boundaries, but recognized for just what they are, "differences."

As symbolized in the three case studies, Evelyn expressed that *feminism* as a movement is perceived or led by upper-class white women. She believes this hurts the cause of feminism throughout the country. She affirmed that her identity is linked more to her cultural background than to gender. Angela supported the notion that the cultural context of her ethnicity defines feminism for her as a woman of color. Conversely, Suyuan believes that feminism needs a new broader definition so that the women's ways of knowing and doing and being can be applied to any human being, whether female or male. Although this belief cannot (and should not) be judged, this is a cultural way of thinking that may suppress the reality of positions of privilege and acknowledgment of who is in positions of power.

I suggest that because ways of knowing are part of our total experience, bringing a feminist perspective to the outdoors may have a cultural component. Outdoor leadership, for instance, does not denote *power-over* for many women; instead, it creates an ethical and inclusive style that encourages rather than limits participation (Mitten, 1992). Because access to social power has traditionally been denied to women of color (Albrecht & Brewer, 1990), when placed in positions of leadership the application is how to flourish this "power" and how to transform it. To be an effective outdoor leader, therefore, the questions for women of color become, Power to do what? And for whom? (Roberts, 1994).

Building Cultural Connections

Greater alliances and deeper coalitions are needed to cross cultural boundaries. How can these be formed? Responses to this question also elicited varying comments. Suyuan indicated that women who choose to work together must start by simply being together until a friendship is developed and the fact of color differences disappear. She stated, "People with a particular need work together; similarity of color is never an automatic criteria for being able to form a coalition."

Angela believed there should be deep and honest discussion of prejudices, biases, and misconceptions between European and African Americans. Although this view is meritorious, it is important to distinguish this from the need for greater discussion of these issues *between* ethnicities. People of color must recognize their responsibility to reduce the myth of the stereotypes which are prevalent in society. Alperin (in Albrecht & Brewer, 1990) concurs that it is imperative for oppressed groups with different viewpoints to form alliances in order to understand how different types of oppression interact. Angela's argument is that if different critical standpoints are more readily available to different oppressed groups through struggle, and if different types of oppression are interrelated, then it would follow that a thorough understanding of the complexity of social relations—in any particular moment—could be most effectively achieved through alliances between groups with different standpoints.

One pertinent connection I want to make relating to experiential education is that the values being taught (i.e., self-confidence, teamwork, compassion, and service to others) ought to have meaning to all people and relate to the rich diversity of individuals venturing into the outdoors. The values being taught and learned perhaps in a challenging wilderness environment are universally important and can be achieved at a greater level if shared across cultures.

Culture and Spirituality

The outdoors can offer a spiritual connection with nature not experienced anywhere else. How can women of color explore their uniqueness and the richness of their particular ethnicity, appearance, and traditions in outdoor activities? A comment offered by Evelyn in response was that newer experiential activities need to be developed, incorporating multigenerational and traditional culture-specific activities of minorities. Angela felt that spirituality can be magnified by using personal heritage to explore the outdoors and "discover the physical bonds we share with our ancestors who first explored the wilderness, and who used the bounty of the woods, fields and streams for medicine and food from what they discovered." Suyuan expressed her personal conviction that it is in being with each other that any minority group finds support and bonding, hence collectively exploring uniqueness and spiritual connections to the environment and to each other.

Discrimination and Racism

Cultural diversity mandates acknowledgment that women act differently to reach certain goals based on the historical impact of racism on their lives. Racism, however, has not affected all people of color in the same way. For instance, many Native American women were coerced off their tribal lands by the U.S. government and forced into white society, whereas African American women have a history of segregation from the white dominant system (Baca-Zinn & Thornton-Dill, 1994; Albrecht & Brewer, 1990).

Every ethnic culture retains a key linked to the power of survival for the women of color. For some Latina women, this may involve speaking only in their native tongue; African American women may find comfort in religion; and some Native women may turn to purification rituals (Boyd, 1990). "For many women of color defining a sense of identity through rituals and traditional customs is paramount in developing a stronger sense of self individually and collectively" (p. 158). I must add that these examples are not intended to reinforce any stereotypes; any method used by women of color to "survive" may not be that distinct or simple, and can be quite complex.

Chavez (as reported in Henderson & Bedini, 1992) explored diversity among various ethnic groups as related to outdoor recreation behavior. She found that groups of European American, Hispanic American, and Mexican American individuals enjoyed and appreciated similar activities and had the same beliefs about crowding issues. The most significant difference between ethnic groups was their "perceived exposure to discriminatory acts." Those individuals identifying as part of a minority group were more likely to perceive themselves as having been subject to these acts, whereas European Americans did not hold the same perception due to their experience in a society that reinforces the myth of "equality." As one of the goals of experiential education is to develop leadership skills, then the process whereby leaders learn, understand, and accept differences may be a catalyst to decreasing the elements of racism and discrimination likely to be perceived by people of color when participating in outdoor activities.

Conclusion

In order to effectively counsel or teach women of color in the outdoors, a relationship must be created across cultural boundaries. Leaders must first be aware of their own cultural heritage and worldview before they will be able to understand and appreciate those of the culturally diverse individuals they serve.

"It is in cross-cultural settings within our own society and internationally that the most powerful, life-changing experiential learning can and often does occur" (Kraft, 1992, p. 14). In his discussion of moral courage, Kraft (1992) contends that it is the power of cross-cultural experience that brings justice into our society. Unfortunately, our communities remain segregated along class, racial, and ethnic lines. Experiential education, according to Kraft, is an extremely powerful tool for helping to bridge those gaps which continuously lead to riots, starvation, homelessness, violence, spread of diseases, and other devastating circumstances. What influence will the growth of such problems have on the roles of educators and leaders? What influence will racism and gender relations have on these roles?

Most of the existing literature of people of color discusses ethnicity from the broader context to include Native, African, Asian, and Latina Americans (NAALAs); it is my conviction that more work needs to look at acculturation, identity as a subgroup as well as the experience of individuals who are biracial (e.g., whether between varying ethnic groups, or between white people and people of color). The existence of biracial people forces professionals and society to re-think the meaning of race and the predicated social order. For instance, skin color and social definitions may run counter to one another when different cultures mix (Root, 1992).

Theories must be developed and research, both qualitative and quantitative, conducted with reference to ethnic diversity and specifically, women of color. Findings must then be put into practice to cross cultural boundaries and ensure that programs are inclusive and optimally beneficial to *all* groups of people.

It is especially incumbent upon women in the field to examine research findings on women of color so that we can assist in the self-empowering of all women involved in experiential education and outdoor recreational activities. Well-developed experiences can inspire women of color to continue to raise their voices, and to refuse to be silenced by traditions carried over from society into the outdoors. But women leaders need to go further; we need to help people connect with one another, share our knowledge, share our skills and our competencies, increase awarenesses and acceptances of all people, and all peoples' experience. This brings us together as one. We need to cross cultural boundaries in order to celebrate our similarities as well as our differences.

We must strive to confirm and support the abilities of women in general. This has to do with understanding some of the barriers that are prevalent in society, and working deliberately and consciously toward ridding society and the field of experiential education of these barriers that tend to oppress all women. Subsequently, it is important that we continue traditions of role modeling and enhance the need for women of color to mentor other young women and provide the necessary opportunities so that we can build upon former traditions, and create new traditions in the area of women of color in the outdoors.

Acknowledgments

The topic of race and culture is both varied and complex; the questions which can be raised by the information and issues presented in this article should lead us to further inquiry in the field of experiential education. I would like to thank Ellen Drogin who offered her insight during the early stages of editing. Special thanks to Karen Warren for encouraging me to persevere, to Nancy Hogan for her valuable feedback, and to the reviewers of this chapter for their comprehensive evaluation. Very special thanks to Sharon Washington for her expertise and assistance; her advice and support was integral to completion of this chapter.

References

Aaron, G. C., & Borgenicht, D. (1993). *Native American wisdom*. Philadelphia, PA: Running Press.

Aguilar, T. E., & Washington, S. J. (1990). Towards the inclusion of multicultural issues in leisure studies curricula. *Schole: A Journal of Leisure Studies and Recreation, 5*, 41-52.

Albrecht, L., & Brewer, R. M. (Eds.). (1990). *Bridges of power: Women's multicultural alliances*. Philadelphia, PA: New Society Publishers.

Ashley, F. (1990). Ethnic minorities' involvement with outdoor experiential education. In J. C. Miles & S. Priest (Eds.), *Adventure education*. State College, PA: Venture.

Baca-Zinn, M., & Thornton-Dill, B. (1994). *Women of color in U.S. society*. Philadelphia, PA: Temple University.

Bialeschki, M. D., & Henderson, K. A. (1993). Expanding outdoor opportunities for women. *Parks and Recreation, 28*(8), 36-40.

Boyd, J. A. (1990). Ethnic and cultural diversity: Keys to power. *Women and Therapy, 9*, 151-167.

Carr, D. S., & Williams, D. R. (1993). Understanding the role of ethnicity in outdoor recreation experiences. *Journal of Leisure Research, 25*(1), 22-38.

Donald, J., & Rattansi, A. (1992). *Race, culture & difference*. Newbury Park, CA: Sage.

Floyd, M. F., & Gramann, J. H. (1993). Effects of acculturation and structural assimilation in resource-based recreation: The case of Mexican Americans. *Journal of Leisure Research, 25*(1), 6-21.

Henderson, K. A., & Bedini, L. A. (1992). NRPA leisure research symposium showcases current park and recreation research. *Parks and Recreation, 1*, 16-25, 90.

Kane, M. J., & Parks, J. B. (1990). Media messages of female athletes: Gender-role expectations as barriers to leisure. National Recreation and Park Association Congress, Phoenix, Arizona. (Abstracts from the Symposium on Leisure Research, p. 47).

Kraft, R. J. (1992). Closed classrooms, high mountains and strange lands: An inquiry into culture and caring. *Journal of Experiential Education, 15*(3), 8-15.

Locke, D. C. (1992). *Increasing multicultural understanding*. Newbury Park, CA: Sage.

Mirande, A. (1985). *The Chicano experience: An alternative perspective*. Notre Dame, IN: University of Notre Dame Press.

Mitten, D. (1992). Empowering girls and women in the outdoors. *Journal of Physical Education, Recreation and Dance, 63*(2), 56-60.

More, A. J. (1987). Native Indian learning styles: A review for researchers and teachers. *Journal of American Indian Education, 27*, 17-28.

Proudman, B. (1992). Experiential education as emotionally-engaged learning. *Journal of Experiential Education, 15*(2), 19-23.

Roberts, N. S. (1994). *Women of color in outdoor recreation: A collection of personal stories.* Unpublished collection. College Park, Maryland.

Roberts, N. S. (1992). *Women of color: Building bridges to adventure.* Unpublished case studies, College Park, Maryland.

Roberts, N. S., & Drogin, E. B. (1993). Factors affecting participation of African American women. *Journal of Experiential Education, 16*(1), 14-18.

Root, M. P. P. (1992). *Racially mixed people in America.* Newbury Park, CA: Sage.

Sue, D. W. (1981). *Counseling the culturally different: Theory and practice.* New York: John Wiley.

Washington, S. J. (1990). Provision of leisure services to people of color. *Journal of Health, Physical Education, Recreation and Dance, 10*, 37-39.

Watanabe, C. (1973). Self-expression and the Asian-American experience. *Personnel and Guidance Journal, 51*, 390-396.

21

Lesbian Baiting Hurts All Women

Mary McClintock

- *Barb is active in the leadership of the Outing Club at her college. She's getting very tired of being "warned" about other women members of the club. Several friends have told Barb that "all those outdoor activities attract lesbians" and to make sure she doesn't share a tent with any of the lesbians.*
- *Lisa is worried that if any of her co-workers see her going to the Women in Experiential Education Professional Group (PG) meeting at the Association for Experiential Education Conference, they'll think she's a lesbian. She's heard some of her co-workers making jokes about what the lesbians in the group do during the women-only meetings.*
- *Clarice decides not to include her extensive volunteer leadership experience with Women Outdoors on her application for a job leading therapeutic outdoor programs for adolescents. Women Outdoors has a reputation as a lesbian organization in the community, and the local school board just made a policy excluding any programs that "support homosexuality" from being part of the school. Clarice knows that some of the school board members are also on the board of the youth service agency with the job opening.*

Barb, Lisa, and Clarice are all experiencing forms of lesbian baiting—labeling women or groups of women as lesbians in order to discredit them and to pressure them to conform to traditional gender roles. Lesbian baiting works because homophobia (the fear and hatred of lesbians and gay men) still exists.

Despite increasing acceptance of lesbians and gay men in some areas of society (including passing gay rights laws and domestic partnership benefits), homophobia is alive and well in many areas of education. The original version of the Elementary and Secondary Education Act passed by the U.S. Senate in the summer of 1994 included an amendment by Senator Jesse Helms that would prohibit schools from receiving federal funds if the schools had any programs or curricula that had "the purpose or effect of encouraging or supporting homosexuality as a positive lifestyle alternative" (Pitsch, 1994). While this amendment was removed in the final version of the Act, the fact that the amendment was approved by the Senate indicates the level of homophobia in public K-12 education. In December 1993, because of concern over increasing harassment and the high suicide rate among lesbian and gay youth, Massachusetts passed a law to protect the civil rights of lesbian and gay public school students and provide programs that support them (Portner, 1994). Some local communities have resisted implementation of these programs, stating that such programs "undermined family values" and "interfered with parents' rights to teach values in the home" (Portner, 1994). The debate in the federal legislature over the Helms amendment and the reaction of communities to attempts to address lesbian and gay issues in schools are just a few recent examples of homophobia prevalent in many areas of education.

One particular form of homophobia that remains prevalent in experiential education is lesbian baiting. While other forms of homophobia and gay baiting affect men, the focus of this chapter is on lesbian baiting and its impact on women. My goal in this chapter is to provide a framework for thinking, talking, and taking action about an issue which hurts all women in the fields of outdoor and adventure education. In all three of the situations described above, it doesn't matter whether Lisa, Clarice, or Barb are lesbians or if any of the women in the Women in Experiential Education PG, *Women Outdoors*, or the outing club are lesbians. What matters is that calling them lesbians or the fear of being called lesbians is causing women to monitor and change their actions in order to avoid being labeled.

Suzanne Pharr, in her pioneering book, *Homophobia: A Weapon of Sexism* (1988), defines lesbian baiting as follows:

> Lesbian baiting is an attempt to control women by labeling us as lesbians because our behavior is not acceptable, . . . lesbian baiting occurs when women are called lesbians because we resist male dominance and control. And it has little or nothing to do with one's sexual identity. (p. 19)

The key is that women are called lesbian because they have done something that appears to be "inappropriate" for women to do, such as excelling at outdoor activities, dressing in clothes that aren't considered feminine, or speaking up for issues that affect women's lives. Being called lesbian or the fear of being called lesbian is used as a tool to get women to change their behavior to more traditional female behavior in an attempt to avoid such labeling.

Lesbian baiting is the intersection of two forms of oppression—sexism and homophobia. Sexism is the systematic subordination of women by men, based on the belief in the inherent superiority of men. Sexism has defined the roles that men and women are supposed to fill in order to keep male dominance in place. Anything that threatens the maintenance of those roles threatens the sexist system. Such baiting is an effective tool to maintain traditional gender roles because the existence of homophobia has made being labeled a lesbian a negative, discrediting action. If being considered a lesbian were not derogatory in the general culture, lesbian baiting would not hold the power that it does.

Lesbian baiting can happen in any situation where women step out of traditional gender roles, including in outdoor and adventure education. Throughout this chapter, I will follow the stories of two situations. The stories are conglomerates of experiences I and other women who work in outdoor and adventure education have had. All of the names have been changed.

Case #1

Louise works as an outdoor educator for an alternative high school, leading outdoor activities for the students at the school. While the students seem to enjoy the activities and to respond well to Louise's leadership, they seem puzzled by her. She is unlike any woman they know. She wears different clothes and likes to do lots of hard, physical activities such as backpacking and rock climbing. The students have asked Louise why she does these activities and why she doesn't dress more like the other women teachers, who often wear dresses and make-up. They also want to know if she has a boyfriend and, if so, what he thinks of her doing this outdoor stuff. Louise told them that the activities are fun and she wears clothes that allow her to do the activities she likes, rather than dressing for fashion. She does not respond to the questions about boyfriends.

One day, after a number of such conversations with her students, Louise started looking at her clothes and thinking that maybe she should wear dresses to work occasionally. She wondered if the students would respect her more if she did. The next week, when Louise walked out the door of the school toward her car to drive home, she noticed four of the girls of her outdoor activity group standing on the sidewalk across from the school. When they saw her, they started to chant, "Lezzie, Lezzie, Lezzie. . . ." They continued until she got in her car.

Case #2

Women's Outdoor Activities (WOA) is a non-profit organization that provides outdoor trips for women and girls. While WOA has been successful in the four years it has been in existence, the WOA Board of Directors is now seeking funding from the local community and from corporations to expand their programs for low-income women and girls.

At the last meeting, the WOA Board discussed recent failures to secure funding from several businesses. The representatives of the businesses said that there were rumors that WOA was really a lesbian organization out to recruit young girls by teaching them masculine outdoor skills, and that their businesses could not be associated with anything to do with lesbians because it would be bad for the company's image. Fran and Beth, the Board members who had approached these businesses, said they thought that the lesbian Board members should be less blatant about being lesbian and that possibly some of the girls' programs should focus on more traditional women's activities.

These two stories demonstrate how lesbian baiting happens both externally and internally on individual and group levels. In Louise's case, other people label her as a lesbian in an attempt to control her behavior—to make her act more like other women in clothing and activity. Furthermore, Louise herself considers changing her behavior to be more typically feminine to avoid such labeling. In the case of WOA, the businesses withhold funding from WOA because of the perception that WOA is a lesbian organization and its involvement in nontraditionally female activities. Some of the Board members internal to WOA suggest changed behavior by lesbian members of the Board and changes in programs.

These stories share elements common to most lesbian baiting situations: an individual or group is labeled lesbian, or some code word for lesbian; a label that is intended to be discrediting or derogatory is used in an attempt to limit or control the behavior of the individual woman or group; and the labeling is based on rigid gender roles or stereotypes.

Lesbian baiting often occurs in more subtle, less overt ways than in these two examples. Rather than directly labeling a woman as a lesbian, questions might be asked about whether she has a husband or boyfriend, code words such as "Amazon" or "mannish" could be used to describe her, or insinuations and whisper campaigns could be started to describe her as being "that way." Sometimes, people don't have the words to describe what they sense, but they know that the woman or group in question is not acting the way women are "supposed" to act, and they equate stepping out of gender role with being other than heterosexual.

Why does lesbian baiting happen in outdoor and adventure education? There are a number of reasons, but the primary reason is that wilderness, the outdoors, and outdoor activities have traditionally been considered the territory of men. Outdoor activities have often been considered an arena for men to prove and exhibit their masculinity.

Joshua Miner and Joe Boldt, in their book, *Outward Bound USA* (1981), describe the concerns of Outward Bound staff when the formerly all-male organization was considering including female students and staff. Outward Bound was not only an all-male organization, but one that equated its activities with masculinity. Bob Pieh is quoted in *Outward Bound USA* as saying, "There was strong feeling at that time among those valuing and cultivating Outward Bound's machismo image that the success of women in similar experiences would diminish that image" (p. 161).

Along with the concerns that "women were not up to hard physical stress or to meeting traditionally male kinds of physical challenge" (p. 160), there were also concerns that being exposed to such programs could have a negative impact on the students and staff. Miner and Boldt describe this concern as "the 'Amazon syndrome'— a concern lest Outward Bound have a defeminizing influence on girl students, or attract 'Amazon types' to staff jobs" (p. 160). These concerns explicitly link the notion of women doing nontraditional activities with the assumption that such women would be "Amazons," which in this case and many others is a code word for lesbians.

The examples mentioned about Outward Bound describe incidents and attitudes in the 1960s. How is lesbian baiting played out in the 1990s for outdoorswomen?

Anne Dal Vera (1994), a member of the American Women's Trans-Antarctic Expedition (AWE), describes the homophobic reactions AWE received when fund raising for and publicizing their all-women's expedition to ski across Antarctica:

> This expedition never received corporate funding, although we approached over 250 corporations. . . . One corporate executive reportedly told Ann Bancroft (AWE expedition leader), "maybe . . . if you take a man along. . . . Other companies were fearful that if the women got hurt, it would be bad for their image. Some didn't want to sponsor a women's expedition because they assumed that all the team members were lesbians. A lot of suggestive remarks were made both directly and indirectly: Two women to a tent? Gonna keep each other warm? Such homophobic assumptions weren't made about Will Steger's 1990 all-male Antarctic Expedition, or the Reinhold Messner/Arved Fuchs ski traverse of Antarctica. (pp. 122-123)

The striking contrast between how this women's expedition and men's expeditions were treated by potential funders and the press speaks loudly of the continued existence of homophobia, sexism, and their by-product, lesbian baiting.

Women are often labeled as lesbians when they work in jobs that have been considered "men's jobs." Outdoor leadership has long been considered men's work. In his book, *Labeling Women Deviant: Gender, Stigma and Social Control*, Edwin M. Schur describes the reaction of men to women entering traditionally "men's jobs" in the following way: "When male workers' conceptions of their 'masculinity' are closely linked to the nature and conditions of their work, they are especially likely to feel threatened by female job entrants" (p. 64). In these situations, Schur says that "more overt derogation may occur" (p. 64).

Similar dynamics occur in the area of athletics, another traditionally male domain. Women who excel in sports are also often labeled as lesbians. Helen Lenskyj (1987), in her article, "Female Sexuality and Women's Sport," addresses this dynamic in the following way:

> The issue of male power is central to the popular association between sport and lesbianism; regardless of sexual preference, women who reject the traditional feminine role in their careers as athletes, coaches or sport administrators, as in any other nontraditional pursuit, pose a threat to existing power between the sexes. For this reason, these women are the frequent targets of labels intended to devalue or dismiss their successes by calling their sexuality into question. (pp. 383-384)

When women engage in any activity that has traditionally been seen as masculine, such as outdoor and adventure education and athletics, they threaten the power dynamics of sexism. Lesbian baiting is used as a tool to attempt to get such women back into roles that support the status quo of sexism, that is, traditional female gender roles.

What are the Effects of Lesbian Baiting?

Case #1

By the time Louise got to her car, she was angry, sad, and afraid. It was clear that the students intended the chanting as derogatory. She didn't know what to think or do. How was she going to face the students the next day? What would she say to them? Did they really think she was a lesbian? Why? Because she was different? Clearly this indicated that the students viewed her difference with suspicion. She was also upset because she had seen one of the school administrators in the parking lot, and she knew he had heard what the girls were chanting. She knew that the Board of Directors of the agency that ran the school, and the community in general, was very politically conservative. She was worried that she might lose her job if the school administration and Board thought she was a lesbian.

Case #2

After the few moments of silence that met Fran and Beth's statement, several Board members started to speak at once. Eleanor expressed outrage that Fran and Beth thought WOA and its Board members should change how they behave to please some businesses. Martha said she was shocked and horrified to hear that WOA had such a "bad" reputation in the community. Claire said that she would quit the Board if she was expected to hide her lesbianism. Suzanne wanted to know if Fran and Beth thought that the lesbians on the Board were to blame for WOA not receiving funding. Instead of discussing fund raising as per the agenda, the Board spent the rest of the meeting discussing whether or how to respond to accusations and how to manage the image of the organization. By the end of the meeting, the only decision that was made was that they would stop seeking funding from businesses while they explored how to respond to the rumors. The tension between Board members was heightened. Lesbian members were upset by the animosity directed at them. Some of the heterosexual members defended their concerns that they would be perceived as lesbian. Progress in setting up the program for low-income women and girls was stopped, effectively keeping them from participating in WOA's activities.

In general, lesbian baiting has a number of effects, both on the individuals involved and on others. Individuals and groups that are targets of baiting, such as the women in these two cases, have to expend energy dealing with the baiting—talking about it, educating about it, or managing their image—rather than putting energy into meeting their own goals. Both Louise and WOA are being pressured to limit their actions to activities that are considered "feminine" and appropriate for women. Such pressure on some women reinforces the limits on all women's behavior. Lesbians are hurt whenever baiting occurs because negative attitudes and behaviors toward lesbians are reinforced. Heterosexual women are hurt because baiting reinforces stereotypes of what behavior is acceptable for heterosexual women.

In adventure and outdoor education, lesbian baiting causes women not to participate in activities that might be enjoyable and beneficial for them in order to avoid being perceived as lesbians. It also limits the abilities of women's programs and organizations to get funding or other forms of support.

Women who are subjected to lesbian baiting often spend a great deal of time and energy trying to correct the image others have of them. They may change their behavior to exaggerate their "femininity," such as by being less assertive, discontinuing participation in "unfeminine" activities such as sports or outdoor activities, avoiding being in the presence of women who are open as lesbians, and making a point of being seen with boyfriends (Blinde & Taube, 1992). In extreme cases, women engage in deep self-hatred and self-destructive behavior when they are lesbian baited.

Taking Action Against Lesbian Baiting

Case #1

As she drove away from school, Louise remembered that she was going out to dinner with several good friends. After telling her story to her friends, Louise realized there were a number of options for how she could react. She considered wearing dresses and talking about a fictitious boyfriend or ignoring it and pretending it never happened. But she still wondered what the students thought of her and realized that both of these options would not address the attitudes of the girls. She decided to call her women friends who lead outdoor activities, to find out if this had ever happened to them and what they'd done. She could also talk to people and read more about women in nontraditional jobs, since part of what was behind this seemed to be the students' reactions to her leading outdoor activities and dressing differently than women were supposed to.

She thought about several things she could do at school the next day. Either she could just tell the students that it was not appropriate for them to call anyone names and that while "Lezzie" is used derogatorily, being a lesbian is not bad. She decided she definitely wanted to talk to the school guidance counselor who had been trying to organize a presentation by the local lesbian, gay, and bisexual speakers' bureau. And she began to consider whether she should plan some activities for the upcoming school Diversity Day on sexism and homophobia in order to help the students develop a broader sense of how women lead their lives and of the lives of lesbians.

As she considered each of these options, Louise realized that she needed to deal with the issue of the conservative, probably homophobic board. She wanted to learn more about how hostile the climate really was for anyone addressing homophobia and to find supportive co-workers.

Case #2

When Deb, one of the WOA Board members, heard about the meeting she had missed, she thought, "Here we go again, another women's organization being lesbian baited!" She had been in other organizations that had been baited, and had done some reading and talking with other women about how to address it. She knew a woman, Anne, who conducted training on issues affecting women, who had taught her a lot about the dynamics of lesbian baiting. Deb called the Chair of the Board and asked to have Anne spend some time with the Board at the next meeting explaining how lesbian baiting worked and helping the Board figure out ways to respond effectively to the baiting.

After hearing Anne explain how lesbian baiting was used as a tool to keep women in gender roles and to support sexism, all of the Board members agreed that they did not want to do anything that supported sexism. Some of the members were still nervous about being called lesbian, but they agreed that maybe they needed to learn more about lesbians and homophobia in general and in their community. The Board agreed that they would continue to seek funding for their programs and continue with the same activities in their programs, and that at the next meeting, they would discuss ways to proactively address homophobia and sexism in the organization and community.

Lesbian baiting will exist as long as homophobia and sexism exist. Along with working against homophobia and sexism in general, individuals and groups can take a number of actions to combat lesbian baiting. In any situation where lesbian baiting has occurred, or has the potential of occurring, there is a whole range of possible responses. Some of the responses actually reinforce the lesbian baiting, while some responses combat it. If one is concerned about combating lesbian baiting, it is important to know the difference between actions that reinforce lesbian baiting and those that combat it. "Defending" oneself by asserting one's heterosexuality, modifying one's behavior to be more "feminine," and not challenging lesbian baiting "rumors" are all actions that reinforce lesbian baiting. Naming baiting for what it is, working against homophobia and sexism in general, and educating oneself about how gender roles limit women are all actions that combat lesbian baiting.

The key to taking action to prevent lesbian baiting and to respond to it when it occurs is to recognize it for what it is, a tool to keep women in line, and to recognize that it operates by drawing on the fear women have of being labeled lesbian. Lesbian baiting does not hold as much power if one is not afraid of being labeled lesbian. Suzanne Pharr (1988) describes this dynamic in the following way: "The word *lesbian* is instilled with the power to halt our work and control our lives. And we give it its power with our fear" (p. 25).

Have you ever experienced lesbian baiting? How did you react? What would you do if you were to be lesbian baited tomorrow? Have you ever spoken with other women who work in outdoor and adventure education about lesbian baiting or homophobia in general? I believe that these are important questions for all women who are outdoor and adventure educators to consider and discuss with other women. One of the major ways that homophobia works is through silence and invisibility. We can counter that silence by talking with other women about how lesbian baiting and other forms of homophobia work to restrict the lives of all women. As Suzanne Pharr (1988) states, lesbian baiting works because of our fear of being called lesbian and because of the existence of homophobia and sexism. In order to effectively combat lesbian baiting, we need to both eliminate our own fear of being labeled lesbian, and to work to end homophobia and sexism in general.

How would you react if you were Louise and had just been called "Lezzie" by students? How would you react if you were a Board member of WOA and had just heard about the rumors about the organization? Louise and the WOA Board were taken by surprise when they were lesbian baited. We do not have to be taken by surprise. We can talk about lesbian baiting and work to prevent it as well as respond to it in a way that empowers women rather than contributes to women's disempowerment. We do not have a choice about whether or how we might be lesbian baited. However, we do have a choice in how we respond when it occurs.

References

Blinde, E. M., & Taub, D. E. (1992). Women athletes as falsely accused deviants: Managing the lesbian stigma. *Sociological Quarterly, 33*(4), 521-533.

Dal Vera, A. (1994). Endurance on the ice: The American Women's Trans-Antarctic Expedition. In S. F. Rogers (Ed.), *Another wilderness: New outdoor writing by women.* Seattle, WA: Seal Press.

Lenskyj, H. (1987). Female sexuality and women's sport. *Women's Studies International Forum, 10*(4), 381-386.

Miner, J. L., & Boldt, J. (1981). *Outward Bound USA: Learning through experience in adventure-based education.* New York: William Morrow.

Pharr, S. (1988). *Homophobia: A weapon of sexism.* Inverness, CA: Chardon Press.

Pitsch, M. (1994). In political season, "social issue" add-ons bulk up E.S.E.A. *Education Week, XIV*(8), 22.

Portner, J. (1994). Districts adopting policies to protect gay students' rights. *Education Week, XIV*(5), 8.

Schur, E. M. (1983). *Labeling women deviant: Gender, stigma and social control.* Philadelphia, PA: Temple University Press.

Additional Reading

Cahn, S. K. (1994). *Coming on strong: Gender and sexuality in twentieth-century women's sport.* New York: Free Press/Macmillan.

Griffin, P. S. (1989). Homophobia in physical education. *CAHPER Journal, 55*(2), 27-31.

Harro, R. L. (1986). *Teaching about heterosexism: A psychological education design project.* Unpublished doctoral dissertation, School of Education, University of Massachusetts, Amherst.

Lenskyj, H. (1986). *Out of bounds: Women, sport and sexuality.* Toronto, Canada: The Women's Press.

Lenskyj, H. (1991). *Women, sport and physical activity: Research and bibliography* (2nd ed.). Ottawa, Canada: Canada Communication Group.

McClintock, M. (1990). How to interrupt oppressive behavior. *Camping Magazine, 63*(2), 32-34.

McClintock, M. (1991). Lesbian baiting and gay baiting: How homophobia is a tool of sexism. In *The 1991 Association for Experiential Education International Conference Proceedings*. Boulder, CO: AEE.

McClintock, M. (1992). Sharing lesbian, gay and bisexual life experiences face to face. *Journal of Experiential Education, 15*(3), 51-55.

Ohle, E. (1990). Putting everyone in the picture: Countering homophobia in the camp setting. *Camping Magazine, 63*(2), 30-31.

Courageous Voices

Courage is the price that life
exacts for granting peace.
The soul that knows it not, knows no release
From little things;
Knows not the livid loneliness of fear,
Nor mountain heights where bitter joy can hear
The sound of wings

Amelia Earhart

When I instructed for the Outward Bound (OB) school in Minnesota in the early 1980s, there was an energetic dialogue about the programmatic use of the metaphor known as the Hero's Quest. Stephen Bacon's book, *The Conscious Use of Metaphor in Outward Bound* (1983), had just been released and seemed to have a key defining influence on the prevailing educational philosophy of OB at the time. The school program director and many senior staff were avid proponents of using the heroic quest as a foundational metaphor for the Outward Bound experience.

Yet amid the clamor, the steady voice of several women arose to question the applicability of the heroic quest to women's experience in the outdoors. As a new staff member, I was awed by the courage these women displayed in going against the groundswell of sentiment for the model. These brave women instructors not only disputed the current literature but also spoke out against those having power in the OB hierarchy. Their only citation was their own experience; their only access to power was through their collective voices. They risked their position and standing in the community to say what they believed to be true about the experience of women and girls.

This is but one example of the ordinary courage women exhibit each day. "To speak one's mind by telling all one's heart," is the definition of courage used in the 1300s that Rogers (1993) resurrected in her work with adolescent girls to reframe how we look at courage. The chapters in this section provide an inspiring view of the ordinary courage of women and girls in experiential education.

Moon Joyce examines the relevance of singing, a risky activity for many, to the experiential education curriculum. She advocates for the use of singing as a tool to connect women to their power and show them a sense of *home,* an incredibly profound metaphor for women. Terry Porter presents an example of a successful program utilizing the new scholarship on girls and women in her chapter on the Connecting with Courage (CWC) program started by women working with the Thompson Island Outward Bound Center. She declares CWC to be an anomaly in the experiential education field as it is a program where the research on the adolescent journey of females served as a foundation of program design. Anne Dal Vera gives a vivid account of the American Women's Trans-Antarctic Expedition (AWE) team's excruciating decision to end the expedition at the South Pole rather than continue their attempt to ski across the Antarctic continent. Dal Vera presents their decision as a lesson in facing women's fear of failure, offering practical applications to experiential educators teaching about risk and failure. The final chapter is the voices of women who speak from the heart about their lives as experiential educators. Nina Roberts and Ellen Winiarczyk have recorded the inspiring stories of five women experiential educators as well as their process of working together to bring the women's stories to print. The collection of stories is a compelling testimony to the extraordinary lives of ordinary women.

References

Bacon, S. (1983). *The conscious use of metaphor in Outward Bound.* Denver, CO: Colorado Outward Bound School.

Earhart, A. (1989). Courage. In M. S. Lovell, *The sound of wings: The life of Amelia Earhart.* New York: St. Martin's Press. (Original work published 1927)

Rogers, A. (1993). Voice, play and a practice of ordinary courage in girls' and women's lives. *Harvard Educational Review, 63*(3), 265-295.

22

Turn off the Radio and Sing for Your Lives! Women, Singing, and Experiential Education[1]

Moon Joyce

Introduction

How does singing relate to women and experiential education? At first glance, this question may appear peripheral or inconsequential. These subjects are often overlooked by a North American mainstream culture that dismisses the role of music in "serious" education, silences or just plain ignores women's voices, sees learning as predominantly a process for the cognitive domain, and supports praxes of both learning and wellness/healing in limited and fragmented ways.

The issue of voice for women is an important one, especially in a North American society where women must struggle for their voices to be heard and valued. This chapter illustrates how singing is an effective and powerful tool for both learning and healing processes and is, more to the point, a tool that is particularly suited for women's use to assist them in their efforts to learn and to move toward more integrated knowledge and wellness *as* women.

Firstly, I explore the holistic nature of singing and its relevance to experiential learning. Secondly, I argue that singing connects women to their power in a way that helps them to act in the world as agents on their own behalf. Finally, I propose that, as a holistic and experiential activity, singing can produce "peak experiences" (Maslow, 1962) for women that I label as experiences of coming *home*.[2]

This chapter is a distillation of a research project (Joyce, 1993) in which I asked seven women to speak about the process of singing and its effects on learning, healing, and transformation. All of the women who participated in the study sing with other women or facilitate singing for women in a variety of contexts, with the common denominator being that they are engaged in some process of change or growth in their lives. As a singer and facilitator of women singing in the context of a wilderness program for survivors of chronic abuse, I included myself in this participatory research project. In this chapter, I include a case study drawn from this work as well as a brief account of my own history with singing.

Background

Singing is generally regarded within North American society as something special; a talent or gift that only some are blessed with. As a result, for many, singing has become an isolated or specialized activity, either left for the "talented" to undertake or to be enjoyed more passively through listening. This is particularly true for white women who are distanced from their European or folk cultural roots. Singing is done in early grade school, in choirs, at summer camp (for those advantaged or lucky enough to go), or in religious gatherings. Apart from places where a folk tradition still flourishes among white North Americans (e.g., Canadian Maritimes), singing has largely become a spectator sport of sorts. It must be stated that this is not true for many women of colour whose communities continue to use music and singing specifically for social, religious, and/or political purposes or where singing is integral to the cultural work of the community and its leaders.[3]

My own experience singing with adolescent and adult learners has been a fascinating journey of experiential learning. Though singing is a natural function, like laughing, somewhere after childhood, that natural ability and compulsion to sing becomes too risky.

For both females and males, the most awkward age for singing is during early adolescence.[4] And for those of us who left the practice of singing or were expelled from it at a tender and vulnerable age, singing became more and more remote and unthinkable; the prospect of singing with, or in front of, others became a terrifying proposition. The fear comes from the risk of exposure, of having one's inner, deeper voice heard and judged as somehow lacking. It's interesting that I will invariably meet adults who claim they have no voice, or that they don't have a "good" voice. And yet, these same people might be found singing in their shower or singing in their cars to the radio while driving alone—only because they think no one can hear them and they are not consciously thinking about how it "sounds." The reality is that, unless we have lost all physical means to make a sound, we all have a voice. The judgment of "goodness" or "badness" comes from an expectation of performance. Singing is an ability that any voice possesses. And like any motor skill, it requires exercise to develop ear/voice coordination. I do believe there are those rare individuals who have inordinate difficulty developing this coordination. (Perhaps this is a kind of "learning disability"?) But for the vast majority of us, I believe the lack of coordination comes from an earlier "choice" or traumatic event causing us to stop singing, thus arresting the development of a natural and common capability.

The Experiential Nature of Singing

As an experiential activity, we can only theorize so much and then we must sing in order to truly know the experience and its effects. Singing, in and of itself, can be understood and structured as an experiential learning task.[5] We, as learners/singers, are provided with a frame within which the task is to be undertaken (lines of melody, key, pitch, lyrics, beat, time, etc.). Then we sing. In reflecting on the experience, we may express emotions, share observations, and pose suggestions for what we can do differently. We may position ourselves to go over the parts we want to experiment with—add harmony, change rhythm, tempo, for instance—and then repeat the piece until we are satisfied with what we have produced. This is a natural progression for learning to sing and learning specific pieces of music.

As experiential educators, we often look for creative ways to engage learners in as holistic a way as possible. Singing as a tool for experiential learning interests me because it intersects so many aspects of a learner's capabilities. Though it may not be the focus of a "lesson," it is surely an aid to learning because it assists learners in staying present and grounded when the degree of risk increases. It helps them to stay connected with others, and indeed themselves, and it opens both the senses and the imagination to intuitive knowledge. Even though singing *itself* is a risky endeavor, a song has its own way of containing itself and participants should be encouraged to decide for themselves what they want to take on.

Unlike open-ended experiential tasks, a song is an entity that has clear boundaries, a structure within which to participate and a clear ending or resolution. In that sense, a feeling of success is concrete and there is satisfaction in completion, which does not always occur in the spiraling process of experiential learning. As a tool in experiential education, singing is also an *enabler*. It enables learners to move through the stages of an experiential model in a more profound and integrated way. The following section briefly describes the holistic nature of singing that leads to its value as a learning enabler.

Singing as a Holistic Experiential Tool

Singing is a process that is difficult to put into words. Through my study of "what happens" when women sing, I found that singing exercises all the human capabilities. For experiential educators hoping to make our methodology holistic, singing provides an effective tool to bring ourselves to a more receptive and imaginative state with which to engage in our learning. (I refer to this as "our learning" in order to recognize that, as facilitators for learning, we are also co-learners with our participants.) In instances where experiential learning tasks occur in groups, singing connects learners in a way that maximizes relational learning and builds the learning community (Kaltoft, 1990).

Holistic learning is an activity that engages all the capabilities we have as human beings to take in information, process it, and "learn." The six capabilities as articulated by Griffin (1990) that define a holistic learning activity are as follows: *physical, emotional, cognitive, intuitional/metaphoric, spiritual,* and *relational.* True to the stages of experiential learning, singing *is* experiential. But it is more than that. As a more holistic activity, it is a connecting force interpersonally (within the person) and intrapersonally (among others). Singing may be done "for it's own sake," but this fails to recognize the myriad purposes to which singing is applied.

Singing is also a very effective enabler for learning generally.[6] As an enabler in experiential learning, singing can be used to support us as we move through the stages of a learning experience. This can be achieved because of the nature of singing itself: it relaxes, refreshes, and energizes, and it encourages and supports lateral thinking and right-brain processes by stirring the imagination through metaphors and imagery, and creating mental space for possibilities.[7] Singing supports creativity by promoting playfulness. As a cognitive process, the structure of singing exercises left-brain functions which assist in sequential, patterned thinking, and serves to increase concentration and memory. Singing also connects right- and left-brain functions.

In support of our spiritual capabilities, the process of "giving voice" is sacred work and as such, promotes the full expression of ourselves as spiritual beings. It connects us to our humanity and sacredness; it grounds and centres us to our own power. Singing is a sublime experience that elicits joy, awe, wonder, and reverence—often in the midst of despair and sadness. Singing can also inspire our individual and collective will and desire.[8]

Singing creates an opportunity for us to open up to one another in order to hear each other in a deep and integral way since it crosses differences of class, race, religion, and sexuality, among others, and creates a space where differences can be seen and acknowledged in a positive and powerful way. In many dramatic ways, singing takes us into our bodies and puts us in touch with our emotions. Singing can relax our body, release physical tension, and provide a vehicle for safe emotional release. It generates physical energy and aerates our bodies through deep and sustained breathing. All our physical senses are stimulated by the process of singing which in turn produces heightened states of sensitivity and arousal. As part of a holistic healing practice, singing can be used explicitly to heal physical and other ailments. One popular technique is *toning* (Keyes, 1973; Halpern & Savary, 1985).

Singing can connect us internally to our own complete inventory of learning capabilities. But even greater possibilities exist when a group of individuals sing en masse. While exercising our individual capabilities, particularly the capacity for relational learning, all members of a group contribute to building a synergistic spiraling of collective energy, insight, and creativity which is extremely compelling and effective.

Women and Singing—Personal and Political Implications

Ann Mortifee (1991) refers to singing as an explicitly feminine act, whether it is done by women or men. She suggests that men would do well to sing and reintegrate their whole selves through the respectful use of song and voice.

For women throughout time, singing has been used as a tool of resistance, a survival strategy, a comfort, a companion, a guide to self, a means to communicate "subversive" information with others, a way to strengthen identity and purpose, and a weapon against despair and alienation. Within society's expectations of what it means to be a woman, there are very strong prescriptions as to what uses of "voice" are appropriate. My own history with singing is an instructive case. As a white female growing up in a working-class family that aspired to and achieved a middle-class lifestyle, I was regularly instructed that "little" girls were to be seen and not heard. The expectation for women to be barefoot and pregnant in the kitchen also included being *silent*. As a child, singing for me was one of the very few, if not the only, places I could have a voice and not be censored. (Now it seems logical to me that, during the history of slavery and intense persecution, African Americans experienced a similar phenomenon: discovering that music and singing were the only "acceptable" uses of voice.)

Though our family was not regarded as a violent one, there was a degree of violence exercised in the name of discipline and "respect." This occurred within a hierarchical pecking order. Like whistling in a thunderstorm, in order to cope with that which frightened me, I learned to sing in the sanctuary of my room. I realize now what a luxury that tiny room was. The louder the fighting, the louder I sang. The sound came from deep inside my body as it was directly connected to the place of fear. It was my flight when I had no arsenal with which to fight. My earliest remembrance of doing this was at the age of three. Perhaps my family thought this cute. At least it was not seen as a threat or overt rebellion. But in my room, I experienced it as my resistance and ultimately part of my emotional survival.

Rather than succumb to the terror and fragmentation of silence, singing gave me the "acceptable" vehicle to remain tangible and whole to myself. If I could sing, I knew I was going to be all right. It was a natural and holistic experience and I learned how to do it by doing it. This was an unconscious exercise in experiential learning.

Like speech, singing is a gendered activity.[9] It has tremendous potential to assist women in reintegrating in the face of the pervasive misogyny that fragments us internally and seeks to isolate us collectively. For women, singing is a way to be powerful, "in our power," and in our bodies where this is often unacceptable within a male-dominated society. Looking at the experience women have of singing and its holistic properties provides valuable insights into the promise that singing holds for women who are seeking to effect change and growth for themselves and the worlds in which they live. By engaging in an activity that is transformative, both individuals and groups are transformed in turn. Each human capability is affected by singing and thus creates a degree of change that is larger than the sum of its parts.

A Case Study

As an Outward Bound[10] instructor working (and learning) with the Women of Courage[11] program over a five-year period, singing has developed as a particularly important component in the courses I co-instruct. This emerged intuitively and was not a conscious curriculum strategy. Singing started out as a way to bring the women to a place of readiness to sleep for their first night in the intimidating new environment of the wilderness. I taught them Cris Williamson's "Lullaby" (1977)—a simple song to learn and sing. It became a most requested song and a popular bedtime practice. From this experience, I introduced "sing-songs" when it seemed that a shift in energy was needed from fatigue or heavy discussion to playfulness and rejuvenation. I remember we sang some dreadful '50s songs of "love gone wrong." But we laughed and hooted and sang with full voices. The more we laughed, the louder we sang. It was at about this point that I wondered about the significance of the context in which we were singing. No men were present and there was something deliciously permissive about singing into the night sky or the open air. Our voices had a place to expand into without bounds. The women talked of feeling a kind of "abandon" that they had long forgotten. A few said they had never felt this way. Energy was certainly raised in these moments and was put to good use helping the group stay present with one another and the work they were engaged in as a group. The outdoors posed a threat, but it also revealed a desire. The threat and desire simultaneously appeared to be to face one's self and be present *to* and *for* one's self. Singing provided moments of connection with self in a way that was at times playful and at other times reverent and solemn. What I noticed was the quality of sound that emerged over the period in which the course ran.

Over time, and many courses, I was able to compare group responses. In those groups where singing is taken up with more enthusiasm, I hear a new quality of sound emerge: deeper, gutsier, emotional. I hear voices rise from the belly and possibly even lower. Talking voices have a different resonance. Laughter starts to come unself-consciously. Although it would be nearly impossible to measure the direct effect that singing has on the experience of women in their Outward Bound experience, there is a noticeable difference that I can only ascribe to the powerful experience that the women have as a result of singing.

Before each course, many of the women are already well into a shift in consciousness about the ways in which their basic human rights are denied through the various forms of abuse and trauma they sustain as individuals and as women specifically.[12] However, many come to recognize, often for the first time, the denial of their rights as they develop a sense of confidence and self-esteem, and a sense of their own selves. As a sense of self emerges, so, too, does the awareness and outrage at having been silenced through abuse. Once women find that they have a *right* to their voice, they can begin to make steps to its reclaiming. This "coming to voice" is a radical shift in consciousness, from which agency flows. Frankie Armstrong (1985) speaks of this shift toward agency:

> I believe that the feeling that we have a *right* to be heard is very closely related to our ability to *make* ourselves heard.... For many women, so much anxiety and inhibition has come to surround our voices, particularly when it comes to raising them in volume—really letting rip—that it is truly difficult for us to make ourselves heard in group settings or public meetings. Hence, although the [singing] workshops started as a way of helping people sing, it soon became very clear that much, much more was being released than the singing voice.
>
> And if so many of us feel robbed of our voices and the right to be heard, it must follow that this has implications collectively and politically. (pp. 22-23)

Although the Outward Bound program is an experiential education program and is not geared to be a form of therapeutic intervention, many of its components will have a therapeutic effect. Singing is clearly one of the components that enables that healing effect.

The Healing Effects of Singing

The passive use of music (listening) in psychotherapy and other forms of healing is well documented. However, making music with the body is also a form of "body work" that has great potential to release tensions, free blockages of energy, and access emotions and memories that are locked in various locations in the physical body. Most therapeutic practices incorporate techniques for their subjects to "get their feelings out" and "express their anger." However, the prospect may be paralyzing for those of us who are either disconnected from our voices (and bodies), unfamiliar with our own emotions, or terrified to really let go with unstructured sound. For survivors of trauma or chronic violence, singing is a contained and structured way to begin making sounds where the ability to make *any* sound has been constricted. The playful use of singing can help survivors move through the terror of making sounds or losing control vocally. In many cases, the process of singing is a doorway to expressing "taboo" or terrifying emotions. The playfulness of singing also offers people who are deeply cocooned in themselves an opportunity to receive some pleasure or a taste of life-affirming joy and the hope of healing. As a tool for group therapeutic work, singing has the ability to connect individuals in a way that encourages attentiveness and focus in order to concentrate on learning.

Singing as a Way Home

Singing, particularly in a context of struggle, learning, or transitional change has the capacity to lead us to high degrees of holistic experience—the highest of which I refer to as "home." This can open us to new ways of seeing and expose us to diverse perspectives of reality, thus promoting compassion and cooperation.

Home is the place where one feels safe, where one is the product of creation as well as experiencing the process of creating. Home is also about connection, relationship, and a sense of being-ness: home is about being at-home in the self, of knowing truly who you are. Knowledge of home encompasses the future, the present, and the past. It is holistic. It is a peak experience and a deep experience. It is the place where the individual and collective experience of identity and agency come together.

> It has been said that all real sickness is homesickness. Who among us fully inhabits the house of his or her particularity? It may be said that a part of every one of us is permanently away from home. That alienation wounds us deeply. We are homesick for wholeness, for at-homeness with ourselves, god and the human family, and all of creation on and beyond what we call planet Earth. We are in need of healing, and healing means coming home. (Winter, 1991, p. 255-256)

Why is "home" so important for women? "Home is that ability to be who you are wherever you are."[13] This ability, or *right* I would say, necessarily involves political action and a commitment to changing contexts where that right is denied through oppression or mistreatment. It is another junction of the personal and the political.[14]

Sandra Butler (1992) states that women in a woman-hating world live in a state of exile.[15] In the instance of oppression as women, the experience of exile is profound—for it forces us to find our way in the darkness, disconnected from one another, from the web of community, and from our whole selves. The opposite to exile is "home." The definition of home is highly subjective: it is a construction of both individual and collective identity and agency in each context where one finds oneself being "at home."

> There is a myth of home for women. In a woman-hating context, they don't have a home. They may have a dwelling place that may act more as a cage as much to keep danger out as to live in.
> Women don't have the freedom to walk out the door.
> Women don't have the freedom to make decisions about our lives.
> Women don't have the means to prevent the rape of ourselves.
> (L. Karch, personal communication, March 1993)

The trauma of oppression is a chronic form of pain and dis-ease. Women as an oppressed group, in *all* our various communities and identities, live in a state of fragmentation and exile. This may be subtle or overt, but it is always there. Thus, any process that can contribute toward a reintegration and healing of our fragmented and alienated selves, is a valuable and necessary process for survival first of all, and also for the development of our full human selves. Singing is one such process.

> The reason why singing is holistic and healing is because, when you have those "peak/wholeness" experiences, they are completely opposite to trauma. Trauma, by its very nature, profoundly violates the conditions of holistic learning [and healing].
>
> Trauma likely violates each of the elements of holistic learning—which is why trauma is such a profound learning experience. So healing then comes from revolution (as in coming around) to a place where the opposite of trauma occurs utilizing all the elements of the holistic learning in a positive and empowering way. (Karch, 1993)

There is a special connection to "home" for women who are engaged in movements of growth, learning, change, transition, or struggle. Women acting on our own behalf are a disruption to the normalization of male domination. In the construction of male domination, women's strength *as* women[16] independent from men and autonomous, is a threat to those very structures and systems. As we become stronger, we ourselves may feel threatened by the loss of what has been our familiar, albeit oppressive or unsatisfactory, relationships. As Michele George (Joyce, 1993) articulates, "They may wonder 'Who will there be to play with?'" As a woman changes the context in which she lives, the context must make room for the changes. If this does not happen, there may be a crisis of identity or a tremendous sense of loss and grief—a new alienation and a new hunger for a better "home." It is in the struggle and search for home that home is realized.

Singing helps us to cope with difficult changes and brings new consciousness "home." In these moments, learning becomes fully integrated because of an intense connection to our own capabilities and to our *femaleness* individually and collectively.

Some Important Considerations for Facilitating Singing

Unfortunately, there are no formulas or recipes for how singing can be used effectively as a tool. But two essential conditions require choosing the "teachable moment" and creating a space that is as safe as possible. Safety ensures that all can stay open, in touch with our intuitive selves and as fully present as possible.

It is important that singing's holistic capacities not be underestimated or missed. The effects of the learning are often very deep, can be mystical, and may overlap into the therapeutic domain (Campbell, 1991). Singing must be used respectfully and responsibly with the understanding that there may be unanticipated consequences.

Therefore, as facilitators of learning and/or healing, we must be explicit about the intent of using music (as with any strategy or tool), sensitive to context and the identities of the participants, and accountable for the consequences of its use.

As facilitators, we need to develop our empathic abilities to be able to sense a group's readiness and the direction that a singing activity must take. This is largely an intuitive process. But if I personally don't have great radar, I can always do an energy or emotion check-in before suggesting a song (e.g., "How are we doing? What do you sense would be helpful right now?"). This gives me clues as to whether singing would be useful and what sort of song is appropriate to lead and/or teach. For example, if energy is low, I go for a familiar, nondemanding kind of song, slow to moderately paced, and reflective. If energy is high, frazzled, or unfocused, I direct energy to teaching a song as a way of refocusing, grounding and reconnecting the group. In some sense, the feel of the songs I choose mirrors the energy and emotional pitch of the group. It's a way of acknowledging in an outward form what is going on inwardly and individually. Participants usually experience this as relaxing, refreshing, and connecting.

Participants need to "have permission" to calibrate the intensity of their own experience, always having the option to decline or to make the sounds they need to make. Making music is not a goal, but a means to a learning process. Those who choose not to sing are also participating as listeners and must be respected for their choice. They are not "resistant" or "non-singers." I consider speculation of someone's reasons for not singing a disrespectful invasion of their boundaries. Any efforts, overt or covert, to force an individual or group to sing will be about as successful as forcing someone to lighten up or have a good time. *Then* you'll see real resistance!

My most successful leading of singing occurs when I am well-grounded in my own power and in touch with what's going on for *me*. Because it's often true that if I'm feeling low-down, chances are the group I'm working with is, too. If my "felt sense" (Gendlin, 1978) feels accurate, I may choose a song that says something that I sense the group is thinking but no one is saying, or a song that captures what we are all saying, but celebrates the work we've done to get there.

Leadership is leadership is leadership. And that goes for singing as well. Each of us has our own personalities, values, and styles. Rather than my attempting to suggest that there is a way to lead singing, I would suggest that you who wish to do so rely on your own leadership skills and style. We cannot be who we are not; insincerity and phoniness will sabotage any efforts, no matter how well-intentioned. I would conclude by saying: Relax, be yourself, stay present to yourself and others, and only sing songs that reflect what you truly believe in.

Conclusion

As experiential educators, we would do well to include singing in our curriculum. It offers a dynamic form of creative engagement and can assist learners in taking risks in their learning and active experimentation. Collective songwriting is one example of an initiative that can assist learners in consolidating the insights gained from their learning. We must also be sensitive to women's ways of seeing the world and living in it. This requires some understanding of the forces that women must contend with that are not present for men. Also, since songs very often reflect cultural identities and histories, we need to be aware of the cultural identities of our participants and ensure that the content being chosen reflects those identities in a respectful and nonappropriating way. Songs are most effectively used when we can connect to the song's context and appreciate its historical, cultural, and political significance. This helps participants to identify with what they are singing and connect to a deeper meaning for themselves. In choosing content, substance must not be sacrificed to rhetoric.

As a tool, singing is very practical. It is easily accessible, portable, requiring few resources, humane, and inexpensive. Leading people in song requires some skill but it is not beyond anyone's learning if they themselves are comfortable singing.

In the context of an experiential curriculum, music and singing cultivate an awareness of holism and one's own capabilities. As such, singing and music should not be peripheral or an add-on to curriculum, but rather a core component to curriculum design and integrated into educational events. This is particularly advantageous when working with women who have experienced being silenced, as it provides the space and a tool with which to be heard in a profound and whole way.

Acknowledgments

I would like to thank the six women who participated in the original research: Jani Lauzon, Delvina Bernard, Michele George, Fely Villasin, Arlene Mantle, and Catherine Glen. As well as performing, these deeply committed and active women facilitate singing with women in various contexts and diverse communities. The common denominator in their work is a sense of singing as contributing to positive change for the women and their communities. I also wish to thank Karen Howe and Louise Karch, for their influential support of this work, and especially Jenny Horsman for her constant encouragement and editorial suggestions.

Endnotes

[1] The idea for the title of this chapter came from my experience driving with the radio on and hearing a steady stream of songs where, as a woman, I felt diminished, insulted, assumed powerless, blamed, and/or just plain erased. That transformative experience taught me that radio's "popular culture" is not good for my health.

[2] Since peak learning experiences are also deeply holistic, there is a broader dimension to the experience that is not completely articulated by Maslow's term, "peak experience." I also feel that the image of a "peak" does not speak to the reality of most women's lives. "Home" represents a more intricately woven depth of connection that is valued highly by women. This shift in metaphor is inspired by Carol Gilligan's study (1982) on the moral development of women, which skillfully points out that women's moral development is based on a set of values that differs from that of men.

[3] In Canada, for example, the community of African Nova Scotians in the Halifax area relies heavily upon the Church as a centre for community activities. In this context, singing is normalized and reflected in family events as well. The concept of singing as something one "has to learn how to do" is a bizarre concept. In a situation where "everyone sings," singing as an *ability* is never questioned. Where there is a history of struggle against multiple forms of oppression, there is very often a history of singing that is *integral* to that struggle, not peripheral.

[4] As we approach puberty, we lose the unself-conscious state of embodiment that is so immediate in infancy and childhood. This is compounded by the self-consciousness that emerges in girls and boys as our bodies go out of control with changes that are both frightening and wondrous. Social conditioning, however, teaches us, as girls, to view our bodies as no longer our own property, but the property of the male gaze. This becomes intensified in adolescence as we are increasingly sexualized. Suddenly, being acceptable or "good" girls pressures us to become very modest about exposing any parts of ourselves. The role of our female voice also undergoes change as we are encouraged to follow a prescribed set of behaviors and attitudes. The consequences for failing to do so escalate. Paradoxically, while struggling to find our own voices, we, as adolescent girls, long to belong. Peer pressure is often swift and cruel if one utters an uncool thought or sound.

[5] Experiential learning is often illustrated using Kolb's cyclic diagram (1984) showing concrete experience, active reflection, abstract conceptualization, and active experimentation.

[6] The use of music in Waldorf schools is an excellent example of an integrated music program that is valued as a learning enabler.

[7] Songs are poems with language that is highly metaphoric. They provide a rich stimulus for divergent and creative thinking. A valuable application of this quality occurs in coded language, where metaphors are used frequently in songs by oppressed peoples to communicate information with one another that would jeopardize their safety if the information were to be transmitted literally.

[8] Music that affects will and desire can be readily misused to promote the worst characteristics of human nature. Songs written as propaganda to instill fear and hatred of the "Other" and glorification of that which is detrimental to human communities is always a serious danger. For example, music and songs were an integral part of the education and indoctrination of youth in Nazi Germany. Once they had captured the imaginations and spirits of the people, it was much easier to rationalize a nationalistic agenda for ethnic genocide and imperial expansionism.

[9] The gendering of singing means that the specific ways and reasons that women sing (or don't sing) are different from those of men. This is not meant in an essentialist way but to be

viewed through an analysis of the social construction of voice for men and women. (See Belenky, Clinchy, Goldberger, & Tarule, 1986.)

[10] "Outward Bound" refers to an international network of outdoor adventure-based schools.

[11] Women survivors who participate in these particular Outward Bound courses are in an enormous transition time that is stressful and produces high levels of anxiety. For women who are survivors of chronic and acute abuse, many tasks are perceived as much higher risks. For example, darkness and sharing a tent with strangers can trigger memories of a perpetrator or past trauma. The successes are experienced, therefore, in a powerful way as the women are more acutely open to learning and personal growth. Their learning is experienced well beyond the comfort zone. However, there are also many supports made available to them that have historically been absent. This is frequently a profound experience in itself.

[12] One of the themes of the Outward Bound program is to assist them in making a distinction for themselves between "victim" as an *identity* and "victim" as an *experience*. The former is inescapable, where the latter is an experience that holds the possibility of change and transformation. For those who grow to refuse seeing their experiences of victimization as defining "who they are," they begin calling themselves "survivor." Therefore, in this paper, I choose to refer to women who have been victimized as survivors rather than victims.

[13] This expression is attributed to a First Nations' man, but his identity is unknown to me.

[14] A visioning exercise I use requires a group of women to imagine what the world would be like if every woman truly had the freedom and material means to be all of who she is.

[15] As both a political activist and a psychologist, Butler is well aware of the collective nature of psychology. In order for individual women to thrive, there must be political change at the collective level to the context in which those women live and are damaged. In failing to transform the context in which women heal, the cause of dis-ease will continue and the need for healing will perpetuate itself.

[16] Sandra Butler was once quoted as saying men are punished for their weakness and women are punished for their strength.

References

Armstrong, F. (1985). Finding our voices. In N. Jackowska (Ed.), *Voices from arts for labour* (pp. 22-29). London, England: Pluto Press in association with Arts for Labour.

Belenky, M. F., Clinchy, B. M., Goldberger, N. R., & Tarule, J. M. (1986). *Women's ways of knowing*. New York: Basic Books.

Butler, S. (1992, March 24). Lecture delivered at The Centre For Christian Studies, Toronto, Ontario.

Campbell, D. (Ed.). (1981). *Music: Physician for times to come*. Wheaton, IL: Quest Books.

Gendlin, E. (1978). *Focusing* (rev. ed.). New York: Bantam.

Gilligan, C. (1982). *In a different voice*. Cambridge, MA: Harvard University Press.

Griffin, V. (1990). *A model of holistic education*. Unpublished manuscript, The Ontario Institute for Studies Education, Department of Adult Education, Toronto, Canada.

Halpern, S., & Savary, L. (1985). *Sound health*. San Francisco, CA: Harper & Row.

Joyce, V. M. (1993). *Singing for our lives: Women creating home through singing*. Master's thesis, Graduate Department of Education, University of Toronto, Toronto, Canada.

Kaltoft, G. (1990). Music and emancipatory learning in three community education programs. (Doctoral dissertation, Columbia University Teachers College, 1991). *University Microfilms International: Dissertation Information Service*, 9033861.

Keyes, L. E. (1973). *Toning: The creative power of the voice*. Marina Del Rey, CA: Devorss & Co.

Kolb, D. (1984). *Experiential learning: Experience as the source of learning and development*. Englewood Cliffs, NJ: Prentice Hall.

Maslow, A. J. (1962). *Toward a psychology of being*. Princeton, NJ: Van Nostrand.

McIntosh, P. (1990). *Interactive phases of curricular re-vision with regard to race*. (Working Paper No. 219). Wellesley, MA: Wellesley College Center for Research on Women.

Mortifee, A. (1992, March 6). Lecture delivered for The Applewood Institute, at the Central YMCA, Toronto, Ontario, Canada.

Williamson, C. (1977). Lullabye on her recording, *Live Dream*. Bird Ankles Music.

Additional Resources

Barnwell, Y., & Brandon, G. (1989). *Singing in the African American tradition*. Woodstock, NY: Homespun Tapes.

Blood-Patterson, P. (Ed.). (1988). *Rise up singing: The group singing songbook*. Bethlehem, PA: A Sing Out Publication.

Buffalo, A. (1993, March/April). Sweet Honey: A capella activists. *Ms. Magazine*, (pp. 25-29).

Hamel, P. M. (Ed.). (1976). *Through music to the self*. Dorset, UK: Element Books.

Wenner, H. E., & Freilicher, E. (Eds.). (1987). *Here's to the women*. Syracuse, NY: Syracuse University Press.

23

"Connecting with Courage," An Outward Bound Program for Adolescent Girls

Terry Porter

I remember that bright January day and the blustery ferry ride in Boston Harbor. Gulls circled around us, the deck swayed beneath my unfamiliar feet, and the bitter wind caught me full in the face. I ducked into the warmer cabin to look for an unobtrusive seat, but there were none; on the in-town subway, I might be invisible, but for that short boat ride, there is only one destination.

Thompson Island is just ten minutes from Boston. It is also home of one of the few urban-based Outward Bound schools in the country. While these facts might add up to an oxymoron for some purists, the staff there prefer to think of them as a challenge and an uncommon opportunity. My purpose on that trip was to learn more about one of their many innovative programs, Connecting with Courage (CWC), through meeting with Program Director Amy Kohut.

As a result of meetings with Amy, conversations with both staff and participants, and my own reading and research, I came to learn that Connecting with Courage is a remarkable program, certainly a significant one in the evolution of experiential education for girls and women. Not only is it the first Outward Bound course to be specifically designed for 12- and 13-year-old girls, but that it is based on still-controversial research about the specific developmental needs of this age group is also significant. In this chapter, a summary of the relevant research precedes a description of the program itself; following these are discussions of offshoots of the original program at Thompson Island and of related issues concerning future directions in the field.

Research Findings

The research that informs Connecting with Courage began with psychologist Carol Gilligan's 1982 publication of *In a Different Voice*. Noting that the major studies and theories of moral development in our Western culture were based on male

267

subjects only, she set out to investigate girls' and women's developmental perspectives. One thing she learned was that the passage through puberty into adolescence was concurrent with a profound shift in the way girls described themselves and their world.

As this 12- to 13-year-old age group had never been systematically studied before, Gilligan, Dr. Annie Rogers, and other researchers at the Harvard Project on Women's Psychology and Girls' Development focused largely on this population, empirically tracing the nature of the adolescent journey for females. To do so, they developed methods of listening that enabled them to delineate different voices within any individual speaker. They also found it necessary to confront their personal histories of adolescent transformation as well. To read their studies is an eye-opening experience, both in terms of a new understanding of women's development in our androcentric American culture and in respect gained for the personal growth the researchers experienced in their process.

When tapes of interviews with many girls were analyzed, the researchers found that "girls watch the human world like people watch the weather" (Brown & Gilligan, 1992, p. 3). Much more attuned to people than they are to objects and accomplishments, girls see "a world comprised of relationships rather than of people standing alone, a world that coheres through human connection rather than through systems of rules" (Gilligan, 1982, p. 29). Where standing theories of moral development placed relational knowing and connectedness as antecedent to a higher plane where ideals and rules of conduct had greater value, new evidence led to the conclusion that there could be both different pathways to maturity and different concepts of maturity itself. Thus, a system where relationships are key to knowing and acting in the world is no less valid than one derived from abstract concepts of justice.

The researchers also learned that 12 or 13 is a watershed age for girls, a time of "central relational crisis" (Brown & Gilligan, 1992, p. 184). Prior to this time, girls are assertive and self-empowered, unafraid to vociferously make their views known. But as their bodies enter the physiological transformations that inevitably culminate in womanhood, their psychological identities undergo dramatic shifts as well. Suddenly there is an onslaught of intense social pressure consisting of norms, expectations, and sanctions about what it means to be feminine in our culture. Reacting to this change in their relational environment, girls go through a process of self-silencing that the researchers have been able to systematically describe.

The first sign of this process is a marked increase in a girl's confusion about what she knows and is willing to discuss. Her speech becomes tentative, often punctuated with disclaimers like, "I don't know" (Brown & Gilligan, 1992; Rogers, 1993). The world suddenly becomes shaky and unsafe at this stage; girls can be seen visibly withdrawing from authenticity in their relationships.

In the next stage, the adolescent girl outwardly adjusts to adhere to social convention but is able to maintain her awareness of doing so. She "finds that she can protect herself by thinking one thing and saying another, by doubling her voice, being in a sense, two people—one private and honest, one public and acceptable" (Brown & Gilligan, 1992, p. 112). A girl might act demure, for example, withholding her opinion in class, when in fact, she has strong thoughts on a certain matter.

While this strategy works for a time, eventually it slips over into what Rogers (1993) has called psychological "resistance," or the dissociation of the experience from awareness. With the passage of time and repeated reinforcement of only the outward personality, the developing girl gradually forgets her internal voice. She becomes to herself the mask she was trying to project. Unfortunately, there is a double tragedy here. Not only is there the loss of a valuable voice to public life, but there is also the private risk of serious psychological problems—either in adolescence or later on in adulthood—as the repressed dissonance between her inner and outer voices festers within (Brown & Gilligan, 1992).

The conclusion of the researchers was that it is next to impossible for a girl of 12 or 13 in this culture to maintain congruence between her inner self and her outer relationships as she moves through adolescence. An overwhelming tide of cultural pressure bears down on her, precisely at a time when she is young, inexperienced, and quite vulnerable. Here then was the challenge for the founders of Thompson Island's Connecting with Courage program: to create an Outward Bound course that would help girls counteract the compromises in relationships that their experience as girls requires, a setting to help them amplify rather than stifle their personal voices.

Connecting with Courage for Girls

Connecting with Courage was birthed in 1992 by Joanne Stemmerman and Helen Fouhey, experiential educators with extensive experience in the field. Some of what makes their vision unique is visible on the surface. Other Outward Bound courses don't accept students under the age of 14, for example, while CWC is designed expressly for 12- and 13-year-olds. And, unlike most other courses where friends are deliberately placed in separate patrols or courses, friends are welcome to do the course together.

The 14-day course length is also shorter than the standard for Outward Bound but much longer than any other courses on Thompson Island, which typically run from one to four days. "I didn't set the length," says Kohut, "but it works. Part of it is the Outward Bound concept of stress—doing a lot of different elements and being able to sink into each element . . . and the longer time you have with the kids, the more the impact of the program will be."

CWC takes much from the Outward Bound style of expeditionary learning. "It's an opportunity to step away from regular life and be introspective," says Betsy Gillespie, another Thompson Island staff member, "and I think Outward Bound facilitates that very well." The good name of Outward Bound has also been a boon.

"The Outward Bound name helps tremendously," according to Kohut. "It gets us in the door, gets us recognized in a positive way with people."

To explore the ways that Connecting with Courage departs from its predecessors, it is helpful to start with its name. In her research, Rogers learned that "in 1300 one definition of courage was 'to speak one's mind by telling all one's heart' . . . the definition of courage drew speaking into relation with mind and heart, intellect and love" (Rogers, 1993, p. 271). Once upon a time, in other words, courage was a quality concerned with personal integrity, both within one's self and in one's relationships.

The modern connotation of valor and bravery in one's conquests—and its application to most adventure programming—is a more recent overlay to this definition. As Kohut explained:

> Lots of high adventure literature is written with conquering words and what feels like masculine language: "conquer the mountain, conquer your own fears, probe your inner desires," lots of wording like that. It's not heart-centered, not relation-centered. . . . We honor the belief that girls are relationship based and we value that within the course. . . . The overall goal is to let them know that we really value who they are; whether we like what they say or not, we just want them to say what they feel and think. (Kohut, 1994)

The challenge in designing CWC was to nurture girls' courage in the earlier sense of the word.

Credit for successful methods of achieving this end go back to the researchers, as Betsy Gillespie explained: "Outward Bound to a great extent has had research follow, and with this program the research is preceding what we're doing" (Gillespie, 1994). Among others, Dr. Annie Rogers has explored and written about what it takes to create "a safe, playful and challenging relational context among women or women and girls together" (Rogers, 1994). She has described two critical ingredients for success.

The first involves using an artistic approach. This was accomplished at Thompson Island by combining traditional course elements with creative initiatives. Woven in with rock climbing, sailing, backpacking, and the ropes course, for example, are activities such as drama, journal writing, drawing, and painting. As Kohut explains: "On the backpacking element in New Hampshire, they'll make friendship bracelets with a commitment to each other for the goals of the course. Or they'll do a group mural one night at the campsite. It all kind of goes hand in hand." Use of the arts brings the girls into relation with each other and encourages them to express their inner selves in uninhibited ways.

The second aspect lies in role modeling, or the instructor's use of herself:

> To invite a girl to reveal herself in my presence, I have found it necessary to make an opening for her courage through mine, revealing myself as someone who struggles as she struggles, breaking conventions of standard

Photo courtesy of Amy Kohut

teaching, research and clinical practice to do so. . . . To learn this practice of courage . . . we need time and space to breathe freely, to be vulnerable, to speak honestly with one another. . . . It also means breaking traditional and time-honored conventions of feminine goodness to create a new order or logic of relationships between women and girls. (Rogers, 1993, p. 291)

Kohut is acutely aware of the value of her excellent staff: "It's a very powerful program to work in staff-wise—the research is very meaningful to them and they are really committed to making it happen and they're incredible."

For each staff member then, it is important to develop relationships with the girls and show them through example that it is okay to speak out, to be playful in questioning convention, and to engage assertively in relationships. As an example, one instructor described her approach: "To go in on the first day of the course and give a lecture about advantages and disadvantages of being a woman—it's not going to fly. But we did it casually over dinner, a few nights into the course."

Connecting with Courage has achieved phenomenal success in its first years of service. For the three years since its inception, demand and numbers of courses offered have risen exponentially. All the more remarkable is the perspective that this is a radical program in many ways. It is a program for females—historically only just over 20% of Thompson Island's enrollment—at an age that has traditionally been considered too young for Outward Bound. It also depends largely on donations, since one of Kohut's goals is to have 50% of the students on some form of scholarship. But in funding for single-gender programs in the Boston area, only 6% of all monies go to girls' programs, the other 94% to programs for boys (Kohut, 1994).

But statistics don't tell the whole story. "I don't think I could really explain how much I like it," said one graduate of the course. "They put a lot of responsibility on you . . . a lot was expected of you. It made you feel really good about yourself, like you could handle this and they were entrusting you with this." The rapid growth of this program is proof that it meets important personal needs while breaking tradition on many levels to do so.

Offshoot Programs

With the success of the girls' courses, the Thompson Island staff wondered about involving adult women in the Connecting with Courage programs. Perhaps adults would also find meaning in the opportunity to connect with themselves and each other through physical challenge and creative expression.

Kohut and her cohorts started with a women's "Invitational," in the summer of 1993, a 3-day program to which they invited a number of women philanthropists and leaders. Following a very positive response, they decided to try several open enrollment weekend courses for women. From just one advertisement in the Boston papers they received over 800 phone calls. "We have totally found a niche and a need," says Kohut. "The response has been tremendous."

Though the women's course is shorter, it is very powerful for the participants. The women use the ropes course and go rock climbing or sailing, camp on the island, and do a mini-solo on their final day. Along with other activities designed to develop trust and encourage sharing, they are also asked to bring a picture of themselves at age 12 or 13. The alchemy of these ingredients is a very exciting weekend where women often make deep connections with themselves and each other. As one instructor put it, ". . . in that short amount of time we've been able to move women to a point where they feel emotionally comfortable . . . my experience in the discussions has been watching a flood of talk."

One participant in the adult course described her experience:

> I was really quite shocked at some of the things I discovered about myself, some things I hadn't been able to put into place. . . . There was a time when I gave up organized sports and had no idea why . . . and I was able to get in touch with that and it was unbelievable.

This description sounds very much like the psychological resistance or self-forgetting process that the researchers have explained. This same woman also had a transforming experience of empowerment on the ropes course:

> I knew it would take a lot to get control and do it, as I was shaking up there, but the sense of "I can do it if I really put my mind to it, or I can fall off and no one's really going to care," is exactly like what it's like at work.

The course helped her literally to remember experiences that she had forgotten, and also gave her valuable support in her current life.

Beyond the women's courses, Thompson Island is experimenting with this material in other ways. "We're building on the connection between women and girls," says Gillespie, "making women more aware of the role that they need to be playing with girls." To this end, they have created courses for mothers and daughters and for classroom teachers—as part of their mission is to make links with the educational system as well.

They have also started a CWC Advisory Council, comprised of girls' and women's course graduates, program staff, and women leaders from the larger Boston community. "What we are doing is saying to girls who have finished the course, 'Your role is to stay involved now; we are inviting you onto the Advisory Council and you will have equal say,'" explains Gillespie. Significantly, the CWC team has gone beyond strict boundaries to build alliances, create new networks, and join with others who are working to empower girls and women through experiential and other modalities.

Conclusion

In this last section, I want to reverse the lens for a moment and take a wide-angle view of Connecting with Courage and women's experiential education in today's landscape.

Perhaps every generation feels itself to be living in a pivotal time, and certainly no less is true for us. We seem to be at a crossroads, where staggering issues of overpopulation, ecological peril, dwindling resources, and social injustice threaten survival, of both our species and our planet. There is also the growing awareness that traditional approaches to problem solving will not work anymore: that what's needed are courageous perspectives and radical paradigm shifts. We are challenged to respond from our hearts and our minds, and in so doing, to reinvent the meaning of responsibility.

Open minded innovators are often finding that they have much in common. Breakthroughs in one area can have relevance elsewhere. This is the stuff of synergy; it offers new outlets for our hope and efforts. I believe that Connecting with Courage is a case in point.

The fact of patriarchy—the cultural hierarchy of men over women that has been in place for an estimated five millennia—has been investigated from many directions in recent years. Feminist thinkers and researchers, both women and men, have established a clear link between our Western patriarchal culture and the unconscious internalization of oppression in individuals:

> As a form of social control, internalization is definitely a long-range strategy. . . . Our conditioning . . . trains us to conform and to assume [patriarchal] values as our own. Given no alternatives, domination and subordination becomes our reality, our universe. . . . We are not consciously aware of making a choice to follow patriarchal values, but we do—of our own volition—choose them. We are not aware of other options, and we are not aware of our own volition. (Hagan, 1993, pp. 85-87)

Others in the field of addictions recovery have approached the same phenomena from a different direction. These days, the term codependency has become a cliché, but its definition sounds very much like the preceding political analysis:

> Codependency is a woman's basic training. That is, in order to be acceptable in the male system a woman is taught to set aside her knowledge, her hopes, her dreams and her power by playing the role of wife, secretary . . . and so on. (Kasl, 1992, p. 39)

Both views describe behavior learned in response to cultural pressure, and the point is made that the learning itself is forgotten once the behavior is ingrained.

If codependency is synonymous with internalized oppression, then the research done by Gilligan, Rogers, and their colleagues seems to document an important way in which this adaptation takes place. In their analysis of the enculturation process that happens to girls at puberty, they have shown us how girls adapt by taking themselves out of an authentic relationship with their own self. This self-silencing amounts to cultural shaping for a subordinate role in patriarchy.

Connecting with Courage was developed as an antidote to the pressure on girls to conform at this age. As such, it is a political program, or at the very least, a program with political implications. It is political because the strong, impassioned, even outraged voices of women are exactly what's needed to fuel the paradigm shifts needed today. Though Kohut is quick to credit other programs with doing similar work in the experiential field, CWC stands out nonetheless. It makes a deliberate link between psychological research and adventure education, and it has also created opportunities for graduates to remain meaningfully involved in ongoing processes of change.

As experiential educators, we are challenged by this example to stay conscious about our ethics and our politics. We can recognize the fact that the work we do has embedded cultural values, and we can make careful choices about how we model and reinforce those values in our work. If we pretend that our field is isolated from other realms of culture, we may be losing valuable opportunities for effectiveness in our work and in our lives. Our choices then remain unconscious, though we will be making them nonetheless.

As the pace of change in our world continues to accelerate, I believe that experiential education will become a more and more powerful tool for helping people change. This is precisely because it overlaps disciplines and impacts us on many levels simultaneously. Our opportunity as experiential educators is to take the lead in much-needed paradigm changes, rather than to be oblivious to them. The challenge is twofold: to become fluent with the experiential tools at our disposal—both their potentials and their ethical uses—and second, to work hard to know and develop ourselves fully, not just as outdoorswomen, but as potential agents of cultural change as well.

References

Brown, L., & Gilligan, C. (1992). *Meeting at the crossroads*. New York: Ballantine.

Gillespie, B. Personal communication in February 1994. Thompson Island Outward Bound School.

Gilligan, C. (1982). *In a different voice*. Cambridge, MA: Harvard University Press.

Hagan, K. L. (1993). *Fugitive information: Essays from a feminist hothead*. New York: HarperCollins.

Kasl, C. D. (1989). *Women, sex and addiction: A search for love and power*. New York: Harper & Row.

Kohut, A. Personal communications from January through October, 1994. Thompson Island Outward Bound School.

Prose, F. (1990, January 7). Confident at 11: Confused at 16. *The New York Times Magazine*, pp. 22-26, 38, 40, 45-46.

Rogers, A. (1993). Voice, play and a practice of ordinary courage in girls' and women's lives. *Harvard Educational Review*, 63(3), 265-295.

24

Facing Women's Fear of Failure: An AWEsome Experience

Anne Dal Vera

We are the ones we have hoped for
We are the women who care
Now is the time to move closer
Separate we lose to despair

Margi Adam

Ann Bancroft pulled on her down coat, took a deep breath, and turned to face the AWE team. Her voice was taut with anger as she described our situation. "We need to use the energy of our sorrow and anger to focus on getting to the Pole. If we don't make it, we will have failed. Other expeditions have gotten this close to the South Pole and have had to turn back. In failing, we will have become severely financially burdened. I speak of 'we' including myself." The sorrow was deep. Ann was determined that the American Women's Trans-Antarctic Expedition (AWE) would be the first women's expedition to ski across the Antarctic continent.

Each of the four women on the expedition had a great desire to complete the traverse. I was burning with curiosity about the land beyond each day's horizon, fascinated with the patterns of waves carved in the snow by the wind. We were 67 miles from the South Pole, moving slowly due to illness and injury. With food for six days left, we had to keep up a steady pace of over 11 miles per day.

I enjoyed Ann's passionate outcry of anger. She always seemed so strong and sure. This was one of the few moments when I felt I knew what she was really feeling. I was confident that we could continue at our established pace of 12 to 14 miles a day. Still, I thrilled to hear Ann's urgent call for each of us to maintain our mental focus on the goal and continue to strive to reach it. Sunniva Sorby responded defensively, "I know you don't believe me, but I am doing the best I can." Sunniva had been struggling with bronchitis for several days, breathing through a cold, damp, neoprene face mask and skiing at a pace that wouldn't force her lungs to develop life-threatening pneumonia.

Sue Giller seemed confused, asking me later if Ann was mad at her for getting too far ahead of Sunniva. Sue's endurance had improved over the 62 days of this expedition until she was zooming ahead, intent on making it to the South Pole.

At the next break, two hours later, Ann apologized for her previous talk. She had meant to be more positive and not give us a downer. She had let her fear of failure, anger, and sorrow about canceling the effort of the ski traverse bring her down. She said that we had done well, in comparison to a previous ski traverse of Antarctica. The men took fewer hours to ski the miles, but we were making significant progress. We hadn't made up the eight-day delay we suffered waiting for plane repairs and the weather to clear before we flew to the start of the journey. We could make the Pole if we focused on that as our goal and worked toward it.

AWE was four-and-a-half years in the planning. The team, lead by Ann Bancroft, age 37, the first woman to cross the ice to the North Pole was supported by the work of hundreds of volunteers. Sue Giller, age 45, expedition navigator and equipment specialist, had spent the previous 20 years mountaineering in the world's highest peaks. I, Anne Dal Vera, age 39, had taught cross-country skiing and guided trips in wilderness year-round for 14 years. I planned, procured, and packed the food for the expedition. Sunniva Sorby, age 31, was in charge of medical supplies and coordinated the research on the expedition.

The team flew from Punta Arenas, Chile, to Patriot Hills in Antarctica, on November 8, 1992. We continued on a short flight to the edge of the continent near Hercules Inlet on November 9. After a very windy introduction to our new "home," we began pulling our seven-foot sleds filled with 185 pounds of food and equipment to the South Pole. Within the first few days, we settled into a routine of sled pulling, cooking, eating, completing the research, and generally taking care of the necessities of life to stay healthy and pull as efficiently as possible. After a month of travel, we were met by plane for a resupply of food and fuel. We arrived at the South Pole on January 14, 1993, after traveling 678 miles. Our original objective of traversing the continent of Antarctica was out of reach, as we would have to travel the remaining 870 miles in 32 days to meet the only cruise ship available to take us off the continent. We succeeded in being the first all-women's expedition to ski to the South Pole, while Ann Bancroft was the first woman to cross the ice to both the North and South Poles. We had failed, however, to cross the continent.

In experiential education, as well as in the society as a whole, success and achievement are highly valued. Challenges are part of experiential education. And sometimes, students fail. The fear of failure is often a barrier for women. The goal of this chapter is to show, through stories of AWE, other accounts of women's outdoor trips, and the research on fear of failure, how fear affects women. How experiential educators can teach about risk and failure in ways that effectively recognize the fear that women and girls have about risking connection and relationship is also examined. A mastery orientation to life's challenges is described and resources available to the educator are noted.

> Fear of failure is an internal experience related to achievement. It is not necessarily related to external, objective measures of success or failure. . . . "Failure" is the experience of falling short, whether or not one actually does so. It is the discrepancy between a self-set expectation or standard and the self-perceived accomplishment. (Yuen & Depper, 1988, pp. 22-23)

Dr. Esther D. Rothblum, at the University of Vermont, has extensively studied women's fear of failure in academia. She has shown that fear of failure leads to procrastination and performance well below the ability of a student. In extreme cases, it can lead to learned helplessness and a paralysis in the face of challenges. Rothblum, Morris, and Weinstock (1995) state, "Although many individuals strive for success, others behave in ways that reduce the risk of failure, even at the cost of success."

Photo courtesy of Woodswomen

Women often question the value of striving for success when a relationship will suffer. In the conclusion of her review of literature in "Fear of Failure," Rothblum (1990) says:

> Women generally report more fear of failure, and behave in ways that express more fear of failure, than do men. What is fearful about failure seems to be the expected interpersonal consequences (such as fear of rejection) rather than the specific academic performance.... Much of the research reviewed suggests that, in many ways, individuals who score high on fear of failure are cooperative rather than competitive, and socially rather than personally oriented.... Perhaps a more important question is whether high striving for success is a desirable goal. (pp. 530-531)

On all-women outdoor trips and expeditions, communication of individual needs and expectations can set the scene for teamwork and cooperative action which allows a group to achieve several goals.

On a Woodswomen leadership course in Colorado, I took part in a discussion among a group of women who were setting out to climb a nearby peak. Denise Mitten, executive director of Woodswomen, asked the skiers to explain what they wanted to get out of the day. After everyone had spoken, she asked the question two more times, phrasing it differently each time, explaining that it was important to her that each person be as clear as possible about her goals. Some of the women realized that although they had a strong desire to reach the summit, on that particular day it was as important to participate in the camaraderie of the group of women and to enjoy the view high above the valley. Later when we reached a high spot, the weather was quite good and although the goals of camaraderie and a good view had been met, there was time to reach the summit as well. That became an added bonus. Decisions were clearer on the mountain and each woman knew what she wanted because we had taken time earlier to look within and see the many possible outcomes for the day. Relationship goals were recognized as being as important as physical goals. The group experienced the process of climbing the peak as rewarding as reaching the summit. This episode also gave these future leaders the skills to facilitate communication and goal setting on subsequent outdoor trips.

When we pay attention to the diverse needs and desires of women, we bring a richness to life. As Rothblum (1990) noted:

> Hoffman has argued that a mentally healthy society needs to emphasize greater flexibility, and the more diffuse achievement patterns of women should serve as a model for a fuller life. Developing affiliative and social skills is preferable to encouraging competitive striving for goals that can be won by, at most, a few individuals. (p. 531)

The AWE team spent four-and-a-half years planning and preparing for the traverse of Antarctica. During that time, the mission and goals of the organization reflected the diverse vision of Ann Bancroft, the team leader. The goals mirrored Ann's commitment to education and a positive impact on her community. Ann stated these goals in the *AWE Fact Sheet*:

Expedition Mission and Goals:

- Focus attention on the existing and potential achievements of women while encouraging people of all ages to take on new challenges.
- Make history as the first all-women's team to traverse Antarctica without dogs or motorized vehicles; and provide Ann Bancroft an opportunity to be the first woman to cross the ice to both the North and South Poles.
- Stretch the physical and emotional limits of team members.
- Promote awareness of the environmental issues facing Antarctica and their global impact.
- Provide a hands-on vehicle for bringing Antarctica, as well as the past and present achievements of women into the classroom.
- Conduct physiological/psychological research pertaining to women under extreme conditions. (AWE Foundation, 1990)

The goal of traversing Antarctica was the most visible and tangible goal of the AWE team. As we approached the South Pole and time was running out, we were faced with the reality of a strict deadline. We had to reach McMurdo Sound by February 17 to meet the only cruise ship available to take us to New Zealand. Eight hundred seventy miles of ice, including the heavily crevassed Beardmore Glacier, wider than the longest glacier in Switzerland, lay between the South Pole and McMurdo Sound. With our efficient UpSki wind canopies, we would need at least 40 days of hard travel to complete the traverse. If we attempted the crossing and missed the ship, our only way off the continent would be an air-pickup by Adventure Network at an estimated additional cost of $350,000 and physical risk to us and the pilots involved.

January 5, 1993, found us 119 miles from the Pole, having spent several days weaving around and over 3- to 6-foot-high sastrugi (waves of snow and ice, packed hard by the wind). That evening, all four of us, crowded into one small tent, assessed our individual conditions, and discussed our strategy.

Amid tears, Sunniva admitted that her sprained ankle and bronchitis meant that in spite of her great desire to do the traverse, it wouldn't be responsible to continue beyond the Pole. Sue was confident that she could endure the emotional hardship involved in the hard push necessary to complete the traverse. She also felt some fear that she would continue to lose weight after the pole and become too physically weak to complete the slog through the deep snow anticipated on the Ross Ice Shelf. We all agreed that Ann Bancroft was the strongest of our group, both physically and mentally. She had gotten stronger throughout the expedition.

Ann and Sue both expressed concern that I would have a great deal of difficulty with the emotional strain of pushing as hard as would be necessary to reach McMurdo Sound by February 17. Emotional outbursts I'd had during a very painful struggle with tendonitis caused them to believe I didn't have an emotional reserve or the ability to shut down to pain. I listened to their comments and said I would give a reply the next day. We concluded the meeting by adjusting our goal to reach the South Pole as a team of four. We planned to ski as hard as possible to try to reserve the possibility of a traverse for two team members. Still, we knew that time was running out.

Exhausted, I crawled into my sleeping bag to sleep on the information. I wanted to work toward the success of the AWE team as a whole and complete the traverse. But I did not want to become an unfeeling automaton (nor could I do so). I also knew deep within me that to accomplish the traverse, the team would have to trust each other implicitly. Travel would be through crevasse fields, where a misstep could plunge a skier deep into an abyss. The other team members would have to be able to rescue the fallen skier. It was no place to doubt the competence of a partner. The next day, I told the others that I would not go on beyond the Pole with them. I cried in anger and frustration with the loss of a big dream.

As I dealt with my sense of failure in not completing the traverse of Antarctica, I grieved the loss of an opportunity to see an incredible part of the world, and the loss of time to enjoy a lifestyle and activity that I treasure. I went through several stages of grieving, much like a person who has lost a loved one.

During the next few days, I went through disbelief to sadness to despair, anger, doubt, loneliness, fear, and a deep connection with the ice and snow over which we traveled. I felt very fortunate that I had the time to deal with all these strong emotions while we were still on the ice. Perhaps that slowed us down at times, while I worked through some of the strongest feelings I'd had since adolescence. I wanted desperately to preserve the slim chance that Sue and Ann had of doing the traverse, and I skied hard, thinking of how my going out could possibly help in fund-raising efforts at home. Still, I felt isolated as I dealt with my fear of how my failure would be seen by others; the media, corporate sponsors, our individual supporters, my family and friends. We pushed hard, pulling sleds ten hours each day, with time only for cooking, eating, and sleep. Communication served to get the daily tasks done. We were operating on survival mode. No time or energy existed to process emotions as we each dealt with our feelings of approaching failure or partial success.

Ann Bancroft, as expedition leader, felt the heavy weight of the decision to end the traverse at the South Pole. She described her experience in an interview:

> In making the decision, I looked at the facts, I looked at the situation, . . . I looked at all the scribbles that I had taken on the backside of my journal: the logistics of a group of three, two, and even a solo option. I looked at all of our options over and over and over again: the miles, the time frame, the money angle, the legacy, all the different aspects to the decision, and it just

kept coming out the same one. I have physically never been in better shape. Never have I been more emotionally ready to take on something in my life. And at that moment I had to separate, and that was very frustrating and very difficult. It has been a long process for me to come to grips with not being able to finish what I set out to do and feel triumphant about what we have achieved. (Rothblum, in press)

On January 14, 1993, the four women of AWE skied the last 12.2 miles to the South Pole. Ann Bancroft became the first woman to cross the ice to both the North and South Poles. We were there—all four of us. And we were still friends. While we didn't list that as one of our goals in our expedition literature, it was important to each of us that we work together as a cohesive unit as we "stretched the physical and emotional limits of team members" (AWE Foundation, 1990, p. 1). We decided to end the expedition at the South Pole. That decision was hard for each of us. It required a great deal of soul searching and self-assessment

Through the AWE expedition, I pushed my limits and lived a very passionate existence. The failure to traverse the continent taught me many lessons: 1) Part of the experience of failure is to grieve the loss of an expectation of oneself. 2) When women fail to reach an objective, we tend to hide from each other, not believing in the power of sharing that experience or the rewards of accomplishing the goals we *have* achieved. 3) When failure occurs, we readjust the goals and go on with life. New goals develop consistent with the values that each of us holds deep within ourselves. 4) I must continue to believe in myself and to know that I am doing what I can to meet my expectations in light of the adjusted goals.

At the South Pole, the AWE team became individualistic, each woman dealing with the impact of suddenly being surrounded by the noise and bustle of a small city, the Amundsen-Scott South Pole Scientific Research Station. I withdrew from the others, not discussing our failure or the goals we had achieved. We had spoken earlier of the hope that our decision could be used by school children to learn about having to make hard decisions about turning back if the risk becomes too great. In their conclusion, Kahn and Leon (1994) described our coping:

A significant issue with which the group had to deal was the decision to terminate the expedition at the South Pole. . . . The interview data confirmed the quantitative information about the high level of functioning of this group. While all were disappointed, the group abided by the ultimate decision made at the South Pole and did not splinter between those who felt physically capable to proceed further, and those who did not. (p. 695)

Whether women dare to present a new concept at a manager's meeting of a Fortune 500 corporation or climb a peak in difficult weather, the risk of failure is present and real. Studies have shown that if women fail, we may try to hide our failures, choosing to believe that women need to see successful role models, not evidence that we can fail. Men often wear their failures as badges of courage to show that they have taken chances. As women, we can give each other significant support by staying near each other and asking what we learned from the experience. We can get beyond our fear of failure and loss of self esteem (Duff, 1993).

Martha McPheeters, a senior staff member at Voyageur Outward Bound School in northern Minnesota, models a learning approach to life as she asks people for constant feedback about her work. She takes many risks and doesn't always succeed, but she loves a life of learning. After being fired from an outdoor adventure program in 1989, Martha requested a meeting with the director to discuss her performance and where she needed to improve. She selected information from that interview to determine what she felt she wanted to develop because she believed in her style and wanted to continue to grow. While it was painful to be fired, Martha chose to make the most of the opportunity to learn from others' experience of her work.

This focus on setting learning goals rather than performance goals is a key to overcoming learned helplessness, an extreme fear of failure that keeps women from actualizing their potential and enjoying life. Marone (1992) describes a woman who developed a "mastery orientation" to life: When Sue Ann's husband hit her after years of verbal and emotional abuse, she started working on a plan to get out. She knew she needed money to survive on her own. Carl wouldn't let her work, so she found ways to squirrel away money, saving from grocery shopping, cutting out lunch, and bumming rides with friends to save gas money. Her friends and family helped by giving her cheap presents she could show her husband and giving her the rest in secret cash. When Carl came home drunk on Fridays and passed out on the couch, she took the opportunity to steal five dollars from his pocket, knowing that he would not remember how much money he had. After two years, during which Carl became more violent and unpredictable, she had saved a little over $700. Following a careful plan, Sue Ann left the house when Carl passed out, slashing his tires so he couldn't follow her. He had threatened to kill her if she left him, so she knew she had to leave town. She rented a studio apartment in a town across the state line, and got two jobs. Through Sue Ann's strategic planning and taking action, she escaped a dangerous situation and created a new life.

Most of the time, we don't develop a mastery orientation to life until we are forced to do so. The skills necessary for taking charge of one's life can also be taught and practiced. I also find it helpful to visualize myself adopting the behaviors of a mastery-oriented individual:

- Offering no explanations for failure nor giving external attributions.
- Refusing to internalize setbacks as personal attributes.
- Keeping failure to a specific area.
- Focusing on the future and seeking solutions in the present.
- Attributing success to internal factors such as effort and ability.
- Striving for success by setting learning goals.
- Being unconcerned with the performance of peers.

- Refusing to compare herself with others.
- Indulging in positive self-talk.

(Marone, 1992)

Developing mastery behaviors empowers us to deal with failure and prevent the devastation that frequently follows failure. At one point in my career, I received a critical evaluation of my performance on an outdoor leadership course. Knowing that the evaluation held the key to future employment, I was devastated. I indulged in negative self-talk and globalized the failure from a few comments into a belief about myself. I spent the evening walking and crying, feeling that I could "never be good enough." The next day, I was told that I would be hired and that the instructors merely wanted me to realize very clearly where I had room for improvement. I could have saved myself the anguish had I learned earlier to look at criticism and failure as an opportunity for growth.

Scientific literature suggests that women and men have been socialized to respond differently in dealing with failure. As noted by Rothblum (1990): "During the early school years, females achieve well in the academic arena. Even by first grade, however, boys prefer repeating previously failed tasks, whereas girls prefer repeating tasks on which they have been successful" (pp. 507-508).

If girls fear failure early in life, they take fewer risks and do not gain the experience of decision making that leads to development of judgment so essential for making important decisions later in life. As experiential educators, we must encourage and support girls in their risk taking, helping them to learn from mistakes and separating the physical risk from social risk. We can create experiences where women consistently support one another through failure, focusing on the benefits of risk taking. We can lessen women's fear of failure.

After the AWE team returned home to a wonderful reception and were able to deal with the media's reaction, which was mostly positive, we began to enjoy the recognition we received. Most were supportive of our decision to stop at the Pole. When failure occurs, we readjust the goals and go on with life. New goals develop consistent with the values that each of us holds deep within ourselves. It is important to feel that I have chosen to deal with the consequences of taking risks, to accept rewards and responsibility. I must continue to believe in myself and to know that I am doing what I can to meet my own expectations.

As I look at these lessons about failure, I ask, "How can we teach the lessons of failure experientially?" It is essential in a world that is constantly changing to be able to deal with the reality that with risk comes the possibility of failure. People must risk as society grows technically and socially. The experience of taking risks and dealing with the consequences of success, failure, and partial success leads to confidence in situations that demand we transcend our limits. As experiential educators, we can teach girls and women about risk and failure in the following ways:

1. Acknowledge up-front that risk involves the possibility of failure.
2. When a woman fails, do not allow her to isolate herself, or others to abandon her. Use the occasion for all to learn from the situation.
3. Encourage learning goals rather than performance goals.
4. When students show risk-avoidance behavior, let them know that their peers also feel those same fears, that their concerns for the well-being of others do not negate their own need to achieve.
5. If a group or an individual fails:
    a. Grieve about the loss of opportunity.
    b. Celebrate achievements!
    c. Learn what skills or knowledge must be gained to succeed in the future.
    d. Adjust goals if necessary, consistent with the values of the individual or members of the group.
    e. Act toward those goals.

In *Women as Pioneers and Risktakers* (Tiernan & Sorenson, 1992), the lesson plans take students through a step-by-step process of team building. Students learn about risk taking, sharing leadership, persevering through difficulties and successes, and seeing old problems in new ways. They share their narratives of success and failure with others and learn from their failure. This curriculum can be adapted for use for 4th grade through college level. Although it is written for indoor classroom use, it could be adapted for outdoor adventure situations as well. Many resources are cited to bring the experience of a culturally diverse history of women into the lessons as well.

Compassionate and caring instructors occasionally encounter students' fears of failure. Golden (1988), a professor in the Department of Psychology at Ithaca College, described her response to women who talk about their fear of failure:

> While I react to each student on an individual basis, there is a general rule I apply when a student presents or manifests fear of failure concerns. Whether it be a reluctance to speak out in class, imposter feelings, or a fear of disappointing some significant other, I share with students my observation of how the same fears exist among their female peers. I want them to know that they are not alone in feeling the way they do, that gender based socialization contributes to their common experience, and in the case of fear of failure in meeting the needs of others, that it is critical to include their own needs among those requiring attention. (pp. 46-47)

As the AWE team flew away from Antarctica, I reflected in my journal:

> Antarctica is a place of my dreams for such a long time now. This has been the experience of a lifetime! I have given all to this venture. I have learned a great deal. I know what it means to push hard day after day and be so tired that I think I can't do it any more. And then to get up and do it anyway. I

know what it is to be lonely and to cry from that and physical weariness. I know what it is to take the risk to be open about my weaknesses. To accept them. And to work with them.

At times I felt bigger than I am—closer to being something I've sensed I might be capable of, but never had the courage to seriously imagine. And those were times born not of great physical achievement but times when I had energy for work, for humor and for love. It may seem odd to speak of love now, but my best work comes from feeling confident that I can give of myself in all ways.

The AWE expedition was a significant part of the risk taking of my life. As I continue to learn and grow, I am more and more excited by the opportunities that life offers us.

As more women risk to accomplish goals not previously attained by women, gender roles become less strictly defined. Women and men find value and satisfaction in pursuing adventure *and* using healthy social skills. As experiential educators, we can encourage students to take risks. If they fail, we can encourage them to discuss their failure with others and add new skills and knowledge to their repertoire. We can encourage groups to stand in solidarity, forging meaningful bonds. We can help them increase self-esteem *because* they have "failed."

References

Adam, M. (1993). *Another place*. Berkeley, CA: Pleiades Records.

AWE Foundation. (1990). *Fact sheet: American Women's Trans-Antarctic Expedition*. Eagan, MN: Author.

Duff, C. S. (1993). *When women work together: Using our strengths to overcome our challenges*. Berkeley, CA: Conari.

Golden, C. (1988). I know this is stupid, but . . .; Or some thoughts on why female students fear failure and not success. In E. Rothblum & E. Cole (Eds.), *Treating women's fear of failure: From worry to enlightenment* (pp. 41-49). New York: Harrington Park.

Kahn, P. M., & Leon, G. (1994). Group climate and individual functioning in an all-women Antarctic expedition team. *Environment and Behavior, 26*(5), 669-697.

Marone, N. (1992). *Women and risk: How to master your fears and do what you never thought you could do*. New York: St. Martin's.

Rothblum, E. D. (1990). Fear of failure: The psychodynamic, need achievement, fear of success, and procrastination models. In H. Leitenberg (Ed.), *Handbook of social and evaluation anxiety* (pp. 497-537). New York: Plenum.

Rothblum, E. D. (in press). *Women's voices in the Antarctic*. New York: New York University.

Rothblum, E. D., Morris, J. F., & Weinstock, J. S. (1995). Women in the Antarctic: Risk taking and social supports. *World Psychology, 1*(1), 83-112.

Tiernan, T., & Sorenson, M. E. (1992). *Women as pioneers and risktakers: A classroom extension to the 1992 Women's Trans-Antarctic Expedition*. Available from: AWE Foundation, 4719 Narvik Dr., Eagan, MN 55122.

Yuen, L. M., & Depper, D. S. (1988). Fear of failure in women. In E. D. Rothblum & E. Cole (Eds.), *Treating women's fear of failure* (pp. 21-39). New York: Harrington Park.

25

Women in Experiential Education Speak Out: An Anthology of Personal Stories across Cultures

Nina S. Roberts and Ellen J. Winiarczyk

In our experience, many of the stories told in circles of experiential educators in past decades lack the voice and flavor of a women's perspective. We know the lives and stories of many of the male founding adventurers in experiential education, but rarely the women. One of our goals as we took on this challenge of recording women's stories, was to record a variety of experiences by a rainbow of women with differences in education, age, sexual orientation, marital status, ethnic background, and experience. A number of the women included here have been involved in the field of experiential education for many years, while others' involvement is relatively recent.

Although we had initial difficulty structuring this collection of stories, it has been the collaborative and cooperative process, with each other and the women interviewed, that has made this a rich experience for each of us. Long discussions at the 1994 International Association for Experiential Education Conference and many phone calls have revolved around how to best unite our ideas, the individual stories, the styles, and the diversity that underlies the collective concerns and successes of women. The choices we had to make were difficult. In order to create an anthology that would give voice to the variety of experiences rising out of ethnicity, race, class, and generational differences as well as out of the simple, irreducible fact of individual histories, we were not able to include all the women we had on our list.

Our collaboration and editing process has been an experience in itself. Part of the difficulty of how best to structure this collection stemmed from the question regarding the need for voices of women of color to be heard and not hidden. While these are women's stories that have surely been told before, they have not been heard in a collection, nor have they been recognized in their magnificent similarity and difference.

We've included personal statements that reflect each of our views about ourselves, this process, and women in experiential education.

Thoughts from Nina

It is critical to recognize that to live, to observe, to write as a woman of color is to live, observe, and write from a position of difference. Although I have a multiracial background, for the sake of simplicity, my identity is from a bi-racial standpoint of primary ancestry (European American father/East Indian mother). Growing up, I was socialized in two distinctly different cultures, yet I still belong to a minority group. As a dark-skinned woman with unique features, people sometimes have difficulty figuring out exactly what my background is. "Are you Black? Portuguese? Latina?" These are questions I am frequently asked.

My experiences and my expressions are different from many of my sisters of color; nevertheless, we share several common threads. That is, we face a certain degree of discrimination and stereotyping, and live in a political framework where white people maintain positions of decision-making power. Consequently, we seek support from our sisters of color to build alliances and strengthen our cultural communities.

As Ellen and I were formulating a method for these interviews, I strongly felt and expressed that, as a woman of color, I should talk with the women of color selected to be included in this chapter. Perhaps some would challenge this with resistance. Through my own research efforts and conversations with numerous professionals, I've learned that it is a common viewpoint that the special insight of minority group scholars (insiders) renders them best qualified to obtain information from minority communities. I am not suggesting that white professionals should not study racial minorities, but I do think that minority scholars have both empirical and methodological advantages. The most important one is that the "lenses" through which they see social reality may allow minority scholars to ask questions and gather information that others could not.

In talking with my sisters of color, there is an exchange of trust and common interest that Ellen could not conceptualize as an "outsider." In experiential education, both gender and race affiliations have made it necessary for women of color to develop strong relationships across cultural lines as a matter of coalition building. The connections we make in this field are often easier, however, due to the genuine and inclusive nature of the professionals involved.

My vision is that as more women of color are trained in experiential education, a field that is still predominantly and historically European American and male, there will be an environment that fosters working together across ideological lines such as class, appearance, skin color, age, sexuality, and community affiliations—issues that have tended to divide all people of color. Culture is, after all, the stories we tell about ourselves, not the stories others tell about us.

Thoughts from Ellen

While the stories contained in this chapter are wonderful and unique, I believe our collaborative process in creating this article has also been each of these things. In our early discussions at the 1994 conference in Austin, I knew intellectually that it was important for Nina to interview the women of color. However, my stubborn and sometimes "blindly equitable" mindset made it difficult to detach myself from wanting to share the women-of-color interviews with Nina, thus splitting the interviews up in some "other" manner. I always thought I saw social reality for "everyone" quite well (how arrogant!). While I am aware of the individuality my Polish/ Irish heritage and lesbian identity bring to my life experience, I know this mindset was shaped by the ease in which my white skin has allowed me to access the privileges of the dominant American culture.

My story as a woman in experiential education has been rather simple, though not entirely. I could always successfully compete, talk, run, climb, play as hard as my fellow brothers and sisters in my suburban Catholic neighborhood and schools. Being in the outdoors and teaching were second nature to me. I worked in the field of education for a while, with the illusion that all women and men regarded each other as equally competent, skilled, and knowledgeable. However, reality struck when I, and other women, were labeled as strident and outspoken by colleagues who became threatened by our confidence and competence. This led me to wonder why there were so few women, and people of color, in the arena of adventure-based and experiential education.

It has been through stories, adventures, and processes with mainly my women friends, and especially my partner, that I have come to recognize my place and identity, as well as those of others. By learning about my identity and trusting my own processes, over the years, I have grown as an educator. As women experiential educators, we must remain open to trusting the process of growth and change, but we must also make our voices heard.

The diversity of experience represented in the stories that follow, I hope, will resonate with each passing reader. Their differences and similarities, like raindrops, nurture each organism on which they fall.

Karen McKinney

> *Karen McKinney is an African American woman from Minneapolis, Minnesota. An ordained Baptist minister, she graduated from Mankato State University in Minnesota with a Master's Degree in Experiential Education. This interview took place during the last quarter of her program. She has since relocated to South Carolina where she is an instructor with the National Civilian Community Corps (NCCC) which is part of the AmeriCorps program.*

When Karen was nineteen years old, she worked at an inner-city Boys and Girls club. "We did a lot of traditional educational things and a lot of experiential things but didn't have the language, we didn't call it that," she explains. "We took kids on Outward Bound-type trips such as eight-day expeditions in the Boundary Waters. We took kids on mission trips and did lots of service learning. Again, I didn't call it service learning because I didn't have that language." Karen left the Boys and Girls club after ten years and went to South America with the intention of improving her Spanish skills. She then traveled to Honduras and worked in a refugee camp on the border of El Salvador.

Upon return, she worked again at the Boys and Girls club before going to The Fuller Theological Seminary in California. Before she left for the seminary, however, she started a program called the Servant Leadership Project which took youth overseas on a mission trip to Haiti. Co-sponsored by her church, church leaders convinced her not to go because of potential dangers. The trip was canceled five days before their departure. Because these inner-city kids had spent their entire summer raising money for this trip and could not go, Karen scrambled to find an alternative.

"I got information from the National Youth Leadership Project (NYLP) and did their ten-day leadership conference," she reports. "That was my first encounter with experiential education in that language. I took these kids on an NYLP program and they later called me up as a consultant and asked me to work at a couple of smaller conferences." The next few summers, Karen was invited back as a staff member and eventually asked to direct the program. Karen emphatically states, "I took the position part-time as the director of the National Youth Leadership Project. I was hiring people who were experiential educators; we did rock climbing, canoeing, biking, service learning, and high and low ropes initiatives. I thought about what was happening: 'I'm hiring people to do these things and I don't know how to do it myself, nor do I know the philosophy.'"

Karen shared the realization of being unknowledgeable about experiential education which had surfaced during her early experience. "I'm just waiting for someone to figure out that I don't know this." She continues, "What the director of the NYLP knew was that I had the people skills. He didn't hire me to be an experiential educator, he hired me to work with people. I could put the staff together, build community, and create a sense of community at these conferences. It wasn't these technical hard skills that were important at the time, I didn't need to know how to do these things. But I thought I did."

In 1992, Karen worked as a chaplain in Minneapolis at a half-way house on forty acres of land. "I was there three days a week and got to use a lot of the initiatives out there," she reports, "and I wanted to do more and learn more." Her supervisor approached her one day and asked, "Have you ever heard of 'The Bush'? That's the Bush Fellowship, you should go for it." Karen decided to apply for the Bush Fellowship Leadership Program in 1993 and won. A prestigious Minnesota state fellowship award for excellence in community leadership, Karen was the only African

American to win the award during that year. Accepting the offer presented by her supervisor to return to school, she explained her interest to him, "I want to get a degree in experiential education because I really want to understand what I'm doing, and get the foundation." Following her goals, she obtained a Master's degree at Mankato State.

Karen maintains that a lack of people of color is a major issue in experiential education. "There are not a lot of people of color to connect with," Karen asserts. "Because there are so few of us, our voice speaks for our people. You're cast into the role of having to teach those who don't know, and you're the token voice. Not only do you have to educate, but you have to tolerate people who are many times either subconsciously or willfully ignorant. There is an isolation factor [as a person of color] and a sense of wondering when these people [from the dominant culture] are going to get with it." Karen feels that many people around her may lack a certain awareness or have a lack of exposure to the perspectives of people of color. She also knows about the importance of educating others, but also informs individuals that she has her own personal perspective and does not represent all African American people. Karen contends, "I have to actually say it: 'This is my perspective, it's not everyone's, we are not a model cultural people. I speak for myself, but I know that because you have no other contact, I end up representing all people of color . . .' and so I have to challenge people. Attempting to inform people about their own narrowness of perspective is a challenge for me. If you're going to be an ally, you can't depend on just my voice. You must ask questions."

For Karen, her main source of support is from circles of women friends. Specifically, a circle of sisters of color provides an opportunity to network and overcome certain barriers and frustrations. "We need a separate space," proclaims Karen. "It's about the dynamics of racism and oppression and how it has place in the common society that we all participate in. I think that white people don't always understand that, so they get suspicious whenever we pull away."

Using the International AEE Conference environment as an example, Karen says, "We hear white people say, 'Why do they have to be together, we want them with us. . . .' We [people of color] must be together," she explains, "because that's where we draw our strengths. We try to tell white people, 'You don't understand how it is; we become bicultural people. We have to be bicultural because we have to operate both in your world and in our own. When you're operating in what is not your own, then you need moments when you need to be with somebody like yourself; otherwise, it drains and strains you. It's rejuvenation when you come together with people who are like you. That's why it is necessary; it's not a conspiracy, it's not about keeping secrets, it's even not about keeping you out, it's about getting something from within and replenishing ourselves from ourselves.'"

Karen described a cultural reality, in part, based on language. In the state of Minnesota, people of color only represent five percent of the population. "I have never lost that sense of always being on the margins," explains Karen. "And I know that influences what I do and how I do it. I could walk into a room and the first thing I notice is who's there. Who's there that looks like me, who's not there, and what kind of situation am I walking into. I'm not even conscious about it, but it's always present. And I know that it influences how I talk. After having been in college for ten years [Bachelor's degree and two Master's], I would go back home and get accused of talking white. People would say to me, 'You talk white. Would you stop doing that.' And so when I'd go into the lingo and slang of my sisters and brothers, my mother would say, 'Would you stop talking like that and talk like you're educated!' So I feel like I can't win."

When asked what empowers women of color and how could she relate this strength and courage to her involvement in experiential education, Karen replied, "Connecting. Affirmation. Having the opportunity to do. Along with the opportunity is being shown how to do something, and then being given the opportunity to do it. Being able to go even a little bit further, and receiving affirmation is empowering. Finding when you get there that what you've done is a validation. Connecting with other women and learning that they've gone through the same kind of struggle, saying 'Yeah,' and recognizing that. Looking back and leaning on our sisters who are back there and knowing that they are trying to push us forward."

Karen states that the audience and the topic determine whether her voice is welcome or not welcome. "Most of the time I think it's welcomed," she says. "At least at Mankato as a student, I bring a piece of [ethnic] diversity that's not there. I'm the only person of color in the whole program in the last two years at Mankato State. My guess is not many people of color have actually gone through the program. So, I bring something different, which is a little bit different for me."

She reports that both the students and professors welcome her voice, yet their occasional use of inappropriate language and cultural stereotyping is more apparent in her presence. "I know that I cause them to change what they say," replies Karen. "I've seen professors use examples [in class], and look directly at me, then they would include an African American example. Just looking at me and seeing this little African American face makes them remember and say, 'Oh, I need to include someone else.' So they do, and that's fine with me because they need to do this better."

Karen tells of another example in a class discussion about an inner-city school. "One of the things the professor said was very derogatory about urban schools. I hit him on it and he immediately apologized, saying he did not mean to perpetuate that kind of an image," Karen says in his defense. "Sometimes this causes people to have to slow down and deal with issues they don't want to deal with because I bring it up. Sometimes I wonder, 'Am I going to always have to be the one to bear the burden of always bringing it up?!' I get tired of that role. I wish someone else would be aware and bring stuff up."

Karen states, "There are few women of color [in experiential education] as role models; therefore, it is difficult connecting with others for advice or for mentoring.

There are not a lot of women in this field in general for this." Despite this barrier, Karen has selected a male mentor from Mankato State and has drawn several strengths from him. "He's dynamic and he's someone who is good in this field. He had something that I wanted to learn. He has a solid philosophy which he operates well from; he's a great facilitator and his bag of tricks is bottomless. I approached this person and asked him to be my mentor because he is in the field of experiential education." He agreed and made opportunities available to her. Karen recounts, "He encouraged me to do, and to go further than I thought I could. For instance, I had the opportunity to be a keynote speaker at the AEE Rocky Mountain Regional Conference. He made the opportunity available to me, and I would not have taken it otherwise. He said, 'Go ahead, do it,' although I didn't think that I was ready."

There was some frustration associated with this offer. "I didn't think I had legitimacy to speak at this event, because I haven't been in this field long enough," Karen explains. "Had I not been a person of color, I know that I would not have been asked to speak as the keynote. I don't have the credentials to be up there yet. But because I'm a person of color, I got this opportunity. So it's frustrating in the sense of asking myself, 'Did I really earn this? Do I deserve to be up there?' On the other hand, it's a good opportunity because it gives me a chance to grow. I do have something to say, so this gives me a voice and a chance to say it. When I got there, I was the only person of color. And that's real frustrating. I go to a large regional conference and I'm the only identifiable person of color there."

Expressing herself with pride, Karen views experiential education as an excellent opportunity and encourages young women of color to get into this field. For young women, particularly young women of color, interested in coming into experiential education, Karen encourages them with determination and vigor. "Although there aren't a lot of women doing this, I would tell them to come anyway," says Karen, "because a lot of the work that we do is work that transforms. It has a power. If anything is going to save our kids, it's going to be us," insists Karen. "This is a way of doing education that can transform them. Education that works, education that does not devalue. I would say to them [young women of color] that if you want to make a difference, this is a way to make a difference. This is a way to learn not just the hard skills, which I see a lot of the young white women doing, but to learn the soft skills and to have the ability to process."

Karen desires to integrate experiential education into what she does for a living because she views it as a way of educating that works. "It values people," she says. "So much of traditional education does not value the learner. And that means that my people, people of color, African American kids are not being valued in the classrooms. The philosophical basis of experiential education values the learner, it's student centered. And so, right from that point it says you are important, you have something to contribute and a space is created to do that."

Karen values facilitation, and believes the reason it is so transformative is because it can be applied to the rest of life. "But you need somebody to ask the right questions," she says. "I would say focus on the soft skills, because we [African Americans] are such a broken people and we need healing. Old people need it, middle-aged people need it, and young people need it because our communities are broken and we need healing. I would say focus on gaining those kinds of skills so that you can be a part of that healing and give back to the community. And you can help facilitate your own healing, because it can do that for you, too. Not only does it transform the participant, it transforms that practitioners as well."

Karen turned 40 in 1994 and, throughout her life, has been engaged in a variety of leadership roles. Her views about diversity in leadership provide more words of wisdom to young people of color: "I think it's important that our people see our people in positions of leadership. This is a much more powerful statement. Young people need to see us doing the programs, not always white people leading the expeditions, and white people doing whatever it is in the position up front. They need to see us up front. So I would encourage them to become the people who are the 'up front' ones."

Her words kept flowing. "It's good to work directly one on one with the kids," she advises, "but don't shy away from moving up and becoming the trainer of trainers. And don't shy away from becoming part of the higher management because that's where the power decisions are made. When you reach the point where you are capable, that's where you have to go. Use what you know and who you know because sometimes that's more important in this world. The fact that I know Craig, my mentor, opens doors. Ethically sometimes I don't like that, but if it's going to get me a voice, and will get me into a position of power and I can use that to help people, then I'm going to go ahead and do it because that's what everyone else uses and, although I don't agree, that's how the game gets played."

Hepsi Barnett

Hepsi Barnett, born and raised in Oklahoma, is a Native American (Osage Indian) currently living in Toronto, Ontario. Her outdoor career began after attending a Colorado Outward Bound School course in 1977. Since then, she's worked at Outward Bound Centers and Schools in New Hampshire, Maine, Florida, Canada, North Carolina, and Colorado. She has also served on the Board of Directors of AEE. Hepsi is currently the Program Director at the Canadian Outward Bound Wilderness School.

Following high school graduation, participating in an outdoor course in the Canyonlands of Utah was a stepping stone to Hepsi's career as an experiential educator. Although she first attended college at Texas Women's University, her wilderness skills were cultivated at Prescott College in Arizona.

She described her experience in the Canyonlands as "life transforming." She was initially frustrated and did not comprehend the meaning of the program. Not knowing anything about experiential education or Outward Bound, Hepsi described her ambivalence: "I thought it was the most ridiculous thing I had ever done and hated it. At one point during the course, I ended up quietly leaving and not telling anybody. I hiked out and got a ride with some hunters. As I was going back to get my stuff, it occurred to me that I was out of there. It also occurred to me that I was quitting. That was really hard so I asked the guys to let me out and I started walking back. I sat by the side of the road for a while and thought about what it would take to finish and why I would want to do that. I ended up walking back and finishing the course."

Her decision to return and finish the course was a turning point in her life. "I needed to do it because I wanted to, there was absolutely no pressure except pressure from myself. And I loved being on the land, being in the canyonlands was great; it's an incredibly spiritual place," describes Hepsi. "I didn't know anybody and was given very little information, yet when I finished, it was this great feeling of accomplishment. But at that time, I never thought this is what I want to do as a profession. It was more like, 'I never want to do this again in my life!' But I did it and never thought I'd do it again."

Hepsi shared that finishing the course was only one of several turning points in her life. Some personally devastating events which occurred while at Texas Women's University prompted Hepsi not to return. "I did not want to go back to TWU so I started doing a lot of introspection," explained Hepsi. "I was searching for something new and having drawn on my paradoxical experience at Outward Bound, I made some decisions and went to Prescott College. I did not go to become an educator necessarily, but to have more freedom and more opportunity to learn about what I wanted to do. And to think less of people telling me what I needed to do."

While at Prescott, Hepsi was approached to assist with an Outward Bound program which had started on a Navajo Reservation. "They had all this funding but they couldn't get the students. And when they did get the students, it was a bit of a disaster." Hepsi was later invited to join the staff. She explained her excitement was due to the fact she would be working with a Native group. "I started working on the Navajo Reservation. Eventually the program died out, but my interest was sparked enough that I wanted to continue in the field."

Hepsi admitted to having a "love/hate" relationship with Outward Bound (OB). "Part of it is the power of the results I have seen from doing the work and how [the programs] can influence people in positive ways. And I think about how it did that for me," she said. She believes Outward Bound is very influential but at the same time has lacked some understanding about cultural adaptation. She described their philosophy, metaphorically, as a mold. "You fit this model versus here is the best model to be in." In other words, the structure of OB has forced individuals to conform to the system rather than opening other avenues. "It seems that with this group [OB], you either fit in or you have nothing to say about it." Hepsi's observation is that Outward Bound is often targeted with negative viewpoints because it is a big organization, but states they are no different from any other. "The most amazing things happen on the courses, yet there are also injustices," she contends.

Her early experiences with Outward Bound were constraining due to a lack of individuality conveyed by the OB system. "I'm really aware of who I am, and how I identify is ever-present," maintained Hepsi. "I identify now and am very open about being a two-spirited Native. When I first came to Outward Bound I was very much acculturated into the [organizational] group. One Outward Bound instructor was the same as another Outward Bound instructor. There was absolutely no mention of who you were, how you identified, or what you could possibly bring or offer that other people could not."

People of color in the field are also beset with "tokenism." Hepsi proclaimed that this is a constant barrier. "It [tokenism] happens every day in experiential education, it happens every day in the corporate world, too. I believe that if there's an experiential education organization which can get away with tokenism, then that would continue. That is, individuals depending on one (or two) people of color in a particular organization to represent, or be the voice of, that particular culture." She also believes that organizations can't get away with it anymore because of an increased awareness of ethnic differences as well as people of color speaking out against "tokenism." She continued by relating this to the importance of change. "Now it's more about challenging the system and the way the system runs."

When available, people of color may be singled out to work with minority groups. There is much validity to this, yet on the contrary, the question may arise as to actual motivation. Similarly, when working jointly with other people of color there are certain mysterious attitudes. "It's hard because I personally get a lot out of working with people of color, as peers as well as on courses," relates Hepsi. "At the same time, I get angry when they think that it's all up to me, that I'm the only one that can do this. Or I hear statements such as 'We are the only ones. . . .' Not only do we have to educate ourselves to be the perfect person and completely understand racism and internalized racism, and work through that on our own, but we have to educate all the people around us in the organization *and* the young people that we're working with." Hepsi expressed that it is a lot to do. "It's hard enough for me to speak for who I am, much less to think that I might be representing Native people. Native people are so different anyway; there are a variety of tribes and we're all different. I go back and forth between being very tired, and very angry, to being very much a learner and really appreciating the opportunities that I've had."

Being a woman of color in the field not only means encountering issues of gender, but learning about the racial-ethnic backgrounds of other people of color. Hepsi has been involved with the Natives, Africans, Asians, Latinos(as) and Allies (NAALA) groups with both Outward Bound and the Association for Experiential Education. "Whether it's with women in NAALA or even in the Native community, I find that we're so divisive and somewhat judgmental of each other," says Hepsi. This barrier is counterproductive to creating unity. "We don't know enough about one another. That's what marginalized groups do to each other, right? Nobody oppresses like the oppressed!" [As people of color] we don't know whether to reach out and embrace each other or be leery of one another. I think you can find that in any group. It hurts us because then you have the dominant group sitting back with their arms crossed, saying, 'Well, we told you so; we gave these people a chance and look at them now.'"

Hepsi recalled a large gathering in 1990 where each Outward Bound School sent nearly every person of color on their staff to Thompson's Island to attend a very important meeting about issues of diversity and funding. Based on a proposal from the office, funding had been allocated to improve diversity within the organization. "Everyone was fighting for this money!" exclaimed Hepsi. "That's really what it was about. For the first time in my life, I saw more people of color than I had ever seen in one place all doing amazing work. We all got together and agreed, 'This is amazing, we had no idea there was this many people of color working for Outward Bound, and we should have lunch together!' Well, it was very threatening to the dominant group. In fact, one of the white professionals said, 'Why can't we have lunch with you?' Many controversial dynamics were happening. As we [NAALA] had lunch together, we talked about such things as 'How can Outward Bound talk about diversity? We should talk about diversity. Because we don't even know what we think yet, we need to wrestle with this and struggle with it and compare our experiences.'" Hepsi explained that safety is a common thread throughout all Outward Bound Schools. When the group came back together with the OB administrators, NAALAs confronted the management by stating that the profile for *diversity* should be equivalent to that of *safety*, and taken just as seriously. Although there are still many unresolved areas, significant outcomes of this gathering include development of the NAALA Steering Committee and establishment of the new position of a National Diversity Director to oversee the newly created NAALA Institute. Many action items regarding issues of diversity are still being addressed; as accountability improves, progress and change will follow.

So what empowers this Native woman? From an early age, Hepsi grew up being proud of who she is. "I grew up being in touch with the traditional Indian culture, being proud of who I am and more or less being related to the land. There were always lots of other Indians where I grew up, and being around lots of relatives created a strong sense of me. I think about how all that relates to everything around me."

Today, Hepsi feels there is a certain expectation or romanticizing, particularly in experiential education, about what it means to be Native American. "I think people are completely disappointed when they meet me," says Hepsi, "because I'm not on a horse, I don't have this long braid. I'm a half-breed, light skinned and people wonder what's it all about. When I think back to when I was younger, that insecurity wasn't there because of where I grew up, which was with my family."

Hepsi describes the women in her family as having courage and fortitude. "Native women are incredibly strong. There were many role models. I think about my grandmother, my mother, and my aunts and they are what has helped feed the culture. They are the teachers; I learned from their strengths. My mother is the one who keeps going; she's the one that's always there and I know she'll take care of whatever situation comes up."

Although her family does not completely understand what Hepsi's work entails, strength and support received has helped her persevere. "I do know that I've always gotten a lot of support from my family, especially from my mother in terms of being strong and standing up for what I believe in, for believing in who I am, and not being afraid to speak out. To them they could never think about paying money to be out on the land. They do know that I work with young people and they completely respect that."

Hepsi has clearly had a variety of experiences and support networks. During her days at Prescott College, she was in a predicament where racial injustice landed her in jail. "One time when I had to deal with paper work to get my dentistry and health care paid for," recalls Hepsi, "I had to go to Phoenix." Because there was a very long wait at the dentist office, she decided to go out for lunch with some other Indian people who were also in the waiting room. "As we were coming back across the alley from lunch, back to the dentist office, we were harassed by these policemen. We were actually provoked based on the fact that we were Indian. I was officially arrested for vagrancy because I didn't have an I.D. and my car was fifty yards away; they wouldn't let me go to my car and so they arrested me and three other Native men."

There was absolutely no reason that should have happened, she insisted. To add salt to her wounds, Hepsi was getting ready to attend a winter mountaineering course which was starting the next day. Luck of the draw and financial assistance from Prescott College sent her on her way. For Hepsi, this was a realization. "Okay, obviously I am different," she states, "and I learned you have to stand up for who you are and for injustices. That was just a small example of things that happen every day to people of color."

Hepsi seeks some of her support from other women and draws much of her strength from other women of color. Francis Rucker, for instance, is an African American woman who came to work for Outward Bound many years ago. "Francis and I ended up working very closely together when she was first hired and, over the years, we've developed a friendship as well as being great resources and strength to each other."

Hepsi's voice has come a long way. "With everything that's happened and every attempt to eradicate Native people, we're still here," she says. "And, there's a huge Native population in Canada with some real political clout," explains Hepsi. When the first Native program came together about ten years ago, she was the only Native instructor. When a decision had to be made whether to blend Native students with non-Natives or keep them together in a group, Hepsi was out-voted and there were one or two Native students with each brigade. "My voice has come a long way since that time," she continues, "and now we're running this Native program that is culturally appropriate. For instance, there are elders who usually start the courses with a prayer, there are sweat lodges, they learn smudges, and teachings are from the instructors as well as the elders from the community. And, there are all-Native brigades with at least one Native instructor on the course."

Hepsi described the background of some of the Native youth who participate in the program. Since the 1960s, many of the young people in Canada have been taken from their families and put up for adoption simply because they're Indian. "These Native kids come through the program and for the first time, they have the opportunity to be proud of who they are and learn about who they are as a Native person in the presence of other Native people," Hepsi reports. "There's this amazing road of exploration that happens out on those courses that I have never seen; it's a rather powerful life-transforming experience."

If any of the young women in her program wanted to pursue experiential education as a viable career, Hepsi would provide as much support and guidance as she possibly could. "I would try to figure out a way for them to work with Outward Bound, or try to hook them up with nearby programs in their communities," shares Hepsi. She also places value in active outreach. "Generally speaking, it has not been my experience that people of color (especially women of color) are lined up at the doors. But they are out there. So when people say, 'I want Native people or I want people of color, our doors are open'—well, you've got to go out there and find them if you really want them, you have to put some energy into it. They are there, you know, we are here," Hepsi states with certainty. "All over, there are organizations who think like that; whether you go to the reservations or inner cities, people of color are around if you really want them."

Hepsi's varied background and venturesome outlook on life has provided her with many unique experiences. She's honest and forthright; her dynamic personality has been a contributing factor to her success. Many of her efforts emphasize community-building, and this is evident in her genuine nature.

Gini Hornbecker

Gini Hornbecker has been an experiential educator for the past 15 years. She has built and managed ropes courses in Portland and Sisters, Oregon, and has worked as a consultant in cultural diversity and organizational change. Over the years, she has worked with a broad spectrum of groups including youth at-risk, women in leadership, and corporate executives.

Gini describes her introduction to experiential education as "somewhat unorthodox." She declares, "I did not consciously choose a path of experiential education. I kind of fell upon it!" She was a junior at the University of Maryland, majoring in psychology, when she left school to devote full-time energy to organizing anti-Vietnam War activities. "We were at the nation's Capitol every other week; there was always so much to do." Gini considers being involved, in this case on the political front lines, essential to experiential learning.

Shortly thereafter, she married a man whom she met in Washington, DC, and in 1972 they moved to Oregon with a newborn son. Frustrated with the lack of quality child care in Portland, Oregon, they "recycled" an abandoned school and opened St. Philip Neri Child Development Center, which Gini managed. Guided in this endeavor by Dr. Mary York, from Portland State University, Gini learned that "if you engage at the heart level, the head will follow." As part of the program, Gini put together classes, field trips, and hands-on learning experiences for children ages two to five. "At the time, I didn't know any experiential theory. I was just operating from the seat of my pants! I was recognizing what was turning kids on, getting them involved, and from there, I could assist them in learning how to be with each other and express themselves."

When Gini first arrived in Portland, she was impressed with the sight of Mt. Hood. "I really wanted to climb it," she says. At the same time, she saw a newspaper article describing the popular south-side climb to the summit. Her interest in summiting Mt. Hood grew with the size of her family. Her husband's fear for Gini's safety, as well as the birth of her daughter, would delay her attempt for another two years. During those years, Gini "developed a dependency on marijuana and began to feel stuck in the traditional wife/mother role." A serious kidney infection in 1976 forced her to recognize that her life needed to change. She took a climbing class, developed her physical conditioning, and finally climbed Mt. Hood. "I absolutely loved everything [climbing] did for me. With climbing, something opened up in me. I felt a renewed passion for my life."

Many of Gini's role models in her life, including in outdoor endeavors, were women. In the early 1970s, she met Helen Cheek while volunteering for the St. Vincent de Paul Association in Portland, and together they had an interesting adventure. Gini recalls, "Helen was a serious backpacker and twenty-five years older than me. She had hiked all over the Northwest and asked me to circumnavigate Mt. Hood with her and a friend. I had never backpacked before except on Mt. Hood. My raingear was a poncho that snapped up the side and a garbage bag."

Gini's story is a classic. "There was a light drizzle when Helen, another friend, Blackie, and I started out from Timberline Lodge at 6,000 feet. We got four or five miles out when Blackie slipped and injured her knee. By this time it was raining heavily. We ran into a ranger who invited us to a Forest Service lodge for the night. As Blackie's knee was quite swollen from the fall, she decided to hike out with the ranger the next morning. Optimistically searching for blue sky, Helen and I decided to continue our trip." As they hiked along, the weather deteriorated rapidly with high winds and rain turning to blinding snow. "Needless to say, it was very cold. By about four o'clock, Helen was hypothermic." Fortunately, Gini had recently been to a lecture by Dr. Cameron Bangs on hypothermia and recognized the symptoms. Gini recalls, "I didn't know where we were, but we managed to find one of the stone shelters on the side of the mountain. I started my first outdoor fire in the corner of the shelter, fired up some hot drinks, stripped Helen down, and climbed into a sleeping bag with her. I did all the basics that I learned in the hypothermia lecture." Gini continued, "Initially, I laid out our rain fly for a ground cloth with our sleeping bags on top of it. The shelter's tin roof was full of holes and leaked like crazy. I realized this is really dumb! I could imagine this article in *Accidents in North American Mountaineering* about two women who froze to death of hypothermia laying on top of the rain fly that might have kept them dry! With the storm raging outside, I put our tent up inside the shelter. The next morning, we awoke to find a foot of new snow completely covering the trail. Fortunately, Helen had recovered that night and in the morning, we figured out which way to go. We had a great trip!" A year later, Helen invited Gini to speak about "accident prevention" at a local trail club meeting.

Gini continued to explore outdoor challenges while balancing motherhood and family responsibilities, with her personal growth and skill development. An interest in ice climbing led her to answer an advertisement for a cook/base-camp manager at Lute Jerstad Adventures ice-climbing seminars held on Mt. Hood's Elliott Glacier during the summer. "I'd done some ice climbing and thought this would be a great opportunity to learn more." She spent the first week hauling loads of equipment and food up to the glacier base camp. It was at this job that she met Catherine Freer, a well-known international climber and instructor who became a significant role model for her.

"Catherine was somebody who had a very 'can-do' attitude." Gini remembers, "There was a craggy outcropping just above our base camp and one evening after dinner [Catherine] said, 'Let's go up and do some bouldering.' She danced up a thirty-five-foot crack, maybe a 5.5 or 5.6. I had never done any solo climbing before that time, but her gentle suggestions and clear confidence in my abilities helped me to find my own confidence and skill." From Catherine, Gini learned about two kinds of fear. "She told me to recognize the kind of fear that stops you dead in your tracks and the fear that sharpens all of your senses—it moves you into total awareness of everything that surrounds you." Gini believes there is a difference in the choices. "In the first choice, one would get nowhere, and in the other, you could see what avenues open up to you." Gini continues to use this notion today in many different situations beyond climbing. "To me, it has a lot of deep metaphoric value."

On Catherine, Gini states, "She made it clear that I could do anything I wanted to. I really wanted to be on the glacier and it didn't make sense that I was doing all the cooking. So I reorganized things to be more equitable between the instructors and by the end of the summer, I, too, was teaching ice climbing."

To create more opportunities for adventure, Gini joined the Mazamas, a Portland-based climbing club. "I was climbing whenever and wherever I could, but mostly with men." Her leadership and climbing skills quickly moved her into a teaching position with the club. She taught climbing "experientially with a lot of support for personal reflection and personal growth."

This was also a time of great personal growth for Gini. Her family was very supportive, often camping out at the trailhead or base camp while she climbed. "My partner wanted to 'do the right thing,' but he was struggling with me coming into my own identity. We had been following a very traditional path doing what [society] expected of us. It became clear that neither of us was happy in these roles."

Climbing became a metaphor for many changes in Gini's life. In 1980, she accepted a position with North Portland Youth Service Center to develop a ropes course challenge program. "I wasn't even sure what a ropes course was, but I thought it might be an opportunity to create a mini-experience in a city park that would duplicate the personal growth I had experienced through climbing." Using guidelines from the book, *Cowstails and Cobras*, Gini, Richard Earnst, and a handful of her climbing friends built both a low and a high challenge course in Pier Park in Portland. Her focus working with the ropes course was to help people "take a look at where they were and reflect on what they wanted as an individual and in group relationships." Proudly, Gini states, "The ropes program at North Portland served over 41,000 people, including adjudicated youth, and adults, during the ten years I was director."

Gini's first experience with the Association for Experiential Education (AEE) took place at the international conference at Humboldt State University, Arcata, California. "I remember meeting Project Adventure folks and hundreds of others doing the same things I was doing." She was amazed to discover people, programs, and a wealth of literature articulating experiential theory and practice. Through her involvement in AEE she came to know women from the Women's Professional Group. "They have been a real salvation for me, over the years. [These women] have always created a tremendous place to feel grounded and supported. For me, this has become a very safe place to be."

Mary McClintock, former AEE Women's Professional Group Chair, and Linda Besant, founder of SOAR, have also been role models for Gini. "Mary is steadfast and completely comfortable being who she is. Mary educated many people at the 1992 AEE International Conference about gay and lesbian history through a timeline she posted on the wall in one of the building corridors." Pertaining to Linda, Gini states, "She founded her own outdoor program for persons with physical and/or mental disabilities. I ran a challenge course and a rock-climbing program for SOAR's participants." To prepare for her work with SOAR, Gini spent time climbing blindfolded and with different limbs immobilized to assist her in developing an understanding of what might be different about the experience for someone who did not have the ability to see or move freely.

Many of the participants in SOAR had disabilities resulting from head injuries. Ironically, in 1988, Gini was in a car accident and experienced a massive head trauma that changed her life. "Essentially, I was killed and resuscitated," according to Gini. Recovery required her to re-learn how to walk, how to talk, and how to organize her thoughts to complete tasks. "I had a condition whereby, in my head, I could see myself or imagine myself saying or doing something and would swear I had done it, only to discover that I had not completed [the task]. I had to make checklists and do tasks in front of the mirror or on a tape recorder." Through this experience, she discovered new ways to train, and "re-direct energy," in her mind. "The accident forced me to look at my life and how I was taking care of myself. I recognized that many of us are disabled in some way, resulting from things that happen to us or what we say and do to ourselves."

Gini would like to see more women in the field of experiential education. "At the risk of sounding sexist, I think women offer another level of balance and openness to situations they are in. Women bring a perspective that is more nurturing, supportive, and accepting."

Some of the barriers that Gini has encountered as a woman in experiential education include not being taken seriously, lack of a formal education, and gender stereotyping. For example, to teach an experiential course at a local college, Gini had to pair up with a male who had a Master's degree. "He was the instructor on record and was paid more. When he no longer wanted to teach the class, the college canceled the course because they would not hire me alone." There were many times she was not taken seriously as a woman in outdoor settings. "Male climbers or rescue students would see me as their instructor and would not really listen until I had led the routes and demonstrated that I could out-climb them."

As a co-founder of the Inclusivity Consulting Group, she often encountered clients who would address their questions to and make eye contact with her male partner first. At one particularly important interview for a contract, she and her partner deliberately took seats next to each other so when clients looked across to us they would be more likely to see both and not just one or the other. "I found I needed to force myself to interrupt conversations and not wait so long for an opportunity to speak. It didn't feel like me, but it seemed to be the norm."

To other women in experiential education, Gini shares that "there is a real strength in looking back over our shoulders, honoring our individual paths, and recognizing the skill and strength it's taken to get here. I'm most successful as an educator when I'm authentic, going by what my head and heart find to be true."

She concludes, "Growing up I received a lot of conditioning around not trusting people and competing with women. Lacking trust creates distance and makes it hard to recognize and accept the support that is available. There are many wonderful people doing wonderful things that go unnoticed. As women, we must be willing to make connections, recognize and value our many perspectives. Using each other's support can make a big difference."

Yuri Kimura

Yuri Kimura is a 22-year-old Japanese woman. She was born in Japan and when she was six, moved to the United States. Yuri is a graduate of Earlham College with a Bachelor's Degree in Human Development and Social Relations.

A young professional to the field, Yuri is exploring her options and career possibilities in experiential education. Earlham College in Indiana was a supportive environment for her while she was a student. She was mentored by some terrific people and gained many valuable skills, including strong leadership skills. Although she has instructed wilderness and basic rock-climbing courses for a variety of programs, working as a leader with Connecting with Courage (an outdoor program for girls in the Boston area) has been the highlight of her experiences thus far.

Yuri explained that Connecting with Courage deals with girls' development and psychological theories. Yuri shared that she struggled with completely understanding if and how American, feminist, and psychological theories would affect someone from a different cultural background. "At these programs [Connecting with Courage], we say, 'Speak from the heart, use your voice, be assertive,' but if a different culture [like the Japanese culture] doesn't allow for that, then this is difficult."

Photo courtesy of Amy Kohut

Yuri described her enjoyment in working with the girls and one other staff person of color while at Connecting with Courage. "The girls' program has a philosophy that allows me to bring up and discuss my culture. There was a half-day during the summer set aside for a culture workshop; having the girls delve into their backgrounds was excellent." This allowed them to open up and be themselves.

Regarding outdoor programs, Yuri believes her experiences have been different from her white allies. "It is clearly different because I've always been in the minority," she reports. "I come from a culture that respects relationships, but women's voices aren't necessarily heard as much as men's. Although I live in America, I still have cultural differences from growing up that are still part of me and it took me a long time to realize it was okay to be assertive." Yuri is very much in touch with her Japanese roots. "The whole Japanese culture is relationship based," she continued, "although you may feel one way, you may express something else just to make sure you're not hurting the basic relationship. Whereas in the [outdoor] field, you have to be totally and completely honest because you're living with other people for an extended period of time. You have to learn to say things with integrity." She explains that Asian women are socialized to be more passive and submissive and not to speak out. "I think people who have come on the [Connecting with Courage] program with cultural stereotypes of who I am are surprised when I become the outgoing, fun instructor who leads trips," Yuri exclaimed.

Yuri has received concrete feedback from others pertaining to her leadership style and skills. An example of this feedback is, "You know you're solid with your skills and you know what you're talking about. You still tend to second-guess yourself and don't speak out when you know that you should." Yuri wonders how much of that comes from her cultural background. For instance, she states, "Maybe I should stay quiet even when I know something is wrong. Avoidance of conflict is very cultural. Don't confront someone with a disagreement, they should just pick up on the signals. This concept of being relationship based has a very strong influence on me."

Overcoming barriers hasn't come easy to Yuri, but she feels that she has been very empowered in the field. "I've done a lot of growing and self-reflecting," she stated. "I feel that I have a strong sense of who I am because of the experiences and encounters that I have had by being in experiential education. I love the teaching that I do and the trust and respect I get from my students." She also maintains that she struggles with the Japanese side of her questioning, "Am I supposed to be heard?" Yuri continued, "I definitely see myself as having a very Japanese side, for instance, quiet, obedient, polite, humble, avoid conflict, and a very American side also. I have struggled in the past figuring out where I am on that spectrum."

For Yuri, women in the field provide sources of support. But she is still frustrated with the issue of racial and ethnic diversity. "It's hard sometimes not having sisters of color around you," Yuri states. "Oftentimes, I'd talk with my women-of-color friends from school where I had a network. Although they're not in the same field, and may not know anything about the outdoors, they understand issues I deal with as a woman of color."

As a Japanese woman, Yuri believes that a crucial part of exploring her ethnicity, uniqueness, appearance, and traditions in the outdoors is finding a self-identity. "What better way than a three-day solo!" she exclaimed. "I did this during my first year in college and wrote forty pages in my journal. I spent a lot of time thinking about me, not about anyone else in my group." She also explained that time in the wilderness provided her with a great deal of personal growth during periods of instruction. "Because you are always on the course yourself, even if you are instructing it," she proclaims.

Yuri believes there are times when she has felt "out of place" in experiential education settings. She said it was difficult to pinpoint specifics but shared one experience: "I remember talking with one of my male colleagues, a Hispanic guy, and we were discussing how we were the only two people of color that were instructors in the field in this particular area [of the program]. Although at one point we were having an argument, we had to be allies. This woman sitting next to me (a friend of mine also on the staff) said, 'I don't really see you as a person of color anyway.' What I felt her saying is that I act white and that she doesn't see me as any different. Maybe I'm assuming that's what she was saying. Basically what she was implying is that I've acculturated myself based on how I say or do things. She was trying to be nice by saying my color doesn't matter. But it does to me. And to disregard that in any way is to disrespect me. This is something I constantly struggle with. Because over ninety-five percent of the people I either worked with or for or have taught in my last four years as an instructor have been white, I feel that I am often the 'invisible minority.' Because I 'talk white, act white, dress white,' I can pretty much conform to the people around me and am often widely accepted as part of that group." Yuri contends that as a result, she is often "caught as the spokesperson for the minority group or the token person of color" and that becomes difficult for her.

One day during a pulling-boat trip, Yuri taught the girls how to count to fifty and sing songs in Japanese while rowing. "This is one way to share my culture, and I had never done that before. It was quite an experience and made me feel like I gave this part of me, this little piece of my culture, to the girls." Yuri has become very aware about how she approaches cultural issues in experiential education. "A facilitator of a culture-and-courage workshop we once had said that I was 'closeted' about my culture on my first course. That really struck me, so I came out as a Japanese woman on the first day of the next two courses."

As a woman of color, Yuri makes every effort to be heard and believes that fundamentally, her voice has been welcome in the field of experiential education. "While working with the girls at Connecting with Courage, I consciously tried to talk about culture or differences and similarities between people," stated Yuri. "Simply because of what I look like, questions are always there for other people. For instance, the girls ask, 'Where are you from?' or 'Do you eat with chopsticks?' Other questions can be inquisitive in another way, such as, 'What do you mean you're Japanese? Can you teach me how to say this or say that?' And so, we've had a lot of good interactions about language and culture." Additionally, Yuri explains how conscious the staff were in placing Asian girls who join the program in her group. As these 12- and 13-year-old girls are at a crucial age of identity development, there is greater value in providing role models with similar backgrounds for them.

Yuri declared that, for the most part, she believes she has been fortunate that her voice has been welcomed. "I think that this may have to do primarily with the fact that I was working with women and girls at Connecting with Courage and before that at Earlham College," says Yuri. "For me, it's sometimes hard to distinguish what is not 'welcome.' Is it because I am a woman? or of color? I know that in some of the coed climbing classes I assisted for a lead male instructor, my voice was not always heard or respected, mostly by the men. This is why I decided to move on to all-women's climbing classes."

Role models for Yuri have been predominantly family members. "Support from my family has been excellent," insists Yuri. "My mom has been a role model in my life. Because of her experiences with the Girl Scouts, she supports me in what I do. She sees my work as good despite all the 'cultural weirdness' that might get brought up about a Japanese woman leading outdoor trips. My grandmother was an amazing role model," continues Yuri. "She knew I was spending time in the mountains and was doing the kinds of things my mom was doing when she was growing up. While some other relatives were skeptical of my work, my grandmother once said to me, 'That's the only place I can really see you—in the woods with a pair of jeans, a T-shirt, and a backpack.'"

Based on racial and ethnic difference, Yuri explained that she felt it is important for her to bring to the field of experiential education who she is and what her culture is. "To be able to be open and honest about my background and my values is important to me," Yuri asserts. "As a leader, I want to be able to share my culture with people in my group and for them to know I am sharing my culture with them."

Peggy Walker Stevens

Peggy Walker Stevens is currently a project director for the research and design firm, Education Development Center, based in Massachusetts. During the past six years, she has developed a network of 450 urban youth leaders in Lawrence, Massachusetts, who are involved in education, service, and adventure. She lives in Lexington, Massachusetts, with her family.

Peggy's introduction to education and the outdoors stemmed from her experience as an avid Girl Scout in both elementary and high school, and by being a Girl Scout leader in college. "I always liked the outdoor type of thing, and I always did a lot of teaching of younger kids. When I was eight years old, I ran a nursery school during the summer mornings in the neighborhood which you could send your kid to for a dime for two hours. So I guess I was born a teacher! I later went to college and became a social studies and English teacher. I taught at an urban high school for three years, later became head of the English department, then taught in a more rural school for three years." This was in the early 1970s. She team-taught with the science teacher and developed an interdisciplinary experiential curriculum which she taught for two years while living in Colchester, Connecticut.

After graduation from the Harvard Graduate School of Education in 1976, she heard Bob Gillette speak at the National Council of Teachers of English Conference in New York City about doing outdoor classroom-based activities. This was one turning point at which Peggy became inspired to get involved in experiential education. "I went on to take a [Colorado] Outward Bound course for teachers in 1978, which also gave me some [teaching] ideas because we had three-and-one-half weeks of Outward Bound, plus a seminar on how to do it with your classes. At that point, it was the first time I had heard of the Association for Experiential Education (AEE), and met some Board members, which is really when I got interested. Because AEE was based in Colorado, Peggy became connected with the experiential educators' network and has worked to combine her love of the outdoors and doing service. "I think it's the idea of outdoors and service and that I was in [scout] troops as a youngster and teenager, that were very service oriented and all that had a big influence on me."

Peggy has always worked in public schools, not in the traditional sense, but in an experiential, interdisciplinary manner. "I'm an English teacher, I'm not an outdoor educator or adventure person." But in 1979, Peggy attended the international AEE conference in New Hampshire which changed her life and her experiential education involvement. At that time, she was teaching five "traditional" high school English classes which was frustrating to her. She remembers the conference because "the group of people were just so exciting." Partially due to frustrations in her teaching situation, she decided to get more involved in AEE. "Along came a ballot where you could nominate yourself or someone else for the board of directors. So I figured what the heck, and I nominated myself. There were approximately twenty-two people running for three spots on the board and there were only two women on the ballot." Peggy won a seat on the board and from that time forward, Peggy catapulted into experiential education and involvement with the Association. "I'd been a member for four months and had gone for one day to a national conference! Nobody who had anything to do with the board had ever heard of me."

This was a tremendous turning point in Peggy's view of herself as an educator. "It changed my idea of myself from a competent teacher who might become a principal, to someone who could operate on the national [education] scene." Through her new friends and colleagues on the AEE board, including Jim Kielsmeier, Bob MacArthur, and Rocky Kimball, Peggy learned a lot about experiential education, personal integrity, and operating an international professional association. "I felt very privileged to work with the people I did on the board. It was a tremendous growth experience for me." About Kielsmeier and MacArthur, she states, "They have a really strong vision, and dreams, and that just stays with them. They are very inspiring to me." Peggy has enjoyed her involvement in AEE and what it has brought to her life. "Everyone shares this passion for learning in an involved way and for a life where you push a little bit to the edge of things."

Not many of her early AEE colleagues were involved in traditional public schools. "They have been much more involved in outdoor leadership or connected with organizations such as Outward Bound. I went for that three weeks [Colorado OB program] and that was it! Other than that, I've always worked in public schools." Through her involvement with AEE in the late 1970s to mid-1980s, Peggy gained ideas about experiential approaches to education. "I was the person who had [a traditional education] voice. I've always been a big spokesperson for the teachers in the organization because that's my orientation. However, I was exposed to some fantastic practitioners. At least by AEE people, public school is sometimes under-rated as a setting for experiential educators."

Peggy continues about the utilization of experiential education in the public schools. "I think that public education is strongly moving in the direction of experiential education. I recently read that ninety percent of what we know about how people learn has been researched in the last ten years. Amazingly, all of [the research on education] is pointing to hands-on experience, people learning by doing." Peggy, however, sees AEE as somehow "missing the boat" in becoming leaders in the public schools movement toward experiential learning.

Regarding experiential education and women today, Peggy states that while there were women in the Association during her time on the board, there were few in leadership roles. "There was Mary Smith, but it was definitely a male-dominated organization. At one point I wrote an article in the *Journal* [*of Experiential Education*] encouraging women to do some of the [leading]. I found the women's group complaining about their lack of a role within the Association. It seemed to me that my story [of getting involved in the Association] was a true exception. Usually, the people getting elected to the board were people who were leading a special interest group or a professional group, or people attending or convening a regional or international conference and that women weren't taking on those roles except in the women's group. And they weren't getting elected to the board when they ran because they weren't taking more visible, lower levels of leadership in the organization. However, on the board, I always felt valued and encouraged. The men leading were very good facilitators . . . every voice was heard and you didn't feel male domination on the board. They encouraged me to become the first woman president of AEE."

Peggy sees education as a profession having a high number of women, but in her experience with AEE, this organization has lacked involvement with women. "All my friends in AEE are men, maybe because there were mostly men when I was on the board and I haven't been involved [with AEE] recently." She believes experiential education has become more diverse because of the rise of therapists and mental health practitioners in the field which are not male-dominated professions. She notes that "you must have people involved on the basic level and they can begin to move forward as their talents and interests develop. If you don't have women or people of color involved at all levels, then you're going to have fewer at the top."

Regarding the arena of awards and recognition, Peggy notes that "there are not many older women in the organization, that is, in their late forties and fifties. Since that's when people tend to be at the height of their career when you would tend to get something like [an] award, it's not surprising that as long as the award is limited to members, you wouldn't have a lot of women nominees for it. Also, look around and you don't see many African Americans in their fifties in the Association." Optimistically, Peggy hopes "that twenty years from now, [awards] won't even be an issue."

As an educator and a leader in AEE, Peggy feels that she brings enthusiasm, organization, and vision. "I think I'm not afraid to say the truth sometimes, even when it's not the 'current line' in AEE." Although women's voices in AEE have had varying involvement and recognition, Peggy believes "you have to roll up your sleeves and show what you can do and say things such as 'I'll convene a conference, I'll show what I can do.'" Peggy notes that she leads with her "interpersonal intelligence." "As a teacher when I work with kids, I always know when one walks in if they're in a bad mood. I'm really tuned in to people."

As a high school teacher, her students would probably remember her because "they were always involved in learning by doing. It was very different than your typical high school class." When teaching government, her students had to work on a political campaign. Her students were "more involved than just sitting on their bottoms." Peggy's classes, and the activities she designed, engaged her student's minds. She was considered to be a really nice, yet really hard teacher. "That's the trick if you have a whole class of kids. How can you have each one stretch, but not so far that they get frustrated, and do that at the same time with twenty-five different people. It's a big challenge in teaching." She thinks that she can be more academic in her style than a lot of AEE people. Her academic curriculum is woven into experiential activities. "I think sometimes there is a problem in how you keep challenging intellectual integrity when the experiences aren't always done well." Currently, Peggy works more with teachers than with kids. However, she believes that the kids in her current program know that she really cares about them and that she will never give up on them.

Influencing Peggy in her early years were her parents. "I believe my parents were a big influence with the service idea; I think that the teacher part of me is just innate. We were raised to be very tolerant." Relating to tolerance, she continues by sharing this story: "One time, I went to a workshop on multicultural awareness and we all had to draw a picture and write what came to mind as your family's motto. I remember I was sitting next to a Mexican woman whose motto seemed to be about beauty and I thought, 'Oh my gosh, BEAUTY!' [My motto] was much more Puritan, Like 'To whom much has been given, much is expected' and 'To make the world a better place.' That's the way were raised." However, she feels that sometimes "people with my Puritan background feel guilty. Guilt trips about my somewhat blessed life, I guess."

In the early 1980s, Peggy stopped teaching when her own children were very young. For the past ten years, she has enjoyed part-time work while still being able to spend time with her children. Prior to her current position, she was the editor of *The Journal of Experiential Education* for five years and was also an adjunct faculty working with beginning teachers. She has made time to be a Girl Scout leader for both her daughters' troops. She says, "I like to have time for doing all the leadership activities with my own kids as well as everybody else's." This ethic is one that has been very important to her. Peggy indicates her belief is that while other professionals, usually men, "have been working toward the height of their career in their 40s, women who choose to spend time as a mother, are somewhat behind professionally." While she is not regretting her choices, she thinks this is important to recognize in the professional scheme of things. Being a mom to her "is the ultimate teaching job."

Philosophically, advice Peggy offers to other women is "to hold your vision of what people can be and choose which battles are important to you." While Peggy started out in college with the goal of making a substantial change in American education, she exclaims, "Now I am happy if I can change just one school."

Acknowledgments

The authors would like to thank the Northwest Regional Council of AEE for funding that supported work on this chapter.

About the Authors

Anne Bell is a graduate student at the Faculty of Environmental Studies, York University, Toronto. A keen amateur naturalist and outdoor enthusiast, she considers nature experience and nature study a focal point of her work in environmental education and advocacy. She is currently involved in ecological restoration initiatives and is a director of the Wildlands League chapter of the Canadian Parks and Wilderness Society. Her research has been published in *Alternatives*, *Trumpeter* and *Pathways* and is financially supported by the Social Sciences and Humanities Research Council of Canada.

Martha Bell has instructed in the outdoors in Canada, the United States, and New Zealand/Aotearoa full-time for seven years. She currently teaches theory of outdoor and experiential education classes at the University of Otago in Dunedin, New Zealand. Her doctoral studies focus on women's social subjectivities and body memories in the outdoors.

Anne Dal Vera has guided outdoor trips for women and taught coed wilderness courses in Alaska and Minnesota. She currently works as a wilderness ranger in Colorado. Anne wrote about the AWE expedition in *Another Wilderness: New Outdoor Writing by Women*, edited by Susan Fox Rogers and published by Seal Press. She has also submitted a piece for the book, *Women's Voices in the Antarctic*, edited by Dr. Esther Rothblum of the University of Vermont. Anne writes poetry and is working on a book about the AWE expedition, integrating her experience with insights about how women work together.

Ellen B. Drogin, Ph.D., is currently a Principal Planner/Research Analyst for the Maryland-National Capital Park and Planning Commission, Information Management Division. She is also an Adjunct Professor in the College of Health and Human Performance at the University of Maryland-College Park. Her research interests include: research methodology; demography and community planning; visitor impact management; and outdoor recreation and behavior.

Rosalind Dutton, M.S.S., L.S.W., is a psychotherapist and consultant with 20 years of experience working with women survivors of interpersonal violence and their families and with women recovering from addictions. She leads wilderness trips for women survivors of interpersonal violence through her group practice, Wissahickon Counseling Associates (1722 Pine St., Philadelphia, PA 19103). Dutton trains professional and community people in these areas of specialization. She is a sexual abuse survivor.

Anjanette Estrellas is a wilderness instructor at the Santa Fe Mountain Center in Santa Fe, New Mexico. She earned her Bachelor's Degree in Social Work from Arizona State University and is currently pursuing her M.A. in Counseling Psychology at Prescott

College. Her Master's thesis will focus on combining group therapy with adventure-based counseling methods for Latina adolescent sexual abuse survivors. Her other research interests include wilderness programming for girls and women and issues of cultural diversity in the field of experiential education.

Karla A. Henderson, Ph.D., is a professor in the Curriculum in Leisure Studies and Recreation Administration at the University of North Carolina at Chapel Hill. Much of her research has focused on issues of women and leisure as they relate to feminism and involvement in activities. She has co-authored two books on women and leisure, *A Leisure of One's Own* and *Both Gains and Gaps*. She is interested in ascertaining ways to help women and girls empower themselves through outdoor pursuits and other leisure interests.

Debra J. Jordan, Re.D., is an associate professor in the Leisure Services Division at the University of Northern Iowa where she studies leadership, gender, and issues of diversity. Deb is a head instructor for the Wilderness Education Association and has been teaching about outdoor leadership for the past 14 years.

Moon Joyce is a 41-year-old, white, lesbian, of mixed English and Ukrainian ethnicity; she was born in Toronto and raised in Scarborough between the "Bluffs" and the Brimley railyard. She spent several years composing, performing, and recording across Canada. Moon's desire to encourage others to sing has led her to become a "cultural animator" with groups wishing to integrate the arts into their collaborative work. Her main challenge is to stay conscious and keep believing that justice can be done. As a writer, artist, educator, and musician, she lives, works, and studies in Toronto.

T.A. Loeffler completed her doctorate in outdoor education and recreation at the University of Minnesota. Her dissertation focused on women's career development in outdoor leadership. She is now an assistant professor at Memorial University of Newfoundland. For the past decade, T.A. has been active in many areas of experiential education, including summer camps, ropes courses, therapeutic wilderness programs, and higher education.

Heidi Mack recently finished her Master of Education at the Faculty of Education at Queen's University in Kingston, Ontario, Canada. Her thesis research and writing were on outdoor programming for women with bulimia. Heidi is building an outdoor and experiential centre in the woods on Crosby Lake in Westport, Ontario, Canada. The centre will run programmes for women dealing with self-esteem and body-image issues.

Mary McClintock, M.Ed., has worked as a leader of therapeutic wilderness groups for adolescents and outdoor trips for women and as an instructor of college and university courses on group leadership and social justice issues. Mary has conducted numerous training sessions on issues related to homophobia and, as a member of Face to Face: A Gay, Lesbian and Bisexual Speakers' Bureau, has spoken on many panels about her experiences as a lesbian, including her experiences of lesbian baiting. She can be reached at 929 South Deerfield Rd., Conway, MA 01341, 413-369-4252.

Wilma Miranda, Ph.D., is Professor of Educational Philosophy at Northern Illinois University where she teaches courses in feminist educational thought, peace studies, and educational policy studies. Her research interests include the professional history and biography of women in the outdoor professions, critical interpretation of the literature of outdoor women writers, and the contributions of women to experiential education thought. She is a former co-chair of the Association for Experiential Education Women's Professional Group, member of the *Journal of Experiential Education* Advisory Board, and presently serves as a regular reviewer for the *Journal*.

Denise Mitten has worked in adventure, outdoor, and environmental education programs for the past 25 years. She has had opportunities to work with women, women offenders, women survivors of sexual abuse, nuns in emotional recovery, homeless people, men, and youth from a variety of ethnic and social backgrounds. Denise brings a comparative perspective regarding the value and uses of various leadership and motivation styles with many different groups. Since 1986, Denise has been Executive Director of Woodswomen, a service organization with a mission to provide adventure travel and teach outdoor living and traveling skills to women. As Executive Director, Denise has combined her breadth of guiding experience with a scientific emphasis (MFS at Yale University) and administrative background. Denise developed and refined Woodswomen's acclaimed leadership program both through Woodswomen programs and as a faculty member at Metropolitan State University. This leadership style focuses on ethical and inclusive leadership. Denise has led workshops all over the U.S. and in Europe, New Zealand, and Australia.

Terry Porter, M.A., is a National Certified Counselor, currently employed as an adventure specialist at the Brattleboro Retreat Psychiatric and Additions Hospital in Brattleboro, Vermont. Prior to entering the experiential education field in 1986, she worked in athletics and recreation, competing as a member of the 1976 Olympic Team in cross-country skiing.

Alison Rheingold graduated from Hampshire College, Amherst, Massachusetts, with a B.A. in Experiential Education. She has worked in a variety of environmental and experiential education programs both in the classroom and the outdoors. Alison currently works at the Children's Institute for Learning Disabilities in Seattle. She is interested in developing environmental/outdoor education curriculum for kids with learning disabilities.

Nina S. Roberts, M.A., is the Assistant Director of the Conservation Career Development Program of the Student Conservation Association. She is formerly an adjunct faculty member in the Department of Recreation at the University of Maryland at College Park. She is a consultant and guide for Expanding Horizons outdoor adventure programs for women in the Washington, DC, area. Nina is the chairperson of the AEE Publications Advisory Committee as well as a regional representative for both the Women in Experiential Education Professional Group and NAALA (Natives, Africans, Asians, Latinos(as) and Allies) Professional Group.

Ruth Rohde is the founder and director of New Routes, a women's wilderness program in the Northeast. Ruth has a Master's in Social Work and one in Environmental Studies and specializes in working with trauma survivors.

Constance Russell is an environmental learner and educator actively involved with the Flesherton Hills Environmental Education Centre. She is a doctoral student at the Ontario Institute for Studies in Education, University of Toronto, whose research interests include the role of experiential learning in the social construction of nature and of animals, ecotourism, the relationship between sense of self and sense of place, critical environmental education, and ecofeminism. She has published articles in *The Journal of Experiential Education, Society and Animals, Trumpeter: Journal of Ecosophy,* and *Pathways,* and co-authored a chapter in the forthcoming *Common Ground: Feminist Collaboration in the Academy.*

Ellen Winiarczyk lives in the Pacific Northwest and has been an experiential educator for the last 17 years. She graduated from the University of New Hampshire in 1981 with majors in Environmental Conservation and Physical Education. Currently, she is pursuing a Master's at The Evergreen State College in Environmental Studies with an emphasis in water policy and issues. She works with the Education and Training Coordinator for the Washington State Service Corps (WSC). WSC is an AmeriCorps National Service grantee and a leader in meeting community needs through citizenship and serving communities. Her interests include sea kayaking, climbing, hiking, bicycling, and adventuring. She is active in the Association for Experiential Education Northwest Region and is active in local environmental issues.

Rita Yerkes, Ed.D., is Dean and Professor, School of Physical Education and Recreation Administration at Aurora University, where she teaches courses in Administrative Practicum in Outdoor Experiences, Outdoor Experiential Education, and Research Methods. Her research interests include women and outdoor adventure, women leaders in the outdoors, and experiential education inter-disciplinary expeditions. She is a former chair of the Women's Professional Group in the Association for Experiential Education, past AEE board member and president, and is an editorial board member for *The Journal of Experiential Education.*

About the Editor

Karen Warren has been actively involved in the field of experiential education for the past 20 years. Currently she is an outdoor instructor for the Outdoors Program and Recreation Athletics and is a Faculty Associate of the School of Natural Science at Hampshire College in Amherst, Massachusetts. She teaches courses in experiential education, outdoor leadership, wilderness studies, and women and girls in the outdoors, as well as serving on students' academic committees in these areas. Karen also serves on the graduate faculty of Lesley College's National Audubon Expedition Institute, teaching courses in environmental psychology and writing for environmental educators. Over the years, Karen has also led hundreds of trips such as canoeing in the Everglades, backpacking in Canyonlands, winter camping in Yellowstone, paddling the Rio Grande, teaching the natural history of the Hawaiian Islands, and telemark skiing in Quebec.

Photo courtesy of Katie Church

Karen holds a Master's of Science in Experiential Education from Mankato State University. She is a co-editor of *The Theory of Experiential Education* and a frequent contributor to the *Journal of Experiential Education* (*JEE*). Karen has guest edited issues on diversity for the *JEE* and on professional outdoorswomen for the *Women Outdoors Journal*. Her research and writing interests include feminist outdoor leadership, diversity and social justice, mentoring, experiential education methodology, and environmental justice.

Karen co-directed Outdoor Trips for Women, a women's outdoor adventure business that specialized in tidal and flatwater canoeing, sea kayaking, caving, rock climbing, and outdoor leadership training. For over 15 years, Karen has taught outdoor leadership workshops and classes for camps, colleges, and universities as well as women's programs such as Women Outdoors, Women's Outdoor Challenges, and Women Outdoors New Zealand.

A former Association for Experiential Education Board member, Karen served on the Executive Committee of the Board for two years. Karen's initiatives while on the Board focused on increasing the spirit of collaboration and enhancing communication between diverse groups and individuals within the organization. In this light, Karen spearheaded the formation of active Professional Group and Publications Advisory Committees.

Karen's active involvement in AEE dates back to 1983 when she and eight Hampshire College students drove cross-country for 22 hours to attend the AEE International Conference at Lake Geneva, Wisconsin. Since then, Karen has been a co-chair of the Women in Experiential Education Professional Group and a regular workshop facilitator at the AEE international and regional conferences. She has also been active in several conference planning committees. Karen was a member of the Project Define group that created the definition of experiential education currently used in AEE. She is also a member of the task force to restructure awards in AEE.

Karen makes her home with her partner and daughter in the hills of Pelham, Massachusetts. She enjoys whitewater canoeing, sea kayaking, telemark skiing, gardening, bird watching, cooking, writing, and natural history in her spare time (which she hopes to have more of with the completion of this book).

Association for Experiential Education Publications

2305 Canyon Blvd., Suite #100, Boulder, CO 80302-5651, USA
Tel. 303-440-8844 FAX 303-440-9581
e-mail: aeemikal@nile.com

Books marked with an asterisk (*) can be ordered directly from Kendall/Hunt Publishing by calling (800) 228-0810 or 319-589-1000. To receive your AEE member discount, when calling please reference AEE and have your membership number ready. If you are outside the U.S., please ask for the international member rate.

BOOKS

ADVENTURE EDUCATION
Available from VENTURE PUBLISHING by calling 814-234-4561—(AEE members receive a discount)
John C. Miles and Simon Priest
ISBN #0-910251-39-8
This book provides the first comprehensive examination of all aspects of adventure education from history, to philosophy, to leadership, to administration. In 53 chapters, it brings together the ideas of many practitioners of adventure education programming to reveal the extent of the literature in the field, providing insight into every aspect of this growing movement.
Member $25.55 / Non Member $31.95

ADVENTURE THERAPY: Therapeutic Applications of Adventure Programming *
Michael A. Gass, Ph.D.
ISBN #0-8403-8272-3
This valuable resource book contains writings by Dr. Gass and other respected practitioners in the growing field of therapeutic adventure programming.

BOOK OF METAPHORS, VOLUME II *
Michael A. Gass, Ph.D.
ISBN #0-7872-0306-8
The use of metaphors in adventure programming often serves as a key for producing lasting functional change for clients. Topics covered include steps for framing experiences, verbal introductions, debriefing, and methods for facilitating adventure experiences.

ETHICAL ISSUES IN EXPERIENTIAL EDUCATION, SECOND EDITION *
Jasper S. Hunt, Jr.
ISBN #0-8403-9038-6
An examination of the current ethical issues in the field of adventure programming and experiential education. Examples of topics include ethical theory, informed consent, sexual issues, student rights, environmental concerns, and programming practices.

EXPERIENCE AND THE CURRICULUM*
Bert Horwood, editor
ISBN #0-7872-1596-1
An anthology where teachers' voices, raised out of hard-won experience and filtered through thoughtful, critical perspectives, provide insiders' views of practice. Unlike the restricted notion that the "experience" in experiential education must comprise some kind of physical adventure, in these stories active experience includes reading and writing, families, the community, and classroom work, as well as out-of-school events.

EXPERIENTIAL EDUCATION IN HIGH SCHOOL: Life in the Walkabout Program
Bert Horwood, with a foreword by Maurice Gibbons
ISBN #0-9293-6104-0
This book is a stirring ethnography of Jefferson County Open High School, an institution based on the revolutionary idea of high school as a right of passage from adolescence to adulthood.

EXPERIENTIAL LEARNING IN SCHOOLS AND HIGHER EDUCATION *
Richard J. Kraft and James Kielsmeier, editors
ISBN #0-7872-0183-9
This updated and expanded anthology addresses the role of experiential education at all levels of schooling. This book is a must for educators, school board members, administrators, professors, and researchers who are still striving to improve education for all our children, young people, and adults.

THE K.E.Y. (KEEP EXPLORING YOURSELF) GROUP: AN EXPERIENTIAL PERSONAL-GROWTH GROUP MANUAL
Karen M. Finch
ISBN #0-7872-2222-4
The K.E.Y. Group is a manual intended for the purpose of facilitating an experiential personal-growth group. Essentially, The K.E.Y. Group focuses on taking care of oneself and introduces, in an enjoyable way, the various tools needed to do that. It consists of information and affirmations integrated into an experiential format for addressing specific issues. The K.E.Y. Group is comprised of 20 sessions that are complete with centering activities, experiential activities, processing questions, and information sheets on topics such as Empowerment, Setting Boundaries, Fear, Trust, Depression as an Opportunity for Growth, and more.

THE THEORY OF EXPERIENTIAL EDUCATION, THIRD EDITION *
Karen Warren, Mitchell Sakofs, and Jasper S. Hunt, Jr., editors
ISBN #0-7872-0262-2
The third edition of this groundbreaking book looks at the theoretical foundations of experiential education from a philosophical, historical, psychological, social, and ethical perspective. The aim of the book is to encourage readers to think about *why* they are doing *what* they are doing.

WOMEN'S VOICES IN EXPERIENTIAL EDUCATION*

Karen Warren, editor

ISBN #0-7872-2059-0

A celebration of women's voices in experiential education and a contribution to the dialogue about gender issues in the profession. The book includes feminist analysis of many topics in experiential education, particularly as it applies to the outdoors and adventure education, as well as practical examples of how women's experiences can contribute to the field as a whole.

OTHER PUBLICATIONS

ADVENTURE PROGRAM RISK MANAGEMENT REPORT 1995: Incident Data and Narratives from 1989 & 1990

Jeff Liddle and Steve Storck, editors

An excellent resource for anyone, from administrators to instructors, charged with managing risk in adventure programming. An annual periodical reviewing the prior year's incident data in adventure programming. A joint project of AEE and the Wilderness Risk Managers Committee.

CONFERENCE PROCEEDINGS MANUALS: 1990-1995

A collection of abstracts from the workshops presented at each International AEE Conference.

GUIDE TO EXPERIENTIAL EDUCATION RESOURCES

A "catalog" with a comprehensive listing of books, journals, organizations, newsletters, and other resources related to the many areas of experiential education. Items are classified and cross-referenced by subject, including Adventure Education; Games, Activities & Initiatives; Youth; Professional Organizations; Technical/Risk Management; Therapeutic Applications; International/Multicultural, and more.

MANUAL OF ACCREDITATION STANDARDS FOR ADVENTURE PROGRAMS 1995

ISBN #0-9293-61-13-X

The most recent issue of the guidelines used to review and accredit programs through AEE's Program Accreditation Services. The *Manual of Accreditation Standards* represents the collective experience of program professionals who have designed and run the activities presented in this book.

PERIODICALS

JOBS CLEARINGHOUSE

One of the most comprehensive and widely used monthly listings of full-time, part-time, and seasonal job and internship opportunities in the experiential/adventure education field. Subscriptions and single issues available.

THE JOURNAL OF EXPERIENTIAL EDUCATION (JEE)

A professional journal for people in the field of experiential education and adventure education. Three issues per year. (Also available: back issues and multi-volume sets.)

JEE BACK ISSUES

Any single issue from 1978-1995.

JEE MULTI-VOLUME SETS

An invaluable reference tool for anyone in the field of experiential education, and a must for your library, school, or organization's collection.

All-Volume Collection: All issues published 1978-1995 (49 issues)

One-Volume Sets (3 issues) for any year from 1978-1995

AEE JOURNAL INDEX

Includes all volumes from 1978-1995, classified by subject, title, and author.

DIRECTORIES

DIRECTORY OF EXPERIENTIAL THERAPY AND ADVENTURE-BASED COUNSELING PROGRAMS

edited by Jackie Gerstein, Ed.D.

A complete biographical breakdown of each organization listed, this directory identifies those programs which use adventure and experiential activities with special needs populations for therapeutic purposes. Lists 257 organizations whose missions include utilizing experiential/ adventure exercises as therapeutic and educational tools.

EXPERIENCE-BASED TRAINING AND DEVELOPMENT: Directory of Programs

edited by David Agran, Dan Garvey, Todd Miner, and Simon Priest

A descriptive listing of over 90 training and development programs in North America and abroad. Also includes chapters on shopping for a program provider, descriptions of activity categories, and services and resources.

SCHOOLS & COLLEGES DIRECTORY

Provides information about many schools, colleges, and universities that have programs or offer degrees related to experiential education. Listings include programs in high schools and independent organizations as well as institutions of higher learning. Most entries list programs offered, contact names and addresses, and degrees available.

The Association for Experiential Education (AEE)

The Association for Experiential Education (AEE) is a not-for-profit, international, professional organization committed to furthering experiential-based teaching and learning in a culture that is increasingly "information-rich but experience-poor." AEE sponsors local, regional, and international conferences and publishes the *Journal of Experiential Education*, the *Jobs Clearinghouse*, directories of programs and services, and a wide variety of books and periodicals to support educators, trainers, practitioners, students, and advocates.

To receive additional information about the Association for Experiential Education, call or write: AEE, 2305 Canyon Blvd., Ste. #100, Boulder, Colorado, USA 80302-5651, (303) 440-8844, (303) 440-9541 (FAX), e-mail: aeemikal@nile.com

Please send information on the following:

❑ Membership in AEE   ❑ Conferences
❑ Program Accreditation Services   ❑ Publications List

Please send the following AEE-K/H books:

Qty.	ISBN #	Author & Title	Price AEE Member	Non-Member	Total
	0-7872-2222-4	Finch/*The K.E.Y. Group*	TBA	TBA	
	0-8403-8272-3	Gass/*Adventure Therapy*	23.00	29.95	
	0-7872-0306-8	Gass/*Book of Metaphors*, Volume II	23.00	28.95	
	0-8403-9038-6	Hunt/*Ethical Issues in Experiential Education*, Second Edition	16.00	23.00	
	0-7872-1596-1	Horwood/*Experience and the Curriculum*	24.00	29.95	
	0-7872-0183-9	Kraft & Kielsmeier/*Experiential Learning in Schools and Higher Education*	30.00	38.00	
	0-7872-0262-2	Warren et al./*The Theory of Experiential Education*, Third Edition	24.00	35.95	
	0-7872-2059-0	Warren/*Women's Voices in Experiential Education*	19.00	23.95	

AL, AZ, CA, CO, FL, GA, IA, IL, KY, LA, MA, MD, MI, NJ, NY, PA, TN, TX, & WI orders, please add your appropriate sales tax.   Tax:

Please add $4.00 shipping and handling for the first book. Add $.50 for each additional book ordered. International customers—call for estimate.   Shipping:

Total:

Ship To:

Name _____

Address _____

City _____ State _____ Zip _____

Phone (____) _____

AEE Membership number _____

Payment:

❑ Check enclosed   ❑ Purchase Order

Charge to: ❑ American Express ❑ Visa ❑ MasterCard

Card # _____ Exp. _____

Name as it appears on card: _____

Signature _____

(Signature required for all charge orders.)

Copy or detach this form and either:

Mail: Kendall/Hunt Publishing Company
Customer Service
4050 Westmark Drive
P.O. Box 1840
Dubuque, IA 52004-1840, USA

Toll-Free FAX: 1-800-772-9165
(24 hours a day/7 days a week)
International FAX: 1-319-589-1046

For a complete listing of available AEE publications and membership information, please see pages 319-322 in this book or contact AEE at the phone number or address listed above.